Homo Prospectus

Homo Prospectus

MARTIN E. P. SELIGMAN

PETER RAILTON

ROY F. BAUMEISTER

CHANDRA SRIPADA

OXFORD
UNIVERSITY PRESS

*On this page Martin Seligman expresses his affection
and profound gratitude to Jack Templeton
(1940–2015)*

Contents

Preface

Martin Seligman

What This Book Is About

We are misnamed. "Wise man" is the intended meaning of *Homo sapiens*, but in contrast to *Homo habilis*, "handy man," and *Homo erectus*, "upright man," our name is not a description, but only an aspiration. And hardly one that we all achieve.

If it is not wisdom, what is it that *Homo sapiens* actually does so well that no other species even approaches? Language, tools, killing, rationality, tasting bad to predators, cooperation—to name a few—have all been proposed. But closer examination of what other mammals, birds, and social insects can do causes us to doubt our uniqueness with regard to each of these. So with Gilbert (2006), we believe that the unrivaled human ability to be guided by imagining alternatives stretching into the future—"prospection"—uniquely describes *Homo sapiens*.

Prospection is the actual ability that, at its best, makes the aspiration of wisdom a reality. Hence, we are better named *Homo prospectus*.

Once you take this name seriously, what follows is much more than semantic. It promotes prospection to the front and center of a new psychological science. The future, particularly cognition about the future, has been very much a back-burner issue in psychology for more than a century. The canonical human being, *Homo psychologicus*, is a prisoner of the past and the present. If you want to know what humans will do in the future, all you need to know are four things:

1. Their history
2. Their genetic makeup
3. The present stimuli
4. The present drives and emotions

Psychoanalysis, behaviorism, and even most of cognitive psychology embody this assumption. But they have left out the pivotal feature, the very fulcrum of human agency, by which we metabolize the past and present into projected futures—prospection.

What happens when the canonical human becomes *Homo prospectus*, and our ability to think about our futures becomes our defining ability?

- What if perception is less about the registration of what is present, than about generating a reliable hallucination of what to expect?
- What if memory is not a file drawer of photographs, but a changing collection of possibilities?
- What if emotion is not agitation from the now, but guidance for the future?
- What if happiness is not the report of a current state, but the prediction of how things are going to go?
- What if morality is not evaluation of the present action, but the prediction of character and its thrust into the future?
- What if treating clinical disorders is less about trying to resolve past conflicts, than about changing the way an individual faces the future?

- What if the mind is not a storehouse of knowledge, but an engine of prediction?
- In short, what if we are not driven by the past, but drawn into the future?

These propositions are what this book is about.

How This Book Came About

This book arose from dissatisfaction with the present. After about a decade of working in positive psychology, studying positive emotions, positive traits, and positive institutions, I sensed that something deeper than the mere neglect of the positive was missing from psychology-as-usual.

What troubles people—what we are sad or anxious or angry about—is for the most part in the present or in the past. What we desire, in contrast, is more often in the future. A psychology that devotes itself to troubles can get away with an epistemology that emphasizes the past and the present and that regards the future as wholly derived from the past and present. Hence, psychology's 120-year obsession with memory (the past) and perception (the present) and its absence of serious work on such constructs as expectation, anticipation, and will. Hence, too, the appeal to some of a "hard determinism" in which behavior is somehow taken out of the hands of the agent and placed under the control of the agent's history.

Roy Baumeister, my kindred spirit, believes the past and the present to be overrated. We were collaborating on mental energy—another sorely neglected topic in psychology—orphaned by psychology's abandoning Freud's hydraulic theory of emotional life. Baumeister suggested that consciousness is, for the most part, the generation of simulations about possible futures—an idea that I fell in love with. We fleshed this idea out in print and a couple of drafts changed hands. In the meantime, Baumeister and E. J. Masicampo (2010) published a learned *Psychological Review* article in which this slant on consciousness was there, but was swamped almost to invisibility by other bowings and scrapings to the reviewers.

In October 2010, I gave the Tanner lecture in philosophy at the University of the Michigan on the topic of positive psychology. Over lunch, Chandra Sripada, an assistant professor of both philosophy and psychiatry, discovered that I had never heard of the *default network* and regaled me with the wondrous discovery of a reliable brain circuit that seemed to be a good candidate for the locus of Baumeister's simulations of possible futures.

That evening a dinner took place joining the Michigan faculties of philosophy and psychology over many bottles of an indifferent red wine. I was seated next to Peter Railton, a well-known moral philosopher. Railton told me that he was interested in how desire seemed to be more about forming a positive image of a possible future than about drives pushing us from behind. At this point, I was called on to say a few words and I was moved to recall Morton White's (1956) *Toward Reunion in Philosophy*'s unfilled promise that philosophy should rejoin hands with its stepchild, psychology.

"Everyone in this room pays lip service to interdisciplinary work," I said. "Let's go around the room and say as a result of this day what we will now do differently? Peter Railton and I will start. We're going to write an article together on being drawn into the future."

This was the very first that Railton had heard of this project. Nevertheless, the project actually began a few days later. Railton and Sripada sent me several articles to read and within 2 weeks, moving at the speed of inspiration, I sent them the very first of what would become scores of drafts that culminated in this book. In this first pass, I made four points:

1. Hard determinism fails because *all* science is at best statistical.
2. Human consciousness is largely about running simulations of the future, perhaps subserved by the default network, and these prospections often have emotional valence.
3. Prospection is the locus of expectation, choice, decision, preference, and free will.
4. The "hard problem of consciousness"—why subjectivity exists—is illuminated by the possibility that subjectivity streamlines making very complex choices among multidimensional simulations.

I concluded that human action is drawn by the future, as well as being influenced, but not driven, by the past. All of this seemed pretty naïve, however, to the Railton, the philosopher, and Sripada, the philosopher who was *also* a working neuroscientist. They were, however, to become the final two of the four horsemen.

Enter the Eagle Scouts of philanthropy: the John Templeton Foundation. I had knocked around science long enough to know my way around funding. By 1996 I had been a supplicant for 40 years and my knees were almost worn out. Then I became President of the American Psychological Association and suggested that psychology turn its attention to what makes life worth living, rather than just to what impedes the good life. Something odd began to happen. Donors came to me.

One of these was the Templeton Foundation. Shortly after my election, I got a warm letter from Jack Templeton, an accomplished neurosurgeon and the head of the Foundation, offering to hold a festschrift in my honor.

"Hold on, dear," warned my wife, Mandy, looking at the Foundation's website. "This foundation has an agenda, a religious agenda. Call them and tell them you are not for rent."

Which I obediently did. The next day the Foundation's executive staff appeared in my living room.

"We do indeed have an agenda," they said. "We fund the intersection of religion and science looking for new spiritual information. Your work is not about religion, but it is about what makes life worth living and we want to fund that aspect. We will never try to co-opt you, and you will not be able to co-opt us." This was their promise, and they have kept it scrupulously and generously. This is the reason for the moniker of Eagle Scouts: They are trustworthy, loyal, helpful, friendly, and all the rest.

Since that time, the Foundation has regularly asked me to spot initiatives that were adventurous, good science, unlikely to be funded by conventional agencies with a pathology agenda like NIMH, and compatible with Sir John Templeton's vision of a science of human flourishing.

"I just happen to have an initiative and I have the four horsemen to do cutting edge research on it." I then explained the idea at length.

"This is just the kind of science that Sir John loved," was Executive Vice President Barnaby Marsh's first reaction. "Sir John thought that imagination—future-mindedness—was the key to success." And in due course, the Templeton Foundation funded us four authors to write this book and to do psychology and neuroscience on prospection. They actually doubled-down and also created a $3 million research competition for the measurement, mechanisms, applications, and improvement of prospection (http://www.prospectivepsych.org/content/projects).

You will learn more about the results of all this in the course of this book.

The four horsemen went to work. We wrote at least 20 drafts of our first paper and we ultimately sent it in to the leading theoretical journal in psychology, the *Psychological Review*. The editor said it was "the most interesting paper he had read since becoming editor," but that it was not theoretical enough. We knew that this was the start of an uphill climb. We then sent it to the *Psychological Bulletin*. The editor said that this was one of the most interesting papers he had read since becoming editor, but it did not review the literature exhaustively. We then sent it to *Perspectives on Psychological Science*, also a leading journal. The editor, Bobbie Spellman, said she could publish anything she wanted to if she thought it was really good and this paper was really good. She published it (Seligman, Railton, Baumeister & Sripada, 2013). This article set forth the history of science's rejection of teleology and several of the implications of taking prospection seriously as a new framework for psychological science.

But it was clear to us that there were many more topics long embedded in the old past–present framework that the new framework of prospection liberates for rethinking: learning, memory, perception, emotion, intuition, choice, consciousness, morality, character, creativity, and mental illness. So we spent the next 3 years meeting together periodically to debate, to argue, and to write. One of us took the lead on each of the 11 chapters, but each one of us commented on each of the chapters. It was then my job to integrate the chapters and smooth out differences of voice and perspective.

So after 4 years of writing, here is the book. The new framework for the future is now in your hands.

References

Baumeister, R. F., & Masicampo, E. J. (2010). Conscious thought is for facilitating social and cultural interactions: How mental simulations serve the animal-culture interface. *Psychological Review, 117*, 945–971.

Gilbert, D. (2006). *Stumbling on happiness*. New York, NY: Knopf.

Seligman, M. E. P., Railton, P., Baumeister, R. F., & Sripada, C. (2013). Navigating into the future or driven by the past. *Perspectives on Psychological Science, 8*, 119–141.

White, M. (1956). *Toward reunion in philosophy*. Cambridge, MA: Harvard University Press.

Part 1
Homo Prospectus

Introduction

Peter Railton

THE FOUNDER OF MODERN PSYCHOLOGY, WILLIAM JAMES, wrote in his magnum opus, *Principles of Psychology*, "My thinking is first, and last, and always for my doing" (James, 1890, p. 960). Certainly, evolutionary considerations argue in favor of this broad idea. Nature is not the College Board—one does not get points simply for coming up with the right answer, rather, getting the right answer matters because it affects how one behaves. Gathering food, seeking shelter, finding mates and allies, caring for the young, and all the while taking risks for uncertain gains—these are the activities that alter the fate of one's offspring and relatives.

But James might have added, ". . . and all of my doing extends *forward* in time, not backward." This seemingly obvious qualification has profound implications for the architecture of mind, whether human or animal, natural or artificial. Imagine an everyday bit of behavior, a deer running across the forest floor, a bird approaching its nest in a tree swaying in the wind, a human hurrying down the hallways of an unfamiliar office building, late for an appointment. Each of these behaviors can be done more effectively and efficiently if the individual anticipates what will come next: The deer moves quickly through the scattered branches and fallen trees by looking a few bounds ahead to anticipate where a clear path lies; the bird avoids missing the edge of the nest by anticipating its movement as the branch sways; and the human avoids wrong turns, doubling back, or having to slam on the brakes by glancing at the office numbers and anticipating how they will change in the hallway ahead. The behavior is more effective because it is likely to be more successful than proceeding without anticipation, and the behavior is more efficient because the same task is typically accomplished in less time, with less effort, and with fewer injuries.

All animals live on a limited budget of energy and time, and so must ensure that they do not expend their last energy before they have found a way to replenish. This constraint is severe. A scrub jay who, over the course of a day, caches too much food and eats too little, will arrive at sunset with insufficient energy stored in its body to escape perishing during the long winter night; another who today caches too little and eats too much will last the night, but perhaps not tomorrow night, if tomorrow turns out to be a poor day for finding food. Modern-day humans are descended from ancestors who faced such limited time and energy budgets, and even today we have not escaped these limitations. In some human populations, finding a way to secure enough nutrition for oneself and one's family is a recurrent problem, while in others, time is the limiting factor, and using anticipation to invest time effectively and efficiently is vital to how well they manage in life. Food deprivation can give a creature hunger and a physiological urge to eat, but anticipation can intelligently regulate motivation to enable a creature to avoid hunger in the first place.

Competition, too, favors anticipation. Predators that are better than their prey at anticipating the other's movement will have a critical advantage. The deadliest predator on the planet is not the strongest or swiftest, but the one with the longest time horizon of anticipation, *Homo sapiens*. For any reasonably healthy animal, predator or prey, adding some capacity to anticipate can be worth more than an increment in strength, speed, or dexterity. Indeed, adding such capacity can itself yield gains in speed, strength, or dexterity, and without adding an ounce of new muscle tissue. As the running deer, returning bird, and hurried human suggest, muscles and joints can be used more effectively and efficiently if guided by an anticipation of what comes next.

And coordination and cooperation can equally benefit from anticipation. How would we coordinate and cooperate if we could not form reliable expectations of what others would do in a range of situations? Or have reliable expectations of what we ourselves will be able to do or be sufficiently motivated to do? Anticipation can even make you smarter in ways that may matter most. Just think of the last time you made what you'd describe as a stupid remark, purchase, bet, promise, or attempted repair and thought, "if only I'd thought ahead just a little bit more." For social animals, intelligent interaction with conspecifics—mates, offspring, relatives, and potential allies or rivals—is just as critical for reproductive success as intelligent interaction with the physical world.

Scarcity and competition, and coordination and cooperation, are two sides of the same evolutionary coin. Coordination and cooperation, whether across generations within a family or across families within a generation, are key ways intelligent animals contend with the threats posed by scarcity and competition. Taken together, they make the case that natural selection strongly favored development of a capacity to anticipate and harnessed this capacity to the regulation of behavior, thus, tying "my thinking ahead" to "my doing," as our amendment to James would put it.

Why, then, aren't all creatures equipped with the long time horizon of human anticipation? Anticipating better-than-chance what will happen next becomes greatly more complicated as one looks further into the future. So do the mental structures needed to make use of such advance information in action, such as imagination, planning, and self-control. The basic mental structures that underlie anticipation are remarkably simple, and so they are ubiquitous in the brains of intelligent animals. But their elaboration into a brain that can think a year or more ahead with some chance of successful prediction, and some chance of actually using this prediction to regulate its life in the here and now, turns out to require a very expensive brain and a very long apprenticeship in life, such as we find in humans. There are, then, trade-offs in developing anticipation, as there are for any capacity worth having. And so there are many ways of making this trade-off to solve problems of scarcity and competition effectively within a given environmental niche without going the whole route to *Homo sapiens*. Hence, the world is full of intelligent anticipators of all shapes, sizes, and time horizons.

We are emphasizing anticipation, but don't intelligent anticipators need past experience to anticipate well? So why say that the mind is forward-looking if it must look backward for its evidence? Or why say that skill has an architecture of anticipation if it must be founded upon a history of practice? Of course, *learning* is required if one is to manage the task of anticipating well; just compare the physical, mental, and social dexterity of typical human adults with that of typical human 2-year-olds. And it is true that at a given moment, all of one's learning took place in the past. Missing from this description, however, is a characterization of *how* we learn.

Anticipation, it turns out, is at the heart of effective learning, for it is through the formation of expectations that an animal is able to detect error and *metabolize* experience selectively into useable information. But what about memory? Surely its essence is not about the anticipation of future experience, but about the preservation of past experience. A growing body of evidence, however, suggests that this is *not* its essence: Memory "retouches" our recollections in a continuing, dynamic interaction with ongoing thought and experience (Nader, 2003). That seems like a fault, but this book is about why that is the right design for memory to have.

In this book we will use the term *prospection* as a label for the mental process of projecting and evaluating future possibilities and then using these projections for the guidance of thought and action (Buckner & Carroll, 2007; Gilbert & Wilson, 2007). Like an old-time prospector searching for gold, the mind's processes of prospection map out not just the physical landscape lying ahead, but an array of possible paths through that landscape. Like an old-time prospector, too, the mind must select among these paths in the face of uncertainty and partial information. So an *estimation* must be made of the promise of the different paths relative to sought-after goals, given the likely risks and costs. Because neither future possibilities nor their estimated value can be seen, heard, felt, or smelled, these are not features of the world that are presented to the mind by perception, past or present. The mind must *add* them. The mind must, therefore, have a way of *representing* these possibilities and anticipated values, making these parts of the mental landscape as real and forceful as the features of the physical landscape presented by the senses. A prospecting mind must do the "seeing" and "feeling" that *simulate* what a future will be like, and thereby place future possibilities on all fours with what is actually seen and felt at present. That is the job of prospection.

And that is why we will be arguing that *Homo sapiens* describes an outcome of human nature, not its origin. For *sapiens* means *wise*, and we are not born wise. Neither do we grow into wisdom the way a seed grows into a sprout and then a plant. We must learn to be wise. And learning is a chancy matter that depends on how well the architecture of expectation operates to extract information from experience. So we are at our beginning *Homo prospectus*, who might or might not make it all the way to *sapience*. But even "*Homo prospectus*" still omits a critical part of the process, for no individual *Homo* could learn to be truly wise entirely on his or her own. Much of what we learn over the course of our lives arises not from solo experience, but from observation of, and interaction with, others. Other species, too, are capable of social learning, although it appears to be confined in ways that might have something to do with some limitations of their ability to project themselves mentally into a standpoint that is not their own. Hence, the true origin of *Homo sapiens* is the distinctive combination of an unprecedented capacity for anticipatory guidance and an unprecedented capacity to live and learn with others—capacities definitive of our ultimate subject matter in this book, *Homo prospectus socialis;* more simply, *Homo prospectus.*

It's time we met him—or her—in person.

Introducing *Homo prospectus*

Imagine that it's a cold clear day in the dead of winter, and we're watching an early human as he emerges into the morning sun from a hut half-buried in drifted snow. In his hand is a spear with a tip he made last summer by flaking flint that he found high on a nearby hill. The spear is freshly mended, using twine braided during long winter nights, from dried grass kept in a pile in the hut.

To our surprise, he walks over to a tree and digs a large rock from the snow, which he carries with him as heads down a path beaten in the snow by frequent passing. We understand why he's lugging this heavy rock when we see his destination—a large, icebound lake. He walks fairly far out, then kneels down and methodically pounds with the rock, brushing away the chips of ice as he goes. His hands are protected from freezing by leather mittens, made in the fall by skinning a fox he'd caught in a snare, turning the fur side inward and stitching the halves together using sinew and an awl split from a coyote's jawbone. Once his hammering has broken through to clear water, he opens the hole by chipping away around its edges. From his sack, he takes a handful of beetles he captured months ago by smearing pine resin on a fallen tree trunk, letting the beetles dry in the sun before plucking them off.

That done, he begins his wait, standing as motionlessly as he can above the hole, his spear hoisted in a cocked arm. Before long, an unsuspecting fish has come to the surface to nibble at the tiny, dried beetles. Only the man's eyes move, carefully following the fish as it slowly circles in the hole. A practiced hunter, he knows that he is unlikely to have a second chance.

This matters. It is late in winter and he and his band are scrawny, like the dried grass that pokes desolately through the snow. Winter came early that year, and now calories and protein are scarce.

We are tempted to describe the miniscule movements of his eyes, which follow the fish, as "trained reflexes" or "automatic." After all, they are happening well below the level of conscious thought, and he is a very experienced hunter. Moreover, it is tempting to say that it is the function of the fisherman's perceptual system to tell him where the fish is, and the function of his memory to accurately represent similar past episodes, so that he will hit his mark by reproducing those motor patterns he executed in the past which were successful and thus reinforced.

Tempting, but this can't be right. Smooth eye movements are voluntary, not reflexive, automatic, or instinctual. They are effortful and even fatiguing. The eye is prone to wander, and it takes active concentration to keep focused on the gently moving fish. And his spear will not strike home if the fisherman knows only how he has thrown his spear in the past or where the fish is now. He needs to transform this past experience into something new, an anticipation of the likely motion of this particular fish at this particular moment, and a corresponding remapping of the motion he will make in tossing his spear. The spear must strike the fish just so, and the exact distance from his arm to the fish, the precise heft and balance of the mended spear in his hand, the toughness of this fish's skin are all things that he has never experienced in exactly this way. To reproduce a past successful throwing motion might yield no more than a glancing blow.

Even if he has hunted for years, he must still read and take into account the particular constellation of facts immediately before him.

Likewise, a skilled baseball batter might be facing a 3-2 count for the thousandth time, but the batter needs to anticipate what this pitcher will do at this point in this game. Hitting a small, spinning, speeding ball with a narrow bat at just the right angle, instant, and force is a highly exacting task, and no *routine* response or mere *habit* will do.

Two Prospective Principles

Here we see a remarkable asymmetry. All of an organism's experience stretches from the present moment *back* into the past, while all of the organism's prospects for meeting its needs or improving its situation start from the present and stretch *forward* in time. Consider the following principle:

> Because action always stretches forward in time, so must a mind that reliably succeeds in action.

There is, moreover, a second, grimmer asymmetry. Why would it be that understanding what it takes to succeed reliably would give us a clue to how *actual* minds operate? Because we know that

> In the game of life, life must win every moment of every day, while death has to win only once.

Having what it takes to succeed, therefore, isn't simply a plus, it is a necessity. Animals run on batteries, the ethologists remind us, and death wins whenever the batteries run out. This means that effectiveness and efficiency in using energy is at a premium and can be enhanced by reliability in anticipation. From these two asymmetries can come a deep reshaping of how we understand all of the key processes of mind—attention, perception, learning, cognition, memory, motivation, and action control—and even the nature of human culture. The implications are system-wide and often surprising.

Prospective Principles of Memory, Perception, and Learning

Let's review a few prospective principles, starting with perception.

At first glance, the perceptual process is a matter of *receiving* information from the environment. It has, however, been a long time since anyone regarded this process as *mere* passive reception. Although our attention is sometimes seized by an unexpected sight or sound, it can also be consciously directed and focused, thereby shaping the perceptual stream, such as when our ice fisherman closely studies the slowly swimming fish. And perceptual processing must impose some organization on the flow of sensory impressions if the mind is to make any sense of what it sees and hears. In both these cases, however, the sights and sounds still flow from the outside in. After all, if the sights and sounds were to come from within instead, then that would be *hallucination* rather than perception, wouldn't it? And yet it increasingly appears that much of our perceptual experience has exactly that character.

Like time and energy, mental processing and nerve channel capacities are limited. So why waste them receiving, interpreting, and storing visual inputs that aren't changing or that could easily be predicted? Information value is the inverse of predictability, so the more a fact could be predicted on the basis of what you already know, the less learning that fact will contribute to what you know. At the limit, wholly redundant information is no information gain at all.

The science of communication theory was born with the recognition of this inverse relationship between information value and predictability. It is this relationship that enables technologists to identify effective and efficient ways of *encoding* information. Morse code, for example, can pack as many messages as possible into a single time interval by choosing shorter and simpler codes for the more frequent letters in English. A single "dot," for example, stands for "e," while "q" is coded with three "dashes" and one "dot." Your perceptual system, too, is designed for efficient coding. For example, if the visual scene is unchanging, or changing in some perfectly predictable way, then there would be no need for the whole of this scene to be recorded directly and passed along the perceptual pathway. Instead, the brain could, like an efficient graphic processor or file compression program in a computer, use prediction to generate what is static or predictable and reserve valuable channel and processing capacity for what is not predictable. This enables the brain to focus its resources where the greatest potential for information gain lies. And a growing body of evidence suggests that perception does indeed follow this principle (Clark, 2013; King, Zylberberg, & DeWeese, 2013), and the following is true:

> Perception is as much about self-generating the information you already know as receiving the information you don't.

The human eye has a "blind spot," corresponding to where the optic nerve attaches to the retina. Yet we never see a blank area in our visual field. The perceptual system uses information about adjacent areas of the visual field to predict what would be present in the blind spot and actively retouches the visual field to fill this spot in. This point can be applied more widely: Efficient perceivers, able to keep up with the potentially huge flow of information from the eye, will also be effective anticipators of what they are about to see and hear, and so be able to triage the incoming signal for what is of greatest interest. Indeed, only a small fraction of our visual field is actually in focus at a given time—the area of the tiny *fovea centralis* in the retina—while the rest is given its full, focused appearance by supplementation from internal sources, much like the blind spot. And, at the limit, a perfectly predictable signal, such as the ticking of the clock in your kitchen, need not be perceived at all once you've been in the room for a few moments. Until your attention turns to the clock—then your perceptual system helpfully puts the ticking back in.

This last point ties the role of anticipation in perception directly to anticipation's role in learning. A rethinking of learning in intelligent animals has taken place within the last generation. The previous generation thought of animal learning as the ingraining of habits by repeated reinforcement of a link between a particular stimulus and a particular response, for example, a rat's turning left and finding food in a simple T-maze. But this theory proved incapable of accounting for the behaviors actually observed in animal learning, because intelligent animals, human infants included, seemed more interested in predictive relations among kinds of events rather than repetitive links among particulars (Aslin, Saffran, & Newport, 1998; Rescorla, 1988). Thus consider the following inference:

> Expectations serve as "hypotheses" about the world around us, and the perceptual system is designed to project these hypotheses and detect errors, generating negative feedback and updating when actual

perceptual input does not match the expectation—all experience is experimentation, and error serves as a "teaching signal."

This implication is foundational in modern formal learning theory. As we will see when we discuss the philosophical case for prospection, "unbiased" learning is a nonstarter. A system that began with no expectations about how the world will be, and simply allowed individual experiences to accumulate, would end up with a pile of disconnected facts and no idea of what might come next. After all, its accumulated information is entirely about particular events that have already taken place and so in itself says nothing about what will happen next. The system would simply draw a blank if asked to guide future action. More effective learners will start off with certain ideas of what to expect, and then use feedback from how well actual experience fits these ideas to reshape their ideas going forward. Expectations thus support both the guidance of "trial" and the possibility of "error" in trial-and-error learning.

Building expectations into the perceptual system, therefore, can serve a dual role: Expectations are the key to efficient coding of incoming information, and they are essential for effective learning from what perception, with help of coding, tells us. It is small wonder that a prospection-based approach to understanding the mind promises to be so powerful.

Let us now turn to a third mental system—memory. Thanks to decades of research and the clinical record of individuals who suffered selective damage in brain regions linked to memory, neuroscientists have come to see memory as a multipart system with a functional division of labor. The mind is not, as some early modern philosophers supposed, a wax tablet upon which experience is simply impressed. Memory and recall are *activities* of the brain, expending energy and tying up resources. So here, too, the demands of efficiency and effectiveness play a shaping role. And once again, we will see how a prospection-based account of memory enables us to make sense of this processing.

In the broadest division, there is short-term and long-term memory. Short-term memory is seen as an on-line mental workspace that holds very recent information, say, the phone number you have just looked up, the last few moments of your experience, or the idea of what you came upstairs to look for. Short-term memory is highly flexible and readily accessible, but has limited capacity—most of us reach a limit at between 4 and 7 separate items. As new items are being pulled into short-term memory, older items are crowded out.

Long-term memory is in many ways the opposite. It is often seen as an off-line archive where information is stored for hours, days, or years, without requiring active attention. It is much less flexible, and for practical purposes, it is almost limitless, so that adding new information need not drive out old. But the resulting massive collection of information is not always easy to access, although the categories used in storing information make following a thread of association or retrieving a given memory easier.

What is kept in long-term memory? Traditionally, it is divided into three kinds. There is "episodic memory," which stores representations of particular events (the time you knocked over a glass of red wine at your first lunch with your boss). "Procedural memory" is a stored repertoire of ways of doing things (such as looking up an unknown word by finding some appropriate source and following alphabetical order). "Motor memory" stores patterns of implementation (such as pedaling a bicycle or writing the letter "q"). (In humans and some other intelligent species there is also "semantic memory," stored concepts, categories, or words, e.g., the distinction between "animate" and "inanimate" objects, or the fact that a "joist" is a beam holding up floors, while a "rafter" is a beam holding up a roof.)

All of this makes good sense from the standpoint of design—a well-built robot would need to perform all three (indeed, if intelligent, all four) of these functions in some coordinated way, too. And yet, memory as we actually find it appears to have a number of peculiar features that make the preceding description a bit misleading.

First consider the "archive" of long-term memory. Papers deposited in an archive might yellow and become brittle, but they are not supposed to be removed or altered in content. This constancy across time enables us to use archives to check our recollections, search land titles, settle lawsuits, and construct and test historical hypotheses. It is a singularly important feature of an archive that the information contained therein is *not* revised in light of more recent events. Researchers are required to leave documents in just the condition in which they find them and can take into archival collections only pencils and cameras to record what they learn. And for good reason—the whole point of an archive would seem to be defeated if users could change what they find to fit their own version of reality. Why, then, is the archive of human memory so different? It is now widely appreciated that human memory is *dynamic*, not static. It is suggestible, prone to conflation, guilty of imposing narrative unity upon what was experienced as a disordered sequence. Recalling an event in a new context, thus pulling the information from episodic memory into working memory, can lead to new information being inserted seamlessly into the memory when it is restored. Coaching of witnesses by police, prosecutors, or defense attorneys need not force the witness to lie about what they remember, instead, it subtly causes them to store revised versions of what they originally recalled, so that when they are called on to testify in court, they sincerely remember the revised version.

Other forms of dynamism in memory are more spontaneous. Newly learned information can silently enrich or delete existing memories. The emotions people felt or the goals they are pursuing will affect what they store from current experience, and how it is interpreted, elaborated, or connected to other memories. In an essay that marked a turning point in oral history, Alessandro Portelli (2010) described how individuals in Terni, Umbria, who had been present at a protest years earlier during which a worker, Luigi Trastulli, was killed, "recalled" different versions of events. These versions did not vary randomly, but displaced the date and cause of the demonstration in ways that invested Trastulli's death with greater symbolic significance for the labor movement as a whole, and reflected the recollecting individuals' differing subsequent relationship to this movement. Memory, it seemed, silently complied with the demands of narrative meaning. Oral history was never the same again.

If the point of memory were to archive history, these would all be defects. And no doubt sometimes they are. But suppose that the main point of memory is to make a positive contribution to one's ability to face the present and future. "Memory is for doing," we might say. And what we need from memory if we are to improve the odds of contending with the present and future is not a warehouse of disconnected documents, but an ability to extract and recombine bits of information in light of subsequent evidence and along lines of relevance to current or anticipated situations, however novel they might be (Genovesio, Wise, & Passingham, 2014; Schacter, Addis, & Buckner, 2007). This process should draw on the full information available to the individual, synthesizing imaginative representations of what is likely or possible by bringing together the old with the new. And this in turn dictates a continual process of enrichment and reorganization in memory, pulling information out of one context to use it in another, correcting past thoughts or perceptions, developing projectable forward trajectories by giving plausible narrative coherence to sequences of events in ways we did not appreciate at the time, and selectively storing and recalling information of greater pertinence upon what we care about or are called upon to do.

A memory made for doing will not be a static archive but a dynamic *relational database*, which permits updating records and projecting and evaluating new possibilities in new settings. An archival memory might be spectacularly accurate in some ways, but would lack all benefit of hindsight and be spectacularly time and energy consuming to use. Just ask any archivally based historian, who labors for months or years to reconstruct sequences of events only to arrive at an outcome that we already know to have occurred. Archival historians typically will, as a matter of fidelity to their sources and their craft, reject demands that they *predict* the future, or say what *would* have happened if things had gone differently. "The archive cannot tell me that," they'll tell you, "I'd be speculating as a rank amateur rather than speaking as a professional." Yet as individuals, we have no choice but to do our best to predict, identify, and learn from ways things might have gone better had we made different choices. If we really had no expertise in projecting from the past into the future, or from the actual to the possible, then accurate memory would do us little good in any event. So it follows that

> Memory must be active and constructive, not passive and fixed—it must metabolize information into forms that are efficient and effective for the forward guidance of thought and action.

Intriguingly, it appears that our mental circuitry for decision-making through imagining the future and counterfactual possibilities is integral with the circuitry for memory (Doll, Shohamy, & Daw, 2015), and this circuitry is alive in all three of these modes in the "default" mode of brain activity (Buckner, Andrews-Hanna, & Schacter, 2008). The brain treats delving into the past and projecting into the future as a unified, ongoing task—because they are. We will discuss this further in the following section, and, especially, in Chapter 4.

The Prospective Regulator

Let us return to our hunter-gatherer. He was left out on the ice, poised motionlessly, his feet going numb, looking for his one chance to spear the fish that had ventured into the hole he'd cracked through the ice. Talk of retouching memory or perception in light of desired goals might suggest a brain that is operating by wish fulfillment, without adequate constraint from reality. But nothing is more real than starvation or freezing, and a furless primate in the depths of a northern winter does not have the luxury of filling his visual field or tampering with his memories in whatever ways he finds most agreeable. Human perception and memory must pay their way by increasing the individual's chance of succeeding in the face of scarce resources and limited time. They, therefore, operate not as autonomous branches of government—the intelligence services, the national archive, and so forth—but in a coordinated way that pulls in information from wherever it can be found and then uses it as efficiently and effectively as possible to guide behavior.

This raises the question: What kind of architecture promotes the most efficient and effective control of behavior? Here we come to the problem of *action control* and one of the most dynamic and exciting bodies of current science and engineering. Again, we can draw on advances in knowledge of how other systems operate to understand better how we operate. According to the good regulator theorem of the systems theorists Roger Conant and Ross Ashby (1970), *a good regulator for a system—one that is both effective and efficient—is a model of that system*. What does this mean for our hunter-gatherer? Ask first, what is the "system" in question? Is it his brain or his organism as a whole? The answer must be neither. The system to be regulated is the hunter-gatherer *in* his environment—an individual with needs, goals, and capacities embedded in an environment with some potential to provide for or obstruct the meeting of these needs or the advancing of these goals, depending on how he uses his capacities. The brain and body of the hunter-gatherer are, then, not the system but the *regulator* for this system, the organism–environment interchange. And the good regulator theorem suggests that in his brain and body there must be built a *model* of that interchange—a model that maps out which causes lead to which effects, with what reliability, and with what implications for drawing down or building up his resources, or for achieving his goals or risking his neck. And, of course, prominent among the causes represented in the model will be the array of possible actions he might take, and prominent among the effects will be the likely outcomes of those actions.

What is a *regulator*? This is, in fact, a broad but technical notion. Think of a home thermostat. It regulates the room's temperature because it sits in the middle of the circuit that turns the heating and cooling system on or off. When the occupant selects a given temperature setting, the thermostat functions as a switch, turning the cooling or heating functions on or off depending on whether the set point chosen is above or below room temperature. Once the room temperature reaches the set point value, it opens the switch, turning off the heating or cooling function, at least until the room temperature or setting changes again.

But such a simple regulator is not very efficient. If occupants return to a stifling house on a hot afternoon and set the thermostat many degrees below room temperature, the cooling function will be instructed to turn on with maximum force. Had the thermostat been able to predict that the occupants usually arrive around this time of day and rarely if ever want to find the house at 85 degrees, then it could cool the house more gradually and efficiently by starting well in advance of their arrival and running at low power. Moreover, the occupants would be spared being uncomfortably hot until the house cools down. Similarly, if the thermostat could predict when they typically leave the house in the morning, then it could begin easing the cooling toward their time of departure, and turn itself down should they forget, avoiding wasted energy. In winter, if the thermostat could predict that external temperature is likely to rise during the day, it could reduce the force of heating gradually as the sun rose, and increase it gradually as the sun was about to set, and so on. The smarter and better informed the thermostat, the less discomfort the occupants will suffer, the more they will save on their utility bill, and the smaller their carbon footprint will be. Notice that these gains in effectiveness and efficiency come because the smart thermostat is building a structured set of expectations—a model, in effect—of the behavior of the small world within which it operates.

How could it *learn* this model? If the occupants don't typically leave the house on weekend mornings, then when they manually adjust the heating or cooling to override the thermostat's gradual cutback, the thermostat will record this override, noting the time and day of week, and modify its expectations accordingly. After they have lived some time with a smart thermostat, a detective could scrutinize its self-reprogrammed expectations and get an idea of the rhythm of their week or the severity of the recent weather. Note that the thermostat learns by using its internal model to guide its action and generate expectations, and then uses discrepancies between these expectations and actual outcomes to readjust its own subsequent actions—using the same model in an "inverse" direction to determine what action would have led to a smaller discrepancy. Thus we can say that

> An effective and efficient regulator of behavior is also an effective and efficient learner—both functions have at their core the building of a working model, encompassing both itself and its environment, and the interactions between them.

Model-based control is an especially powerful way to learn because acting upon the world is an especially good way to give the world a chance to send us a signal if we are in error. Animals that forage for food in a risky and changing environment—as natural environments typically are—are simultaneously foraging for *information*. Their hunger for information is as potent a force in their behavior as their hunger for food.

We should expect intelligent animals to be more like smart machines than like the preprogrammed machines typical of today. Behavior is likely to be largely model-based and flexible rather than instinctual, hardwired, or based on mere stimulus-response associations and rigid habits. If feedforward–feedback learning of, and guidance by, a model can be implemented by the relatively simple electronic circuitry found in a smart thermostat, should natural selection not have favored the emergence of animal brains at least this complex? Given the relentless pressure for effectiveness and efficiency in fast-metabolizing warm-blooded animals that must forage for their living, and given the evidence that such animals can relatively rapidly develop nearly optimal foraging patterns in a complex and chancy environment (Dugatkin, 2004), it would be surprising if we did not find in such animals refined capacities to learn and use models of their world. In the next chapter, we will see that the evidence for this has mounted impressively in the last decade and a half. As systems theorists Conant and Ashby predicted in 1970, the good regulator theorem

> ... has the interesting corollary that the living brain, so far as it is to be successful and efficient as a regulator for survival, *must* proceed, in learning, by the formation of a model (or models) of its environment. (p. 1)

And in the case of intelligent animals that are also social, we can add something more: learning from others' experiences as well as one's own. This greatly accelerates and enriches learning, especially in those animals, such as humans, who can communicate what they have learned directly to one another. Suppose that all of the thermostats in all of the rooms of a large hotel could share information. Then they could each have a model that is more predictive of a wider range of guests, perhaps even breaking the guest population down into types who display particular patterns of preference and behavior. Thus we arrive at the kind of smart system that produces the recommendations you receive from the algorithms at Amazon or Netflix. Consider that

> Learning about an environment with many dimensions of variability is enhanced by sharing information across individuals with diverse experiences—so that social animals have the best chance of accurately modeling their environment and interactions with it.

An ability to share information is not enough—the animals must also communicate honestly, at least, in the main. Bees can rely on the dances of other bees in their colony when setting out to find pollen, and thereby pool and use the whole information acquired from all the searching of all their hive-mates, because all the bees in the colony are closely related genetically. Bees are at the extreme end of relatedness, because they all have the same mother, but most highly communicative social animals live in groups with some degree of relatedness. Humans appear to be unique for their ability to exchange information and live mostly peacefully with very large populations of unrelated individuals, coordinating well enough to make towns, cities, and countries possible and productive. And we see some striking results, from the existence of institutions, such as universities, the international market, and the Internet, to the astonishingly rich and predictive models attained by modern science. But powerful models with long time horizons are not merely the result of such large-scale coordination and cooperation. As we will see, they play an indispensable role in making such relationships among strangers possible and reliable in the first place.

Thermostats, even thermostats that share information, live in a restricted world. The tasks they perform are narrowly defined; their ability to act is limited to a few behaviors; their production and reproduction are taken care of by someone else; and they have no goals of their own to decide among. When the electricity fails, this it is not a problem *they* are called on to fix. Neither do they suffer, die, or go extinct when this occurs, but simply lie dormant, ready to come back to regulative life as soon as power is restored. This is very unlike the organism–environment interchange typical of intelligent animals, who must care for their own maintenance and reproduction, devise novel behaviors for changing environments, and shift their priorities as their needs and goals come and go. In short, they must regulate their behavior in light of the full array of possible costs and benefits of a life, and this makes prospective modeling all the more essential, but at the same time all the more advantageous over preprogrammed or merely reactive, stimulus-bound minds.

What does a model look like? We have spoken of expectations, which can be thought of in an *if-then* form, for example, connecting actions and contexts to possible outcomes, costs, and benefits. But models have more structure than that. We can start by thinking of a *mental map* that individuals might form of their environment, showing its features, their location, and the paths or actions available to them. But the model is also *evaluative*, and so with these paths will be associated whatever benefits, costs, and risks they have learned from taking them, or others like them. Or, from the experience of their parents, siblings, or fellow creatures in taking similar paths themselves.

Unlike the maps with which we are familiar, however, the "paths" in this map do not just correspond to spatial trajectories, but to potential *actions* leading with some probability not only to places, but to possible goals. Thus the maps will include cause-and-effect relationships that will support both forward-looking initiation and monitoring of behavior and inverse inferences from goals to the behaviors requisite to achieve them. All this may seem barely credible when talking about the minds of mice and rats, yet one of the great surprises of recent research is that the more we know about how to challenge and observe the brains of such animals, the more the idea of real-time prospective mapping fits what we observe.

It is a prospective mapping of this kind that explains why our hunter decided, after several days of finding his snares empty, to try fishing in the lake. And why, having made this change of mind, he could work backward from his new goal to the need to repair his spear the night before and to remember to take his pounding stone and dried beetles. Before venturing out into the cold, while still warm in his hut, he could imaginatively explore the paths of his mental map and see that having a working spear improves the odds of catching a fish, that having a pounding stone improves the chance of having a hole in the ice in which to fish, and that using bait improves the chance of luring a fish to that hole. Compared to wandering out onto the frozen lake with no resources—hoping to find a hole in ice that is nonetheless solid enough to stand upon or trying to lure and catch a fish by dangling his hands in the freezing water—this at-home, *simulated* trial-and-error process is a gain in effectiveness and efficiency he can readily appreciate.

Spear, stone, and beetles are themselves the results of earlier prospective mapping by himself and by those from whom he's learned. Thanks to them, he now has promising paths open before him he would not have had if his time horizon, or theirs, had been shorter. It is true that one's mental map is thus a function of one's past, but the more advanced human culture and technology have become, the more it is past *prospection* that determines the shape and branching pathways of the map as we will see in detail in Chapter 5. Sitting in their hut the night before, warm in their clothing and blankets, chewing dried meat and berries from the stock accumulated in fall, the family was surrounded and sustained by the work of prospection. That's also how our hunter had grass to braid a string strong enough to mend a spear, just as his mother had shown him. And that's how today he has something of his own invention: Having seen a beetle trapped by pine resin last summer, he stripped back some more bark and saved the captured and desiccated insects as bait to attract fish.

Importantly, his projective ability enabled him not only to contemplate a new behavior, but to *motivate* it through an *imagined* future reward. Although he had never before seen or performed such behavior, much less been rewarded by it or punished for failing to do it, this structured, effortful, time-consuming sequence of actions could emerge in the face of incentives to do something that would be more immediately rewarding:

> To be effective, prospection requires a motivational system that can give present motivational force to *imagined* future benefits and costs, and this *prospective motivation* is what is distinctive about desire: It is not a mere urge, conditioned drive, or magnetic attraction to something immediately tempting, but rather an ability to be moved by images of possibilities we create—to *want* to take an action because we like the *idea* of what that action might yield, even if that is remote in time or novel in character.

Such a capacity to mobilize motivation in the present on behalf of the mere idea of a future benefit or cost plays a clear role in underwriting human innovation, as our fisherman shows, but it also lies at the foundation of human social, moral, and economic life (Railton, 2012). For example, it enables us to be *trustworthy*, to be motivated to keep the agreements we've made, even when facing incentives to cheat. And it enables inspiration by *ideals* and *principles* to translate into the force and resolve to hold ourselves to them in the face of costs, challenges, and disappointments. Morality, social norms, and laws thus join technology in adding structure to the future, making actions and outcomes possible, which otherwise would simply be unavailable:

> Intelligent action over time involves not only taking choices in light of a causal model of possibilities, but *creating* possibilities—"working backwards" from distant goals to the proximate actions that are preconditions for them, and "working forward" by conceiving and acting upon ideas and ideals that will sustain new ways of acting in the future.

By now prospection is looking very complicated—not just beyond the minds of mice and rats, but also very unlike the minds of humans as we go through our days. How many of us engage in this sort of active prospection of possible pathways, costs, benefits, and risks in more than a tiny fraction of our lives? As James wrote, "Not one man in a billion, when taking his dinner, ever thinks of utility. He eats because the food tastes good and makes him want more" (1890, Vol. II, p. 386).

However, the response offered by contemporary developmental psychology and cognitive and affective neuroscience is that we *all* naturally think in these ways, as do our intelligent mammalian relatives. Does this sound preposterous? Thinking, after all, is not simply conscious deliberation, it is information-processing that is done by representations. Very young children construct causal models of their world (Gopnik et al., 2004; Gopnik & Wellman, 2012), as do rats, according to some recent research (Blaisdell, Sawa, Leising, & Waldmann, 2006). And contemporary neuroscientists have found evidence that systems of neurons in the brains of rats and other mammals (as well as related areas of the human brain) generate multidimensional "cognitive maps" and continuously form and update conditional action–outcome expectations (Moser, Kropff, & Moser, 2008; Stern, Gonzalez, Welsh, & Taylor, 2010; Tobler, O'Doherty, Dolan, & Schultz, 2007). These processes take place in areas of the brain not directly accessible to consciousness, but fully capable of representational thought, computation, and simulation. The fascinating story of this research and the representationally rich "prediction engine" it has revealed will be told in the chapters to come.

Our fisherman's distinctive way of creating future options is more than simple tool use, which we find in birds and monkeys. How did humans *get* into this godforsaken frozen clime in the first place? They certainly did not evolve their way into this niche by natural selection. Compared to the animals around them, they lack the endowment of specialized adaptations for winter life. Except for one endowment, which shortcuts natural selection and makes adaptation possible to wildly diverse environments. Growing fur is not necessary to adapt to the north if one can appropriate the fur of northern animals. Growing sharp claws, spring-like legs, and massive teeth is not necessary to adapt to catching and eating the fish and game in northern winters if one can flake flint into keen blades to carve and tip spears, bend branches and braid grass to make snares, or heat wood shavings with the friction of a fire drill made from sticks and twine, to start a fire to cook meat too tough to chew. *Creativity*, then, in which humans build actively upon statistical learning, can generate the new ideas that become the tools and other artifacts that make new adaptations possible (even as we grow old, as we'll see in Chapter 11).

The power of creativity is familiar to us all. But less obvious are two features even more basic than the creativity we rightly celebrate.

Prospection, Evaluation, Emotion, and Motivation

Beings with excellent maps but no goals can wander, but only by chance will they stumble upon what they want or need. This means that the *evaluation* of possible destinations or pathways is as basic a function of the mind as mapping them out and fully on a par with perception and cognition. We have remarked that prospective mapping involves evaluation, but how is this accomplished? And how does evaluation turn into the motivation needed to realize those values? After all consider that

> For intelligent behavior in living systems, biology must find a way
> of representing not only the physical and social environment and its
> possibilities, but of representing and comparing the values at stake—
> benefits and costs must function as *weights* in the selection of actions
> and in the allocation of effort.

The brain's way of representing value cannot be inert. To reshape behavior, it must affect attention, perception, memory, inference, and action-readiness in a coordinated way. Our values must serve to *orient* and *move* us, if they are to be more than pious hopes. They must have *valence*—positive versus negative force—which moreover must vary in *degrees* of strength and urgency. They must have a spectrum of *characters* corresponding to the wide range of potential costs, benefits, and risks: from harm to health, from loss of a parent or partner to gaining a friend, from threat to one's social standing to the receipt of help from others, from lacking information to gaining understanding, from violation of social norm to upholding a shared value, and so on. They must, like the *if-then* expectations that model the causal relations in prospective maps, be sensitive to patterns in experience, otherwise we won't be able to learn what to value or unlearn what we shouldn't be valuing.

The system biology built with all these features—valence; degrees of strength and urgency; spectrum of character; sensitivity to experience; and direct, coordinated connections with attention, perception, memory, inference, and action—is *emotion*, the affective system, broadly understood. Since Robert Zajonc's pioneering work on "affective primacy" (1980, 1984), emotion has moved from the periphery to the center of our understanding of the mind and brain. Emotion, it seems, is the brain's first line of response to new experience. The fear response to incoming sensory information indicating a potential threat comes on line in the perceptual stream before declarative belief and immediately reorients attention, primes relevant memories, and ramps up vigilance and action-readiness, which is an example of "affective primacy" at work, *attuning* mental responses to new information. And affect appears to enter virtually all subsequent mental processing, from the way that interest affects memory retention to the way that surprise launches new lines of reasoning. And so we come to yet another way in which a forward-looking perspective can reshape the way we think about our minds and ourselves:

> If emotion is built to contribute to successful anticipation and action, then the primary function of emotion will not be *agitation* but *information* and *evaluation, not arousal,* but *orientation* and *guidance.*

Emotion, then, is as much a part of our intelligence and representational capacity as cognition, as classically understood; increasingly, neuroscientists are questioning the emotion–cognition dichotomy (Pessoa, 2008).

But emotion does its work not only in the here and now. Thoughts about ways things *might* go wrong elicit the doubts and fears typical of anxiousness: Contemplating an underhanded act elicits prospective guilt over one's action and prospective shame at the possibility of being caught; deciding between spending time with a friend in the hospital and fishing down at the lake sends one through a succession of feelings of projected discomfort, pleasure, regret, guilt, pride, ingratitude, and more, which remind us of the many values at stake in relationships in the longer run. Our ability, then, to *empathically simulate* emotions that are responses to imagined possible or future acts or outcomes is vital in keeping us in touch with things that matter.

The demands of the representational, memorial, creative, and evaluative tasks we have just described are great, and a special kind of brain had to be built to make them possible. As it turns out, it was a brain built around affect. After all, it is one thing to predict an outcome or another's behavior and something else to appreciate its significance. This is the work of the human capacity for *empathy*, for simulating the thoughts and feelings of others, whether the "other" is ourself at a future time, a current friend, or past foe.

Empathy is not *sympathy*: It is a general-purpose capacity to simulate the lives of others "from the inside" (Buckner & Carroll, 2007; Ruby & Decety, 2001) that helps us gauge a stranger's intentions, predict a rival's likely next move, intuit whether a friend is distracted or distant, or sense whether a child is dissimulating or merely shy or a future self is likely to be pleased with a clever bit of opportunism or distraught at having betrayed another's trust. Empathy is integral to our capacity to anticipate and to make anticipation effective in the guidance of current choice by inducing a current emotion in the self that models a potential emotion in the future or in another. A decision theorist friend who tried for years to quit smoking one day came across a cheerful brochure at the doctor's office, "You and Your Emphysema," which gave an upbeat presentation of how to get through the day with the disease. For the first time, he could vividly, empathically simulate what it would be like to live the life of the future self that his continued smoking would bring into existence, and the effect was to kill his enthusiasm for smoking more effectively than dire warnings ever had, and he quit for good. Improved anticipation led to improved action-guidance through more accurate *emotional* representation of what before had been represented with cool precision.

Humans appear to be remarkable in the extent of their empathic capacity. After all, it had to develop along with our anticipatory horizon and social scope if seeing farther into the future or associating with larger numbers of others was to deliver the benefits they promise:

> Empathy brings together our capacity to simulate possibilities and our capacity to acquire information and to evaluate and understand through feeling; the extensive development of empathy in humans is an essential part of the learning capacity needed for accurate and effective prospection—in one's own life or one's life with others—and for translating future thoughts into present action.

Humankind's greater self-intelligibility and mutual intelligibility go hand in hand in enabling humans to coordinate and cooperate in ways apparently unprecedented in the animal kingdom. Not only are we capable of acting on shared intentions on a large scale (Decety & Stevens, 2009), but we can assess those intentions morally and even take that seriously:

> Some of the persistent puzzles about morality—how evolution might have equipped man for morality, how morality might have emerged and been an important force in people's lives despite the sharp conflicts of interest that seem inherent in social life, what "moral intuitions" might be, and whether such intuitions should inspire much confidence—can be made more tractable once the prospective–empathic character of social evaluation is taken into account.

All this suggests that we should be able to better understand the workings of the mind and body if we shift away from the tempting and familiar past- and present-oriented perspective and toward a future-oriented framework.

With this framework more fully in mind, let us return a last time to the ice fisherman, *Homo prospectus*, at work.

Suppose now that the fisherman, having missed the fish with his spear—prospective guidance isn't perfect—is trudging home, lugging his rock and spear, downcast. His eyes are scanning the landscape, looking for any sign of life. Hungry and cold, the unbidden and unwelcome thought of his family's hunger and cold also comes to mind, and the image of their disappointment when he returns to the hut with empty hands pains him more than his own empty stomach. He thinks, "I'll put down the rock and spear before I re-enter the hut, and gather some firewood and bark for tea. If I can't bring them real food, at least I'll bring them warmth. I just can't enter empty-handed." He starts looking around for birch bark and dried branches in the snow.

But as he looks down, another image intrudes on his mind, that of the dried beetles floating in the water of the hole in the ice. In his frustration and exhaustion, he had left them there, and yet they could be recovered and dried out for an attempt tomorrow. Wearily, he puts down the rock to lighten the trudge back, but as he's putting down the spear, he notices how the low evening sun is sending his shadow far behind him on the white expanse of the snow-covered ice, and another thought occurs to him. While hunting, he has seen animals return to where they were startled, as if to see what had frightened them or to have a second chance at the bait they saw. Perhaps a fish, too? At this one thought, his whole manner changes. Forgotten are the hunger and cold, as energy flows back into his limbs and mind. His grip on his spear firms up and he heads back, stepping lightly but quickly; the heavy shuffling step he had before is gone. He notices that his shadow is about to reach the ice hole, and so he deftly steps sideways to prevent the shadow from crossing the hole, perhaps startling the returned fish. He traces a delicate, circular path to approach the hole from the other side.

As he nears the hole, he stops briefly again. "This time," he thinks, "I will throw the spear quickly, immediately, with all my force." He bends down to tie a long piece of twine from the spear to his ankle as a tether—a trick he'd seen others use to keep a spear thrust deep into the water from being lost under the ice. Now he approaches yet more quietly and carefully, taking care not to trip on the tether. But before he sees down into the hole he sees ripples on the surface of the water, winking in the low, yellow sunlight. "The fish is there," he thinks, "nibbling at the beetles." And now he takes the final steps, his arm cocked. Before he even reaches the edge of the hole, he has flung his spear toward it, bending over double with the exertion. The suddenly stopped, staggering motion of the spear tells him he has hit his prey. The fish was struck hard, sideways, and thrashes to shake free, but the fisherman makes a fast, shoveling motion with the spear, scooping the fish from the hole and sending fish and spear sliding across the ice's surface while he slips and falls backward when the tether tugs his foot out from under him on the now-wetted ice. He is suddenly sitting in cold water but laughing aloud at the pratfall. He thinks of his family again, but now feels a warm flush of pride and affection. Snug in their tiny hut, they will be happy and full tonight.

Here we have seen a wide array of the abilities of *Homo prospectus* on display in a simple scene. Our fisherman could blend in his action what he'd learned from others, what he'd done in the past, and what he improvised on the spot, to outsmart the fish he needed so desperately to catch. He imagined possibilities he'd never tried, and then worked them into a novel sequence of behaviors by thinking forward from where he stood and backward from the goal yet to be realized. He was able to look at things from the fish's point of view, and imagine what a hungry fish might do and what he couldn't or wouldn't see or hear. He used anticipatory signs: his prospective emotions when thinking how it would look to his wife and children when he returned without food; his quick inference from the glistening of the water in the fish hole to the presence of the fish, vigorously occupied with eating and so unlikely to startle if he could launch the spear entirely without warning; his ability to place himself in a location he had yet to occupy and to adjust his behavior to what he saw there in his mind's eye; and his capacity to use prospective mental imagery to generate motivation when it seemed all his energy was gone. He came to the scene with products reflecting the experience of generations past, but was also able to extract bits of memory from their original context and recombine them and construct new possibilities. He had the self-control and focus needed not to let his excitement with the future prevent being attentive to the present, so that he noticed his shadow about to fall across the fishing hole and remembered the need for a tether.

For now, this is enough prologue—and prospection—of what is to come. In the following chapters, we will look at this remarkable constellation of capacities in greater detail, and make the case for thinking we really are *Homo prospectus* and how this makes us into the peculiar creatures we are.

References

Aslin, R. N., Saffran, J. R., & Newport, E. L. (1998). Computation of conditional probability statistics by 8-month-old infants. *Psychological Science, 9*, 321–324.

Blaisdell, A. P., Sawa, K., Leising, K. J., & Waldmann, M. R. (2006). Causal reasoning in rats. *Science, 311*, 1020–1022.

Buckner, R. L., Andrews-Hanna, J. R., & Schacter, D. L. (2008). The brain's default network. *Annals of the New York Academy of Sciences, 1124*, 1–38.

Buckner, R. L., & Carroll, D. C. (2007). Self-projection and the brain. *Trends in Cognitive Sciences, 11*, 49–57.

Clark, A. (2013). Whatever next? Predictive brains, situated agents, and the future of cognitive science. *Behavioral and Brain Sciences, 36*, 181–204.

Conant, R. C., & Ashby, W. R. (1970). Every good regulator of a system must be a model of that system. *International Journal of Systems Science, 1*, 89–97.

Decety, J., & Stevens, J. (2009). Action representation and its role in social interaction. In K. D. Markman, W. M. P. Klein, & J. A. Suhr (Eds.), *The Handbook of imagination and mental simulation* (pp. 3–20). New York, NY: Psychology Press.

Doll, B. B., Shohamy, D., & Daw, N. D. (2015). Multiple memory systems as substrates for multiple decision systems. *Neurobiology of Learning and Memory, 117,* 4–13.

Dugatkin, L. A. (2004). *Principles of animal behavior.* New York, NY: W. W. Norton.

Genovesio, A., Wise, S. P., & Passingham, R. E. (2014). Prefrontal–parietal function: From foraging to foresight. *Trends in Cognitive Sciences, 18,* 72–81.

Gilbert, D. T., & Wilson, T. D. (2007). Prospection: Experiencing the future. *Science, 317,* 1351–1354.

Gopnik, A., Glymour, C., Sobel, D. M., Schulz, L. E., Kushnir, T., & Danks, D. (2004). A theory of causal learning in children: Causal maps and Bayes nets. *Psychological Review, 111,* 3–32.

Gopnik, A., & Wellman, H. M. (2012). Reconstructing constructivism: Causal models, Bayesian learning mechanisms, and the theory theory. *Psychological Bulletin, 138,* 1085–1108.

James, W. (1890). *The principles of psychology* (Vols. I & II). Cambridge, MA: Harvard University Press.

King, P. D., Zylberberg, J., & DeWeese, M. R. (2013). Inhibitory interneurons decorrelate excitatory cells to drive sparse code formation in a spiking model of V1. *The Journal of Neuroscience, 33,* 5475–5485.

Moser, E. I., Kropff, E., & Moser, M.-B. (2008). Place cells, grid cells, and the brain's spatial representation system. *Annual Review of Neuroscience, 31,* 69–89.

Nader, K. (2003). Memory traces unbound. *Trends in Neurosciences, 26,* 65–72.

Pessoa, L. (2008). On the relationship between emotion and cognition. *Nature Reviews Neuroscience, 9,* 148–158.

Portelli, A. (2010). *The death of Luigi Trastulli and other stories: Form and meaning in oral history.* Albany, NY: State University of New York Press.

Railton, P. (2012). That obscure object: Desire. *Proceedings and Addresses of the American Philosophical Association, 86,* 22–46.

Rescorla, R. A. (1988). Pavlovian conditioning: It's not what you think it is. *American Psychologist, 43,* 151–160.

Ruby, P., & Decety, J. (2001). Effect of subjective perspective taking during simulation of action: A PET investigation of agency. *Nature Neuroscience, 4,* 546–550.

Schacter, D. L., Addis, D. R., & Buckner, R. L. (2007). Remembering the past to imagine the future: The prospective brain. *Nature Reviews Neuroscience, 8,* 657–661.

Stern, E. R., Gonzalez, R. Welsh, R. C., & Taylor, S. F. (2010). Updating beliefs for a decision: Neural correlates of uncertainty and underconfidence. *The Journal of Neuroscience, 30,* 8032–8041.

Tobler, P. N., O'Doherty, J. P., Dolan, R. J., & Schultz, W. (2007). Reward value coding distinct from risk attitude-related uncertainty coding in human reward systems. *Journal of Neurophysiology, 97,* 1621–1632.

Zajonc, R. B. (1980). Feeling and thinking: Preferences need no inferences. *American Psychologist, 35,* 151–175.

Zajonc, R. B. (1984). On the primacy of affect. *American Psychologist, 39,* 117–123.

2

Intuitive Guidance: Emotion, Information, and Experience

Peter Railton

The Question of Psychological Realism—Could We Really Be Homo prospectus?

The reader may by now feel a growing skepticism: If prospection is such a fundamental feature of the architecture of the human mind, and if a prospective mind proceeds by acquiring information to generate and evaluate diverse possible future courses of action, then why does our actual psychological life *seem* so different from this? Why does everyday thinking seem to be so preoccupied with the present moment and the recent past, devoting so little time to any explicit planning for the future? Often one thing just runs into another, and we operate in a manner that seems to be largely a mixture of habit (when things are familiar) and guesswork (when they are not). And even when we stop to make a decision with an eye toward the future, we seldom consider more than one or two alternatives, without attempting anything like a systematic accounting of the benefits, costs, and risks of the options before us. One might strengthen this last point: Hasn't psychology over the last several decades told us that people are conspicuously *weak* at the rational estimation of probabilities or the coherent comparison of expected values over time? And finally, if we're so smart, why ain't we rich? Humans—individually, socially, and globally—seem to be plagued with the regrettable consequences that result from failure to think ahead.

Is our notion of prospection, therefore, simply *psychologically unrealistic*? In Chapter 1, we drew attention to some of the core components of prospective guidance of action, but it was more by storytelling than hard evidence. And we did not spell out how ordinary conscious experience might relate to the prospective processes we mentioned. In this chapter, we will begin to remedy these defects, providing a fuller picture of the psychology of *Homo prospectus*, trying to make him or her more recognizable in our own lived experience.

Our explanation will involve three key elements and their related challenges:

- *Intuition*—The moment-to-moment guidance of thought and action is typically intuitive rather than deliberative. When we're having a conversation, for example, almost fully formed thoughts come spontaneously to mind as the conversation evolves. We speak our thoughts with little forethought or reflection, sometimes with a quick aptness or wit that surprises even ourselves, and sometimes with an inaptness that we very much regret.

- *Affect*—According to the prospection hypothesis, our emotional or affective system is constantly active because we are constantly in the business of evaluating alternatives and selecting among them. Yet when we think of emotion—fear, anger, joy, surprise, sadness, guilt—these seem to be episodic, discontinuous, more often reactions to departures from the normal course of events than an ongoing condition. True, some affective states, such as moods, are more persistent (think of the person who is chronically depressed, anxious, or angry). Yet such states are blanket responses to the world, not finely tuned sensitivities to the changing scene.

- *Information*—A system of prospective guidance is *information-intensive*, calling for individuals to attend to many variables and to update their values continuously in response to experience.

Yet the amount of information we can take in, hold in active awareness, or retain for any length of time, seems much more limited. In ordinary thought and action, we seem to rely excessively on the most recent information or unrepresentative scraps from the past or to fall back on a limited array of basic schemes, rules of thumb, or habitual responses.

What do intuition, affect, and information have to do with one another, and how do they fit into the picture of *Homo prospectus*?

Intuition and Information

We go through much of our lives with a sense of what we're doing and why, a feel for what to make of a situation, an inkling of how well a situation is going, or a hunch of how likely a proposed solution is to work. We often call such states of mind *intuitions*, a venerable term whose Latin roots mean "seeing within." "Seeing" because intuition seems to be more like immediate perception than like deliberate reasoning or calculation. It is a spontaneous sense, often unbidden and quite quick, of how things *look* or *seem*. This is attested by the sensory words we use to describe intuitions: a *sense, feeling,* or *impression*. Whereas intuition, like perception, often takes an external object, the sensory impression is to a large extent supplied from "within." This presumably is why intuitions are so often described as "gut feelings," "instinctive responses," or a "feeling in the bones."

Moreover, also unlike the senses, intuitions can occur even with objects that are *absent* or *abstract*. We can have an intuition about a proposed action, a hypothesized scenario, or a purported explanation. Similarly, intuition, unlike the five senses, is not confined to a particular palette or range. Intuition can present its objects as seeming to have an indefinite array of descriptive and evaluative features. You can have a reliable intuitive sense that the boss' proposal for boosting employee morale is going to make things worse, that a person is timid but strong underneath, that you should pass the ball rather than drive to the basket, that a choice of words for a condolence letter is a bit too abrupt, that the music you are improvising needs to shift back into the major key, or that a sales pitch is simply too good to be true. Despite the visceral language we use to describe them, and even though intuitions can certainly *give* us visceral feelings, it is difficult to believe that such specialized and nuanced notions actually originate from the workings of the stomach or intestines.

Intuitions often come unbidden, and we can seldom explain just where they came from or what their basis might be. They seem to come prior to judgment, and although they often inform judgment, they can also stubbornly refuse to line up with our considered opinions. For example, I might appeal to a moral principle to reason my way into taking an action and yet find that the action still does not feel right at all and feel, too, that it would be a mistake to ignore this feeling (we will discuss cases like this in Chapter 9, on morality). Yet if asked to provide a reasoned justification for this intuitive resistance to judgment, I might find I have little or nothing to say. As Aristotle pointed out in his *Posterior Analytics* (trans. 1941, II.19) and Wittgenstein argued in his *Philosophical Investigations* (trans. 1953, section 98), reasoning can never be wholly self-standing, because it always starts from premises and relies on inferential rules or relationships. On pain of regress, reasoning itself cannot supply these. So a faculty other than reasoning must supply our sense that some starting points are more legitimate, plausible, or promising than others, or else reasoning will never get underway. Intuition, Aristotle claimed, is the answer to how we obtain these "first premises" and "first principles."

But that forces the question: What are these intuitions, and why should they have any authority to guide how we think or act? Couldn't an intuition simply be an internalized prejudice stemming from one's upbringing or culture, or from a basic, incorrigible impulse of human nature—the product of evolutionary or historical accident?

We do not treat all intuitions as on a par. Some people, we know, have better intuitions than others. We see this in the reliability of these intuitions in guiding their judgments or conduct. Typically, those with good intuitions have had a lot of relevant experience—not just as observers, but as engaged and usually skillful and successful practitioners. And typically they show sensitivity to situational variation as well as some creativity and ability to think ahead. Moreover, someone can have good intuitions in one domain but not another: Political reporters might have good intuitions about whether a bit of legislation will pass, but poor intuitions about how to get on with their fellow journalists. In these respects, intuitions appear to be much like many other forms of knowledge.

What differentiates intuitions from many other forms of knowledge is that we typically acquire them implicitly rather than through explicit instruction, and we often are unable to explain how we arrived at them. Budding mathematicians can be taught a large number of proofs in full detail, along with successful proof techniques. But the intuition they will need to have a reliable *sense* that that technique can be applied in an unexpected way or to an unanticipated class of problems is not likely to come from classroom instruction alone. Indeed, it often seems that intuitions, rather than explicit inferences, take the lead when one makes a significant breakthrough or achieves a novel synthesis, and the processes underlying the intuition can elude explanation even after the fact. In these respects, intuition seems more like *skill, expertise,* or *creative talent* than mastery of method and fact. But intuition isn't only for the *most* skilled or creative. We all have some measure of intuition, and in nearly all of us, that intuition is more reliable in the areas where you'd expect it to be: where we have the greatest experience and background knowledge.

But surely there must be more to be said about where intuitions come from and why they have the features they do. We believe that the answer is closely linked to the operation of prospection; understanding the one will help us understand the other.

First consider one of the areas where the idea of intuition has been most extensively used, *linguistic intuitions,* which are the spontaneous judgments of native speakers about the grammaticality or acceptability of sentences. For example, a native speaker will immediately distinguish:

(1) Oscar pushed the toy car along the floor.
(2) *The floor along the toy car Oscar pushed.

To native speakers, (2) will sound wrong or seem odd, but can they say what principles of language (2) violates? Linguists have argued that speakers' open-ended, spontaneous, intuitive ability to distinguish well-formed from ungrammatical or otherwise anomalous sentences—their *implicit knowledge* of their native language—must be *generative,* a tacit mastery of the language's rules and regularities that can extend indefinitely to many novel cases and is not simply a repertoire of acquired sentences or patterns.

A tacit mastery of this kind could explain another notable fact: Native speakers can *produce* an indefinitely large number of sentences without ever thinking about grammatical rules or principles, and the sentences they produce will be comprehensible to other speakers. So the underlying competency must be similar in important respects across individuals, and it must be something that nearly anyone can acquire and not the preserve of rarefied experts. After all, virtually everyone growing up in a culture becomes fluent and capable of novelty in their speech and understanding. The human mind, it seems, must be set up in such a way that a shared, structured, largely unconscious generative competency can be acquired simply on the basis of ordinary experience. And this complex competency can produce at the conscious level spontaneous novel intuitions and fluent, inventive speech at the speed of thought without special effort or calculation.

Language is perhaps special, and some have argued that it depends on dedicated brain modules or faculties, although increasingly language learning is seen as integrated with other cognitive capacities (for discussion, see Chater & Manning, 2006; Fodor, 1983; Griffiths, Steyvers, & Tenenbaum, 2007; Hauser, Chomsky, & Fitch, 2002; Markson & Bloom, 1997). And what about all the other domains in which people appear able to develop spontaneous intuitions capable of generating or comprehending novel forms of thought and action? Do each of these domains require special modules, or might they be manifestations of a more general capacity to acquire through experience complex, largely unconscious, structured systems of knowledge that confer "generative" competencies upon the agent (Tenenbaum, Kemp, Griffiths, & Goodman, 2011)?

Because intuition is spontaneous and rapid, there has been a tendency to think of intuitions as *direct, immediate, non-calculative, non-analytic* reactions, not the product of an underlying, complex computation within a structured system of knowledge or information. Certainly intuitions often seem to arrive as completed wholes, but perhaps this is just a "user illusion, a reflection of how they strike the conscious mind, not an indication of their true nature.

To pursue this thought, think first of your reliable companion, your laptop or tablet computer. Let's say you're sitting at the kitchen table, staring at the screen, working through your email. Listed in the crowded inbox is a message from someone you know casually, bearing the subject line, "Invitation to my place on Saturday." Your heart sinks, but you go ahead, click on the message, and read the invitation to a gathering of friends your colleague is hosting. And now you don't know how to respond. You immediately feel both that you'd prefer not to attend and that it would be a problem to say no. Your relation to this person hasn't been easy, making this invitation a matter that requires some delicacy. You sit motionless, letting the question roll around in your mind, with no immediate answer popping up.

What about your computer? Because you are not typing, there is no new information to process, so it should be idle, waiting for you to make something happen. But if your computer has an indicator light for hard drive activations, or if you open the resource monitor, you will see signs of constant activity. Apparently underneath its calm surface and sleek casing, the computer is engaged in some intensive activity (indeed, the machine's cooling fan might just have come on).

What's happening is that the machine's own programs are running, indexing files, updating data and programs, establishing links among related data and programs, reorganizing disk space, allocating resources among the many housekeeping programs, talking to the network, checking for viruses or reminders, and so on. It is a beehive of activity, and like a beehive, the activity is structured and stratified in that many different, interdependent things are going on at once in ways that enable the whole system to continue to function effectively and efficiently. The product of this beehive is not honey but *ability*, for example, the ability to provide you with prompt answers to search queries you've never made before, to spontaneously send you a reminder of an appointment you've forgotten about, or to make information from one program available to another, seemingly effortlessly.

Still stumped for a response to the invitation, you decide to use the search function to call up past exchanges. The "Loading" icon barely has time to appear before a lengthy, chronologically ordered list of messages, marked for whether you responded to them, and perhaps tagged for what the email program calls "importance" shows up on your screen. (Was the message sent directly to you? Was it sent by someone you often correspond with?) Compare this almost instantaneous search outcome with the old days, when you would have had to rummage around in your papers looking for your past correspondence—if you even kept it. If you were well organized or lucky enough, you might find the relevant folders or piles, and by leafing through them and scanning the pages, locate the messages needed to answer your question about whether or when you had turned down your colleague's previous proposals. And when you'd finished the search, whether you found what you wanted or not, you'd have to refile all the messages and folders in accord with your organizational scheme (to the extent that you had one). Email, seemingly, is a great improvement over your own memory system.

In fact, in the old days, it was much more likely that you wouldn't have tried to undertake a systematic search of the past at all. Instead, you'd have taken a shortcut, relying on what Paul Slovic and colleagues call the "affect heuristic" (Slovic, Finucane, Peters, & MacGregor, 2007). You'd ask how you feel about attending the gathering, but also whether you feel you've been a bit too resistant to the host's previous requests, how you'd feel about saying no this time, and whether it feels on balance as if this time you'd better say yes.

However, let's ask whether email gave you the answer you needed. It served you a well-ordered list of past messages, tagged in a way that's rather unrelated to your current concern. But what are you to do with these messages? It would be just as cumbersome to sort through them as it would be to leaf through your old paper files. You might have better luck figuring out some particular facts, but they are unlikely to tell you whether you've been excessively negative. You will soon tire of trying to sort through exchanges and find you still have to ask yourself how you feel about what you've ascertained, whether it seems adequate for a decision, whether you'd better err on the side of caution, and so on. In short, you're right back with the affect heuristic.

So, what *does* feel right? The idea of spending an evening with this colleague and his friends holds no appeal; it seems to you that they drink more than they can hold, and the jokes they tell leave you a bit queasy. Your host would soon notice that you're not enjoying yourself, but just try to fake enjoyment to a colleague who already seems to view you with some suspicion. Still, it feels like a bad idea to say no. And then it occurs to you that you recently received a promotion, while he was passed over. It becomes immediately clear that you really *can't* say no. You feel too keenly how that would look to him, and you lose heart about finding some excuse that you sense he almost certainly wouldn't find convincing. So you type, "Sure—Saturday works. What time were you thinking of?" With a sigh, you push "Send."

In making your decision, you didn't do an elaborate calculation, but rather proceeded in a largely intuitive manner, responding to the thoughts that came to you as they emerged, not working out all the possibilities, costs, and benefits, but following your feelings as an "affective shortcut." But remember your computer's busyness while you mulled over your colleague's invitation. Perhaps your brain was not taking a shortcut after all, but rather the thoughts that came to your conscious mind and the feelings you experienced reflected underlying processes that *were* keeping track of possibilities, costs, and benefits. When you tossed the question into your mind to let it roll over a bit, perhaps you were letting your mind set itself to work, pulling in relevant information and memories, running scenarios, taking up viewpoints—making you feel at one moment inclined to say no, at the next, to say yes. This tacit churning through relevant, conflicting experience and information could have begun the instant you saw the subject line of your colleague's email and would explain why, almost as soon as you got to the end of the subject line, you already were experiencing a mixture of feelings and hesitancy about responding. This churning, even if not under your direct control, need not be random. It could, like your computer's indexing system, follow connections with "importance," depending on who wrote the message, what relationship you have with that person, what sort of thing the message is asking you to consider, what responses might be available to you, and so on. In this way, while you let your thinking take its own course, your mind could be chasing down paths of strongest relevance and so quickly cut through the mass of data. Within a moment, a range of conflicting considerations is coming into conscious awareness, and soon afterward, a fact emerges from memory with enough weight to settle the matter: his failure to be promoted while you succeeded. This is not bad for aimless mulling.

The personal computing revolution did not arise solely from the development of smaller and smaller chips capable of larger and larger numbers of operations per second, or even from this plus the development of amazingly complex and powerful programs. What opened the door of the computer world to those with no knowledge

of engineering or programming was the development of the graphical user interface (GUI), for example, the familiar desktop or start
screen of your computer or tablet. In the old days of mainframe computing, conducting a search required writing computer code to set
the search parameters and instruct the machine about the sorting or
selection function that was to be performed on the data recovered,
punching the code onto cards, debugging the code and checking its
syntax, adding job-control cards to allocate core processing space and
to designate the tapes and drives to be used, physically mounting the
tapes (which could not all be mounted at once, and which themselves
had to be updated regularly by taking time to run special-purpose
maintenance programs), and formatting the desired output. Now the
user need only type a word or two in a search box to receive a nearly
instant answer.

A good GUI is said to be *intuitive*, because it allows users to find
and focus on what most interests them, getting the results they want
with the least frustration or need for insight into the inner workings
of the machine while the device handles the rest.

Think of human intuition, then, and the conscious experience in
which it appears, as the brain's GUI. An intuitive "sense" provides a
readily recognized and easily used summation of what can be syn-
thesized from the resources available to the brain, which include
recent experiences, relevant memories, preferences, social norms,
degrees of uncertainty, commitments, knowledge of particular persons and situations, and of the social and physical world in general,
ability to imagine options, motivational force, and so. These all must
be brought together if you are to make the best use of your brain's
resources to solve the problems you face, but you do not need to see
anything like the totality of this information if instead you can be
responsive to its upshot through a *sense* of what's at stake, what's
more important or urgent, what would be a good or bad outcome,
what would be risky, and so on.

But isn't it unrealistic to imagine that the non-conscious brain
could be racing through large amounts of information, projecting alternatives, keeping track of the relevant benefits and costs, and so on,
fast enough to produce in some organized way that distinctive set of
feelings and thoughts you experienced as you read your colleague's
message?

For a start, the brain need not start from scratch for each search, any more than your computer, or Google, does. It is the job of an intelligent operating system or search engine to keep at work tracing connections, updating information, tracking and predicting the demands made upon it, and the like, even when you are busy on the GUI clicking through mildly distracting blog posts. A tiny hint of this capacity in the human brain emerged in 1984, when Lynn Hasher and Rose Zacks found that the mind, seemingly unconsciously, kept track of relative frequencies in the environment, even while engaged in other tasks (Hasher & Zacks, 1984). The explosion of work on the unconscious mind that has taken place since the early 1980s will be discussed more fully in the "Looking Under the Hood" section, but for now it is worth noting that Hasher and Zacks' finding need not surprise. Our sense that the brain can only work on a small number of tasks at the same time and that it cranks along at the pace and in the manner of conscious thought is an illusion generated by never peering behind the GUI of consciousness.

It is astonishing that if we pose to Google the query, "What do you call the little spinning blue circle that appears on the screen when my computer is searching for a file?," it can search the Web and in 1.49 seconds offer 240,000 results. But Google didn't wait until the question was sent to link together information relevant to answering a query about file searching, waiting, and the icons used to symbolize this. It is the bread and butter of a search engine to work constantly setting up such relations among potentially relevant items while no one is asking, and thereby have answers at the ready when they do. The more queries the search engine receives and processes and the more it tracks the users' responses to the results it delivers, the better it gets at creating links people are most likely to be curious about and supplying answers they are most likely to read. (Another search engine, Bing, posed the same question, arrived at only 94,000 items in about 1.5 seconds.)

But Google's accomplishment is less impressive than what your brain does all the time. For a start, Google wasn't selective enough. The top items proffered were about how to get rid of the spinning blue circle and (of course) related complaints about Windows. The sought-after name, "throbber," wasn't near the head of the list, and it took a lot of picking through the items Google retrieved to find it. If "semantic memory," which is our memory for concepts, words, names, and meanings, were this cumbersome, then we'd never be fluent in speech.

But calling up words and names is a simple matter compared to what ran through your mind when you saw the invitation message in your inbox. In about the time Google arrived at a cumbersome, long list of items with some relevance to our question, your brain recognized the name of the person sending it, called this particular person to mind, interpreted the words in his subject line, began to anticipate the content of the message, set in motion conflicting ideas and feelings reflecting past experience with this person, and generated a sense of uneasiness about how to respond, which cued you to the delicacy of the situation and the need for some thought. That is a tremendous amount of information and evaluative assessment to locate, retrieve, and pack into your ongoing experience in such a short period, and it happened in a much more effectively focused manner than Google's answer to our query about the little blue circle's name.

How could this be possible? The adult human brain has some 80–90 billion neurons, each of which can project to hundreds or even thousands of others, resulting in trillions of synaptic connections. Moreover, because processing can be taking place in many brain regions active at once, the effective cycle time for the "human computer" is estimated to be in the range of 80 billion to 15 trillion action potentials *per second*. The estimated storage capacity of human memory ranges from 10 to 100 terabytes of data, though some estimates range up to 2.5 petabytes (i.e., 2.5 million gigabytes). For comparison, 2.5 petabytes is sufficient to store 300 years of continuous color television, if that's your idea of a good time (Reber, 2010).[1] These estimates are, of course, speculative, but even so, they do not include the additional processing and storage capacity that might depend on astrocytes—glial cells in the brain that outnumber neurons and can have tens of thousands of connections involving dozens of chemical pathways, and which also play a role in neuron activation in long-term potentiation and memory formation (Henneberger, Papouin, Oliet, & Rusakov, 2010; Suzuki et al., 2011). The result is a system for storage and retrieval that is rivaled in capacity and complexity only by supercomputers made up of a thousand or more high-powered individual computers working in parallel.

It is often said that there is a sharp trade-off between speed and complexity in mental processing, and this, of course, has to be right. But a brain that is capable of making billions of synaptic connections in a second can handle a great deal of complexity in what constitutes, by normal human standards, a very short time.

Most human thought and action is guided by implicit or intuitive processes rather than explicit deliberation and decision (Bargh & Chartrand, 1999; but see also Baumeister, Bratslavsky, Muraven, & Tice, 1998). This would be a disaster for us if implicit or intuitive thought relied on simple shortcuts without careful attention to the statistics of the world. Of course, the implicit mind isn't cheap. Whether you are focused on a conscious task or letting your mind wander aimlessly, the metabolic activity in the brain remains remarkably constant, burning through 15%–20% of your body's oxygen and calories, despite constituting only about 2% of your body weight (Raichle & Gusnard, 2005). Why would we grow a brain with this amazing computational speed and storage capacity and keep it active almost constantly at great metabolic expense only to rely, when doing most of what we do all day, on no more than stimulus-response associations, habits, or shortcuts that avoid extensive calculation?

The answer lies in two seemingly unconnected places: the "server farms" that dot our landscape and in the famous remark of Luis Pasteur's that inspiration comes to the prepared mind. Search engines, as we've noted, do not await your query before searching. Unlike a print encyclopedia that offers only fixed, stored answers, search engines are intensely interested in what is going on moment to moment in the world of inquiry, whether this is a matter of monitoring and seeking access to formal publications, informal posts, trends in queries, shopping patterns, or user response patterns. This is possible only by processing, storing, and updating a tremendous amount of information at any one time, and the energy demands of this are fierce. Still, this is the only way to keep up with a rapidly changing virtual community's demands for information. Computers are expensive, and so interlinked systems are designed to allocate and reallocate tasks in a way that keeps the computers operating at a high level, placing a "metabolic demand" on the earth's resources that was recently estimated to consume 10% of the world's electric power (Walsh, 2013).

The implicit mind likewise makes a high, continuous metabolic demand on the body to fuel the large memory and rapid computations needed to keep up with our information demands—not just in answering queries, but in guiding thought and action without grinding to a halt. During its "default" mode of operation, which is the state the brain enters when task demands let up, it has been theorized that the brain is occupied in consolidating, organizing, and anticipatory tasks, just like computers (Bollinger, Rubens, Zanto, & Gazzaley, 2010; Buckner, Andrews-Hanna, & Schacter, 2008; Lewis, Baldassarre, Committeri, Romani, & Corbetta, 2009). (This topic will be discussed in detail in Chapter 4.) The expensive human brain is also a resource far too valuable in coping with the world to waste or leave idle.

So it isn't unreasonable to imagine that the brain—just as much as your computer or search engine—is an informational beehive full of activity while you sit trying to create a response. The idea that we can often solve problems by *not* thinking about them explicitly, and instead by letting them percolate through our minds while we work on other tasks or "sleep on it," isn't just a bit of mythology, but one of the most familiar facts of life. Rarely, if ever, do we deliberately work our way step by step to a solution to a problem without relying at some point on ideas or possibilities that spontaneously "occur to us" and "seem plausible enough" to be pursued or on memories or analogies with previous experience that "come to mind" without our knowing to go look for them. Such intuitions and "inspirations" might work, not by magic, but through the same sorts of experience-based, data-intensive, conceptually organized processes that have made search engines our regular companions throughout all aspects of contemporary life.

Although they appear quickly and effortlessly on our screens, we do not think of Google's deliverances as based on "gut feelings," "instincts," "habits," "associative reflexes," or "simple heuristics." The search engine, like the GUI, skillfully masks complex mechanisms and algorithms behind a user-friendly, intuitive surface. Why should we think that the implicit mind runs a metabolically expensive, high-powered computer only to ignore it?

It might seem that emphasizing the metabolic demand of the brain runs contrary to our emphasis on effectiveness and efficiency. What's become of energy saving? But the answer is obvious from the old saw: "If you think learning is expensive, try ignorance." If a brain calculation can generate and evaluate a potential action sequence and eliminate it as having lower expected value than other available sequences in a fraction of a second, this takes energy, but much less energy than would enacting that sequence and learning from experience of its low yield. It is a general feature of well-designed regulators that they *do* consume energy that could be put to other uses, but the amount of energy is tiny compared to the amount they save. Running the circuits of a smart thermostat for an hour consumes much less power than running a cooling system at a higher-than-needed power for a minute. So the efficiency gain of smart technology is very real, and as we enter the world of the "Internet of things," its share of the world's energy footprint will surely grow, for reasons any hard-nosed accountant will understand. The speed in historical time with which the Internet has spread across the world and into virtually every aspect of our waking lives is matched only by the speed in geological time with which *Homo sapiens* has overrun the planet and even cluttered up nearby space.

What of the second point, which is that "inspiration comes to the prepared mind"? Talk of a prepared mind risks obscuring a subtle but vital distinction. By pausing briefly to consider it, we can perhaps make clearer the difference between *Homo sapiens* and *Homo prospectus* as frameworks for understanding the human mind. Consider the most well-prepared intuitive responses, such as those of chess grand masters, elite athletes, top jazz musicians, commanders of firefighting teams, and highly skilled artisans. Psychologists have long been fascinated by the ability of such individuals to size up situations and produce an exceptionally adept response without pausing for conscious deliberation. One influential model of expert intuitive behavior has been that experts acquire, through thousands of hours of experience, a vast repertoire of <situation-action> "pattern recognition" and "motor programming," which is stored in memory. Such <situation-action> pairs are then recalled and put into effect when triggered by the perception of specific features of circumstances. For example, in an influential essay, the Nobel laureate Herbert Simon wrote, "The situation has provided a cue: This cue has given the expert access to information stored in memory, and the information provides the answer. Intuition is nothing more and nothing less than recognition" (1992, p. 155). And according to the psychologists Gary

Klein and Daniel Kahneman (another Nobel laureate), "Intuitions that are available only to a few exceptional individuals are often called creative. Like other intuitions, however, creative intuitions are based on finding valid patterns in memory, a task that some people perform much better than others" (Kahneman & Klein, 2009, p. 521). These stored patterns and motor procedures or routines save the conscious mind from having to build up a response for each situation anew, and that is why the transition from being a novice to being expert is marked by a gradual "off-loading" of control from effortful, self-conscious thought to effortless, implicit processes. We might think of this as a *Homo sapiens* model of expert intuition. Expertise *is* knowledge or wisdom, but in the concrete form of patterns stored in memory, accessible on cue by well-trained recognitional abilities.

This idea of expert or exceptional performance is, however, quite unlike the idea of optimal behavior held by contemporary normative decision theory, the most influential form of which is Bayesian decision theory (Berger, 1980; Jeffrey, 1965; Raiffa, 1974). According to normative decision theory, optimal behavioral responses are achieved by calculation and comparison of the costs and benefits of an array of possible actions, drawing on a continuously updated model of one's situation and its prospects and risks, and selection of the action with the highest expected value at the moment. The action selected might never have been previously performed or observed, and the information and evaluations on the basis of which it was chosen, too, are changing in the face of new information. This would be, if you will, a *Homo prospectus* model of expertise: Expertise lies in a capacity for dynamically evolving prospective modeling, simulation, evaluation, and choice.

It has long been thought that this second, Bayesian model of expert or exceptional performance, while in some formal sense optimal, is simply not psychologically feasible within the tight time constraints imposed on expert decision-making in actual circumstances. In competitive sports or games, for example, the speed and skill of opponents make it necessary that one respond within a fraction of a second, leaving no time for the simulation and evaluation of multiple alternatives, much less optimal selection among them. Hence the idea of turning expertise into recognition: cue-based recall of stored solutions, which could, if well trained, occur within a split second without requiring conscious deliberation. Experts are those who have more stored solutions, are quicker at spotting cues, and more adept at calling them up and putting them into practice.

If we are right, that is, if *Homo prospectus* is to portray actual humans realistically, then we should expect the second decision-theoretical model to underlie truly expert or exceptional intuitive performance, since it is in fact more optimal *if feasible*. But is it feasible? The point of the analogy we've been making with smart, dynamic, computationally, and informationally intensive artificial systems is that, increasingly, we are able to see how it could be. Such systems can perform the needed computations and comparisons in real time, given current levels of computational speed and capacity. The flurry of computation is simply hidden behind the simple, intuitive GUI that is seen by the user.[2]

Let's now try to bring the analogy closer to home by thinking about a naturally occurring example of intuitive expertise, the product of which is precisely an intuitive GUI—the perceptual system. This system is expert at translating a potentially overwhelming stream of noisy sensory information into the well-organized phenomenon that is our normal perception of the external world. A two-dimensional retinal input that changes every few milliseconds is transformed into a relatively stable, three-dimensional world populated by persisting objects, which appear to us to stand out against the background, and to retain their identity, shape, size, and color despite continually changing perspective, proximity, and incident light. We know from attempts to design artificial object-recognition systems that this requires a tremendous amount of computation, and drawing in of non-visual information about the world or about the movement of the individual in it. Of course, an expert object-identification system, like your own visual system, does not bother you with this vast array of information and probabilistic computations, but instead provides a cleanly organized, largely ambiguity-free intuitive graphic interface with the external world. Could such expertise take the form of cue-based recall of stored visual responses? Hardly, because the variation we encounter in the world is indefinitely large and dynamically evolving into arrays we have never before encountered. Instead, evidence is accumulating that object identification and tracking in the visual system operates in real time through hierarchically structured networks based on learning algorithms similar to Bayesian inference and resolves ambiguities and inconstancies through processes similar to Bayesian decision theory (Kersten, Mamassian, & Yuille, 2004; Najemnik & Geisler, 2005).

If our highly structured visual field is the GUI provided by vision, what is the interface provided by expertise? We speak of *seeing* that a particular action would not be a good idea or *sensing* that a particular person is sincere, but such things as bad ideas or sincere behavior do not literally show up sensorily, as special colors or textures. Instead, they show up *affectively*, in the spontaneous *feelings* we have as we face choices, meet people, and act, or the degree of *confidence* we have in a belief we've formed or an analogy we make. But how could affect do this?

Affect and Information

Emotion is a topic so central that it will be treated at length in Chapter 8. Here we need to see in a general way how and why emotion, or affect more generally, plays a pivotal role in the mental architecture of *Homo prospectus*.

Emotion has been contrasted with cognition and reason by philosophers and psychologists alike. But the last few decades have seen a revolution in thinking about affect, a revolution that places affect squarely in the middle of our capacity to represent the physical and social world, to evaluate prospects or perils we face there, and to guide thought and action accordingly (de Oliveira-Souza, Moll, & Grafman, 2011; Pessoa, 2008).

Why would *affect* (i.e., *feeling*) be suited for such a central role? Let's start with Robert Zajonc's work, which began the "affective revolution" in psychology. He offered experimental evidence that affective responses preceded and shaped cognitive responses—the hypothesis of "affective primacy"—and constituted a source of information relevant to the organism's needs and goals (Zajonc, 1980, 1984). Zajonc's painstaking experiments took place prior to the massive development in brain imaging capability in the 1990s and were largely based on the long-standing method of measuring reaction times. Evolutionarily, it makes a great deal of sense that a reaction of fear, anger, or surprise should take place fast enough to enable one to contend with the threat, harm, or unexpected event they signal. For example, within a 10th of a second after exposure to the presence of a threatening animal—even if the visual information is wholly unexpected and not at the center of attention—the mammalian fear response is already underway, beginning to reorient attention, intensify alertness, accelerate brain activity, prime memories of similar prior events, increase heart rate and slow digestion, ramp up action-readiness, and prepare a response (Luo et al., 2010). It is characteristic of affect that it can act simultaneously and directly upon all of the mind's key systems—attention, perception, cognition, memory, motivation, felt experience, and action—as well as the body itself. Affect therefore can *orchestrate* the individual's response to a wide variety of challenges or opportunities in the physical and social environment (for a summary, see Rolls, 2007).

Today in cognitive social psychology, it has become customary to speak of *valence*—degrees of positivity or negativity—as an essential and distinguishing feature of affect, making it possible for affect to function as the brain's *currency* for evaluation or appraisal (Shuman, Sander, & Scherer, 2013). The idea that affect is evaluative flows naturally from affective responses playing the same sort of role in adjusting one's thought and action to a situation that evaluation would play. Liking and loving, hoping and trusting, respecting and admiring, are positive in valence, directly inducing attraction, approach, acceptance, and credence. Fear and distrust, disgust and revulsion, hatred and contempt, are negative in valence, directly inducing aversion, avoidance, rejection, and disbelief. As Jonathan Haidt describes the affective revolution that has swept social psychology, "the basic point was that brains are always and automatically evaluating everything they perceive, and that higher-level thinking is preceded, permeated, and influenced by affective reactions" (Haidt, 2007, p. 998).

Some affective states, such as fear, anger, and surprise, involve arousal, shifting our psyche from "business as usual" to heightened and refocused activity. When consciously felt, these tend to have a distinctive, attention-grabbing phenomenology. Other affective states, however, are low arousal, such as confidence, interest, liking, and satisfaction, which underwrite everyday living and encourage us to get on with our lives. Such everyday, unaroused emotions function as a kind of "default" setting of the psyche, to which a healthy psyche returns when more agitated, aroused emotions fade. The default character of these attitudes helps explain their "thin" phenomenology—to do their job, they should (like the default programs of a personal computer) be able to process information and ready responses in systematic, task-relevant ways without creating a distraction on the user interface. For example, everyday confidence in one's eyes and ears sustains spontaneous perceptual learning and belief formation while being barely noticeable. Only when some unusual circumstance or condition undermines this confidence, as when vision suddenly becomes blurry, the ears seem to "hear voices" we know are not there, or an anxiety attack pulls the rug from under self-assurance, is it clear what it is like to *have* such baseline trust in our faculties and their deliverances.

It seems clear why the default emotions must be in the positive register on the whole: If we were generally disposed *not* to have confidence in our perceptions, thoughts, or capacities for action, *not* to trust others, *not* to enjoy satisfying our needs or accomplishing our goals, *not* to take a positive interest in life, we would be in a dangerously self-defeating condition. Unable to trust our senses, we would be unable to learn from experience; incapable of sustaining confidence in our thoughts, we would be unable to follow a line of reasoning or to draw on our memory; lacking desire or pleasure in satisfying our wants, we would lose motivation to keep ourselves well, maintain our relationships, or pursue our goals. We would be boxed out of life and learning by our own psyches. It is, therefore, interesting that across many nations and tens of thousands of informants, 86% of informants reported themselves above neutral in subjective well-being, with an average life satisfaction in developed countries ranging from 6 to 7 or higher on a 10-point scale (Diener & Diener, 1996). In short, if we were not generally positive, we would be in a state of affective *dysfunction*, similar in its effects to the ways chronic depression erodes learning, memory, thought, motivation, and action. As we will see in Chapter 10, there are profound links between affective dysfunctions and dysfunctions of *prospection*. Here we are concerned primarily with how affect works in tandem with prospection when things are going reasonably well.

The evaluative role of affect includes not only the *learning* and *representation* of value, but also the *value-based guidance* of thought and action. Much of the content of affect is itself prospective. Part of what it is to have a goal, for example, is to have a positive affective attitude toward the thought of attaining it and a positive affective expectation from its realization. These in turn translate into a positive affective attitude toward *means* to realize that goal. Because affect is intrinsically linked with motivation as well as valence, this favorable attitude in turn motivates the effort needed to perform the means of attaining the goal or overcome the obstacles that stand in the way. The anticipation of effort and obstacles, too, has an affective expression, and this dispreference motivates us to look for means that are less demanding or difficult, if they can be found. When obstacles prove difficult to overcome, the negative affect of frustration makes us discontent with accepting failure and motivates us to invest the additional effort needed to find a solution, or, if that proves unavailing, to revise our plans. By contrast, making progress toward a goal is satisfying, but as encouragement rather than mere satiation. Successful effort is thus rewarded, but further effort is made more attractive as well. In these ways and more, affect gives values the practical force needed to turn them into planning and action.

If the affective system is indeed evolved to inform and help guide action, then we should expect that it does more than shape how we respond to the environment; it should reshape itself in response to the environment in order to remain as informative as possible. Experiments with rats suggest that the brain's "affective keyboards" for risk and reward are not fixed, but can be "retuned" in response to changes in the level of risk and reward it faces. In a more dangerous environment, for example, a greater portion of the nucleus accumbens shell becomes devoted to fear-generation, to permit greater discrimination among degrees of risk; when risk is removed and the environment made friendlier, a greater portion of the shell becomes devoted to the discrimination of degrees of positive valence and appetitive motivation (Reynolds & Berridge, 2008). Like any biological system, these tunings are not perfect; particular kinds of experiences or drugs can result in the keyboard being out of tune in various ways. Chronic insecurity and stress in early childhood or severe trauma in adolescence or adulthood can result in individuals being hypersensitive to particular kinds of situations or drugs. A normally flexible, adaptive system that helps individuals cope with the vicissitudes of life can become distorted in ways that make life much more difficult. This can cause various kinds of disorder or addiction (Herman, 1992; Knudsen, Heckman, Cameron, & Shonkoff, 2006; Lupien, McEwen, Gunnar, & Heim, 2009). Proper attunement of paired forms of affect, such as confidence and fear, liking and disliking, anger and amiability, is as essential in daily life as it is in emergency situations or situations of great risk. Excessive confidence can render us foolhardy, socially insensitive, overly certain of our own opinions, and oblivious to evidence and to the feelings of others, whereas excessive fear can render us anxious, withdrawn, irresolute, suspicious, defensive, and mean-spirited. Out-of-tune affective responses are often just as great an obstacle to successful navigation of the physical and social world as poor sensory perception or physical coordination. Indeed, recent research relates a number of psychological disorders to failures of the learning processes of the affective system.

What we increasingly find in contemporary psychology, then, is a conception of the affective system as an experientially calibrated information-processing system. This system makes a key contribution to our ability to learn about, anticipate, evaluate, estimate, and act upon the prospects or perils of the world (Nesse & Ellsworth, 2009). The idea of "affect as information"—shaping cognition and helping guide behavior—has gained increasing support (Schwarz & Clore, 1983, 2007). Thus, although everyday life does not *seem* full of emotion, once we take into account default, as well as aroused, affect and think about what life is like in those moments when we *lose* default affective responses for whatever reason, we realize that an emotional tone—when healthy, typically mildly positive—is always there.

This conception of the affective system also helps explain a number of puzzling findings in the psychology of *happiness* or, more precisely, subjective well-being, which is an average of an individual's self-evaluation of two variables: recent affective state and overall sense of life satisfaction. We have already seen why a positive score on the typical 10-point scale of subjective well-being should be expected to be the norm in most human societies, even those with relatively low standards of living. But social scientists have been puzzled that once individuals attain a reasonable level of material sufficiency (around $60,000–$80,000 in the United States in 2008–2009), their expressed level of satisfaction increases only with *exponential* increases in income, and their overall positive affect does not really increase at all (Diener, Sandvik, Seidlitz, & Diener, 1993; Kahneman & Deaton, 2010). Why doesn't greater wealth make us happier? Equally intriguingly, even though average levels of subjective well-being are relatively constant within a population or over relatively long spans of individual lives, there is noticeable variation within individuals over shorter periods of time, such as the course of weeks and even days, in response to *changes* in their condition or information state (Eid & Diener, 1999, 2004; Schimmack & Oishi, 2005). When workers learn that they have just received a healthy raise, this characteristically results in a higher level of life satisfaction, but the effect usually fades with time, and after some number of months, they will typically report a level of subjective well-being essentially the same as it was before the raise. This has been called a "hedonic treadmill," as individuals strive to increase their well-being while always reverting to a personal "set point," which varies somewhat from individual to individual (Brickman & Campbell, 1971; Watson & Clark, 1994). At the same time, finely grained daily events cause fluctuations in subjective well-being (Suh, Diener, & Fukita, 1996). Thus, a morning frustration, even relatively small, can send one's life satisfaction down, while an afternoon success, even relatively small, can send it up. But not all of life's changes work this way—some changes in condition leads to a persistent loss of life satisfaction, as for example, among those involuntarily unemployed in highly developed countries (Lucas, Clark, Georgellis, & Diener, 2004).

This all seems very difficult to fit into a coherent picture of subjective well-being until one thinks of affect as information. Default affect, we argued, must typically fall in the positive range if the individual is to sustain the ordinary business of life. Fine-grained fluctuation, however, makes sense if subjective well-being is telling us how well things are going from moment to moment in our lives and whether our prospects are improving or deteriorating— whether we should make some changes or adjustments in our behavior or to simply keep doing what we are doing. Return to a set point is a generic feature of many effective information-sensing systems. If the system ratcheted upward with each gain and stayed there until some decrement occurred—in the case of well-being, say, if the better one's life had gone, the higher the level would be, right up to the top of the scale—then the "needle" on the gauge of the sensing system would be pushed up against the top of its range, with less and less ability to signal the next gain. However, if there are conditions that one must persistently seek to find a way to overcome (i.e., obstacles to getting by), such as involuntary unemployment, a more persistent decrement is found on subjective well-being, because one is *not* able to return to business as usual (Lucas et al., 2004). All this is speculative, but it suggests how thinking of affect as functioning primarily to provide thought- and action-guiding information related to the meeting of life's large and small challenges, affords us a new lens for viewing what had been a very unclear picture of a central fact about human life. Moreover, it points directly toward the *prospective* character of affect: Affective states coordinate mental and bodily states to prepare the individual for *what is to come*, not simply to register a response to what *is present now* or *what has come before*.

Think back on your reaction to the email invitation and your mulling over how to respond. Perhaps, when you first saw the message, you felt almost instantly that you'd like to decline. But no sooner had this idea crossed your mind than you felt unsure about it and unhappy with it. So your mind ranged a bit further and turned up a complex interplay of personal and social feelings, each of which can be seen as attentive to one or more dimensions of the problem and each of which exerts some force in shaping the overall "feeling" that eventually led to your decision to accept. These responses drew directly on your own "affective palette," but they imaginatively "tried on" possible responses and used this palette to paint a psychic portrait of what those possibilities might be like, to which, in turn, one could react positively or negatively, confidently or anxiously. This process involved an immediate and involuntary form of empathic projection, a simulation of how things might look or feel from your coworker's standpoint, using your own affective system as a "test bed," whether or not these reactions on his part would be justified in your view. Just as our perceptual system keeps us in touch with what is happening to the objects around us, empathy keeps us in touch with what is happening to the people around us, and each is a vital stream of information needed in real time if we are to flourish as social beings.

In the normal case, these streams of information flow continuously without need for conscious intervention: We'll "see" the anger or sadness on colleagues' faces when we encounter them in the hallway, even though we were concentrating on something else at the time. And during a fluent conversation, we will "see" each other's shifting responses to what has been said almost as soon as they occur. Indeed, when this breaks down, conversation can become awkward and ineffective: "Yes, we talked about it. But I don't think they heard what I was saying." Part of what makes your quandary over how to respond to your colleague's email difficult is that you must anticipate his reaction without the visual information face-to-face communication would make possible. Empathy has limits and is, of course, entwined with our own cognitive, imaginative, and affective limitations. Various circumstances and attitudes will tend to inhibit empathy, and we may lack the responsive range in our own affective system to understand each other spontaneously if our differences in culture or life experience are sufficiently great.

From the standpoint of prospection, what is notable about empathy, however, is that spontaneous empathic simulation of others generates a predictive internal model of them, which can be more or less accurate depending on the psychological resources we can bring to bear. The more effectively we empathize, the better we will be at modeling and predicting. In our discussion of linguistic competence, we noted that positing some implicit, organized body of knowledge that speakers can spontaneously draw on is thought to be necessary in order to understand how humans can so universally and effectively learn their native languages and go on to produce and understand an enormous number of novel sentences. But producing and understanding sentences is hardly a grammatical task alone: The hardest parts in conversation are knowing what to say, how to phrase it, when to speak, what others' words mean, or what they are thinking and feeling and how to adjust to this. For such *sociolinguistic competence* to be an open-ended capacity that most humans achieve to some degree—they could hardly get on in the social world or even make sense of one another's words if they did not—the amount of implicit, organized knowledge and information they are able to spontaneously draw on must be huge. This seems possible only if individuals also spontaneously form multidimensional internal models of one another as they move through the social world. As in the case of language, we can speculate that the human mind is set up by evolution to be able to extract information from others' behavior to form such generative internal models of what they are thinking and feeling. For example, evidence from developmental psychology suggests that even at a very early age, human infants are able to distinguish the feelings and intentions of others (e.g., Barrera & Maurer, 1981; Meltzoff, 1995; Onishi & Baillargeon, 2005; Serrano, Iglesias, & Loeches, 1992; Southgate, Senju, & Csibra, 2007).

Looking Under the Hood—Do the Processes Underlying Our Conscious Experience Fit Homo prospectus?

We have been speculating about psychological processes and their connection to prospection. We've suggested, for example, that conscious feelings and intuitions about language or about others' thoughts, feelings, and likely behavior might be manifestations of unconscious, but informationally rich, model-building, projective, evaluative, and decision-making mental processes. That is a lot to ask of the human brain, imperfect as it often seems to be. Such suggestions on our part make predictions about what neuroscientists will find as they penetrate beneath the conscious surface of mind. The last two decades in neuroscience have given an emphatic answer: There is a great deal of evidence that the brain is involved in just these sorts of informationally rich processes, even if our conscious mind has no clue of this.

Let's start with a look at the findings regarding the spontaneous empathic modeling of one another. Experiencing a mild shock, anticipating the arrival of such a shock, watching another person undergo such a shock, and imagining inflicting such a shock upon another appear to activate extensively overlapping or adjoint regions of the affective system (Decety & Ickes, 2009; Ruby & Decety, 2001; but see Singer & Lamm, 2009 for more detailed analysis of the areas involved). That is, the same or very similar core affective responses are observed in all these cases, and where they differ is what use the brain then makes of this affective encoding of "what it is like" to feel an electric shock. This information can serve to guide one's own immediate behavior, one's expectations and feelings about one's future possibilities, or one's expectations for and feelings about others. Moreover, those with profound deficits in these capacities find the "intuitive" ability to anticipate their own futures or to spontaneously understand the state of mind of others exceptionally difficult to acquire or use effectively (Baron-Cohen, 1997; Decety & Ickes, 2009).

Regarding actions, systems engineers had discovered the effectiveness of a control process for complex movements in which the issuance of a motor command is accompanied by generating a "forward model" of the predicted outcome of executing the command, permitting detection of discrepancies with desired outcomes even before sensory feedback can occur. And such anticipatory discrepancy in turn can be fed back via an "inverse model" to determine what changes in motor command might bring the system closer to the desired state (Craig, 1986). Underlying this capacity is, as we might suspect, a capacity to construct and update a causal model of the situation, available actions, and likely outcomes. Soon this approach was being applied theoretically to motor control in living systems (Lacquaniti, Borghese, & Carrozzo, 1992; Miall & Wolpert, 1996), and immediately the search for actual neural mechanisms began.

Within a decade, the theorized model-based motor control had been given substantial empirical grounding, and still more sophisticated versions of dynamic model-based control using Bayesian approaches to uncertainty and principles of optimality in behavior selection had come into play (Körding & Wolpert, 2006; Liu & Todorov, 2007; Todorov & Jordan, 2002). The slowness of actual sensory feedback means that the system's reliance on expectations is critical. It appears that this same predictive and inverse modeling capacity is used empathically to simulate internally and thereby predict and interpret the observed behavior of others. It can then be used to generate the expectations needed to guide our own actions with respect to them, preparing responses to actions not yet performed and immensely facilitating tasks, such as social learning and cooperation, although the mechanisms involved in such simulation remain subject to debate (Calvo-Merino, Glaser, Grèzes, Passingham, & Haggard, 2005; Lamm, Batson, & Decety, 2007).

A causal, predictive internal model thus provides an integrated way of interpreting recent experience and selecting a response to it, which can be used equally for the self or others. Empathy is not a simple replication of the attitude or behavior of another by a kind of "emotional contagion." We don't just become angry when someone else is angry or bored when we see that someone else is bored. The simulation of empathy uses our own affective system, but "off line," so that the connection with action is mediated by representations of the self versus others. Anatomically, these differences in simulation appear to be neurally correlated with differences in self- versus other-representation in general (Ruby & Decety, 2001).

Given the tight social conditions under which humans and their immediate ancestors have come into the world, grown to maturity, lived, and reproduced, it would be surprising if a capacity to be attuned in real time to the evolving thoughts, feelings, intentions, and likely behavior of those around us were *not* part of the core functioning of the brain. What could be more important in small-scale human societies for the meeting of one's needs or accomplishing of one's goals than one's relations with others?

This picture of the working of empathy requires, however, that our minds be capable of sophisticated kinds of learning necessary to build and update the underlying predictive models. We must somehow acquire sufficient information about the causal and intentional structures of the world. And these learning processes must be able to proceed via "unsupervised" as well as supervised learning, both because explicit instruction or correction are comparatively rare in social situations, so that implicit learning is more the norm, and because, at the very beginning, the infant must herself learn which gestures or words of others correspond to instruction or correction. Could the learning systems we inherit from our animal and hominid ancestors be up to such an informationally intensive and computationally complex task?

As long as implicit personal and social learning were regarded as purely associative processes, an ingraining of stimulus-response dispositions on the basis of past reward or punishment, such a task seemed far out of reach. Such processes acquire information slowly, adapt poorly to changing environments, and effect "local" links between stimuli and responses, which do not support higher-level modeling of the explanatory mechanisms behind what is experienced.

However, a revolution has occurred in learning theory, profoundly enriching our picture of how intelligent animals actually learn. A breakthrough came when neuroscientists using microelectrode readings of the behavior of single neurons began to assemble a picture of the neural infrastructure of reward learning. Wolfram Schultz and co-investigators (Schultz, Dayan, & Montague, 1997) placed microelectrodes in so-called dopamine neurons in the midbrain of macaques, and they were able to record the train of spiking activity that took place when an animal first received an unexpected reward (a squirt of sweet fruit juice). Later, they conditioned the macaque to expect this reward by turning on a light 1.5 seconds before the arrival of the juice. They observed, perhaps unsurprisingly, that the dopamine neurons initially underwent a spike in firing when the unexpected juice arrived (the "unconditional stimulus"). After all, isn't dopamine about pleasure? But with increased exposure to the "conditioning stimulus" of the light, the spike moved from the time of the arrival of the juice to the time of the coming on of the light. And then when the juice arrived 1.5 seconds later, there was no spike. Had the macaque become indifferent to the juice, getting pleasure instead from the light? Schultz et al. (1997) tried turning on the light, and then, 1.5 seconds later, giving *no* juice. When this occurred, an extraordinary event took place. Normally in any collection of neurons, a certain amount of seemingly random firing is taking place, often seen as a minimal, baseline neural noise. But when the juice failed to arrive, the dopamine neurons fell nearly silent—nothing—right on cue at 1.5 seconds.

So the initial spike in the dopamine neurons was not pleasure or reward, it was *information* about prospective reward (Brooks & Berns, 2013; de la Fuente-Fernández et al., 2002). Prior to the introduction of the conditioning stimulus, the unexpected arrival of the unconditioned stimulus, a squirt of sweet juice, was good news—a "better than expected" event. But after conditioning, the news value attached instead to the coming on of the light, which interrupted an otherwise boring bit of time in the lab. So the light became the good news, and when the squirt of juice was delivered right on time, 1.5 seconds after the light came on, its arrival was "no news"—the juice was neither better nor worse than expected, so no spiking behavior was observed. And then, when the juice failed to arrive 1.5 seconds after the light came on, this "worse than expected" result immediately induced a dramatic suppression of the normal activity of the dopamine neurons—a pronounced and distinctive neural "error signal." This error signal also functioned as a "teaching signal" for the macaque, and if the failure to deliver a squirt of juice continued, the spike associated with the coming on of the light would attenuate and disappear.

The macaque did not simply "associate" juice with the light, but internally generated a specific expectation of how the world would be, given the information provided by the light. This forward-looking representation set the macaque up to expect juice in 1.5 seconds, created a state in which the absence of juice in 1.5 seconds was not simply one more boring moment in a boring day, but a *mistake*, a distinctive neural event signaling an *error* in the forward representation. Through such "prediction-error" based learning, the animal seemed able to acquire and retain an internal representation of the probabilities and rewards of the world through error-reduction learning. Here's a schematic way of picturing the process:

(*) *representation* → *expectation* → *observation* → *discrepancy detection* (feedback) → *error-reducing representation revision* → *revised expectation* → *observation* → *discrepancy detection* ...

By repeated application of a process of this kind, the animal's internal representations will tend to become "tuned" to the actual frequencies in its environment.

Researchers asked what would happen if one varied the probability with which juice followed the light, so that it was received 75%, 50%, or 25% of the time. Studies by Schultz and many others showed via individual neural recordings of spike rates that the primate and rat brains can keep accurate track of all of these variations. For example, when the probability is 50%, the spiking activity is roughly half as high as when the probability is 100%; when the probability is 75%, the spiking activity is midway between the two (Fiorillo, Tobler, & Schultz, 2003). And what would happen if one varied the *value* of the reward from time to time, increasing it from one squirt to two, or two to one? Neural firing activity in the orbital prefrontal cortex was monitored, and again, the cells' responses tracked variations in magnitude—not just absolute, but relative to prior expectations and preferences (Tremblay & Schultz, 1999). Further research found that macaques and rats not only formed separate representations of probability versus reward value, but also computed a joint product, *expected value* (probability × reward) that appears to guide choice behavior (Preuschoff, Bossaerts, & Quartz, 2006; Schultz, 2002; Singer, Critchley, & Preuschoff, 2009; Tobler, O'Doherty, Dolan, & Schultz, 2006). Eventually, a complete and coherent "marginal utility function" could be reconstructed from the monkeys' choices in gambles between banana slices and squirts of sweet juice (Stauffer, Lak, & Schultz, 2014).

Contrary to years of thinking about the animal mind, it appeared that intelligent mammals respond to information and rewards in their world very much in the manner rational decision theory would recommend.[3] Moreover, their learning pattern closely resembled the behavior of idealized models of Bayesian probabilistic learners, for whom expectations are updated in light of experience via "conditionalization," a mathematical function that takes into account prior expectations as well as the likelihood of the new evidence, given what was antecedently expected. Successive episodes of updating will tend, as evidence grows, to generate an increasingly accurate array of forward expectations of outcomes. Indeed, there is something more: The brains of intelligent animals and humans respond to experience by forming expectations not only about individual events, but about *higher-order regularities* and *types* of events and outcomes, thus creating causal-explanatory models of the world much as a scientist does (Badre & Frank, 2012; Courville, Daw, & Touretzky, 2006; Frank & Badre, 2012; Gershman & Niv, 2015; Tenenbaum et al., 2011).

Philosophers, mathematicians, and statisticians had previously shown that Bayesian learning has a number of singularly important features for creatures such as ourselves and for the foraging mammals from which we descended. First, it links learning directly to the guidance of behavior by making *expectation* be at the center of learning: Learning is not about assembling a massive archive of past events, but about efficient extraction from ongoing experience of probabilistic information used to update model-based expectations. A record of past events, however accurate, is mute about what will happen next (the "time/date" coding of stored information will always be *earlier* than the present moment). The expectations resulting from (*)-like or Bayesian processes are, in effect, running summaries of the impact of past information, and thus afford instantaneous access to the net result of what one has learned without requiring an extensive search of memory in order to determine "the weight of evidence." For a creature living on the edge of existence, this is a tremendous saving of the neural structures it must grow and sustain. And for humans who ordinarily deliberate using intuitively "felt" strengths of belief or degrees of uncertainty, such processes suggest a mechanism by which such intuitions could be sensitive to what we have learned implicitly as well as explicitly, and how reliable this has been.

Second, (*)-like and Bayesian processes are "self-correcting." Expectation always introduces an element of bias, because it anticipates outcomes without waiting to see what actually happens. However, if expectations are consistently modified in the face of experience in a (*)-like or Bayesian manner, then over time, the influence of initial expectations will tend to diminish as new experiences "tune" expectations to actual frequencies through the reduction of prediction error. As experience grows in magnitude and diversity, Bayesians point out, initial expectations tend to "wash out," and individuals who began from different starting assumptions, but encountered similar experience, will tend to converge in their expectations. And importantly, they will tend to converge on the actual "natural statistics" of their environment (for further perspectives on the "Bayesian brain", see Chater & Oaksford, 2008 and Hohwy, 2013).

Associative learning, we noted, has been criticized as far too slow to permit fine-tuning to a rapidly changing environment. Such learning is cumulative in character, and the great weight of past experience tends to offset changes in recent experience (Lieberman, 2000). But statistical learners employing (*)-like or Bayesian methods see things differently; the *more strongly* a certain outcome is expected, the more *surprise* one experiences when the expected outcome does not occur, and the more one revises one's expectations going forward. If animals and humans are (*)-like or Bayesian learners, then they should pay greatest attention to *incongruous* rather than familiar experiences, as these afford the greatest potential information value for learning. And when researchers look at the attention patterns of very young infants, they find just this pattern. Even at a few weeks of age, infants show greater interest when they hear scrambled patterns of phonemes in their native language as opposed to normal speech (Saffran, Aslin, & Newport, 1996). And by 8 months, infants are able to discriminate incongruities in an artificial language and appear to update their conditional expectations accordingly (Aslin, Saffran, & Newport, 1998). More recent research indicates that infants in the first year of life use statistical information across contexts to resolve the reference of words (Smith & Yu, 2007) and exhibit quite general capacities for causal and statistical learning across a variety of domains (Kirkham, Slemmer, & Johnson, 2002; Sobel & Kirkham, 2006). Studies of causal learning by rats suggests that even they abjure purely associative learning and statistically learn to distinguish different causal models of situations and to discriminate between the absence of events and the lack of evidence (Blaisdell, Sawa, Leising, & Waldmann, 2006; Waldmann, Schmid, Wong, & Blaisdell, 2012). Recent work on "deep learning" models of object recognition and on Bayesian causal learning shows how the development of hierarchical information structures in the face of experience can even result in the formation of new categories. Drawing on the large amount information about objects encoded in learned "deep" hierarchies, it becomes possible to correctly identify examples in a new category even after experiencing a few instances—the way that children quickly spot the difference between a bicycle and a scooter, even after seeing only a few samples of each (Lake, Salakhutdinov, & Tenenbaum, 2015).

The importance of statistical learning sheds light on the difficult problem of *implicit bias* in human social interactions. The bad news is that children appear to learn over time to make implicit evaluations of the abilities and aptitudes of groups based on the biased samples of the total population to which they are typically exposed when growing up in the United States, which remains significantly segregated in residence and primary education. By age 6, children already show implicit learning of the biases of their society, even children who belong to the stigmatized group itself (Baron & Banaji, 2006). Because this learning is implicit, it can shape behavior even when the individual is trying consciously *not* to be prejudiced (Macrae, Bodenhausen, Milne, & Jetten, 1994). Is implicit bias, therefore, an intractable problem? The good news is that the same kinds of statistical learning mechanisms can operate to weaken implicit bias if individuals are exposed to samples less biased in their representation of abilities (Dasgupta, 2013). If bias is learned in a (*)-like or Bayesian implicit way from living in unequal social relationships, then it can be unlearned in a (*)-like or Bayesian implicit way by living in more equal social relationships. What looks like an intractable social problem arising from hardwired or inbred ingroup/outgroup attitudes seems instead to reflect, and thus be amenable to, statistical learning. We will return to the problem of implicit bias, and to a remarkable "natural experiment" that illustrates how learning can change even centuries-old biases, when we discuss morality in Chapter 9.

Reinforcement learning, so long as it involves a rich and varied environment, is not about entrenching habits by hammering them home by repetition, but about attending to the most informative cues in the environment to construct probabilistic representations of what to expect (Gallistel, Mark, King, & Latham, 2001; Rescorla, 1988). In Chapter 1, we introduced the idea of a "good regulator" and suggested that we should think of the challenge individuals face in the world as one of regulating their interchanges with their physical and social environment so as to meet their needs and realize their aims. A good regulator, we noted, must build an *internal model* of the system as a whole and make its decisions by consulting this model to understand how its actions will affect its world and itself.

(*)-like learning is not enough for a good regulator to build an accurate model of the system as a whole. The regulator would need to *use* the probabilistic information thus acquired to construct structural models of causal relationships (Tenenbaum et al., 2011).[4] And considerable evidence attests that human children engage in this kind of causal modeling from early on (Gopnik et al., 2004; Sobel & Kirkham, 2006), and that intelligent animals develop and use model-like representations of spatial relationships and potential actions in navigating their environment (Moser, Kropff, & Moser, 2008). Recently, work indicating the use of causal-explanatory models by intelligent animals has also begun to appear (Blaisdell & Waldmann, 2012). Model-based learning is of special importance in understanding the pervasive *dynamic flexibility* of behavior in real time—a flexibility that is difficult to accommodate on habit-based models (Balleine & Dickinson, 1998), and even behaviors traditionally seen as habitual are being rethought as more complex (Smith & Graybiel, 2014).

In thinking about the ice fisherman's actions in Chapter 1, we appealed to the flexibility of model-based action to suggest how he was able to intelligently improvise a new approach and capture the fish (Gillan, Otto, Phelps, & Daw, 2015). He not only caught a fish, he caught a new *way* of catching fish. And he will be able to use this new approach the very next time he fishes, without waiting for a long history of reinforcement in that new pattern of behavior. But this does not require departure from broadly Bayesian learning. For (*)-like or Bayesian responses to causal events of diverse kinds over the course of his lifetime has given the fisherman not only first-order expectations about ways of catching fish, but higher-order expectations about the ways in which the world is regular, and this general knowledge can be brought to bear to permit extrapolation even from individual instances. That is, the fisherman has used something like Bayesian hierarchical learning to develop and assess causal models of his world. This is how, it seems, actual humans solve the age-old problem of induction—they *don't*. Instead of induction, they use causal modeling, starting off with prior expectations and updating these on the basis of experience (Gopnik et al., 2004). In the intensely social human world, the experience of exchanging information with others is of special importance. We speculate that humans can accomplish their remarkable adaptive improvisation not only because of their brains, but also because of the language and culture they inherit (the *socialis* in *Homo prospectus socialis* and the topic of Chapter 5). This inheritance enables them to acquire rich representations of the physical and social world that extend far beyond the course of first-person experience.

But humans are not the only ones good at adaptive innovation. To understand how deep the idea of prospection is in understanding the evolved brain and the great advantages it confers, we need to see how key powers of prospection earned their way into the minds of our ancestors long before the emergence of culture as we know it. Where better to start than the favored species of experimental psychology, the white rat? Rats suffered through decades of maze running to test the associative theory of learning, and a large research program, behaviorism, was built upon their backs. On the associative theory, a rat learns to turn right in a maze because the motor response of executing a right turn was soon followed by a reinforcement—a bit of food. By repeated running of the maze, this motor response was "trained" into the rat. But the great experimentalist Karl Lashley made an observation in 1920, in the heady early days of behaviorism, which raised questions about this idea of what the rat had learned. One day, a rat escaped the start box of its maze, climbing up on top of the structure. What would it do? The conditioned response model would predict that the rat would walk (say) 10 steps forward, turn right, walk 5 steps, turn right again, and find the food. After all, that was the motor pattern that had been so assiduously reinforced.

But instead the rat scampered *diagonally* across the top of the maze, directly to the food station (Lashley, 1929). Laboratory conditions prevented the rat from "following its nose" to the food—somehow, it was following something else, something more abstract that it had *learned* while running trials in the maze. Thus began the idea that rats might not be slaves to stimulus-response conditioning, they might form mental representations of *locations and paths* extending in space, permitting them to respond flexibly and intelligently to entirely novel opportunities afforded by the world. Not only that, but the novel behavior had never been reinforced. Could learning really take place in light of *internally represented values or goals ("purposes")*, without the external carrot of reward or stick of punishment?

It was the Berkeley psychologist Edward Tolman who took the next step. He held that rats could learn about their environment from exploration alone, without external reinforcement, and posited that rats developed a "cognitive map" of the spatial layout of the maze that was not tied to any specific pattern of motor responses. In a series of experiments in which rats had to perform novel actions to get to the food, such as swimming or managing to put together a sequence of rolling or rotating movements enabling them to turn right after their ability to turn right directly had been surgically removed, his hypothesis held up (Tolman, 1948). Tolman came to see rats as *purposive* creatures whose cognitive maps enabled them to pursue goals in a manner he called "autonomous": They can extract information from their confined experience of the maze to build general-purpose mental representations that give them an ability to shift the way they pursue their goals without new incentives.

Ironically, it was Tolman's concern with autonomy, not just running down the channels laid down for him, which led him to refuse to sign the loyalty oath required by the Regents of the University of California. Despite his eminence as a researcher, his refusal to sign the loyalty oath on grounds of academic freedom led the McCarthy-inspired Regents to seek his dismissal in the early 1950s. Tolman, of course, had the scientific accomplishments needed to obtain a position elsewhere, and he was able to continue his research at McGill University in Canada. But his commitment to autonomy wouldn't let him stop there, and he sued the California Regents in *Tolman v. Underhill* (1955), in which the California Supreme Court struck down the loyalty oath and ordered Tolman's reinstatement. Today, the building on the Berkeley campus built to house the departments of psychology and education is named Tolman Hall—a monument to standing up for the freedom to pursue one's own paths.

Tolman's cognitive maps, like the notions of "autonomy" and "purposive behaviorism" that went with them, were greeted with great skepticism by hard-core behaviorists, who remained steadfastly loyal to the stimulus-response, engrained motor-pattern model. Direct experimental testing of Tolman's ideas of rat mentation would await the development of sophisticated neuroscientific techniques seven decades later. And when testing did come, Tolman's "cognitive maps" hypothesis turned out to be true, in spades. As a rat explores the environment, "place cells" in the hippocampus and "grid cells" in the entorhinal cortex respectively construct relational and absolute maps of the environment. The system keeps track of where the animal currently is, but also represents a totality of possible locations (Ainge, Tamosiunaite, Wörgötter, & Dudchenko, 2012; Derdikman & Moser, 2010; Langston et al., 2010). These maps have substantial independence from direct experience and show repeated activation when the rat is waiting its chance to run the maze or in rapid eye movement (REM) sleep after a day of training in the maze (Ji & Wilson, 2007). During these episodes, activation preferentially occurs in the areas the rat spent *less* time in, and follows *backward* as well as forward trajectories. These are patterns you would expect if animals make use of past experience to build a richer representation of the world behind experience, and the opposite of what you'd expect if animals operated by associationist principles. And Lashley's rat was finally explained: During REM sleep, activation in the maze includes the construction of shortcut paths across the grid, so that these actions can be readily available should circumstances permit them (Gupta, van der Meer, Touretzky, & Redish, 2010). Moreover, in the aftermath of these periods of brain activity *simulating* the running of the maze, performance improves: Learning takes place without external reinforcement, again, the opposite of what the behaviorists for so long preached must *obviously* be the case. Disrupt these periods of "off-line" activation, and performance deteriorates (Ward et al., 2009), a result that has been duplicated with human sleep and learning (Stickgold, 2013).

Now, the real test of the idea of prospection is: Does a rat actually running the maze *consult the map prospectively* when making its way through? Does it engage in prospective guidance by simulating alternate possible paths and using evaluative information to select among them? Do mapping and expected value estimation combine in the rat mind to yield genuinely prospective guidance? David Redish and colleagues at Minnesota tested this idea by watching activation patterns in the rat's cognitive maps as the rats reached choice points during the period when they were actively learning the maze. They found that prior to the rat turning left or right, while still poised at the junction, activation in its mental map spread alternately down the two arms of the maze, ahead of the rat's current location. These "sweeps" of possible pathways appear to serve as prospective models of possible actions that afford a projective frame to guide evaluation and action selection (Johnson & Redish, 2007; Johnson, van der Meer, & Redish, 2007). Without leaving the choice point, the rat has "looked down" both of the paths; and drawing on what it learned thus far about the probability and value of the rewards it received in prior exploration, it elects the arm of the maze with the higher expected value. Rats are not only good at Bayesian learning of probabilities and values, they are good at modeling this information in a spatially mapped array of possible actions to guide actual choices in line with maximizing expected value.

A key task for testing such a hypothesis about the guidance of animal behavior by causal modeling and expected value computations comes with *foraging*. Mammals need to gain their nutrition from the environment around them, and prior to the human invention of agriculture, this called for hunting and gathering (like our ice fisherman from Chapter 1). Foragers need to figure out the shape of their environment, the location and reliability of possible sources of food, the costs and risks of obtaining food from the different sources, the balance of nutritional needs, the trade-offs between exploring for new resources and exploiting known resources, and so on. Ethologists have observed that mammals and other intelligent species are able to develop nearly optimal foraging patterns via sampling the physical and social environment for food as well as other vital resources, such as partners for cooperation and mating (Dugatkin, 2004). An account of the mechanisms by which they do this has been missing. In effect, the animals face an *optimal control problem*, and systems theory tells us that we should look to model-based control as an effective way of solving such optimization-under-constraint problems (Braun, Nagengast, & Wolpert, 2011; Conant & Ashby, 1970). The very machinery that neuroscience has been discovering is ideally suited in the real world for animals to forage effectively.

And what about humans? Recent experiments in which human subjects face simulated foraging tasks, involving risk and money, rather than food and predation, indicate that given time to explore and sample, humans can also develop nearly optimal foraging patterns (Kolling, Behrens, Mars, & Rushworth, 2012) and can use the volatility of rewards to adjust decision-making for uncertainty in an optimal manner (Behrens, Woolrich, Walton, & Rushworth, 2007).

Model-based control theory has also come to play a central role in the study of *skilled movement* in animals and humans. Elite athletes appear to differ from merely excellent athletes not in the speed of their reflexes, ability to jump, or degree of training of basic motor patterns. The crucial difference appears to be that they possess more detailed and accurate models of complex movements and competitive situations, which allow them to get the drop on their rivals (e.g., placing a tennis shot where it can't be returned, identifying a fast-emerging scoring opportunity before the opponent can spot and close it) and to achieve more efficiency and effectiveness in exploiting the body's resources (just how to take off and twist in a high jump) (Yarrow, Brown, & Krakauer, 2009). Intriguingly, the elite athletes continue to show variability in large-scale motor performance (swinging a bat, golf club, or raquet) even when some of the small-scale components of such performance have achieved a high level of consistency (Yarrow et al., 2009). It appears that they are constantly, implicitly, experimenting. Famously, artisans expert at making cigars showed continued improvement in performance even after rolling cigars for 7 years (Crossman, 1959). Finally, expert models in competitive sports and games must include accurate *evaluative* information, because successful competitors must make trade-offs involving risks, benefits, and costs.

We are still at the beginning of the emerging understanding of how animals and humans are able to construct and use evaluative-causal models to perform effectively and efficiently in the face of the challenges facing them. But thanks to research in psychology and neuroscience, underpinned by a solid foundation in philosophy and systems theory, for the first time we are getting a unified account of how this might actually work, whether in a foraging field mouse, a skilled athlete, or an excellent diagnostic physician.

Intuition Revisited

Let us now return to the question of intuition. Optimal guidance by "evaluative mapping" of future possibilities must combine stored and computed information of a large variety of kinds with the representations furnished by perception and spatial mapping. For greatest functionality, efficiency, and effectiveness in regulating the organism/environment interchange (e.g., guiding action selection), the predictive and explanatory models thereby created must forge together evidence from:

- Our different senses
- Information about causal relationships or similar patterns of events, drawn from memory of particular incidents (episodic memory) or general tendencies (semantic memory)
- "Interoceptive" information about the internal state of the organism, including available resources, more or less urgent needs, and longer-term goals
- Representations of the physical and social surroundings, whether proximate or distal
- Indicators of personal location and trajectory
- Imaginative representation of an array of possible actions and outcomes and the ways in which values or likelihoods depend on which action is taken

Could all of this really be going on as you sit at your kitchen table, pondering how to respond to your coworker's invitation? Don't we know that such responses tend to be based on relatively simplistic thinking and blunt "gut feelings?" The reader versed in contemporary social psychology will know of the huge body of research based on "dual-process" models of the mind (Bargh & Chartrand, 1999; Haidt, 2001; Kahneman, 2011). In this model, system 1 is *intuitive*. It is largely an implicit system, fast, automatic, and affective rather than calculating, and it is dominated by such simplifying heuristics as "anchoring," "representativeness," and "salience," with "little understanding of logic and statistics" (Kahneman, 2011, pp. 21, 24). System 2 is *conscious and deliberative*. It is the "declarative" system of conscious thought; it is capable of logical and statistical reasoning, but it is slow and effortful, placing demands on attention. In ordinary life system 2 plays a much more restricted role in our behavior. How does the dual-process picture square with our picture of the implicit, intuitive system as actively engaged in prospective assessment via expected value representations and causal modeling?

We have already seen that although our affective system is "ancient" and grounded in brain systems we share with our mammalian ancestors, this need not make it unsophisticated at learning and using information about probabilities and values or modeling the prospects and perils of a complex physical and social environment. Why *wouldn't* millions of generations of natural selection for optimal foraging have evolved and improved mechanisms that would be effective and efficient at evaluation and action-selection? And given what we know about the brain's power and speed, the rapidity of intuitive responses need not mean that they do not involve complex processing of information or calculation of expected value and risk (see Quartz, 2009). Intriguingly, humans who are given a chance to engage intuitively in implicit learning using representative samples and feedback seem not to make some of the errors with probability that have been well-documented in the "heuristics and biases" literature (Behrens et al., 2007; Pleskac & Hertwig, 2014). Perhaps the right moral to draw is that the "intuitive" system, like any system that *projects* on the basis of experience, needs good data to yield good results.

There are many limitations of probabilistic learning. For example, while such systems can yield new categories through learning, in solving life's practical, social, and theoretical problems we often must introduce new categories or hypotheses in a *directed* fashion, ahead of learning. Language and declarative thought are well-suited to provide this sort of cognitive scaffolding, especially since they enable us to *share* what we have learned and to deliberate or innovate *together*—even though they cannot do so effectively or efficiently without relying extensively upon the intuitive attitudes we have acquired through experience. We are brought back to Aristotle's observation in the *Posterior Analytics* (trans. 1941, II.100b) that reasoning cannot supply its own premises. As Paul Slovic put it, "analytic reasoning cannot be effective unless it is guided by emotion and affect" (Slovic, Finucane, Peters, & MacGregor 2004).

What then would our experience be like if we actually were guided by prospection? It would be like the experience of our ice fisherman in Chapter 1 or like ourselves when faced with an unanticipated email invitation. It would be like the bad feeling of returning home to a hungry family empty-handed, or like the feeling that it just might be a good idea to make a second try at catching the fish. It would be like sensing that the fish might be startled by your shadow, and that you'd have a better chance if you snuck up from the other side of the ice hole. And it would be like the strong sense that turning down your coworker's invitation, even though you have mixed feelings about accepting it, is nonetheless not the thing to do.

Finally, it would be like your growing sense that this chapter has gone on long enough to make its point: human simulation and evaluation of possible futures—prospection—can take place implicitly as well as explicitly, and such implicit prospection could underlie intuition and explain why it is so central, and so often effective, in human life.

Notes

1. For some discussion, see "Neurons and synapses" (n.d.).
2. Of course, in the real world—even the real world of high-powered artificial computation—optimization is to some degree relative to a set of constraints on speed, power, and data. What is important for our purposes is whether the decision-making process is psychologically realized by a mechanism of the recognition-and-recall sort described by Simon, Klein, or Kahneman, or one that takes the form of a dynamic, real-time, model-based optimization. (We might add that, in practice, even building a recognition-and-recall expert requires building pattern-recognition and pattern-abstraction abilities in the face of noisy data, which, in modern machine intelligence, is typically accomplished by Bayesian or statistical optimization procedures. For a seminal discussion see Tenenbaum, de Silva, & Langford, 2000; for a summary of techniques, see Webb & Copsey, 2011.)
3. Animals can become "overtrained" if the pattern of probabilities and rewards remains static over an extended period, and the behavior of dopamine neurons will be relatively slow to adjust dynamically if the probabilities or rewards change, resulting in purely habitual behavior (Adams & Dickinson, 1981; Dickinson, 1985). Humans, too, appear to exhibit such behaviors (Tricomi, Balleine, & O'Doherty, 2009)—we will, for example, flip the light switch on the wall in order to see better what we're doing, even though what we're doing is changing the burned-out light bulb in the fixture controlled by the switch.

4. One important current line of research distinguishes between "model-free" and "model-based" reinforcement learning, though this terminology can be confusing. The "model-free" process involves the formation and updating of expected value representations of potential actions and selection among actions in light of these representations. The "model-based" processes draw on the probability and value estimates of the "model-free" system (Balleine & O'Doherty, 2010; Doll, Shohamy, & Daw, 2015). Two recent studies of Pavlovian conditioning suggest that a model-based account provides a better fit with a range of neural data in a range of cases (Dayan & Berridge, 2014; Prévost, McNamee, Jessup, Bossaerts, & O'Doherty, 2013), and in any event the two systems seem to overlap extensively (Doll, Simon, & Daw, 2012). For our purposes, we distinguish the expected-value representations of (*)-like learning from full-scale causal and spatial modeling of alternative pathways.

References

Adams, C. D., & Dickinson, A. (1981). Instrumental responding following reinforcer devaluation. *The Quarterly Journal of Experimental Psychology, 33*, 109–121.

Ainge, J. A., Tamosiunaite, M., Wörgötter, F., & Dudchenko, P. A. (2012). Hippocampal place cells encode intended destination, and not a discriminative stimulus, in a conditional T-maze task. *Hippocampus, 22*, 534–543.

Aslin, R. N., Saffran, J. R., & Newport, E. L. (1998). Computation of conditional probability statistics by 8-month-old infants. *Psychological Science, 9*, 321–324.

Badre, D., & Frank, M. J. (2012). Mechanisms of hierarchical reinforcement learning in cortico-striatal circuits 2: Evidence from fMRI. *Cerebral Cortex 22*, 527–536.

Balleine, B. W., & Dickinson, A. (1998). Goal-directed instrumental action: Contingency and incentive learning and their cortical substrates. *Neuropharmacology, 37*, 407–419.

Balleine, B. W., & O'Doherty, J. P. (2010). Human and rodent homologies in action control: Corticostriatal determinants of goal-directed and habitual action. *Neuropsychopharmacology, 35*, 48–69.

Bargh, J. A., & Chartrand, T. L. (1999). The unbearable automaticity of being. *American Psychologist, 54*, 462–479.

Baron, A. S., & Banaji, M. R. (2006). The development of implicit attitudes: Evidence of race evaluations from ages 6 and 10 and adulthood. *Psychological Science, 17*, 53–58.

Baron-Cohen, S. (1997). *Mindblindness: An essay on autism and theory of mind.* Cambridge, MA: MIT Press.

Barrera, M. E., & Maurer, D. (1981). The perception of facial expressions by the three-month-old. *Child Development, 52*, 203–206.

Baumeister, R. F., Bratslavsky, E., Muraven, M., & Tice, D. M. (1998). Ego depletion: Is the active self a limited resource? *Personality Processes and Individual Differences, 74*, 1252–1265.

Behrens, T. E. J., Woolrich, M. W., Walton, M. W., & Rushworth, M. F. S. (2007). Learning the value of information in an uncertain world. *Nature Neuroscience, 10*, 1214–1221.

Berger, J. (1980). A robust generalized Bayes estimator and confidence region for a multivariate normal mean. *The Annals of Statistics, 8*, 716–761.

Blaisdell, A. P., Sawa, K., Leising, K. J., & Waldmann, M. R. (2006). Causal reasoning in rats. *Science, 311*, 1020–1022.

Blaisdell, A. P., & Waldmann, M. R. (2012). Rational rats: Causal inference and representation. In E. A. Wasserman and T. R. Zentall (Eds.), *Handbook of comparative cognition* (pp. 175–198). Oxford, England: Oxford University Press.

Bollinger, J., Rubens, M. T., Zanto, P., & Gazzaley, A. (2010). Expectation-driven changes in cortical functional connectivity influence working memory and long-term memory performance. *The Journal of Neuroscience, 30*, 14399–14410.

Braun, D. A., Nagengast, A. J., & Wolpert, D. M. (2011). Risk-sensitivity in sensorimotor control. *Frontiers in Human Neuroscience, 5*(1), 1–10. doi:10.3389/fnhum.2011.00001

Brickman, P., & Campbell, D. (1971). Hedonic relativism and planning the good society. In M. H. Apley (Ed.), *Adaptation-level theory: A symposium* (pp. 287–302). New York, NY: Academic Press.

Brooks, A. M., & Berns, G. S. (2013). Aversive stimuli and loss in the mesocorticolimbic dopamine system. *Trends in Cognitive Sciences, 17*, 281–286.

Buckner, R. L., Andrews-Hanna, J. L., & Schacter, D. L. (2008). The brain's default mode network. *Annals of the New York Academy of Sciences, 1124,* 1–38.

Calvo-Merino, B., Glaser, D. E., Grèzes, J., Passingham, R. E., & Haggard, P. (2005). Action observation and acquired motor skills: An fMRI study with expert dancers. *Cerebral Cortex, 15,* 1243–1249.

Chater, N., & Manning, C. D. (2006). Probabilistic models of language processing and acquisition. *Trends in Cognitive Sciences, 10,* 335–344.

Chater, N., & Oaksford, M. (Eds.). (2008). *The Probabilistic Mind: Prospects for a Bayesian Cognitive Science.* Oxford: Oxford University Press.

Conant, R. C., & Ashby, W. R. (1970). Every good regulator of a system must be a model of that system. *International Journal of Systems Science, 1,* 89–97.

Courville, A.C., Daw, N.D., & Touretzky, D.S. (2006). Bayesian theories of conditioning in a changing world. *Trends in Cognitive Sciences, 10,* 294–300.

Craig, J.J.(1986).*Introduction to robotics.*Reading, MA: Addison-Wesley.

Crossman, E. R. F. W. (1959). A theory of the acquisition of speed-skill. *Ergonomics, 2,* 153–166.

Dasgupta, N. (2013). Implicit attitudes and beliefs adapt to situations: A decade of research on the malleability of implicit prejudice, stereotypes, and the self-concept. In P. G. Devine & E. A. Plant (Eds.), *Advances in experimental social psychology* (Vol. 47, pp. 233–279). Oxford, England: Academic Press.

Dayan, P., & Berridge, K. C. (2014). Model-based and model-free Pavlovian reward learning: Revaluation, revision, and revelation. *Cognitive and Affective Behavioral Neuroscience, 14,* 473–492.

Decety, J., & Ickes, W. (Eds.). (2009). *The social neuroscience of empathy.* Cambridge, MA: MIT Press.

de la Fuente-Fernández, R., Phillips, A. G., Zamburlini, M., Sossi, V., Calne, D. B., Ruth, T. J., & Stoessi, A. J. (2002). Dopamine release in human ventral striatum and expectation of reward. *Behavioural Brain Research, 136,* 359–363.

de Oliveira-Souza, R., Moll, J., & Grafman, J. (2011). Emotion and social cognition: Lessons from contemporary human neuroanatomy. *Emotion Review, 3,* 310–312.

Derdikman, D., & Moser, E. I. (2010). A manifold of spatial maps in the brain. *Trends in Cognitive Sciences, 14,* 561–569.

Dickinson, A. (1985). Actions and habits: The development of behavioural autonomy. *Philosophical Transactions of the Royal Society of London, 308,* 67–78.

Diener, E., & Diener, C. (1996). Most people are happy. *Psychological Science, 7,* 181–185.

Diener, E., Sandvik, E., Seidlitz, L., & Diener, M. (1993). The relationship between income and subjective well-being: Relative or absolute? *Social Indicators Research, 28,* 195–223.

Doll, B. B., Shohamy, D., & Daw, N. D. (2015). Multiple memory systems as substrates for multiple decision systems. *Neurobiology of Learning and Memory, 117,* 4–13.

Doll, B. B., Simon, D. A., & Daw, N. D. (2012). The ubiquity of model-based reinforcement learning. *Current Opinion in Neurobiology, 22,* 1075–1081.

Dugatkin, L. A. (2004). *Principles of animal behavior.* New York, NY: W. W. Norton.

Eid, M., & Diener, E. (1999). Intraindividual variability in affect: Reliability, validity, and personality correlates. *Journal of Personality and Social Psychology, 76,* 662–676.

Eid, M., & Diener, E. (2004). Global judgments of subjective well-being: Situational variability and long-term stability. *Social Indicators Research, 65,* 245–277.

Fiorillo, C. D., Tobler, P. N., & Schultz, W. (2003). Discrete coding of reward probability and uncertainty by dopamine neurons. *Science, 299,* 1898–1902.

Fodor, J. A. (1983). *The modularity of mind: An essay on faculty psychology.* Cambridge, MA: MIT Press.

Frank, M. J., & Badre, D. (2012). Mechanisms of hierarchical reinforcement learning in cortico-striatal circuits 1: Computational analysis. *Cerebral Cortex, 22,* 509–526.

Gallistel, R., Mark, T. A., King, A. P., & Latham, P. E. (2001). The rat approximates an ideal detector of changes in rates of reward: Implications for the law of effect. *Journal of Experimental Psychology, 27,* 354–372.

Gershman, S. J., & Niv, Y. (2015). Novelty and inductive generalization in human reinforcement learning. *Topics in Cognitive Science, 7,* 391–415.

Gillan, C. M., Otto, A. R., Phelps, E. A., & Daw, N. D. (2015). Model-based learning protects against forming habits. *Cognitive, Affective and Behavioral Neuroscience, 15*, 523–536.

Gopnik, A., Glymour, C., Sobel, D. M., Schulz, L. E., Kushnir, T., & Danks, D. (2004). A theory of causal learning in children: Causal maps and Bayes nets. *Psychological Review, 111*, 3–32.

Griffiths, T. L., Steyvers, M., & Tenenbaum, J. B. (2007). Topics in semantic representation. *Psychological Review, 114*, 211–244.

Gupta, A. S., van der Meer, M. A. A., Touretzky, D. S., & Redish, A. D. (2010). Hippocampal replay is not a simple function of experience. *Neuron, 65*, 695–705.

Haidt, J. (2001). The emotional dog and its rational tail: A social intuitionist approach to moral judgment. *Psychological Review, 108*, 814–834.

Haidt, J. (2007). The new synthesis in moral psychology. *Science, 316*, 998–1002.

Hasher, L., & Zacks, R. T. (1984). Automatic processing of fundamental information: The case of frequency of occurrence. *American Psychologist, 39*, 1372–1388.

Hauser, M. D., Chomsky, N., & Fitch, T. (2002). The faculty of language: What is it, who has it, and how did it evolve? *Science, 298*, 1569–1579.

Henneberger, C., Papouin, T., Oliet, S. H. R., & Rusakov, D. A. (2010). Long-term potentiation depends on release of D-serine from astrocytes. *Nature, 463*, 232–236.

Herman, J. L. (1992). Complex PTSD: A syndrome in survivors of prolonged and repeated trauma. *Journal of Traumatic Stress, 5*, 377–391.

Hohwy, J. *The Predictive Mind.* Oxford: Oxford University Press, 2013.

Jeffrey, R. C. (1965). *The logic of decision.* New York, NY: McGraw-Hill.

Ji, D., & Wilson, M. A. (2007). Coordinated memory replay in the visual cortex and hippocampus during sleep. *Nature Neuroscience, 10*, 100–107.

Johnson, A., & Redish, A. D. (2007). Neural ensembles at CA3 transiently encode paths forward of the animal at a decision point. *The Journal of Neuroscience, 27*, 12176–12189.

Johnson, A., van der Meer, M., & Redish, A. D. (2007). Integrating hippocampus and striatum in decision-making. *Current Opinion in Neurobiology, 17*, 692–697.

Kahneman, D. (2011). *Thinking, fast and slow*. New York, NY: Farrar, Straus and Giroux.

Kahneman, D., & Deaton, A. (2010). High income improves evaluation of life but not emotional well-being. *Proceedings of the National Academy of Sciences, 107*, 16489–16493.

Kahneman, D., & Klein, G. (2009). Conditions for intuitive expertise: A failure to disagree. *American Psychologist, 64*, 515–526.

Kersten, D., Mamassian, P., & Yuille, A. (2004). Object perception as Bayesian inference. *Annual Review of Psychology, 55*, 271–304.

Kirkham, N. Z., Slemmer, J. A., & Johnson, S. P. (2002). Visual statistical learning in infancy: Evidence for a domain general learning mechanism. *Cognition, 83*, B35–B42.

Knudsen, E. I., Heckman, J. J., Cameron, J. L., & Shonkoff, J. P. (2006). Economic, neurobiological and behavioral perspectives on building America's future workforce. *Proceedings of the National Academy of Sciences, 103*, 10155–10162.

Kolling, N., Behrens, T. E. J., Mars, R. B., & Rushworth, M. F. S. (2012). Neural mechanisms of foraging. *Science, 336*, 95–98.

Körding, K. P., & Wolpert, D. M. (2006). Bayesian decision theory in sensorimotor control. *Trends in Cognitive Sciences, 10*, 319–326.

Lacquaniti, F., Borghese, N. A., & Carrozzo, M. (1992). Internal models of limb geometry in the control of hand compliance. *Journal of Neuroscience, 12*, 1750–1762.

Lake, B. M., Salakhutdinov, R., & Tenenbaum, J. B. (2015). Human-level concept learning through probabilistic program induction. *Science, 350*, 1332–1338.

Lamm, C., Batson, C., & Decety, J. (2007). The neural substrate of empathy: Effects of perspective-taking and cognitive appraisal. *Journal of Cognitive Neuroscience, 19*, 42–58.

Langston, R. F., Ainge, J. A., Couey, J. J., Canto, C. B., Bjerknes, T. L., Witter, M. P., . . . Moser, M.-B. (2010). Development of the spatial representation system in the rat. *Science, 328*, 1576–1580.

Lashley, K. S. (1929). *Brain mechanisms and intelligence*. Chicago, IL: University of Chicago Press.

Lewis, C. M., Baldassarre, A., Committeri, G., Romani, G. L., & Corbetta, M. (2009). Learning sculpts the spontaneous activity of the resting human brain. *Proceedings of the National Academy of Sciences, 106*, 17558–17563.

Lieberman, M. D. (2000). Intuition: A social cognitive neuroscience approach. *Psychological Bulletin, 126,* 109–137.

Liu, D., & Todorov, E. (2007). Evidence for the flexible sensorimotor strategies predicted by optimal feedback control. *The Journal of Neuroscience, 27,* 9354–9368.

Lucas, R. E., Clark, A. E., Georgellis, Y., & Diener, E. (2004). Unemployment alters the set point for life satisfaction. *Psychological Science, 15,* 8–13.

Luo, Q., Holroyd, T., Majestic, C., Cheng, X., Schecter, J., & Blair, R. J. (2010). Emotional automaticity is a matter of timing. *The Journal of Neuroscience, 30,* 5825–5829.

Lupien, S. J., McEwen, B. S., Gunnar, M. R., & Heim, C. (2009). Effects of stress throughout the lifespan on the brain, behaviour, and cognition. *Nature Reviews Neuroscience, 10,* 434–445.

Macrae, C. N., Bodenhausen, G. V., Milne, A. B., & Jetten, J. (1994). Out of mind but back in sight: Stereotypes on the rebound. *Journal of Personality and Social Psychology, 67,* 808–817.

Markson, L., & Bloom, P. (1997). Evidence against a dedicated system for word learning in children. *Nature, 385,* 813–815.

Meltzoff, A. N. (1995). Understanding the intentions of others: Re-enactment of intended acts by 18-month-old children. *Developmental Psychology, 31,* 838–850.

Miall, R. C., & Wolpert, D. M. (1996). Forward models for physiological motor control. *Neural Networks, 9,* 1265–1279.

Moser, E. I., Kropff, E., & Moser, M. B. (2008). Place cells, grid cells, and the brain's spatial representation system. *Annual Review of Neuroscience, 31,* 69–89.

Najemnik, J., & Geisler, W. S. (2005). Optimal eye movement strategies in visual search. *Nature, 434,* 387–391.

Nesse, R. M. & Ellsworth, P. C. (2009). Evolution, emotion, and emotional disorders. *American Psychologist, 64,* 129–139.

Neurons and synapses. (n.d.). In *The human memory: What it is, how it works, and how it can go wrong.* Retrieved from http://www.human-memory.net/brain_neurons.html

Onishi, K. H., & Baillargeon, R. (2005). Do 15-month-old infants understand false beliefs? *Science, 308,* 255–258.

Pessoa, L. (2008). On the relationship between emotion and cognition. *Nature Reviews Neuroscience, 9,* 148–158.

Pleskac, T. J., & Hertwig, R. (2014). Ecologically rational choice and the structure of the environment. *Journal of Experimental Psychology: General, 143,* 2000–2019.

Preuschoff, K., Bossaerts, P., & Quartz, S. R. (2006). Neural differentiation of expected reward and risk in human subcortical structures. *Neuron, 51,* 381–390.

Prévost, C., McNamee, D., Jessup, R. K., Bossaerts, P., & O'Doherty, J. P. (2013). Evidence for model-based computations in the human amygdala during Pavlovian conditioning. *PLoS Computational Biology, 9*(2), 1–13.

Quartz, S. (2009). Reason, emotion and decision-making: risk and reward calculation with feeling. *Trends in Cognitive Sciences, 13,* 209–215.

Raichle, M. E., & Gusnard, D. A. (2005). Intrinsic brain activity sets the stage for expression of motivated behavior. *The Journal of Comparative Neurology, 493,* 167–176.

Raiffa, H. (1974). *Analysis for decision making: An audiographic, self-instructional course.* Chicago, IL: Encyclopaedia Britannica Educational Corporation.

Reber, P. (2010, April 1). What is the memory capacity of the human brain? *Scientific American.* Retrieved from http://www.scientificamerican.com/article/what-is-the-memory-capacity/

Rescorla, R. A. (1988). Pavlovian conditioning: It's not what you think it is. *American Psychologist, 43,* 151–160.

Reynolds, S. M., & Berridge, K. C. (2008). Emotional environments retune the valence of appetitive versus fearful functions in nucleus accumbens. *Nature Neuroscience, 11,* 423–425.

Rolls, E. T. (2007). *Emotion explained.* Oxford, England: Oxford University Press.

Ruby, P., & Decety, J. (2001). Effect of subjective perspective taking during simulation of action: A PET investigation of agency. *Nature Neuroscience, 4,* 546–550.

Saffran, J. R., Aslin, R. N., & Newport, E. L., (1996). Statistical learning by 8-month-old infants. *Science, 274,* 1926–1928.

Schimmack, U., & Oishi, S. (2005). The influence of chronically and temporarily accessible information on life satisfaction judgments. *Journal of Personality and Social Psychology, 89,* 395–406.

Schultz, W. (2002). Getting formal with dopamine and reward. *Neuron, 36,* 241–263.

Schultz, W., Dayan, P. & Montague, P. R. (1997). A neural substrate of prediction and reward. *Science, 275,* 1593–1599.

Schwarz, N., & Clore, G. L. (1983). Mood, misattribution, and judgments of well-being: Informative and directive functions of affective states. *Journal of Personality and Social Psychology, 45,* 513–523.

Schwarz, N., & Clore, G. L. (2007). Feelings and phenomenal experiences. In A. Kruglanski & E. T. Higgins (Eds.), *Social psychology: Handbook of basic principles* (2nd ed., pp. 385–407). New York, NY: Guilford.

Serrano, J. M., Iglesias, J., & Loeches, A. (1992). Visual discrimination and recognition of facial expressions of anger, fear, and surprise in 4- to 6-month old infants. *Developmental Psychobiology, 25,* 411–425.

Shuman, V., Sander, D., & Scherer, K. R. (2013). Levels of valence. *Frontiers in Psychology, 4*(261). doi:10.3389/fpsyg.2013.00261

Simon, H. A. (1992). What is an "explanation" of behavior? *Psychological Science, 3,* 150–161.

Singer, T., Critchley, H. D., & Preuschoff, K. (2009). A common role of insula in feelings, empathy, and uncertainty. *Trends in Cognitive Sciences, 13,* 334–340.

Singer, T., & Lamm, C. (2009). The social neuroscience of empathy. *Annals of the New York Academy of Sciences, 1156,* 81–96.

Slovic, P., Finucane, M. L., Peters, E., & MacGregor, M. (2004). Risk as analysis and risk as feelings: Some thoughts about affect, reason, risk, and rationality. *Risk Analysis, 24,* 311–322.

Slovic, P., Finucane, M. L., Peters, E., & MacGregor, M. (2007). The affect heuristic. *European Journal of Operational Research, 177,* 1333–1352.

Smith, L. B., & Yu, C. (2007). Infants rapidly learn word-referent mappings via cross-situational statistics. In D. S. McNamara & J. G. Trafton (Eds.), *Proceedings of the 29th annual conference of the Cognitive Science Society* (pp. 653–658). Austin, TX: Cognitive Science Society.

Smith, K. S. & Graybiel, A. M. (2014). Investigating habits: strategies, technologies and models. *Frontiers in Behavioral Neuroscience, 8,* Article 39, 1–17.

Sobel, D. M., & Kirkham, N. Z. (2006). Blickets and babies: The development of causal reasoning in toddlers and infants. *Developmental Psychology, 42,* 1103–1115.

Southgate, V., Senju, A., & Csibra, G. (2007). Action anticipation through attribution of false belief by 2-year-olds. *Psychological Science, 18,* 587–592.

Stauffer, W. R., Lak, A., & Schultz, W. (2014). Dopamine reward prediction error responses reflect marginal utility. *Current Biology, 24,* 2491–2500.

Stickgold, R. (2013). Parsing the role of sleep in memory processing. *Current Opinion in Neurobiology, 23,* 847–853.

Suh, E., Diener, E., & Fukita, F. (1996). Events and subjective well-being: Only recent events matter. *Journal of Personality and Social Psychology, 70,* 1091–1102.

Suzuki, A., Stern, S. A., Bozdagi, O., Huntley, G. W., Walker, R. H., Magistretti, P. J., & Alberini, C. M. (2011). Astrocyte-neuron lactate transport is required for long-term memory formation. *Cell, 144,* 810–823.

Tenenbaum, J. B., de Silva, V., & Langford, J. C. (2000). A global geometric framework for nonlinear dimensionality reduction. *Science, 290,* 2319–2393.

Tenenbaum, J. B., Kemp, C., Griffiths, T. L., & Goodman, N. D. (2011). How to grow a mind: Statistics, structure, and abstraction. *Science, 331,* 1279–1285.

Tobler, P. N., O'Doherty, J. P., Dolan, R. J., & Schultz, W. (2006). Reward value coding distinct from risk attitude-related uncertainty coding in human reward systems. *Journal of Neurophysiology, 97,* 1621–1632.

Todorov, E., & Jordan, M. I. (2002). Optimal feedback control as a theory of motor coordination. *Nature Neuroscience, 5,* 1226–1235.

Tolman, E. C. (1948). Cognitive maps in rats and men. *Psychological Review, 55,* 189–208.

Tolman v. Underhill, 39 Cal.2d 708 (Cal. 1955).

Tremblay, L., & Schultz, W. (1999). Relative reward preference in primate orbitofrontal cortex. *Nature, 398,* 704–708.

Tricomi, E., Balleine, B. W., & O'Doherty, J. P. (2009). A specific role for posterior dorsolateral striatum in human habit learning. *European Journal of Neuroscience, 29,* 2225–2232.

Waldmann, M. R., Schmid, M., Wong, J., & Blaisdell, A. P. (2012). Rats distinguish between absence of events and lack of evidence in contingency learning. *Animal Cognition, 15,* 979–990.

Walsh, B. (2013, August 14). The surprisingly large energy footprint of the digital economy (Update). *Time.* Retrieved from http://science.time.com/2013/08/14/power-drain-the-digital-cloud-is-using-more-energy-than-you-think/

Ward, C. L., McCoy, J. G., McKenna, J. T., Connolly, N. P., McCarley, R. W., & Strecker, R. E. (2009). Spatial learning and memory deficits following exposure to 24 h of sleep fragmentation or intermittent hypoxia in a rat model of obstructive sleep apnea. *Brain Research, 1294,* 128–137.

Watson, D., & Clark, L. A. (1994). Emotions, moods, traits, and temperaments: Conceptual distinctions and empirical findings. In E. P. Ekman & R. J. Davidson (Eds.), *The nature of emotion: Fundamental questions* (pp. 89–93). New York, NY: Oxford University Press.

Webb, A. R., & Copsey, K. D. (2011). *Statistical pattern recognition* (3rd ed.). Chichester, England: Wiley.

Wittgenstein, L. (1953). *Philosophical investigations* (G. E. M. Anscombe, Trans.). London, England: Macmillan.

Yarrow, K., Brown, P., & Krakauer, J. W. (2009). Inside the brain of an elite athlete: The neural processes that support high achievement in sports. *Nature Reviews Neuroscience, 10,* 585–596.

Zajonc, R. B. (1980). Feeling and thinking: Preferences need no inferences. *American Psychologist, 35,* 151–175.

Zajonc, R. B. (1984). On the primacy of affect. *American Psychologist, 39,* 117–123.

3

Deliberative Guidance: Intuitive Guidance in the Counterfactual Mode

Chandra Sripada

IN CHAPTER 2, WE EXPLORED INTUITIVE GUIDANCE. THIS is perhaps the usual mode by which we guide action, but it is not the only way. People sometimes deliberate. They look at the options that are available and try to evaluate them step by step. Unlike intuition, which is immediate and spontaneous, deliberation unfolds over time. It feels effortful. It requires attention and working memory (Fincham, Carter, van Veen, Stenger, & Anderson, 2002). Doing too much of it leaves a person feeling drained (Vohs et al., 2008).

Thus commonsense understands that there are two different ways for guiding action: intuition and deliberation, and the behavioral sciences are in complete agreement. Summarizing a lot of theory and findings, psychologist Seymour Epstein writes,

> There is no dearth of evidence ... that people apprehend reality in two fundamentally different ways, one variously labeled intuitive,

automatic, natural, nonverbal, narrative, and experiential, and the other analytical, deliberative, verbal, and rational. (Epstein, 1994, p. 710)

The main question in this chapter is the relationship between guiding one's actions by intuition versus guiding one's actions by deliberation. Two possibilities are of particular interest.

One view, which we call the *separate processors* view, says intuition and deliberation are separate, distinct modes of thought. If we were to open up a person's head, we would find two different processors: one that delivers intuitive judgments and one that delivers deliberative judgments. If we peak inside the processors themselves, we would see they operate according to very different principles. The idea is already apparent in the preceding quote from Epstein where the intuitive processor is "nonverbal" and "experiential" whereas the deliberative processor is "verbal" and "rational." The cognitive scientist Steve Sloman says the hallmark of the intuitive system is that it is "associative" while the deliberative system is "logical" and "rule-based" (Sloman, 1996). The psychologist and Nobel laureate Daniel Kahneman adds that the intuitive system is "emotional" while the deliberative system is "neutral" (Kahneman, 2003). In addition to operating in different ways, the separate processor view says intuition and deliberation operate independently. They are sealed off from each other; each processor chugs along largely in isolation.

An opposing view says intuition and deliberation are thoroughly intertwined; deliberation is constructed with intuition as a main ingredient. This view starts out with the claim that people can imagine episodic representations of the future. These are vivid and rich in sensory information, concrete details, and spatial context. They can be thought of as mental images or even as mental movies. We call these *episodic prospections* and we say more about how they are built a bit later. According to this second view, episodic prospection is fundamental to deliberation, and it provides the bridge that links deliberation with intuition.

Here is how it works: Suppose a woman is deliberating about whether to vacation in Alaska or Las Vegas. She starts with Alaska and imagines getting up close to a massive glacier. There is perfect silence all around except for an icy breeze whipping around her ears. She evaluates this episode affectively, in particular with the very same affective mechanisms that would have responded were she in fact standing before an awesome glacier. Her heart beats a little faster; she likes this prospect quite a bit. Next, she creates an episodic prospection in which she is at Las Vegas, drawing on memories of prior trips. It is too hot, the casinos are crowded, and every activity requires waiting in lines. Her affective system finds Las Vegas unappealing and she decides on Alaska.

On this second view, there aren't two independent processors. Rather, deliberation depends fundamentally on intuitive affective evaluations. The same intuitive processes that deliver affective evaluations of ongoing actual situations are *reused* during deliberation, but they are now directed at situations constructed in the mind. We call this view, which understands intuition and deliberation as deeply interconnected, the "massive reuse model."

It is important to see that with the massive reuse model, deliberation isn't just a supporter for intuition. The two can certainly disagree. Suppose the waiter puts a luscious cheesecake right in front of you. Your affective systems might spontaneously respond by motivating you to have a large slice. However, you can stop yourself and engage in deliberation. You can bring to mind negative consequences of eating the cake, like your belly bulging out of your swimsuit when summer comes around. Or you imagine the positive consequences of restraint, such as the wry smile on your partner's face when viewing your chiseled figure. Here, affect is playing a critical role in deliberation by supplying the needed evaluative information about these imagined prospects. Moreover, it is possible that by considering these downstream prospects, you reach a verdict opposed to your initial reaction. Hence, according to the massive reuse model, although deliberation is fundamentally reliant on affective systems, the two can nonetheless disagree.

So we have two models available, the separate processors view and the massive reuse view. These represent extreme positions, but they are useful nonetheless because the positions are stated with clarity and they are sufficiently distinct that one can start to sort through the evidence and see which has better support. Over the last 10 to 15 years, evidence has started to accumulate that strongly supports the massive reuse model, and we review some of this evidence in the following two sections.

Episodic Prospection

The massive reuse model says imagining sensorily rich prospective episodes is fundamental to deliberation. One line of evidence in favor of this view is that the brain houses an elaborate system for constructing just these kinds of episodic prospections. This system has been intensively investigated over the last decade. Let us get better acquainted with its workings.

Much of our knowledge of how the brain constructs episodic representations of the future builds on an understanding of how it constructs episodic memories of the past (Schacter et al., 2012). Long-term memory is usually divided into procedural memory, (knowing *how*) and declarative memory (knowing *that*). The latter is then divided again. "Semantic memory" is memory for facts. It resembles pulling data from a file: Carson City is the capital of Nevada; 13 squared is 169. "Episodic memory" is memory for autobiographical personal experiences (Tulving, 2002). Episodic memory has a rich quasi-sensory phenomenology and contains information about the "w"-questions: What happened and who was involved? Where did it occur; what was the context? When did it occur and in what order did it unfold? Episodic memory fuses together information about what, where, and when into a single composite representation of the overall event.

Interestingly, the brain appears to maintain relatively separate stores of information for each component of episodic memory (Allen & Fortin, 2013). "What" information—information about persons or things that were involved—is stored in the perirhinal and entorhinal cortex, regions deep in the medial temporal lobe of the brain. "Where" information is stored in other regions, including the parahippocampal and post-rhinal cortex and in the medial temporal lobe. Less is known about how "when" information is stored: Very short time scales—seconds to minutes—have been tied to an internal pacemaker in the striatum, a set of structures underneath the cortex. Time information over much longer scales—weeks to months to years—is much harder to study and much less is known.

In episodic memory, these three streams of information—what, where, and when—are fused together to create a complex, composite representation of an overall episode (Allen & Fortin, 2013). Orchestrating this union is the hippocampus, a seahorse-shaped region deep in the medial temporal lobe (Davachi, 2006; Konkel & Cohen, 2009). The hippocampus plays a central role in relational memory. When items are presented with others, for example as pairs, the perirhinal and entorhinal regions—the "what" regions discussed earlier—are needed to recall the identity of the individual items. The hippocampus, especially its anterior regions, is required specifically to recall *that the items co-occurred*. More generally, the hippocampus stores all sorts of spatial, temporal, and other abstract relationships between items.

An emerging hypothesis says imaginative prospection uses the brain's vast storehouse of episodic memories as raw material; the elements in these memories are recombined to create the imagined scenario (Schacter, Addis, & Buckner, 2007). Initial evidence in favor of this account arises from the observation that states or conditions that impair episodic memory seem to have similar effects on episodic prospection. For example, individuals with damage to the medial temporal lobe experience a loss of episodic memories of past personal experiences *and* these individuals are reliably found to also be impaired in constructing rich and detailed episodic simulations of the future (Hassabis, Kumaran, Vann, & Maguire, 2007; Race, Keane, & Verfaille, 2011; Squire et al., 2010; Tulving, 1985). Developmental studies similarly find that it is only once children gain an ability to recall personal experiences from the past that they are able to construct episodic prospections about the future (Busby & Suddendorf, 2005).

Perhaps the most remarkable evidence comes from neuroimaging. During retrieval of episodic memory, distributed regions of the brain's default mode network are activated. The various regions contribute to a complex integrative process that has been called *scene construction*. During imaginal prospection, this very same set of regions is activated, suggesting that highly similar scene construction processes are engaged (Buckner & Carroll, 2007; Hassabis & Maguire, 2007; Schacter & Addis, 2007; Schacter et al., 2007; Spreng & Grady, 2010; Suddendorf & Corballis, 2007). There appears to be an important difference, however. Imagined scenes can't simply be replays or attempts at replaying what happened before. Rather, one must engage in additional activity to recombine elements from prior episodes. The persons, things, and places from episodic memories are the raw materials from which entirely new, never-experienced scenes are generated.

Donna Addis, Daniel Schacter, and their colleagues examined the neural substrates of this recombination process using fMRI. Before scanning, participants were asked to provide episodic memories of actual experiences that included details about a person, object, and place. During a subsequent fMRI scan, they were instructed to either (a) recall events that had actually occurred; or (b) imagine a novel scene in which the person, object, and place from separate prior episodes had to be recombined. Consistent with the idea that episodic memory and imagination draw on a common brain network, default network regions were activated in both conditions.

Several regions, especially the anterior hippocampus, were more vigorously activated during imagined scenarios, suggesting they are the substrates for the recombination process (see also Gaesser, Spreng, McLelland, Addis, & Schacter, 2013). Given the anterior hippocampus's role in relational memory noted earlier, it is possible that during imaginative prospection existing links between persons, places, and times are broken and new links are temporarily formed. Thus a person regularly located in one context is "unlinked" from it and instead placed in a different context at a different time. Through this unlinking process, the elements in existing memories could provide the "ingredients" to construct an unlimited array of novel scenarios.

Let us return to the massive reuse view. Notice that it requires that the brain be outfitted with a mechanism to generate detailed sensorily rich prospective episodes that represent what would be the case were the person to undertake various candidate actions. Only then will affective systems have something concrete and detailed enough that they can target, thus delivering up emotional evaluations of these episodes. There is now abundant evidence that the brain does in fact have the machinery required by the massive reuse view.

Affective Redeployment

A second key claim of the massive reuse model is that the same affective systems that operate during our ordinary transactions with the world and that deliver ongoing evaluative information are reused during deliberation. How could decision-making work if it were not true? In Chapter 2, we saw that affective systems maintain a rich and detailed map of the evaluative landscape. These systems use sophisticated statistical machinery to maintain and rapidly update representations of the goodness or badness of situations, allowing them to intelligently shape behavior in real time. For example, if a person is on a quiet beach with a bright sun overhead and cool drink at hand, this person's affective system rapidly registers this as a very good situation. There is an abundance of positive affect, what might be described as an affective "inner glow."

It is entirely natural to think that during deliberation when people bring to mind the prospect of going to the beach versus an alternative (say, staying at home), these very same affective reactions are called up as a way of registering how good or bad these prospects are. When they think about going to the beach, they experience a bit of this same inner glow that they would have experienced had they actually been at the beach, and this helps to explain why they chose the beach. This picture fits with the phenomenology of deliberation and the common sense understanding of how deliberation works.

The alternative model, the separate processors view, is that there is some other entirely distinct set of "cool" representations of value that come on line during deliberation. Affective systems guide ongoing action in real time but with a different set of nonaffective representations coming on line during slow, serial, deliberative reflection. This picture is rarely explicitly articulated by separate processor theorists, but nonetheless, it seems implicit in the model. For example, a model along these lines appears to be suggested by Kahneman in his discussion of the affect heuristic, which he calls "probably the most important development in the study of judgment heuristics in the past few decades" (Kahneman, 2003). Drawing on the work of his colleague Paul Slovic and others, Kahneman says that when presented a hard choice, people often use their quick affective reactions as a guide to what to do. This is contrasted with the alternative process of going through a slower and more difficult "analytic" cost–benefit calculation (Slovic, Peters, Finucane, & MacGregor, 2005). Neither Kahneman nor Slovic say how this cost–benefit calculation works in any detail, but if it is supposed to be a genuinely different way to arrive at a judgment than consulting one's affect, then one must assume that it is a process that is nonaffective. That is, it must use some other kind of "cooler" representation of value.

Kahneman's picture—if we understand it correctly—is implausible. Why would the mind be built this way with both rich and detailed hot representations of value as well as a separate set of cool, nonaffective representations of value? There is already an elaborate and sophisticated system designed for tracking the value of actually encountered situations: the affective system. Wouldn't it be wasteful (and redundant) to cast this system aside during deliberation and instead rely on some other system to track the value of prospective situations?

There is neurobiological evidence that supports the idea of affective redeployment that is central to the massive reuse model. Antonio Damasio, Antoine Bechara, and their colleagues have pursued a long-standing research program examining patients with selective damage to discrete regions of the brain as a way to illuminate the role of affect in decision-making.

In one line of research, they investigated the Iowa Gambling Task. This is a task in which participants make repeated selections from four decks of cards (Bechara, Damasio, Tranel, & Damasio, 1997, 2005; Damasio, 1994). With each card selected, participants receive a potential reward (gain of money) or punishment (loss of money). Unbeknownst to the participants, two decks have relatively favorable payoffs ("good" decks) while two are unfavorable in that they have initially high rewards but thereafter have even larger punishments ("bad" decks). Healthy participants rapidly learn to move away from the bad decks and select from the good ones and they appear to learn to do this mostly nonconsciously. Skin sensors that measure emotional responses reveal that participants rapidly acquire quick, spontaneous affective responses, what are often called "gut feelings," as they make choices from the decks, and these affective cues guide them away from the bad decks and toward the good ones. These affective reactions emerge quite early in the task, well before participants can explicitly articulate why they are favoring certain decks and avoiding others.

Damasio, Bechara, and their colleagues found that patients with damage to their ventromedial prefrontal cortex (vmPFC), a region that houses important affective valuation circuits, do not generate anticipatory affective reactions as they perform the task. Moreover, they fail to switch away from the bad decks. They lack knowledge of the costs or benefits of the various decks and continue to select from all decks—good and bad—alike. Of course, these results should be not at all surprising to our readers because they fit nicely with our argument from Chapter 2 that affective systems are sensitive to hidden patterns of rewards and punishment. These systems use sophisticated statistical routines to rapidly calculate and update the goodness or badness of the person's options, thus providing critical ongoing intuitive guidance for action.

If the separate processors view were correct, then the problems of these patients would be relatively specific to contexts requiring affect to provide rapid intuitive guidance of action. When these patients step back and engage in slow, effortful deliberation about what to do, then a separate processor with a distinct set of "cool" nonaffective value representations should come on line. In contrast, the massive reuse view says that when affective systems are compromised, then not only is intuitive guidance by affect impaired, but deliberative guidance will also be impaired because it makes massive reuse of affect.

Damasio and colleagues' observations strongly support the predictions of the massive reuse view. The famous case of Phineas Gage provides one illustration. After a tamping iron pierced his skull, destroying his vmPFC, he subsequently became impulsive, inappropriate, and made a series of disastrous decisions (Damasio, 1994). Gage, of course, was a historical figure and surely has been subject to the accumulation of distortions and hyperbole. Damasio and his colleagues were able to undertake comprehensive neuropsychological investigation of other patients with vmPFC damage (Damasio, 1994). This includes studies of Elliot, a patient with selective damage to the vmPFC established by modern day radiographic imaging.

Comprehensive testing showed that Elliot's general intellectual abilities were unimpaired:

> The standardized psychological and neuropsychological tests revealed a superior intellect. On every subtest of the Weschler Adult Intelligence Scale, Elliot showed abilities that were either superior or average. His immediate memory for digits was superior, as were his short-term verbal memory and visual memory for geometric designs. His performance on the Multilingual Aphasia Examination, a battery of tests which assess various aspects of language comprehension and production, was normal. His visual perception and construction skills were normal on Benton's standardized tests of facial discrimination,

judgment of line orientation, tests of geographic orientation, and two- and three-dimensional block construction. . . . In short, perceptual ability, past memory, short-term memory, new learning, language, and the ability to do arithmetic were intact (Damasio, 1994, p. 41).

Despite this, Elliot's decision-making was seriously compromised.

His knowledge seemed to survive, and he could perform many separate actions as well as before. But he could not be counted on to perform the appropriate action when it was expected. Understandably, after repeated advice and admonitions from colleagues went unheeded, Elliot's job was terminated. Other jobs—and other dismissals—were to follow ... No longer tied to regular employment, Elliot charged ahead with new pastimes and new business ventures. . . .. In one enterprise, he teamed with a disreputable character. Several warnings from friends were of no avail, and the scheme ended in bankruptcy. All of his savings had been invested in the ill-fated enterprise and were lost. It was puzzling to see a man with Elliot's background make such flawed business and financial decisions. His wife, children, and friends could not understand why a knowledgeable person who was properly forewarned could act so foolishly ... (Damasio, 1994, pp. 36–37).

According to Damasio's descriptions, Elliot's social world also began to disintegrate. He left his wife, entered into several unwise relationships, had several subsequent divorces, and ended up drifting from place to place without an income.

Based on the experiments with the Iowa Gambling Task, neurological case studies such as Elliot, as well other lines of evidence, Damasio proposed the somatic marker hypothesis (Bechara & Damasio 2005; Damasio, 1994). This is a complex model, but for our purposes, the most relevant point is that Damasio draws a deep connection between affect and deliberation. He proposes that affective systems are called on during consideration of options, biasing action away from bad prospects and toward good ones. It is precisely this affective guidance during contemplation of what do that is absent in Gage and in Elliot, accounting for their disastrous decision-making.

The idea that affect is redeployed during deliberation also finds support from neuroimaging studies. Most imaging studies have examined rapid, on line selection of action; that is, in our terminology, they probed intuitive guidance. In these studies, participants are presented with dozens, sometimes hundreds, of choices and have a very brief period, usually just 2 to 3 seconds, to respond to each choice. Areas known to be implicated in intuitive, affective processing— vmPFC regions—are reliably activated, and they appear to supply evaluative signals that guide choice (Montague & Berns, 2002; Montague, King-Casas, & Cohen, 2006; Rangel, Camerer, & Montague, 2008).

Other studies look at more challenging decisions where options have multiple attributes, some of which are positive and some negative (Basten, Biele, Heekeren, & Fiebach, 2010; Hare, Camerer, & Rangel, 2009; Kahnt, Greuschow, Speck, & Haynes, 2011). This more closely resembles deliberative decision-making where each outcome has a novel combination of attributes and the person must sum across various dimensions to arrive at an overall valuation. These studies reliably find activity in the vmPFC region and, moreover, the magnitude of activation in this region strongly correlates with the overall summed values across the multiple attributes (Kahnt et al., 2011). This suggests affective mechanisms in vmPFC, which are known to operate during intuitive guidance of action, continue to provide the key evaluative signals during slower, more deliberative decisions.

Additional evidence for affective redeployment comes from studies examining episodic future simulation (Gerlach, Spreng, Madore, & Schacter, 2014; Johnson, Nolen-Hoeksema, Mitchell, & Levin, 2009; Johnson et al., 2006; Mitchell et al., 2009; Spreng & Schacter, 2012). Researchers instructed participants to either construct detailed episodic prospections that involve the person's own goals or prospections that are not goal-relevant. There are, of course, intimate connections between one's goals and evaluative processing. When envisioning a goal-relevant scenario, it is expected that evaluative processes will activate, while a scenario that is not goal-relevant will not elicit strong evaluations. These studies find that vmPFC valuation regions, the regions that subserve intuitive affective processing, are activated during goal-relevant episodes (see Stawarczyk & D'Argembeau, 2015 for a recent meta-analysis). This finding supports the idea that during deliberation when prospective episodes are called to mind, affective systems are deployed to provide evaluative information about these episodes.

The massive reuse view provides an intriguing view of the relationship between intuitive guidance of action and deliberation. The model says we do *not* have two separate processors operating by very different principles. Rather, intuitive guidance and deliberation are fundamentally connected. There is extensive evidence from psychology and neuroscience that supports the model. First, there is clear evidence that humans have the mental machinery to construct sensorily rich episodic prospections. Second, there is evidence from neurobiology, neuropsychology, and neuroimaging that affective systems are redeployed during deliberation, and they deliver evaluations of these sensorily rich prospective episodes.

This calls into question the claims by many theorists that deliberation is vastly different from intuition. Deliberation is "verbal," "logical," "rule-based," and "neutral," whereas intuition is just the opposite: "nonverbal," "irrational," "associative," and "emotional." This bifurcated picture—two minds built from wildly different materials—is wrong. Rather, the difference between intuitive guidance and deliberative guidance is much more subtle: It consists in the direction of the "mind's eye." During our ordinary transactions with the environment, intuitive affective systems are tuned to the world and they supply ongoing automatic guidance of action. During deliberation, intuitive affective systems once again take center stage. The only difference is that the "gaze" of these systems is pointed away from the actual situation and instead toward episodic prospective representations constructed in the mind.

References

Allen, T. A., & Fortin, N. J. (2013). The evolution of episodic memory. *Proceedings of the National Academy of Sciences, 110,* 10379–10386.

Basten, U., Biele, G., Heekeren, H. R., & Fiebach, C. J. (2010). How the brain integrates costs and benefits during decision making. *Proceedings of the National Academy of the Sciences, 107,* 21767–21772.

Bechara, A., & Damasio, A. R. (2005). The somatic marker hypothesis: A neural theory of economic decision. *Games and Economic Behavior, 52,* 336–372.

Bechara, A., Damasio, H., Tranel, D., & Damasio, A. R. (1997). Deciding advantageously before knowing the advantageous strategy. *Science, 275,* 1293–1295.

Bechara, A., Damasio, H., Tranel, D., & Damasio, A. R. (2005). The Iowa Gambling Task and the somatic marker hypothesis: Some questions and answers. *Trends in Cognitive Sciences, 9,* 159–162.

Buckner, R. L., & Carroll, D. C. (2007). Self-projection and the brain. *Trends in Cognitive Sciences, 11,* 49–57.

Busby, J., & Suddendorf, T. (2005). Recalling yesterday and predicting tomorrow. *Cognitive Development, 20,* 362–372.

Damasio, A. (1994). *Descartes' error: Emotion, reason, and the human brain.* New York, NY: Avon.

Davachi, L. (2006). Item, context and relational episodic encoding in humans. *Current Opinion in Neurobiology, 16,* 693–700.

Epstein, S. (1994). Integration of the cognitive and psychodynamic unconscious. *American Psychologist, 49,* 709–724.

Fincham, J. M., Carter, C. S., van Veen, V., Stenger, V. A., & Anderson, J. R. (2002). Neural mechanisms of planning: A computational analysis using event-related fMRI. *Proceedings of the National Academy of Sciences, 99,* 3346–3351.

Gaesser, B., Spreng, R. N., McLelland, V. C., Addis, D. R., & Schacter, D. L. (2013). Imagining the future: Evidence for a hippocampal contribution to constructive processing. *Hippocampus, 23,* 1150–1161.

Gerlach, K. D., Spreng, R. N., Madore, K. P., & Schacter, D. L. (2014). Future planning: Default network activity couples with fronto-parietal control network and reward-processing regions during process and outcome simulations. *Social Cognitive and Affective Neuroscience, 9,* 1942–1951.

Hare, T. A., Camerer, C. F., & Rangel, A. (2009). Self-control in decision-making involves modulation of the vmPFC valuation system. *Science, 324,* 646–648.

Hassabis, D., Kumaran, D., Vann, S. D., & Maguire, E. A. (2007). Patients with hippocampal amnesia cannot imagine new experiences. *Proceedings of the National Academy of Sciences, 104,* 1726–1731.

Hassabis, D., & Maguire, E. A. (2007). Deconstructing episodic memory with construction. *Trends in Cognitive Sciences, 11,* 299–306.

Johnson, M. K., Nolen-Hoeksema, S., Mitchell, K. J., & Levin, Y. (2009). Medial cortex activity, self-reflection and depression. *Social Cognitive and Affective Neuroscience, 4,* 313–327.

Johnson, M. K., Raye, C. L., Mitchell, K. J., Touryan, S. R., Greene, E. J., & Nolen-Hoeksema, S. (2006). Dissociating medial frontal and posterior cingulate activity during self-reflection. *Social Cognitive and Affective Neuroscience, 1,* 56–64.

Kahneman, D. (2003). A perspective on judgment and choice: Mapping bounded rationality. *American Psychologist, 58,* 697–720.

Kahnt, T., Greuschow, M., Speck, O., & Haynes, J. D. (2011). Perceptual learning and decision-making in human medial frontal cortex. *Neuron, 70,* 549–559.

Konkel, A., & Cohen, N. J. (2009). Relational memory and the hippocampus: Representations and methods. *Frontiers in Neuroscience, 3,* 166–174.

Mitchell, K. J., Raye, C. L., Ebner, N. C., Tubridy, S. M., Frankel, H., & Johnson, M. K. (2009). Age-group differences in medial cortex activity associated with thinking about self-relevant agendas. *Psychology and Aging, 24,* 438–449.

Montague, P. R., & Berns, G. S. (2002). Neural economics and the biological substrates of valuation. *Neuron, 36,* 265–284.

Montague, P. R., King-Casas, B., & Cohen, J. D. (2006). Imaging valuation models in human choice. *Annual Review of Neuroscience, 29,* 417–448.

Race, E., Keane, M. M., & Verfaille, M. (2011). Medial temporal lobe damage causes deficits in episodic memory and episodic future thinking not attributable to deficits in narrative construction. *The Journal of Neuroscience, 31,* 10262–10269.

Rangel, A., Camerer, C., & Montague, P. R. (2008). A framework for studying the neurobiology of value-based decision making. *Nature Reviews Neuroscience, 9,* 545–556.

Schacter, D. L., & Addis, D. R. (2007). The cognitive neuroscience of constructive memory: Remembering the past and imagining the future. *Philosophical Transactions of the Royal Society B: Biological Sciences, 362,* 773–786.

Schacter, D. L., Addis, D. R., & Buckner, R. L. (2007). Remembering the past to imagine the future: The prospective brain. *Nature Reviews Neuroscience, 8,* 657–661.

Schacter, D. L., Addis, D. R., Hassabis, D., Martin, V. C., Spreng, R. N., & Szpunar, K. K. (2012). The future of memory: Remembering, imagining, and the brain. *Neuron, 76,* 677–694.

Sloman, S. A. (1996). The empirical case for two systems of reasoning. *Psychological Bulletin, 119*, 3–22.

Slovic, P., Peters, E., Finucane, M. L., & MacGregor, D. G. (2005).
Affect, risk, and decision making. *Health Psychology, 24*,
S35–S40.

Spreng, R. N., & Grady, C. L. (2010). Patterns of brain activity supporting autobiographical memory, prospection, and theory of
mind, and their relationship to the default mode network. *Journal
of Cognitive Neuroscience, 22*, 1112–1123.

Spreng, R. N., & Schacter, D. L. (2012). Default network modulation
and large-scale network interactivity in healthy young and old
adults. *Cerebral Cortex, 22*, 2610–2621.

Squire, L. R., van der Horst, A. S., McDuff, S. G., Frascino, J. C.,
Hopkins, R. O., & Mauldin, K. N. (2010). Role of the hippocampus
in remembering the past and imagining the future. *Proceedings of
the National Academy of Sciences, 107*, 19044–19048.

Stawarczyk, D., & D'Argembeau, A. (2015). Neural correlates of personal goal processing during episodic future thinking and mind-
wandering: An ALE meta-analysis. *Human Brain Mapping, 36*,
2928–2947.

Suddendorf, T., & Corballis, M. C. (2007). The evolution of fore-
sight: What is mental time travel, and is it unique to humans?
Behavioral and Brain Sciences, 30, 299–313.

Tulving, E. (1985). Memory and consciousness. *Canadian Psychology,
26*, 1–12.

Tulving, E. (2002). Episodic memory: From mind to brain. *Annual
Review of Psychology, 53*, 1–25.

Vohs, K. D., Baumeister, R. B., Schmeichel, B. J., Twenge, J. M., Nelson,
N. M., & Tice, D. M. (2008). Making choices impairs subsequent
self-control: A limited resource account of decision-making, self-
regulation, and active initiative. *Journal of Personality and Social
Psychology, 84*, 883–898.

4

Imaginative Guidance: A Mind Forever Wandering

Chandra Sripada

IN CHAPTER 3 WE DISCUSSED THE MANY FORMS OF prospection that are deliberate and controlled. We now turn to the kinds of prospection that are spontaneous and discursive.

Think about what goes consciously through your mind during idle moments. Thoughts of various kinds spontaneously pop into your head. You think about your recent experiences. You gaze into the future. Many of your thoughts are accompanied by images and quasi-perceptual content. The train of thoughts is discursive: It meanders from topic to topic. There are some associative connections and thematic links between successive thoughts, but there are also substantial discontinuities, leaps, and odd transitions.

This is *mind-wandering,* and it is deeply puzzling to theorists (Callard, Smallwood, Golchert, & Margulies, 2013; Smallwood & Schooler, 2006, 2015). The biggest puzzle is why we do so much of it. One study, which used experience sampling methods with 2,250 adults, found mind-wandering occurred in a remarkable 46.9% of the time points sampled (Killingsworth & Gilbert, 2010).

Neural evidence tells a complementary story. Mind-wandering has been tied to the default mode network, a set of brain regions that are involved in episodic memory and imagination (Buckner, Andrews-Hanna, & Schacter, 2008). This network was identified from observations of brain activation during prolonged functional imaging tasks. These tasks often provide for intermittent rest intervals, and it was noticed that during these rests, a network of midline and medial temporal lobe structures reliably turn on (Raichle & Snyder, 2007). These regions were dubbed the default network because their ongoing operation appears to be the brain's default state of activity (Raichle et al., 2001). It was subsequently shown that this network subserves mind-wandering activity (Andrews-Hanna, Reidler, Huang, & Buckner, 2010; Christoff, Gordon, Smallwood, Smith, & Schooler, 2009; Mason et al., 2007). The overall picture, then, is that when nothing else is going on, people don't simply "power down" and let their minds go idle. Rather, they engage a network of brain regions specialized for a distinctive activity: churning out discursive trains of episodes from the past and prospections into the future. The question is: *Why?*

An increasingly common explanation for mind-wandering says it serves the purpose of planning. Thus Jonathan Smallwood and Jessica Andrews-Hanna write:

> From an evolutionary perspective, prospection allows us to simulate plausible outcomes to alternative future events, including the emotional states of ourselves and other people in response to ... events (Gilbert and Wilson, 2007). In this way self-generated thought [i.e., mind-wandering] is an adaptive process that helps us select the optimal course of action, prepare for upcoming events, and achieve our upcoming goals (Schacter et al., 2007; Suddendorf and Corballis, 2007; Suddendorf et al., 2009; Szpunar, 2010). (Smallwood & Andrews-Hanna, 2013, pp. 3–4; see original for references)

While we think Smallwood and Andrews-Hanna are right, there is a need for additional specificity in the proposal. How specifically can engaging in discursive trains of thought help to prepare us for the future? In addressing this question, there is a useful distinction to be made between *planning* and *learning*, which can be illustrated with an example.

Suppose you have a map of New York City and need to get from LaGuardia Airport to lower Manhattan. You can look at the map and plan the best route. One route takes the Long Island Expressway through Queens and crosses the Brooklyn Bridge. Another crosses Harlem and then heads down the Henry Hudson Parkway. A third route takes a bus to 145th street and then the A train south. You can evaluate these options and figure out which is best. Planning, then, takes a circumscribed body of knowledge and uses it to answer a specific action-directed question.

Learning, at least the kind of learning being emphasized here, is different; it is the process by which this body of domain knowledge is generated in the first place. Learning isn't usually done for answering a specific action-directed question. It is *ultimately* useful because later one can interrogate the "map" that is learned and address an open-ended array of specific action-directed questions whenever they happen to come up. But the rationale for learning can't be identified with its utility for answering any one of these specific questions; the utility of learning is far more indirect and diffuse.

We agree that people sometimes engage in prospective thought to plan for their futures and thereby achieve their goals. But notice that prospection for the purposes of deliberate planning, such as planning routes from LaGuardia to lower Manhattan, is not very much like mind-wandering. When engaged in planning, the mind doesn't discursively move from one topic to the next, following associative links (or digressively jump without any obvious links at all). In addition, planning is usually effortful. It requires sustained attention and working memory (Fincham, Carter, van Veen, Stenger, & Anderson, 2002; Newman, Carpenter, Varma, & Just, 2003), and it leaves a person cognitively fatigued (Vohs et al., 2008). Mind-wandering, in contrast, is not effortful. Trains of thought during mind-wandering occur spontaneously, without conscious supervision or control, and without placing substantial demands on attention and working memory (McVay & Kane, 2010). There thus appear to be substantial differences between mind-wandering and structured planning in terms of discursivity, phenomenology, cognitive processes, and neural substrates. This suggests that mind-wandering is unlikely to prepare us for the future by itself being a form of planning.

In this chapter, we advance the view that mind-wandering is not (directly) for planning but rather plays a pivotal role in learning;

it contributes to building a highly general "map" of the world that can later be queried for whatever specific purposes a person happens to have. More specifically, our view sees mind-wandering as involving in a highly interesting and widely underappreciated process for facilitating certain kinds of learning: the process of *repeated presentation of learning examples*. We will argue that in the right sort of learning contexts, presenting discursive ongoing streams of learning examples can facilitate identification of the deeper hidden patterns. We call this the "deep learning" account of mind-wandering.

We begin this chapter with an extended discussion of the complementary learning systems (CLS) model, one of the most influential views of memory to have emerged in the last several decades. In the second section, "The Extended CLS Model," we propose various refinements and extensions to the CLS model and locate mind-wandering as a critical driver of deep learning within this extended model. With the third section, "Trains of Thought," we delve further into the distinctive discursive quality of mind-wandering. The fourth section provides evidence that mind-wandering enhances deep learning, and the fifth section draws links between mind-wandering and dreaming. We suggest that daydreaming and night dreaming form part of a continuum of mind-wandering states that differ importantly.

Complementary Learning Systems

Our starting point is the seminal work by James McClelland, Bruce McNaughton, and Randall O'Reilly on the CLS view of memory (McClelland, McNaughton, & O'Reilly, 1995; Norman & O'Reilly, 2003; O'Reilly & Norman, 2002). This view divides the cognitive architecture for memory into two systems. First, there is a high-fidelity "surface" system, located primarily in the hippocampus and associated regions of the medial temporal lobe. It keeps detailed records of experiences as they transpire. This system has a sizable storage capacity but has minimal learning and conceptualization abilities; it doesn't try to make sense of patterns within these records. Second, there is a "deep" system that is primarily located in the neocortex. This is a high intelligence, high abstraction system that is specialized for extracting statistical regularities, generalizations, and patterns from the data. Importantly, for the deep system to do its work, it needs to be presented with a large number of examples from the domain of interest. The sur-face system is well positioned to provide these examples because it stores detailed records of experience in its high-fidelity library. The CLS framework proposes complementary interactions be-tween the two systems, with the surface system feeding examples from its sizable library in an ongoing way to the deep system and thereby facilitating high-level pattern learning.

Importantly, the idea of *repeated presentation* plays a central role in the CLS architecture. This is the idea that certain forms of learn-ing, especially learning of patterns and generalizations across a set of examples, are substantially facilitated by presenting these examples multiple times and in multiple ways. We will discuss the computa-tional advantages of repeated presentation as we proceed.

The CLS picture is widely accepted by memory researchers (Frankland & Bontempi, 2005; Moscovitch, Nadel, Winocur, Gilboa, & Rosenbaum, 2006; Squire & Bayley, 2007) and is supported by multi-ple lines of evidence. First, there is excellent neurobiological evidence for a functional dissociation between the hippocampal and neocorti-cal systems proposed in the CLS model. The hippocampus exhibits a number of "design features" that enable it to play the role of the high-fidelity surface learner. Regions of the hippocampus, especially region CA3, have reduced cellular density, regular latticed arrange-ment of neurons, and lower levels of neuronal firing compared to the neocortex (Barnes, McNaughton, Mizumori, Leonard, & Lin, 1990; O'Reilly & Norman, 2002). These features are well suited for creating sharply demarcated memory representations in which even highly similar stimuli get distinct representations.

The hippocampus is also unique in being highly plastic (Marr, 1971; McNaughton & Morris, 1987); that is, it exhibits a remark-ably rapid learning rate, which is essential if it is to store *in real time* high-fidelity representations of experience. Perhaps the best known and most extensively studied example of rapid plasticity in the brain is the phenomenon of long-term potentiation (Bliss & Collingridge, 1993), which occurs in multiple subregions of the hippocampus and associated structures. This is a Hebbian learning process (fire together, wire together) in which groups of temporally co-active neurons ex-hibit persistent strengthening of their synaptic connections lasting for weeks to months. Long-term potentiation is thought to explain the ability of the hippocampus to rapidly learn arbitrary associations between two stimuli or between stimuli and spatiotemporal context, including various instances of "one shot" learning in which associations are formed within a single training episode (Nakazawa et al., 2003).

With respect to all of these design features, the neocortex is almost precisely reversed (O'Reilly & Norman, 2002) It has high cell density, irregular neuronal arrangements, and rapid firing rates, all of which produce overlapping representations for similar stimuli. In addition, rather than rapid Hebbian learning, the neocortical system uses various forms of error-correction learning of the sort we saw in Chapter 2. This kind of learning is slow and iterative, and we will discuss it in more detail in a moment.

In short then, consistent with the CLS model, the neurobiological evidence supports specialization in the hippocampus and neocortex: The hippocampus is optimized for the separation of representations and retention of detail while the neocortex is optimized for integration of representations and forming abstractions from the details.

Turning now to a second line of evidence supporting the CLS model, a key postulate of the model is that that the hippocampus *repeatedly presents* high-fidelity records of experience to the cortical deep learning system. There is compelling neurobiological evidence that this process in fact occurs (O'Neill, Pleydell-Bouverie, Dupret, & Csicsvari, 2010). A vivid illustration comes from studies (Davidson, Kloosterman, & Wilson, 2009; Lee & Wilson, 2002) of the firing patterns of so-called hippocampal place cells that fire selectively to certain locations as an animal explores its surroundings. As a consequence, when the animal travels a certain trajectory, these place cells fire in a distinctive sequence. During subsequent periods of quiet rest or slow wave sleep, these same place cells are repeatedly reactivated in brief burst patterns (Buzsáki, 1989; Girardeau & Zugaro, 2011) with concurrent increased hippocampal-cortical communication. Critically, the order of place cell activation during each burst is the same as during previous rounds of exploration (although the firing rate is dramatically speeded up, with a "virtual speed" of roughly 8 meters per second; Davidson et al., 2009). This supports the idea that the hippocampus is repeatedly presenting trajectories from previous rounds of exploration in a way that would facilitate cortical deep learning of the gist, in this case, abstract spatial relations.

A third line of evidence for the CLS model comes from human lesion studies. It has long been known that lesions to the hippocampus produce retrograde amnesia for declarative memories, especially for memory of autobiographical episodes. Interestingly, amnesia is often time-limited with memories from the more remote past spared (Squire & Alvarez, 1995; Squire & Bayley, 2007). The CLS framework nicely explains this pattern. The neocortical system stores generalizations and statistical regularities from hippocampal inputs, resulting in partial redundancy and overlap in the mnemonic contents of the two systems. The formation of neocortical memory traces, however, is slow and iterative, and thus requires extensive time for consolidation. This explains why there is preferential sparing of remote memories with hippocampal damage; only those memories that have had sufficient time for neocortical stabilization and consolidation are spared. If the neocortex has not had time to extract patterns from hippocampal memories of relatively recent events, then there will be complete amnesia for these events.

A fourth line of support for the CLS model comes from considering its computational rationale; there are excellent computational reasons for why a two-tiered learning architecture makes sense. It might seem initially strange that learning can be facilitated by presenting memories of prior experiences again and again. Rather, it seems more plausible that once an experience has occurred, the learner should extract whatever lessons it has and then move on; little is to be gained by replaying a memory of that experience, let alone replaying it repeatedly. Perhaps McClelland, McNaughton, and O'Reilly's most penetrating insight is that there are certain learning contexts—in particular, contexts involving the learning of abstract patterns—in which repeated presentation of memories dramatically enhances learning.

McClelland, McNaughton, and O'Reilly model this kind of high-level "pattern learning" of an artificial neural network consisting of an input layer, output layer, and multiple hidden layers (McClelland et al., 1995). The network is initialized with random weights between the nodes. Training examples consist of specific input-output pairings; if the network fails to generate the correct predicted output with the presentation of the input, then this leads to small, incremental adjustment of the weights in the network in a direction that reduces the discrepancy. Over time, the network faithfully reproduces the input-output mappings with which it was trained.

Artificial neural networks can uncover hidden patterns of similarity among inputs and generalize learning to new unseen inputs, and there is evidence they do this in ways that more closely resemble human learners (Elman, 1998; Rumelhart, McClelland, & PDP Research Group, 1986; White, 1989) Patterns of similarity are encoded in the weights in the hidden layers; inputs that are similar share similar configurations of weightings. For example, McClelland et al. (1995) discuss the example of a network that learns about living things (plant, animal, pine, oak, robin, sunfish, etc.) and their properties (is big, can fly, has gills, etc.). After training, the network weightings reflected that oak is similar to pine, and both are quite different from a canary or a robin.

Training of an artificial neural net must proceed in a slow and iterative way. Weights are adjusted a small amount at a time. Large adjustments would "overfit" the network to the current example while the goal is for the network to uncover patterns of similarity that hold across a range of examples. In addition, McClelland et al. (1995) discuss a second critical feature of artificial neural net training: Learning should be *interleaved*.

Consider two ways of training a neural network to learn 10 examples (i.e., 10 input-output pairings). The first presents blocks of each example serially, say 40 times for the first example, 40 for the second, and so on. The second presents the examples in a fairly random interspersed fashion: Two or three presentations of one example are followed by another and then by another until each of the 10 examples are presented 40 times. The first scheme—the serial scheme—ultimately fails because it generates the problem of "catastrophic interference" (McClelland et al., 1995; Spivey & Mirman, 2001). The network learns the current example, but then the weights are overwritten to learn the second example, and so on. In contrast, the interleaved presentation allows learning of all the examples and will result in optimal generalization to new unseen examples. In effect, interleaved presentation allows the network to "see" a number of examples in close proximity and thus identify the hidden patterns that the examples have in common.

McClelland et al. (1995) locate the computational rationale of the CLS architecture in the need to produce iterative, interleaved trains of examples for the purposes of neural net learning. This can most readily be achieved with a two-tier architecture: One system specializes in storing high-fidelity examples and thereafter repeatedly presents them in an interleaved fashion, and the other system specializes in slow iterative learning of hidden abstract patterns in the example set.

The Extended CLS Model: Mind-Wandering as Deep Learning

Our goal in this section is to use the McClelland et al. (1995) CLS architecture as a starting place to explain mind-wandering. To do this, we will need to propose several refinements and extensions to the CLS model, resulting in a new model that we call the *extended CLS model*. A number of these extensions concern psychological functions (e.g., episodic memory, conceptual learning systems, consciousness) that are likely to be uniquely human, or at least elaborated to a unique extent in humans.

Episodic Memory in the Surface System

In formulating the original CLS model, McClelland, McNaughton, and O'Reilly assumed the hippocampal surface learner records discrete semantic items (e.g., *robins are birds, penguins cannot fly*) and repeatedly replays these items to the deep neocortical system. In the extended CLS model, our focus is on a more complex type of memory—episodic memories (Allen & Fortin, 2013; Tulving, 2002). These are memories of personal experiences that have a rich quasi-perceptual phenomenology. They contain conjoined information about the "W questions": What happened and who was involved? Where did it occur and what was the context? When did it occur and in what order did it unfold? There is extensive evidence that the hippocampal system does indeed play a critical role in encoding and recall of episodic memories (Burgess, Maguire, & O'Keefe, 2002; Squire, 1992), so our extension of the CLS model to emphasize this type of memory is plausible.

Multiple Deep Learning Systems

A second refinement of the original CLS model concerns how to understand the neocortical deep learning system. McClelland et al.

(1995) treat the deep learner as a single network. They recognize, however, this is an expository convenience and that it does not reflect the actual organization of the neocortical system: "We view the neocortex as a collection of partially overlapping processing systems; for simplicity of reference, however, we refer to these systems collectively as the *neocortical processing system*" (p. 422–423). For our purposes, however, we want to be more specific about the kinds of relatively distinct neocortical deep learners. There is now substantial evidence—drawn from studies of differential developmental trajectories during youth, studies of the effects of localized brain lesions, comparative studies across animals, and studies using neuroimaging—that humans have a number of partially dissociable "conceptual learning systems" (Carruthers, 2006). A list of these systems should at least include the following four categories, with multiple subsystems grouped under each.

Statistical learning systems. These systems maintain and update degrees of belief in prospects and calculate confidence bounds on these probabilities (White, Engen, Sørensen, Overgaard, & Shergill, 2014). They also compute decision-guiding signals, including riskiness of outcomes, absolute and relative value, expected value, and discrepancies between expected and actual outcomes (Montague & Berns, 2002; Montague, King-Casas, & Cohen, 2006; Schultz, 2000).

Causal learning systems. These systems generate graphical maps of a domain with links representing causal relations (Gopnik & Glymour, 2002; Gopnik et al., 2004). The graphical causal maps are produced by tracking statistical information about correlations and conditional probabilities among observed events as well as information gained through active interventions (e.g., pushing a button on a machine to see what happens next).

Analogical reasoning systems. These systems apply strategies and models learned in one domain to other domains. This is made possible by identifying abstract similarities at the level of the relations between objects, even when the relevant objects are dissimilar (Gentner & Markman, 1997; Holyoak & Thagard, 1996).

Social cognition systems. These systems keep track of other peoples' mental states as well as underlying character traits that give rise to long-term patterns of behavior (Brüne & Brüne-Cohrs, 2006; Gallagher & Frith, 2003; Karmiloff-Smith, Klima, Bellugi, Grant, & Baron-Cohen, 1995). Additional systems keep track of reputations (e.g., a person's moral reputation) and information about friendships, alliances, coalitions, and benefits and burdens implicitly or explicitly accruing from social contracts (Carruthers, 2006). All the preceding systems interact to produce high-level explanations and interpretations of complex social interactions.

In our extended CLS framework, episodic memory-based learning examples stored and reactivated by the hippocampal surface system are "consumed" by these conceptual learning systems. These multiple conceptual systems separately engage in various forms of deep learning, including such things as detecting generalizations, constructing causal explanations, predicting downstream consequences, identifying cross-domain relationships and similarities, assigning social meanings, and so forth.

Consciousness

The original CLS architecture proposes that the hippocampal surface system delivers ongoing trains of learning examples to the deep learning cortical system. McClelland et al. (1995) did not discuss the subjective correlates of activating these learning examples, that is, *what it would be like* to be a creature in which ongoing reactivation of these hippocampal states is occurring. Given that repeated reactivation of hippocampal memory items is known to occur in rodents and other lower mammals, it seems unlikely that this reactivation must necessarily be accompanied by any type of conscious experiences.

Our extended CLS architecture, however, differs in a crucial respect: We propose that episodic memory examples generated by the hippocampal system are consumed by a variety of neocortical deep learning systems. This requires widespread *dissemination* of these memory states; only if these episodic memory-based learning examples are widely disseminated can they be consumed by multiple disparate neocortical systems. This brings consciousness into the picture.

On the global workspace model, consciousness is a mechanism for accomplishing widespread dissemination of information to multiple consumer systems (Baars, 2002, 2005; Dehaene, Kerszberg, & Changeux, 1998; Dehaene & Naccache, 2001). Informational states that enter the global workspace are amplified and "broadcast" rapidly

across long-range recurrent cortico-cortico and cortico-thalamic connections (Dehaene & Naccache, 2001). Such broadcast, it is claimed
by defenders of workspace theory, is necessary for a state's being
consciously experienced, and according to some theorists, also sufficient. Because the extended CLS model proposes that episodic
memory examples from the hippocampal surface system are typically consumed by multiple, disparate cortical deep learning systems,
we assume these hippocampal memory states use the mechanism
of global broadcast to be disseminated widely, and thus they are
conscious.

After these refinements, we are now in a position to locate mind-
wandering. To recap a bit, the extended model proposes that there is
a hippocampal surface system that stores sensorily rich and detailed
episodic memories. There is also a neocortical deep system, which
itself consists of a number of disparate conceptual learning systems,
and the neocortical system requires an ongoing stream of learning examples. Using the mechanism of conscious broadcast, the hippocampal surface system delivers these examples to the neocortical system
thereby driving deep learning (including generalization, explanation,
abstraction, gist-finding, and social interpretation). Because the deep
system requires interleaved inputs, the stream of examples from the
surface system must vary in content and be drawn from the domain
of interest in a semi-random way—it must meander in order to work.
Mind-wandering is located within this architecture as the ongoing,
discursive series of episodic memory examples from the hippocampal
surface system that are consciously broadcast to, and consumed by,
the neocortical deep system.

Why is mind-wandering so ubiquitous; why does it occupy nearly
half of our waking lives? We theorize in the extended CLS model
that the neocortical deep learning system is slow and that it learns
only incrementally. If it is to extract useful generalizations, explanations, abstractions, gists, and interpretations, the hippocampal surface
system must deliver a massive number of meandering memories.
Thus, there must be an abundance of mind-wandering activity.

Notice, however, that though neocortical deep learning is ultimately valuable, engaging in it is rarely *pressing*. So the mind-
wandering activity that drives neocortical deep learning should
operate as a default activity. That is, it is an activity that should be
conducted throughout "rest" periods and when engagement with a

demanding task is required, mind-wandering should be suspended, with an immediate resumption of mind-wandering as soon as the resting state resumes. The fMRI findings we discussed earlier, in which mind-wandering is subserved by the (appropriately named) default mode network, provides strong support that mind-wandering follows precisely this predicted on-and-off pattern.

Trains of Thought: Distinctive Characteristics of Mind-Wandering

John Locke observed that "[W]hilst we are awake, there will always be a train of ideas succeeding one another in our minds" (Locke, 1689/ 1979, II.19, section 1). We can distinguish these trains of thoughts along at least two dimensions: (a) types of links between thoughts (i.e., how the individual items in a train of thought are linked together) and (b) types of thoughts (i.e., the kinds of thought elements that are linked together in the train). Mind-wandering involves *discursive links* that connect *episodic thought*, and each is discussed in turn.

Discursive Links

Mind-wandering involves trains of thought that are linked together in a substantially discursive fashion; thoughts appear to be drawn somewhat randomly from some relevant domain (Irving, 2015). Contrast this with "focused" trains of thought that arise during certain other tasks: doing mental arithmetic with three-digit numbers, planning next week's dinners, or solving the Tower of Hanoi problem. In these tasks, the mind stays focused on a particular topic and follows a structured sequence of operations. A frontoparietal brain network implements a number of critical functions for sustaining these sequences. For example, the network performs executive functions, such as maintaining the instructions for producing the task-specific sequences (often referred to as *task sets*) (Baddeley 1996; Monsell, 2003). It is also the source of attentional signals for selecting certain representational contents to be sustained and manipulated (Corbetta & Shulman, 2002; Woldorff et al., 2004), as well as monitoring and control signals that regulate the flow of thought so that it does not deviate from prescribed lines (Miller, 2000; Miller & Cohen, 2001).

There is evidence that mind-wandering also activates certain regions of this same frontoparietal network (Christoff et al., 2009; Fox, Spreng, Ellamil, Andrews-Hanna, & Christoff, 2015; Smallwood, Brown, Baird, & Schooler, 2012; Teasdale et al., 1995). This finding may initially seem to be at odds with the claim that the discursivity of mind-wandering is to be contrasted with the organized sequencing of focused modes of thought. The seeming tension, however, can be reconciled by noting that the frontoparietal network in question performs a number of distinct storage, executive, attentional, monitoring, and control functions. Mind-wandering and focused modes of thought might engage distinct processes that fall under these headings, or, even if the very same processes are engaged, they might be engaged in substantially different ways.

To illustrate these possibilities, consider that mind-wandering appears to involve conscious awareness of trains of discursive thoughts (as was noted in "The Extended CLS Model" section). According to a number of leading theories (Baars, 1997; Carruthers, 2015; De Brigard & Prinz, 2010; Dehaene & Naccache, 2001; Prinz, 2012), the deployment of attention is required for conscious awareness; when attention targets certain mental representations, those representations are selectively strengthened, rendering them conscious. Focused trains of thought also involve conscious awareness, in this case of tightly sequenced thoughts that are organized by task sets and sustained against distraction by cognitive control signals. For focused trains of thought, then, in addition to using attention for conscious awareness, additional frontoparietal resources are required, including executive resources to maintain the task sets (Baddeley, 1996; Baddeley, Chincotta, & Adlam, 2001) and monitoring and control resources to generate cognitive control signals (Miller, 2000; Miller & Cohen, 2001). If this understanding is correct, mind-wandering and focused trains of thought should both engage frontoparietal regions, but they should exhibit distinct, though potentially partially overlapping, neural signatures. Moreover, focused thought, because it engages more extensive frontoparietal resources, would plausibly activate frontoparietal regions more vigorously. To test these predictions, it would be particularly useful to perform studies that examine the neural underpinnings of mind-wandering and focused trains of thought in the same individuals, thus allowing head-to-head comparison of their respective neural profiles.

The claim that mind-wandering is discursive might also, at first pass, seem to fit poorly with evidence that mind-wandering is strongly influenced by personal goals. For example, Morsella and colleagues (Morsella, Ben-Zeev, Lanska, & Bargh, 2010) found that when people are told they will later face a quiz about certain geography facts, their subsequent mind-wandering was concerned with geography 70% of the time. In comparison, control subjects, who were told of an upcoming geography test and then immediately after told they would not in fact have to take it, subsequently thought about geography only 10% of the time. Other studies using experience sampling (Baird, Smallwood, & Schooler, 2011) and diary methods (Klinger & Cox, 1987) also corroborate the connection between mind-wandering and personal goals.

Does this body of evidence contradict the claim that mind-wandering is discursive? No, the two claims can be reconciled. The key to seeing this is to note that interleaved learning requires the specification of a domain of examples. Recall that in the extended CLS architecture, the discursivity of mind-wandering is explained through the computational advantages of interleaved learning: When the elements from some domain of learning examples are repeatedly rebroadcast (and the order of broadcast is substantially varied), this greatly facilitates deep learning of the meaningful patterns in the learning set. The present proposal is that personal goals can influence mind-wandering by biasing the selection of a domain of examples from which interleaved sampling subsequently occurs. For example, if a person is concerned with doing well on a geography test, then the relevant domain of examples might consist of the set of one's geography-relevant experiences, and mind-wandering will discursively draw from this set. If an important relationship, perhaps with a spouse, is threatened, then the relevant domain of examples might include experiences with that person, or experiences with significant others more broadly. There is no need to suppose the person intentionally or explicitly selects a certain domain of examples for the purposes of mind-wandering. Rather, the proposal is that one's personal goals have an automatic and nonconscious biasing effect in selecting a relevant domain of examples from which mind-wandering discursively samples.

It is interesting to speculate that rumination represents a limiting case of this phenomenon. If personal goals bias and constrain the domain from which mind-wandering mechanisms sample, it might be possible for certain goals, especially goals that are relatively strong and specific, to constrain this domain excessively. The result will be that one's spontaneous thoughts take on the repetitive, perseverative quality that is characteristic of rumination. As was noted earlier, trains of topic-constrained thought can also be generated via the maintenance of task sets and the generation of cognitive control signals, as occurs during focused activities such as planning, deliberation, and problem-solving. On the current proposal, however, the mechanism that maintains trains of topical thought during rumination is quite different. Rumination has the spontaneous quality of mind-wandering; ruminative thoughts simply pop into one's stream of consciousness unbidden. The maintenance of topical focus is achieved, it is proposed, by the biasing effects of personal goals; they constrain the domain of experiences from which mind-wandering mechanisms discursively sample sufficiently tightly that there is little space for the mind to wander to a variety of internal episodes. Some tentative initial evidence for this "constrained mind-wandering" model of rumination comes from a number of neuroimaging studies that link hyperactivity of the default network, a brain network centrally implicated in mind-wandering, with ruminative thoughts (Berman et al., 2011; Kross, Davidson, Weber, & Ochsner, 2009) as well as depression (Nejad, Fossati, & Lemogne, 2013; Sheline et al., 2009), a disorder characterized by rumination.

Episodic Thought: Autobiographical and Prospective

The thoughts that discursively pop into one's mind during mind-wandering are characteristically episodic (Klinger & Cox, 1987; Delamillieure et al., 2010). As noted earlier, this kind of thought involves quasi-perceptual representations of events, including information about who was there, what happened, where it occurred, and other kinds of contextual information (Allen & Fortin, 2013; Tulving, 2002) Many of the episodic thoughts that appear during mind-wandering are autobiographical and concern prior personal experiences. However, a substantial number, by some estimates, the majority, are prospective episodes (Baird et al., 2011; Delamillieure et al., 2010; Klinger & Cox, 1987). This kind of episodic thought is constructed from elements of autobiographical memories; these elements are recombined to build new representations of future scenarios (Addis,

Pan, Vu, Laiser, & Schacter, 2008; Buckner & Carroll, 2007; Seligman, Railton, Baumeister, & Sripada, 2013; Suddendorf & Corballis, 2007). The hippocampus appears to play a critical role in implementing the recombination process that produces the prospective episodes (Addis, Cheng, Roberts, & Schacter, 2010; Gaesser, Spreng, McLelland, Addis, & Schacter, 2013), although general knowledge, likely drawn from neocortical systems, is also required to ensure that prospections are realistic extrapolations from experience. If mind-wandering serves the function of driving deep learning, what roles do prospective episodes play in the learning process?

One possibility is that including prospective episodes in mind-wandering serves to boost the number of examples in the learning set. Thus far, we have seen that discursive sampling from one's autobiographical episodic memories can facilitate extraction of deep patterns in the learning set. Let us now suppose the person also has reasonably accurate information, likely implicit information but potentially also explicit, enabling the individual to generate episodic prospections about what will happen in the future. In this case, it is possible to combine these episodes, both autographical and prospective, thus substantially augmenting the set of learning examples available to drive implicit pattern learning.

Consider an illustration. A therapist is driving to work and his mind wanders. He thinks about a pair of patients he saw yesterday, Mr. *A* and Mrs. *B*. He reflects on how little progress has been made. He prospects that the upcoming slate of patients for later in the day will be more of the same. An image of Mr. *C* passes before his mind. He will cry as he perseverates on his sick daughter. An image of Mrs. *D* appears. She will complain about how she is worse off than when she first walked in. The therapist sees patterns and trends across all these episodes, two that have already occurred and two that are yet to occur. He detects pessimistic trends in these examples. Following this train of thought, he thinks of other ways outside the clinic that things have gone wrong and ways they might unravel in the future. He is implicitly picking up on trends and patterns across all these episodes—retrospective and prospective—and building models of how things have gone wrong and why.

It must be emphasized that prospective episodes are not confined to mind-wandering. They are also a crucial component of more structured modes of cognition such as deliberation and planning.

Thus the preceding claims about the functional purpose of prospective episodes should be seen as domain-limited. It is claimed that when prospective episodes appear as part of the discursive train of thoughts *during mind-wandering,* they serve the function of boosting the size of the learning set available for deep learning. This is fully consistent with the claim that prospective episodes play other quite distinct roles when they occur during more structured modes of cognition such as deliberation and planning.

Evidence That Mind-Wandering Enhances Deep Learning

There is a growing body of evidence arising from distinct methodologies that links mind-wandering with behaviors and outcomes that are indicative of improved deep learning. In an early research program that anticipates key elements of contemporary research into mind-wandering, J. L. Singer and his colleagues investigated the psychological correlates of a person's propensity for daydreaming. They found daydreaming was positively correlated with a number of psychological measures of social health as well as higher levels of creativity (Singer, 1974; Singer & Antrobus, 1963; Singer & Schonbar, 1961). These results are well explained on the hypothesis that mind-wandering facilitates improved learning of underlying hidden patterns in one's experiences, including one's social experiences.

Another line of research takes advantage of mind-wandering having a reliable neural correlate, activity in the default mode network (Fox et al., 2015), in order to assess the psychological consequences of increased mind-wandering. For example, Wig and colleagues (Wig et al., 2008) examined the extent of default network activation during breaks during a cognitive task, with greater activation plausibly indicating more vigorous mind-wandering. They found higher default network activity was linked to measures of recognitional memory performance, suggesting a link between mind-wandering and the formation of more stable and efficient associative links between memory items (see also Yang, Bossmann, Schiffhauer, Jordan, & Immordino-Yang, 2012, for an analogous finding that coupling within the default network predicted greater depth of social understanding).

Perhaps the strongest kind of evidence for a link between mind-wandering and deep learning directly manipulates the quantity of mind-wandering and measures the consequences for deep learning-related constructs. In an elegant study, Baird and colleagues (2012) presented participants with the unusual uses task (UUT), which asks participants to list as many unusual uses as possible for a common object, such as a toothpick, in a set amount of time. They received the same UUT twice, at baseline as well as at a later "time 2." By having participants perform cognitive tasks of different levels of difficulty during the intervening period, the quantity of mind-wandering during this period was successfully manipulated. They found that participants in the undemanding task condition, who exhibited the most mind-wandering during the intervening period, had significantly improved scores on their time 2 UUT. A natural explanation of this finding is that, consistent with the deep learning model, mind-wandering during the intervening period served to extract hidden patterns from prior experiences with the relevant UUT object thus enabling better performance when given the UUT a second time.

Mind-Wandering and Dreams

There are interesting similarities between mind-wandering that occurs during the day and nighttime dreaming. Both involve conscious experience of a stream of imagistic sensorily rich episodes, both arise spontaneously, and both are mostly undirected and discursive. In addition, we spend substantial amounts of time engaged in each, which has separately puzzled thinkers working on each topic for quite some time. Might the deep learning account of mind-wandering offer insights into the nature and purpose of dreams?

Let us start with recent influential accounts of dreaming that emphasize its role in facilitating memory and learning. It has long been known that sleep preserves and strengthens memories in their original form, as occurs in rote memorization of a list of words. Thus Quintilian (as cited in Stickgold, 2005, p. 1272), addressing the benefits of sleep, notes, "what could not be repeated at first is readily put together on the following day; and the very time which is generally thought to cause forgetfulness is found to strengthen the memory."

More recently, it has been appreciated that some forms of deep learning discussed earlier—generalization, explanation, abstraction, and interpretation—are facilitated by sleep and in particular by dreaming. For example, Wagner and colleagues (Wagner, Gais, Haider, Verleger, & Born, 2004) presented participants with a mathematical rule-following task in which they apply certain rules to strings of digits to produce an answer, a somewhat tedious task. In addition, there is a hidden shortcut in the task that allows computing the answer with less time and effort. Remarkably, 59% of the subjects who slept for a night between training and retesting discovered the shortcut rule. By contrast, no more than 25% of subjects in any of four different control groups who did not have a night's sleep, but were matched on such things as alertness at the time of testing and duration of time between training and testing, had this insight.

Neuroanatomical and neuroimaging evidence also supports connections between daytime mind-wandering and nighttime dreaming, and, more specially, supports the idea that the extended CLS architecture plays a role in both. Fox and colleagues (Fox, Nijeboer, Solomonova, Domhoff, & Christoff, 2013) performed an activation likelihood estimation (ALE) meta-analysis of six studies that examined brain activation during rapid eye movement (REM) sleep in healthy, nonclinical populations. Of eight significant cortical clusters of activation identified, all but one overlapped to at least some extent with core regions of the default mode network, the network that is repeatedly implicated in mind-wandering. There was particularly prominent activation during REM sleep in the medial temporal lobe encompassing the hippocampus. This is notable because the extended CLS architecture proposes that this region houses the high-fidelity surface system that engages in repeated reactivation of memories; that is, it produces streams of episodic memory-based examples for further processing by neocortical deep learning systems.

Further evidence for hippocampal reactivation of memories during sleep comes from animal studies. Earlier we discussed place cells in the hippocampus that fire in sequence as an animal moves along a specific trajectory. We noted that these cells repeatedly fire in the same sequence during waking periods of quiet rest and also during sleep (Davidson et al., 2009; Lee & Wilson, 2002). This suggests the existence of a common hippocampal memory reactivation mechanism that operates during both of these quiescent states.

Other studies found similar effects of sleep, especially REM sleep, in facilitating other types of deep learning processing including: spatial learning tasks in which portions of a landscape are presented and must be integrated into a generalized map, lexical learning tasks in which new word items must be integrated into existing semantic networks, gist learning tasks in which individual items are presented and thematic links must be identified, inference tasks in which selective premises are presented and additional permissible inferences must be recognized, and probabilistic learning tasks in which underlying statistical patterns in large sets of examples must be detected (see Stickgold & Walker, 2013 for reviews of these and other tasks). This body of evidence provides a compelling case that both daytime mind-wandering and nighttime dreaming play a pivotal role in deep learning.

We spend a substantial portion of our lives engaged in mind-wandering, and there is growing recognition that it serves adaptive functions. The deep learning account developed here provides a novel perspective on how mind-wandering achieves functional ends. Building on the seminal work of McClelland, McNaughton, and O'Reilly, the core insight of the deep learning model is that mind-wandering emerges from the interaction between complementary brain systems that implement reactivation-based learning, a powerful process for facilitating pattern learning. The model illuminates a number of aspects of mind-wandering including its adaptiveness, pervasiveness, discursivity, pattern of onset and offset, connection to rumination, and relation to nighttime dreaming.

References

Addis, D. R., Cheng, T., Roberts, R. P., & Schacter, D. L. (2010). Hippocampal contributions to the episodic simulation of specific and general future events. *Hippocampus, 10,* 1045–1052.

Addis, D. R., Pan, L., Vu, M. A., Laiser, N., & Schacter, D. L. (2008). Constructive episodic simulation of the future and the past: Distinct subsystems of a core brain network mediate imagining and remembering. *Neuropsychologia, 47,* 2222–2238.

Allen, T. A., & Fortin, N. J. (2013). The evolution of episodic memory. *Proceedings of the National Academy of Sciences, 110,* 10379–10386.

Andrews-Hanna, J. R., Reidler, J. S., Huang, C., & Buckner, R. L. (2010). Evidence for the default network's role in spontaneous cognition. *Journal of Neurophysiology, 104,* 322–335.

Baars, B. J. (1997). Some essential differences between consciousness and attention, perception, and working memory. *Consciousness and Cognition, 6,* 363–371.

Baars, B. J. (2002). The conscious access hypothesis: Origins and recent evidence. *Trends in Cognitive Sciences, 6,* 47–52.

Baars, B. J. (2005). Global workspace theory of consciousness: Toward a cognitive neuroscience of human experience. *Progress in Brain Research, 150,* 45–53.

Baddeley, A. (1996). Exploring the central executive. *The Quarterly Journal of Experimental Psychology Section A: Human Experimental Psychology, 49,* 5–28.

Baddeley, A., Chincotta, D., & Adlam, A. (2001). Working memory and the control of action: Evidence from task switching. *Journal of Experimental Psychology: General, 130,* 641–657.

Baird, B., Smallwood, J., & Schooler, J. W. (2011). Back to the future: Autobiographical planning and the functionality of mind-wandering. *Consciousness and Cognition, 20,* 1604–1611.

Baird, B., Smallwood, J., Mrazek, M. D., Kam, J. W. Y., Franklin, M. S., & Schooler, J. W. (2012). Inspired by Distraction: Mind Wandering Facilitates Creative Incubation. *Psychological Science, 23*(10), 1117–1122.

Barnes, C. A., McNaughton, B. L., Mizumori, S. J. Y., Leonard, B. W., & Lin, L.-H. (1990). Comparison of spatial and temporal characteristics of neuronal activity in sequential stages of hippocampal processing. *Progress in Brain Research, 83,* 287–300.

Berman, M. G., Peltier, S., Nee, D. E., Kross, E., Deldin, P. J., & Jonides, J. (2011). Depression, rumination and the default network. *Social Cognitive and Affective Neuroscience, 6,* 548–555.

Bliss, T. V. P., & Collingridge, G. L. (1993). A synaptic model of memory: Long-term potentiation in the hippocampus. *Nature, 361,* 31–39.

Brüne, M., & Brüne-Cohrs, U. (2006). Theory of mind—evolution, ontogeny, brain mechanisms and psychopathology. *Neuroscience and Biobehavioral Reviews, 30,* 437–455.

Buckner, R. L, Andrews-Hanna, J. R., & Schacter, D. L. (2008). The brain's default network: Anatomy, function, and relevance to disease. *Annals of the New York Academy of Sciences, 1124,* 1–38.

Buckner, R. L., & Carroll, D. C. (2007). Self-projection and the brain. *Trends in Cognitive Sciences, 11,* 49–57.

Burgess, N., Maguire, E. A., & O'Keefe, J. (2002). The human hippo-campus and spatial and episodic memory. *Neuron, 35,* 625–641.

Buzsáki, G. (1989). Two-stage model of memory trace forma-tion: A role for "noisy" brain states. *Neuroscience, 31,* 551–570.

Callard, F., Smallwood, J., Golchert, J., & Margulies, D. S. (2013). The era of the wandering mind? Twenty-first century research on self-generated mental activity. *Frontiers in Psychology,* 4(891), 1–11.

Carruthers, P. (2006). *The architecture of the mind.* New York, NY: Oxford University Press.

Carruthers, P. (2015). *The centered mind: What the science of work-ing memory shows us about the nature of human thought.* New York, NY: Oxford University Press.

Christoff, K., Gordon, A. M., Smallwood, J., Smith, R., & Schooler, J. W. (2009). Experience sampling during fMRI reveals default network and executive system contributions to mind wandering. *Proceedings of the National Academy of Sciences, 106,* 8719–24.

Corbetta, M., & Shulman, G. L. (2002). Control of goal-directed and stimulus-driven attention in the brain. *Nature Reviews Neuroscience, 3,* 201–215.

Davidson, T. J., Kloosterman, F., & Wilson, M. A. (2009). Hippocampal replay of extended experience. *Neuron, 63,* 497–507.

De Brigard, F., & Prinz, J. (2010). Attention and consciousness. *Wiley Interdisciplinary Reviews: Cognitive Science, 1,* 51–59.

Dehaene, S., Kerszberg, M., & Changeux, J.-P. (1998). A neuro-nal model of a global workspace in effortful cognitive tasks. *Proceedings of the National Academy Sciences, 95,* 14529–14534.

Dehaene, S., & Naccache, L. (2001). Towards a cognitive neurosci-ence of consciousness: Basic evidence and a workspace framework. *Cognition, 79,* 1–37.

Delamillieure, P., Doucet, G., Mazoyer, B., Turbelin, M.-R., Delcroix, N., Mellet, E., . . . Joliet, M. (2010). The resting state question-naire: An introspective questionnaire for evaluation of inner experience during the conscious resting state. *Brain Research Bulletin, 81,* 565–573.

Elman, J. (1998). Generalization, simple recurrent networks, and the emergence of structure. In M. A. Gernsbacher & S. Derry (Eds.), *Proceedings of the twentieth annual conference of the cognitive science society* (p. 6). Mahwah, NJ: Erlbaum.

Fincham, J. M., Carter, C. S., van Veen, V., Stenger, V. A., & Anderson, J. R. (2002). Neural mechanisms of planning: A computational analysis using event-related fMRI. *Proceedings of the National Academy of Sciences, 99*, 3346–3351.

Fox, K. C. R., Nijeboer, S., Solomonova, E., Domhoff, G. W., & Christoff, K. (2013). Dreaming as mind wandering: Evidence from functional neuroimaging and first-person content reports. *Frontiers in Human Neuroscience, 7*(412), 1–18.

Fox, K. C. R., Spreng, R. N., Ellamil, M., Andrews-Hanna, J. R., & Christoff, K. (2015). The wandering brain: Meta-analysis of functional neuroimaging studies of mind-wandering and related spontaneous thought processes. *NeuroImage, 111*, 611–621.

Frankland, P. W., & Bontempi, B. (2005). The organization of recent and remote memories. *Nature Reviews Neuroscience, 6*, 119–130.

Gaesser, B., Spreng, R. N., McClelland, V. C., Addis, D. R., & Schacter, D. L. (2013). Imagining the future: Evidence for a hippocampal contribution to constructive processing. *Hippocampus, 23*, 1150–1161.

Gallagher, H. L, & Frith, C. D. (2003). Functional imaging of "theory of mind." *Trends in Cognitive Sciences, 7*, 77–83.

Gentner, D., & Markman, A. B. (1997). Structure mapping in analogy and similarity. *American Psychologist, 52*, 45–56.

Girardeau, G., & Zugaro, M. (2011). Hippocampal ripples and memory consolidation. *Current Opinion in Neurobiology, 21*, 452–459.

Gopnik, A., & Glymour, C. (2002). Causal maps and Bayes nets: A cognitive and computational account of theory-formation. In P. Carruthers, S. Stich, & M. Siegal (Eds.), *The cognitive basis of science* (pp. 117–132). Cambridge, England: Cambridge University Press.

Gopnik, A., Glymour, C., Sobel, D. M., Schulz, L. E., Kushnir, T., & Danks, D. (2004). A theory of causal learning in children: Causal maps and Bayes nets. *Psychological Review, 111*, 3–32.

Holyoak, K. J., & Thagard, P. (1996). *Mental leaps: Analogy in creative thought*. Cambridge, MA: MIT Press.

Irving, Z. (2015). Mind-wandering is unguided attention: Accounting for the "purposeful" wanderer. *Philosophical Studies*, 1–25.

Karmiloff-Smith, A., Klima, E., Bellugi, U., Grant, J., & Baron-Cohen, S. (1995). Is there a social module? Language, face processing, and theory of mind in individuals with Williams syndrome. *Journal of Cognitive Neuroscience, 7*, 196–208.

Killingsworth, M. A., & Gilbert, D. T. (2010). A wandering mind is an unhappy mind. *Science, 330*, 932.

Klinger, E., & Cox, W. M. (1987). Dimensions of thought flow in everyday life. *Imagination Cognition and Personality, 7*, 105–128.

Kross, E., Davidson, M., Weber, J., & Ochsner, K. (2009). Coping with emotions past: The neural bases of regulating affect associated with negative autobiographical memories. *Biological Psychiatry, 65*, 361–366.

Lee, A. K., & Wilson, M. A. (2002). Memory of sequential experience in the hippocampus during slow wave sleep. *Neuron, 36*, 1183–1194.

Locke, J. (1979). *An essay concerning human understanding.* P. Nidditch (Ed.). Oxford, England: Oxford University Press. (Original work published 1689)

Marr, D. (1971). Simple memory: A theory for archicortex. *Philosophical Transactions of the Royal Society B: Biological Sciences, 262*, 23–81.

Mason, M. F., Norton, M. I., Van Horn, J. D., Wegner, D. M., Grafton, S. T., & Macrae, C. N. (2007). Wandering minds: The default network and stimulus-independent thought. *Science, 315*, 393–395.

McClelland, J. L., McNaughton, B. L., & O'Reilly, R. C. (1995). Why there are complementary learning systems in the hippocampus and neocortex: Insights from the successes and failures of connectionist models of learning and memory. *Psychological Review, 102*, 419–457.

McNaughton, B. L., & Morris, R. G. M. (1987). Hippocampal synaptic enhancement and information storage within a distributed memory system. *Trends in Neurosciences, 10*, 408–415.

McVay, J. C., & Kane, M. J. (2010). Does mind wandering reflect executive function or executive failure? Comment on Smallwood and Schooler (2006) and Watkins (2008). *Psychological Bulletin, 136*, 188–197 (Discussion pp. 198–207).

Miller, E. K. (2000). The prefrontal cortex and cognitive control. *Nature Reviews Neuroscience, 1*, 59–65.

Miller, E. K., & Cohen, J. D. (2001). An integrative theory of prefrontal cortex function. *Annual Review of Neuroscience, 24*, 167–202.

Monsell, S. (2003). Task switching. *Trends in Cognitive Sciences, 7,* 134–140.

Montague, P. R., & Berns, G. S. (2002). Neural economics and the biological substrates of valuation. *Neuron, 36,* 265–284.

Montague, P. R., King-Casas, B., & Cohen, J. D. (2006). Imaging valuation models in human choice. *Annual Review of Neuroscience, 29,* 417–448.

Morsella, E., Ben-Zeev, A., Lanska, M., & Bargh, J. A. (2010). The spontaneous thoughts of the night: How future tasks breed intrusive cognitions. *Social Cognition, 28,* 641–650.

Moscovitch, M., Nadel, L., Winocur, G., Gilboa, A., & Rosenbaum, R. S. (2006). The cognitive neuroscience of remote episodic, semantic and spatial memory. *Current Opinion in Neurobiology, 16,* 179–190.

Nakazawa, K., Sun, L. D., Quirk, M. C., Rondi-Reig, L., Wilson, M. A., & Tonegawa, S. (2003). Hippocampal CA3 NMDA receptors are crucial for memory acquisition of one-time experience. *Neuron, 38,* 305–315.

Nejad, A. B., Fossati, P., & Lemogne, C. (2013). Self-referential processing, rumination, and cortical midline structures in major depression. *Frontiers in Human Neuroscience, 7*(666).

Newman, S. D., Carpenter, P. A., Varma, S., & Just, M. A. (2003). Frontal and parietal participation in problem solving in the Tower of London: fMRI and computational modeling of planning and high-level perception. *Neuropsychologia, 41,* 1668–1682.

Norman, K. A., & O'Reilly, R. C. (2003). Modeling hippocampal and neocortical contributions to recognition memory: A complementary-learning-systems approach. *Psychological Review, 110,* 611–646.

O'Neill, J., Pleydell-Bouverie, B., Dupret, D., & Csicsvari, J. (2010). Play it again: Reactivation of waking experience and memory. *Trends in Neurosciences, 33,* 220–229.

O'Reilly, R. C., & Norman, K. A. (2002). Hippocampal and neocortical contributions to memory: Advances in the complementary learning systems framework. *Trends in Cognitive Sciences, 6,* 505–510.

Prinz, J. J. (2012). *The conscious brain.* New York, NY: Oxford University Press.

Raichle, M. E., MacLeod, A. M., Snyder, A. Z., Powers, W. J., Gusnard, D. A., & Shulman, G. L. (2001). A default mode of brain function. *Proceedings of the National Academy of Sciences, 98,* 676–682.

Raichle, M. E., & Snyder, A. Z. (2007). A default mode of brain function: A brief history of an evolving idea. *NeuroImage, 37,* 1083–1090 (Discussion pp. 1097–1099).

Rumelhart, D. E., McClelland, J. L., & PDP Research Group. (1986). *Parallel distributed processing: Explorations in the microstructure of cognition. Volume 1: Foundations.* Cambridge, MA: MIT Press.

Schultz, W. (2000). Multiple reward signals in the brain. *Nature Reviews Neuroscience, 1,* 199–207.

Seligman, M. E. P., Railton, P., Baumeister, R. F., & Sripada, C. (2013). Navigating into the future or driven by the past. *Perspectives in Psychological Science, 8,* 119–141.

Sheline, Y. I., Barch, D. M., Price, J. L., Rundle, M. M., Vaishnavi, S. N., Snyder, A. Z., . . . Raichle, M. E. (2009). The default mode network and self-referential processes in depression. *Proceedings of the National Academy of Sciences, 106,* 1942–1947.

Singer, J. L. (1974). Daydreaming and the stream of thought. *American Scientist, 62,* 417–25.

Singer, J. L., & Antrobus, J. S. (1963). A factor-analytic study of daydreaming and conceptually-related cognitive and personality variables. *Perceptual and Motor Skills 17,* 187–209.

Singer, J. L., & Schonbar, R. A. (1961). Correlates of daydreaming: A dimension of self-awareness. *Journal of Consulting Psychology, 25,* 1–6.

Smallwood, J., & Andrews-Hanna, J. (2013). Not all minds that wander are lost: The importance of a balanced perspective on the mind-wandering state. *Frontiers in Psychology, 4*(441).

Smallwood, J., Brown, K., Baird, B., & Schooler, J. W. (2012). Cooperation between the default mode network and the frontal–parietal network in the production of an internal train of thought. *Brain Research, 1428,* 60–70.

Smallwood J., & Schooler J. W. (2006). The restless mind. *Psychological Bulletin, 132,* 946–958.

Smallwood J., & Schooler J. W. (2015). The science of mind wandering: Empirically navigating the stream of consciousness. *Annual Review of Psychology, 66,* 487–518.

Spivey, M., & Mirman, D. (2001) Retroactive interference in neural networks and in humans: The effect of pattern-based learning. *Connection Science, 13,* 257–275.

Squire, L. R. (1992). Memory and the hippocampus: A synthesis from findings with rats, monkeys, and humans. *Psychological Review, 99*, 195–231.

Squire, L. R, & Alvarez, P. (1995). Retrograde amnesia and memory consolidation: A neurobiological perspective. *Current Opinion in Neurobiology, 5*, 169–177.

Squire, L. R., & Bayley, P. J. (2007). The neuroscience of remote memory. *Current Opinion in Neurobiology, 17*, 185–196.

Stickgold, R. (2005). Sleep-dependent memory consolidation. *Nature, 437*, 1272–1278.

Stickgold, R., & Walker, M. P. (2013). Sleep-dependent memory triage: Evolving generalization through selective processing. *Nature Neuroscience, 16*, 139–145.

Suddendorf, T., & Corballis, M. C. (2007). The evolution of fore-sight: What is mental time travel, and is it unique to humans? *Behavioral and Brain Sciences, 30*, 299–313 (Discussion pp. 313–351).

Teasdale, J. D., Dritschel, B. H., Taylor, M. J., Proctor, L., Lloyd, C. A., Nimmo-Smith, I., & Baddeley, A. D. (1995). Stimulus-independent thought depends on central executive resources. *Memory & Cognition, 23*, 551–559.

Tulving, E. (2002). Episodic memory: From mind to brain. *Annual Review of Psychology, 53*, 1–25.

Vohs, K. D., Baumeister, R. F., Schmeichel, B. J., Twenge, J. M., Nelson, N. M., & Tice, D. M. (2008). Making choices impairs subsequent self-control: A limited-resource account of decision making, self-regulation, and active initiative. *Journal of Personality and Social Psychology, 94*, 883–898.

Wagner, U., Gais, S., Haider, H., Verleger, R., & Born, J. (2004). Sleep inspires insight. *Nature, 427*, 352–355.

White, H. (1989). Learning in artificial neural networks: A statistical perspective. *Neural Computation, 1*, 425–464.

White, T. P., Engen, N. H., Sørensen, S., Overgaard, M., & Shergill, S. S. (2014). Uncertainty and confidence from the triple-network perspective: Voxel-based meta-analyses. *Brain and Cognition, 85*, 191–200.

Wig, G. S., Grafton, S. T., Demos, K. E., Wolford, G. L., Petersen, S. E., & Kelley, W. M. (2008). Medial temporal lobe BOLD activity at rest predicts individual differences in memory ability in healthy young adults. *Proceedings of the National Academy of Sciences, 105*, 18555–18560.

Woldorff, M. G., Hazlett, C. J., Fichtenholtz, H. M., Weissman, D. H., Dale, A. M., & Song, A. W. (2004). Functional parcellation of attentional control regions of the brain. *Journal of Cognitive Neuroscience, 16*, 149–165.

Yang, X.-F., Bossmann, J., Schiffhauer, B., Jordan, M., & Immordino-Yang, M. H. (2012). Intrinsic default mode network connectivity predicts spontaneous verbal descriptions of autobiographical memories during social processing. *Frontiers in Psychology, 3*(592), 1–10.

5

Collective Prospection: The Social Construction of the Future

Roy Baumeister

I N CHAPTER 2, WE EXAMINED HOW AN INDIVIDUAL PROSPECTS the future by intuitive guidance, which is not conscious. In Chapters 3 and 4, we examined how an individual consciously imagines the future and uses mind-wandering to adjust behavior accordingly. But these omit a crucial dimension. Human beings are social animals, indeed social in a way that is unprecedented in nature. Human beings use culture to organize their social life. Thinking of prospection as a matter of a solitary individual imagining things forward in time is seriously deficient and perhaps slightly absurd. One only learns how to think about the future from other people. Moreover, the future itself is socially and culturally constructed. Most of the future, as it exists in the present and can be used by living things to organize their own actions and affairs, is created by others—indeed not just particular others but the culture in general. This chapter will flesh out the non-individual nature of the future.

Reality and Social Construction

The future is socially and culturally constructed, but nonetheless real. This view sits uncomfortably with many scholars who have come to think that things are only real if they are physical events and caused by physical events.

There is certainly some appeal in thinking that reality consists solely of hard, physical facts. Physical events can be objectively verified. There is not much that clever reinterpretation can do to alter physical facts, such as that the ice has melted, the window is broken, the dog is alive, and the fire is burning. In contrast, whether a particular ruling is fair or not, whether someone is behaving inappropriately, whether immigration and gay marriage should be encouraged, and whether the President is doing a good job are things that people can legitimately disagree about. There is no objective fact that can settle the matter for all concerned, unlike the question of the dog's life or the broken window.

Half a century ago, a classic book by Berger and Luckmann (1966) argued that much of reality is socially constructed. People do not figure out what is real in their world as isolated minds apprehending physical facts. Rather, they share understandings and work together to create a model of how the world works. Along the way, they create social systems that include some arbitrary designations. Who is eligible for citizenship? Trying to define that in purely physical terms is impossible. Some other social constructions, such as national borders and life histories, are needed to define citizenship.

To construct a theory about the future, it is necessary to understand the difference. In a literal, physical sense, only the present moment is real. Moreover, physical causality moves only forward in time, and only in very small steps (i.e., from one moment to the next). It is thus impossible for the future to exert any causal influence on the present. But the theme of this book is that much behavior is based on the future. People can construct a shared understanding of the future and base their current actions on it, showing that a social construction (of tomorrow) can change physical reality (what one does today).

The view of social reality as second-class reality, or even as a sneaky attempt to treat fiction as truth, has gained ground in recent decades (Mallon, 2013). Leading the charge were radical feminists, who angrily rejected the view that differences between men and women reflected any sort of biological facts. Instead, feminist theory proposed that men and women are basically the same, but gender stereotypes were invented by men in their conspiracy to oppress women and reduce them to inferior status. In many social sciences, it is still unacceptable to propose that there are any innate differences between the genders other than the few obvious physical ones. Radical feminist theory is motivated by the political goal of advancing the status of women, especially at the expense of men. It confronts the issue of women holding social status inferior to men in all known cultures, and it argues that this is essentially arbitrary and unfair—hence based on false ideas about gender that societies have invented without any compelling reality or factual basis.

Abraham Lincoln, often ranked as America's greatest president, liked this joke: "How many legs does a dog have, if you call a tail a leg?" One was inclined to answer five, but the punch line was, "No, four! Calling a tail a leg doesn't make it a leg!" His joke exemplifies the distinction between social construction and physical reality. There are really four legs, and no amount of interpersonal discussion can change that fact.

Against that view, there are realities that are purely social. Searle (1995) pointed out that a cocktail party—or a war—is not a description of purely physical events but rather depends on how the people taking part in it understand it. A person may fire a gun, but whether this is an isolated crime, a recreational entertainment, or an act of war depends on how it is interpreted. The rotation of the earth and the resulting alternation of day and night do not. Nonetheless, war and cocktail parties really do happen. They are not fictions nor illusions, as the people whose lives are altered by them can attest.

Let us explore the idea that the future is socially constructed, but nonetheless real. Yes, next year's election is not a physical fact that one can point to today. But it is really going to happen, and plenty of what is happening today is shaped by the collectively shared understanding that there will be an election next year.

Monday Is Real

The authors of this book met to plan it in the wilds of South Australia in 2013. We earnestly discussed how an individual might envision the future and act on that basis. But as we discussed the actual processes, we noticed that this is hardly a solitary enterprise. To illustrate, one of us had plans to fly home the Monday after the week-long meeting. The very idea of Monday is a cultural construction. Solitary beings would not have Mondays. Moreover, the precise definition of Monday is subject to social construction, indeed it is very officially set by the culture as a whole. The Monday of the flight home corresponded to the day that the United States switched to daylight savings time, so the 24-hour daily schedule shifted forward by an hour. Australia, being in the southern hemisphere, was already on its own daylight savings time, and it was preparing to revert to normal time, although that would not happen until April. The flight home would depart from Australia on Australian time and land in the United States on the forward-shifted daylight savings time, thus an hour earlier than the previous day's same-numbered flight landed. Of course no actual hour disappeared from reality, and the flight from Sydney to Los Angeles took the same amount of time as ever. Only the official time of landing would be different because of the cultural convention of skipping one of the wee hours between late Saturday night and Sunday morning.

That was the least of it. The plane reservation on Monday was not something a solitary individual could have made or even contemplated. The ticket was purchased months in advance. It was not a solitary or solipsistic fantasy: There really was going to be a particular flight on that particular Monday, with a limited number of seats to be bought and reserved well ahead of the actual date of flight. Reserved seats on airplane flights are only possible in a social world that has structured its future quite precisely. Because of these precise plans, remarkable things happen in human social groups. An assortment of strangers show up at a preordained time and place, line up to climb into a big metal tube, and sit in specifically designated seats. The metal tube blasts into the sky and comes down at a far distant place, whereupon the passengers separate and go their separate ways, mostly never to see each other again. The airplane itself is only possible because of a cultural accumulation of knowledge that has been built up over decades, using science and technology and regulated by the government's laws, paid for with money and yet now functioning to increase total wealth. Without a culture that has an established future, nobody would build, let alone invent, an airplane. Certainly no one except in the most advanced human civilizations ever did.

The point of this example is that the future is created and mapped out not by individual persons but by the social group. If you lived alone and never interacted with another person, you would have no Mondays, no reservations, and certainly no airplane flights. Humans label themselves "*Homo sapiens*" based on their ostensible individual intelligence, but the solitary human mind can accomplish very little. The great progress of human culture comes from the accumulation of many, many different individuals contributing to a common stock of knowledge. The greatest individual minds operate within a system, and their achievements simply move the collective enterprise forward rather than accomplishing something that is truly individual. That is, they take what many others have already built and learned, and they add to it, using methods they have learned from teachers and others. If you started from scratch, you could hardly figure out addition and subtraction, let alone trigonometry, calculus, and the iPhone.

The future is neither an objective, inhuman prospect nor a product of solitary imagination. Airline flights are a good example. They are not mere fantasy, nor are they up to individual thinking. There will really be one particular plane flying from Sydney to Los Angeles on a given Monday morning, and it has a fixed number of seats, and a given person may or may not be able to sit in one. Likewise, the future really does contain political elections, final exams, holidays, and deadlines. These are neither a figment of one person's imagination nor a purely physical fact. Plane flights and elections can be delayed. Exams are scheduled on an ad hoc basis by school and college administrators, and exceptions are permitted in some cases (e.g., taking the exam a day later because one was ill). There is a real future, but its existence rests on the shared understandings of the social group. We already know that February 2063 will have 28 days, but February 2064 will have 29 days. It is even slightly possible that governments will revise that. Long ago, Europe's ruling bodies decided that there would be no October 10, 1582, when they switched from the Julian to the Gregorian calendar and simply skipped over a couple weeks.

In fact, it's even weirder. Some countries didn't make the change right away, but eventually they all did, so October 10, 1582, actually took place and existed in some countries but not others, and the stragglers had other phantom calendar dates. Had the discrepancy been the other way, it's doubtful that they would have skipped backward and repeated a couple weeks, so that two different days would have had the same date. Instead they probably would have just tacked on a dozen extra days at the end of one month. The principle here, which could not be deduced directly from the physical movements of the planet, was that duplicate dates would create more problems than skipped ones. Having two October 10ths in a particular year would complicate birthdays, contracts, historical records, and more. (Note, however, that when a country shifts into daylight savings time, it does duplicate an hour, although it tries to minimize scheduling hassles by picking the least eventful hour of the week. Imagine the chaos that would stem from doubling a really busy hour.)

In a sense, the future is a product of collective imagination and agreement. The group imagines it together. Early humans probably made simple plans together, such as for a group hunt or a battle. The modern construction of the calendar is similar. That is, the people in the group cooperate to impose their collective imagination on top of some physical or anticipated facts. The planet does continue to rotate and revolve around the sun, regardless of our imaginings. But we use our collective imagination to count and calculate and label those movements. That's how we get Mondays (and all the rest).

Culture as Biological Strategy

All living things die. Life inherently seeks to continue life, which means grappling with the fundamental problems of survival and reproduction. Survival means sustaining the individual life as long as possible. But creating permanent life (immortality) has proven impossible, so the key to long-term sustenance of life is reproduction. Natural selection has favored organisms that can survive and, even more important, can reproduce.

Human beings have adopted a rather unusual strategy for surviving and reproducing (see Baumeister, 2005). We create social systems established on shared information, exchange and trade, morality, and group effort based on interlocking roles. In a word, we rely on culture to produce survival and reproduction. It has worked quite well for our species. Human beings survive and reproduce much more effectively than any other mammals on the planet. It's why we put the other mammals in zoos rather than vice versa. No other creature has tripled its average life expectancy, because no other one has mastered the cultural practices of accumulating scientific knowledge and using it to inform medical treatments and public health practices. And while the populations of most other creatures on earth, and certainly all other mammals, has declined in recent centuries (with a few exceptions that are overseen by human intervention, such as breeding chickens and keeping dogs as pets), the human population has ballooned to an astonishing degree and continues to increase. Culture has greatly increased human life.

The future is culturally constructed. Time will proceed regardless of culture, and even if humankind commenced a nuclear war and wiped itself out of existence, there would be a physical future in the sense that the earth would continue to rotate and each place on earth would undergo an alternation of night and day. But without humankind, that alternation would lose most of its meaning. Human conventions construct the future, with national and religious holidays, weekends, and more. Individuals fill in their specific details, such as anniversaries, appointments, deadlines, and travel plans.

The individual human mind learns to operate within the socially created structure of past, present, and future. It is safe to predict that citizens in Western civilization will celebrate Christmas on a particular date in 5 years. That date is based on a presumptive but almost certainly erroneous calculation of the date of birth of a particular individual a couple thousand years ago. Even people who have no belief in Christian doctrine will celebrate the holiday: They will stay home from work, give gifts to their children and relatives, and eat a holiday feast of some sort. Thus their individual beliefs about the validity of religious doctrines are somewhat irrelevant to altering their actions on a particular, prearranged day.

How Natural Selection Actually Selected

Central to this book, we have proposed that being able to base one's behavior on the future rather than the past would be highly adaptive. Hence any evolutionary progress in mental capacity to better predict the future and adjust behavior accordingly would confer a big advantage in natural selection. In the simplest terms, creatures who acted on the basis of the past would not survive and reproduce as well as creatures who could base their actions on the future.

One can develop this argument in purely individual terms. An animal that can adjust its actions based on reasonably accurate expectancies would have an advantage over rivals whose actions were driven by the past. Over time, across a species, animals with better forecasting and prospecting abilities would survive and reproduce better than ones who were terrible at those tasks.

But perhaps that simple analysis misses a key dimension. Yes, predicting the future benefits and individual contingencies would be useful and adaptive. Human beings, however, work together. The evolutionary benefits of prospecting may come not just from solitary forecasts but also from group planning and committing.

After all, what pushed humankind to become able to rule over all other animals? It was not the prowess of individuals. A single human being is no match for a lion, tiger, bear, or any other large hunting animal. But groups of humans worked together to take over the world. To do that, they needed more than a capability of an individual brain to imagine and plan the future. They needed to do that together.

Most likely, we think, natural selection favored humans who could participate in families and other small groups that prospected together. They could make group plans and follow them. To do this, they needed not only to be able to project what could happen in the future but also to communicate those ideas to others, who could understand them. Members of the group might argue about which plan should be followed. To do that, they needed to share an understanding not just of the various possible sequences of future events but also of some criteria for favoring one plan over the alternatives.

Humans seem to approach strangers with an attitude of being wary but hoping to establish a relationship. For example, thousands of hours of research with the prisoner's dilemma game (based on a choice of whether to go for oneself or take a risk by cooperating with another person) have established that the most effective strategy is to start off cooperating but then reciprocate based on what the other person does (Axelrod, 1980; Axelrod & Hamilton, 1981). The initial cooperation shows the openness and it is necessary to make possible the establishment of a relationship.

Relationships benefit both parties in long run, but in the short run, there is advantage to be gotten from betraying trust, so you have to watch out for whether the other person might succumb to these temptations. The first or default plan when you meet someone is to form a cooperative relationship with that person (e.g., Rand, Greene, & Nowak, 2012; see also Dunning, Anderson, Schlösser, Ehlebracht, & Fetchenhauer, 2014). That can be quickly set aside if there is anything negative about him or her. One acts in the present based on what one thinks the future will hold.

Earning Trust

The ability to project forward into the future may have been crucial for the development of the kinds of social relationships that constitute human society. This section builds on the idea that humans evolved to create culture.

Cooperation and competition are two basic ways that creatures can relate to each other. They are not on a par, however. Competition is much older and more fundamental, in evolutionary terms. It was the emergence of cooperation that may have depended on becoming able to forecast the future.

In *A Natural History of Human Thinking*, Tomasello (2014) pointed out that most of the great apes have very sophisticated, effective minds for dealing with competition, but not for cooperation. Nonhuman apes understand competition instinctively and become highly skilled at anticipating what rivals are doing. The idea that strangers might want to cooperate with them, however, does not come naturally. That is the human innovation.

Cooperation, however, requires considerably more mental competence than competition. Prospection is also needed.

Because hunting is an important source of food and presumably something that both humans and other primates engaged in, consider competitive versus cooperative hunting. In a competitive mindset, hunters see each other as rivals seeking the same prey. That makes group hunting a bit more complicated than solitary hunting, but not by much. Other hunters represent simply one more way that one's hunt can be thwarted.

Cooperative hunting requires considerably more in the way of mental processing and social competence. Cooperative hunters understand that they are working together, performing different roles to produce a joint result. Presumably they must understand that this leads to sharing the prey.

Tomasello (2014; Tomasello & Call, 1997) points out that non-human primates do engage in group hunts, yet each ape or chimp is really out for him- or herself. Primates participate in the group hunt because doing so presents them with opportunities for individual gain, not because the hunters make a pact to perform complementary roles and then share the proceeds. There is no pact and no real sharing, although when one makes a kill, the others do come over to help themselves by grabbing what they can.

Something like cooperation can emerge from purely selfish, competitive creatures. Tomasello (2014) gives the example of what happens when a group of chimps spots a monkey and give chase, hoping to catch and eat it. If the monkey runs up a tree, the chimp closest will go after it. A chimp at the far end of the group knows it will not be the first one to reach the monkey, so there is no point in trying. Instead, it might block off a possible escape route. Human groups may do this, so that all escapes are blocked, but that is based on an agreement to share the prey, regardless of who makes the kill. The chimp guarding the escape route has no such guarantee. If the monkey comes its way, it will kill it and start eating the best parts as fast as it can. If the monkey doesn't come near, the chimp has no claim, but it can make its way over to where another member has killed the monkey and try to grab a few bites.

When early human ancestors began to develop cooperation, it proved much more effective than the pseudo-cooperation of the chimp group hunt. Cooperation, however, involves risk and vulnerability. If you agree to stand guard to block off a possible escape route and the prey does not come your way, you have still contributed to the success of the hunt, and presumably the others have agreed to share the meat regardless of who makes the kill. The hunter who does make the kill might not share, in which case your standing guard was a fool's errand (despite its contribution to making the kill). You performed a role in the system based on trust that the rewards would be shared, and others betrayed your trust.

Trust is an important foundation of cooperation in particular and culture in general. Trust is inherently prospective: It is about the future. Trust is a matter of expecting that someone will at some point in the future do what is good for you rather than what might bring that person some benefit or advantage then. Trust is an expectation. The development of trust as a moral foundation of human culture likely depended on the ability to think about the future, usually far beyond the next 5 or 10 minutes.

The chimps can perform their quasi-cooperative roles without any agreements or expectations. As Tomasello (2014) explains, each one is simply out for itself, even though that leads some to play complementary roles. But an agreement to share the spoils—common among human groups, but absent in all other primates—invokes a shared understanding of the future, indeed of an event that is not yet in sight. Blocking an escape route can be improvised on spur of the moment, as the chimp sizes up its own best chances for catching the monkey given that others are already in hot pursuit. In contrast, agreeing to share the spoils at the end of the hunt is something that presumably happens before the hunt starts, thus requiring more prospection.

And cooperation may push for even longer time frames. As Tomasello (2014) explains, if the group flourishes by means of cooperation (as early human groups presumably did), then each person's success depends partly on inducing others to cooperate. You have to worry about whether others will want to cooperate with you, not just today but in the long run into the indefinite future.

Consider the group hunt from the perspective of the successful individual. Among the chimps, there is no question what to do. The one who made the kill is the fortunate one and so eats as much as it can, before the others arrive to dig in. There is no thought of waiting till all are present and then sharing the food equally, like a suburban family meeting to enjoy dinner together.

In a cooperative human hunt, if you made the kill, you would have reached some kind of understanding with the other hunters that sharing is expected. You would likely be tempted to break that agreement. After all, you would be hungry, and the food would be in your possession. What's to restrain you? Why wouldn't you eat all you can and leave the others to fend for themselves?

The drawback of that selfish strategy is that others will soon stop cooperating with you. Betraying trust brings an immediate gain but carries significant long-term costs. If you alienate all potential cooperators by such acts, you may end up losing the benefits of cooperation, and that loss could prove fatal. (Remember that early hunter-gatherers did not have the luxury of the modern city dweller, with thousands of other people nearby, so that any lost cooperator can be replaced with an endless stream of others. Early humans lived in small, stable groups, so it was vital to stay on good terms with most members of the group.)

In short, cooperators have to worry about their reputations in ways that competitors do not. Cooperation greatly improved the effectiveness of human groups, but living in a cooperative environment enhances the importance of prospection. One's reputation as a trustworthy partner is sustained by resisting the temptations to do the selfish act of betraying others for one's own immediate advantage. The here-and-now benefits of betrayal must be resisted for the sake of one's future attractiveness to other potential cooperators.

Reputation extends the self into the future. Roberts (2002) concluded that hardly any animals are capable of thinking more than a few minutes ahead. But a reputation is something that extends days, months, even years into the future. The emergence of the self as a moral agent probably required a mental capability for imagining the future and adjusting current behavior on that basis. The chimp hunter who captures the prey commences to devour all it can, as fast as it can. The human hunter waits to eat until the others have arrived and the food can be shared, as agreed. Waiting is costly and would reduce your own consumption for the moment, but you would do this based on anticipating that on other occasions, when other members of the group make the kill, they would wait and share with you.

Thus, human social life was able to take off in new, highly profitable directions *because of prospection*. Being able to understand how others will treat you in the future based on how you behave right now was extremely helpful, if not indispensable, for the evolutionary emergence of human cooperation.

Culture, Time, and Possibility

Thus far this chapter has focused on how culture improves and facilitates prospection. This section will look at the other side of the coin: how prospection improves and facilitates culture. If constructing culture is the human way of solving the basic biological problems of survival and reproduction, then prospection benefited humans by strengthening culture.

Culture is possible without prospection. Ethnologists estimate that several dozen species have some degree of culture (e.g., de Waal, 2001), and most of them have no sign of being able to think about the future (let alone do so collectively, sharing their understanding of the future with each other). Culture is understood as learned behavior that is shared socially. That can work just by having individual animals copy and mimic each other's behavior, so that something that one of them learns or invents can be transmitted to others in the group.

But prospection greatly improves the power of groups to share information. Collective planning becomes possible when group members can share a vision about the future. Learning and even teaching can occur without an immediate problem to solve: People can share information that is not immediately useful but is likely to be useful in the indefinite future.

Before fleshing this out with examples, we point out one more feature of the contribution of prospection to culture. To take advantage of prospection, it may generally be necessary for cultures to acknowledge the indeterminate nature of the future. That is, culture must work with the realization that the future is a matter of multiple possibilities rather than a fixed pathway.

We have already covered some examples of this. Trust is only meaningful in a world of multiple possibilities. Whether someone is trustworthy is a matter of whether that person will treat others fairly and honor promises *despite the tempting possibility of doing otherwise*. Both the trustor and the trustee understand that what is at stake is how the person will choose when there are multiple options and alternatives later.

Even when it seems that culture is about knowing what is inevitable, usually there is some aspect of multiple possibility that is relevant. For example, in recent decades meteorologists have become much more effective at predicting major storms, such as hurricanes. These predictions do not enable people to prevent the hurricane (at least not yet). But people can reduce the damage caused by the hurricane by making preparations and taking precautions. Otherwise, what's the use of knowing that a hurricane is coming? Knowing about future events that one cannot control is useful for enabling us to control the things we can control. In the hurricane example, those are things like loading the refrigerator with extra ice (to sustain freezing in case of power failure), filling the tub with water (in case water service is disrupted), and putting the pool furniture into the pool (where it won't blow away or break windows).

The calendar might seem an exception to the principle that culture constructs the future as possibilities rather than certainties. But the calendar is useful as a framework for organizing the possibilities. It is pretty much guaranteed that there will be a day known as March 12th next year, and another one the following year. For practical purposes, that much is a certainty. But that certain fact provides a basis for constructing possibilities. Members of the culture can use that date to make plans.

Let us return briefly to the earlier example of the air travel and the reality of Monday. Without a precise map of the future, one could not make airplane reservations, and indeed the airline business really depends on having the calendar structuring the future in order to operate profitably. The airline commits itself to organizing a particular flight on next March 12th, and doing that is a matter of ensuring that there will be an airplane with fuel and staff, as well as the rest of the support structure. The plane has a limited number of seats, each of which contains the possibility of taking one person from the departure point to the destination. These are possibilities. People wishing to travel from the departure to that destination can buy seats on that plane if they want to travel on that day. When all the seats are sold, the possibilities for other people to get on the flight are sharply reduced.

Airline flights are one of many ways in which the collectively shared understanding of the future contributes to how culture can improve the lives of individuals. The next section will cover an even more important and pervasive one of these: money.

Money and Time

Money is purely a cultural invention. Money does not exist in nature, and no other species has been found to have anything approaching a genuine economy. Even humans did not have money during our evolutionary history. Historians estimate that money only came into being about 3,000 years ago (Weatherford, 1997). Nonetheless, its usefulness was quickly recognized. Money was rapidly adopted by one culture after another, and today all countries in the world have and use money.

Money is inherently prospective. Money stores value for some indeterminate point in the future.

To appreciate the prospective aspect of money, it is useful to contrast it with how trade occurred before money. Animals do not trade, but early humans seem to have figured out how to do it and enjoyed its benefits. A good trade makes both parties better off, and so there is an incentive for (or at least a benefit from) learning how to trade. Before money, however, trade was restricted to barter: Each person gave one of his or her possessions to the other.

That trade benefits both parties even without money is important to understand. The benefit stems from various reasons that economists have illuminated. To illustrate: A fishing village may catch more fish than it can consume or store, but it lacks grains. Nearby, perhaps, a farming village grows more grain than it needs, but it lacks fish. If they trade, both are better off, not least because their diets improve. More important, each side gets something more valuable than it gives up. The people in the fishing village already had enough fish, and the surplus would have been wasted, but instead of letting the fish rot, they can trade them for something they want and need.

But notice the drawbacks of barter. It is only possible when and because both sides have something the other wants. Moreover, as the fish example reveals, what one has to barter might not last very long. The surplus fish need to be traded right away, for whatever happens to be available. The trading partner likely knows this and can use it to get a better bargain. For example, if traders are offering knives in exchange for fish, they know their knives will still be good next week, whereas the fish will be useless by then. They knows the alternatives for those who caught the fish are to get something or nothing, and so the people in the fishing village are better off making even an unfair deal than no deal.

Still, the prospects for barter are often limited. If you have fish, and the other person has knives, you might make a trade. But then suppose you already have a knife? You want to unload your fish before they go bad, but you don't need any more knives. The other person doesn't have anything else to offer, so no trade is made.

Money solves all these problems. Money, unlike fish, does not expire in a few days. Money does gradually lose value in many cases, as governments print more of it, but it took ancient civilizations many centuries to understand this. Hence money seemed like a safe and permanent store of value, even if little by little its value did erode, mostly unnoticed. So instead of trading something that would quickly lose its value, one could trade for money, which seemingly would retain its value into the indefinite future (and money doesn't have to be refrigerated).

Thus, money is inherently prospective. With barter, each side has to get something that it wants, or else there is no deal. With money, only one party gets a good or service that he or she wants. The other gets money, which can be kept for a long time and then exchanged for something else—something not yet wanted or envisioned. Money is a repository of value in the future. Without the future, money would not have been invented.

The uses of money have likewise built heavily on prospection. Capital markets enabled people (and large groups of people) to spend more money than they have, because they can borrow the money now and pay it back in the future. Some economic historians think the Dutch windmills were an important spur to this innovation (Bernstein, 2004). Farmers could benefit from windmills for draining fields and managing water. But the farmers were quite poor, and none would ever have been able to save enough money to pay for building a windmill. (Indeed, the windmill was essential for creating profits, so without it, their chances of saving were even slimmer and grimmer.) But a farmer could borrow the money to build the windmill and pay back the loan over many years with the increased profits that the windmill made possible. Again, everyone was better off.

Over time, money's many uses have become even more future-oriented. Credit card debt, long-term investments, tax planning, pension plans, mortgages and reverse mortgages, amortization, and plenty of other phenomena involve the prospective application of money.

We have also emphasized that trust is inherently about the future. Money is about trust. Indeed, it has become a truism in economics that all financial transactions require some degree of trust. Money enables people to have mutually beneficial interactions with complete strangers, something that has proven elusive in nonhuman nature. But some trust is required. You purchase a meal from a restaurant with money. You trust that the food will be what you ordered and that it has been properly protected from infections and contaminations that might poison you. You trust you will get the quantity that you paid for. The restaurant owners also trust you: Not least, they serve the food and let you eat it before they see any of your money, so they trusted that you would pay your bill. They may also trust that you will not only pay the agreed price, but that you will use real rather than counterfeit money. The waitperson trusts that you will give a suitable tip. And so on.

Trust is sustained partly by other prospective factors. In the modern economy, law enforcement helps to sustain trust, because those who betray the trust can be prosecuted. That is why trust is lower and deals become harder to arrange in cases when the government is not available to step in and punish anyone who fails to do what he or she was trusted to do. Illegal drug deals, for example, are far more precarious than restaurant meals. If your dealer sells you phony cocaine, you cannot really go to the police for help in getting your money back, unlike what happens if the restaurant serves you phony food.

Effective law enforcement is a recent invention. Yet economic trade began centuries earlier and indeed flourished. How was trust sustained then? The answer to that involves another social phenomenon, which the next section will address.

Religion

The relevance of prospection to morality will be discussed in Chapter 9. For many people, morality is closely intertwined with religion. Religion is an important cultural activity. One may even propose, if in oversimplified manner, that morality is discovered, whereas religion is invented. As one sign, moral rules are broadly similar across all cultures, with quite similar ideas about fairness, reciprocity, and the like, whereas the content of different religions is fundamentally different. People fight wars over differences of religion, but hardly ever over differences in morality. No known culture is against the Golden Rule or would go to war to uphold the opposite principle.

From its earliest days, religion has been both retrospective and prospective. Early religions offered explanations of how the earth and universe were created, but also typically presented some views of life after death (Eliade, 1978). Some notions of life after death may not have been primarily attempts to project into the future about one's own death. Rather, they may have sought to explain why deceased persons, especially ancestors and rulers, could still be active in the present. Still, it seems likely that people wondered about their own fate beyond the grave, and religious ideas provided some ways of anticipating what awaits each person.

Early religions did not, however, seem to have much concern with morality (Eliade, 1978). Anyone familiar with ancient stories of gods, such as the Greek myths, knows that the gods were mainly concerned with their own affairs, which were hardly exemplars of dutiful virtue. The early gods fought each other and humans, engaged in illicit sex, tricked and swindled, and so forth. They may have wanted humans to make sacrifices to them, but they did not generally produce lists of moral principles that humans were expected to obey. The Ten Commandments and similar edicts came from a later generation of gods.

The transition has been described and analyzed by Norenzayan and colleagues (Norenzayan 2013; Norenzayan et al., 2015). The amoral nature of early religion does not indicate that society was amoral. On the contrary, early human groups had both morality and religion, but these were separate. They merged much later. The shift was linked to another huge change in religion, namely the spread of monotheism. Early religious practices typically celebrated multiple gods, and in some cultures each family had its own pantheon of multiple gods. But today, most religious people believe in only one god (although they disagree about that god's identity and attributes).

Why the change? The answer, according to Norenzayan et al. (2015), has to do with the human project of expanded cooperation and its need for trust. The switch occurred as trade and other forms of cultural exchange were expanding. Large-scale networks of people had to work together to advance society, but cooperation requires trusting that the other will also contribute and not simply take advantage of one's vulnerability. As we said, there was not much in the way of reliable law enforcement, so the police were not an adequate source of confidence in trustworthiness.

Big gods filled this gap. Early gods were often ancestors and were thus linked to particular families. Most evolutionary theorists have proposed that people (and many other animals) have some innate predisposition to trust and cooperate with kin. That's the idea behind the "selfish gene" theory (Dawkins, 1976; from Hamilton, 1964a, 1964b), which is that natural selection's unit is the gene rather than the individual. Creatures will make sacrifices and accept risks so as to benefit others who share their genes (most notably offspring). These gods encouraged the family to stay together, work together, and be loyal to each other. They encouraged trust, but only among relatives.

Big gods extended trust to a far wider circle. You travel to a distant city and want to trade, but can you trust the strangers who live there? *Trust is easier if they believe in the same god that you do.* Moreover, you trust them all the more if the god you both believe in happens to be a god who cares about human moral virtue. If they cheat you, your god will punish them.

Hence not only did the number of gods change drastically from many to one: The new big gods became interested in human life in new ways. They expected people to behave according to moral principles. The big gods made moral rules, most famously giving stone tablets with Ten Commandments to a human man who had climbed a mountain for a special audience with his god (Yahweh). And the big gods enforced these principles, or at least people believed that they would.

The rising importance of morality, and its divine sanction, transformed the religious views about life after death. Early Jewish religion did not have an afterlife, and early Christian views tended to see it as collective. These simple views were replaced by the view that individuals will be judged after their death based on the moral quality of all the actions during their lifetime (plus possibly some other factors, such as having participated in church rituals). To return to the example of early citizens traveling to another city and hoping to trade with strangers: You can trust them a little better if you and they share the belief that anyone who cheats or betrays the other will be punished with eternal hellfire.

Religions also increased trust by invoking the genetic-selfishness heuristic. Our travelers do not have any family bonds with the strangers in the other city. But if they believe in the same god, they are pseudo-related. Christianity is not the only religion to treat God as a parent and insist that all believers are brothers and sisters, but it is an especially obvious one, to the extent that people address clergy with family titles such as "father," "brother," and "sister." Would you cheat your own brother or sister?

Religion has been a powerful cultural construction, and it served vital functions in facilitating large-scale cooperation, long before law enforcement was up to the task. It enabled people to work together for mutual benefit in large social groups and networks. Sharing a god as a common ancestor or parent, indeed a god who watched people constantly and set rules for morally proper behavior, facilitated the trust needed for such cooperation. It would hardly have been possible without prospection, however. Part of the power of religion was that it could explain the entire time span of the universe, from its origins to its end. Big gods made sure that each individual's role in that universal saga would involve moral judgment, with immense rewards or punishments awaiting each individual on the basis of how morally virtuous his or her actions were.

References

Axelrod, R. (1980). Effective choice in the prisoner's dilemma. *Journal of Conflict Resolution, 24,* 3–25.

Axelrod, R., & Hamilton, W. D. (1981). The evolution of cooperation. *Science, 211,* 1390–1396.

Baumeister, R. F. (2005). *The cultural animal: Human nature, meaning, and social life.* New York, NY: Oxford University Press.

Berger, P., & Luckmann, T. (1966). *The social construction of reality: A treatise in the sociology of knowledge.* New York, NY: Doubleday.

Bernstein, W. (2004). *The birth of plenty: How the prosperity of the modern world was created.* New York, NY: McGraw-Hill.

Dawkins, R. (1976). *The selfish gene.* New York, NY: Oxford University Press.

de Waal, F. (2001). *The ape and the sushi master: Cultural reflections of a primatologist.* New York, NY: Basic Books.

Dunning, D., Anderson, J. E., Schlösser, T., Ehlebracht, D., & Fetchenhauer, D. (2014). Trust at zero acquaintance: More a matter of respect than expectation of reward. *Journal of Personality and Social Psychology, 107*, 122–141.

Eliade, M. (1978). *A history of religious ideas, Volume 1: From the Stone Age to the Eleusinian mysteries*. (W. Trask, Trans.). Chicago, IL: University of Chicago Press.

Hamilton, W. D. (1964a). The genetical evolution of social behavior. I. *Journal of Theoretical Biology, 7*, 1–16.

Hamilton, W. D. (1964b). The genetical evolution of social behavior. II. *Journal of Theoretical Biology, 7*, 17–52.

Mallon, R. (2013). Naturalistic approaches to social construction. In E. N. Zalta (Ed.), *The Stanford encyclopedia of philosophy* (Fall 2013 edition). Retrieved from http://plato.stanford.edu/archives/fall2013/entries/social-construction-naturalistic/

Norenzayan, A. (2013). *Big gods: How religion transformed cooperation and conflict*. Princeton, NJ: Princeton University Press.

Norenzayan, A., Shariff, A. F., Gervais, W. M., Willard, A. K., McNamara, R. A., Slingerland, E., & Heinrich, J. (2015). The cultural evolution of prosocial religions. *Behavioral and Brain Sciences*. Advance online publication. doi:10.1017/S0140525X14001356

Rand, D. G., Greene, J. D., & Nowak, M. A. (2012). Spontaneous giving and calculated greed. *Nature, 489*, 427–430.

Roberts, W. A. (2002). Are animals stuck in time? *Psychological Bulletin, 128*, 473–489.

Searle, J. R. (1995). *The construction of social reality*. New York, NY: Free Press.

Tomasello, M. (2014). *A natural history of human thinking*. Cambridge, MA: Harvard University Press.

Tomasello, M., & Call, J. (1997). *Primate cognition*. New York, NY: Oxford University Press.

Weatherford, J. (1997). *The history of money*. New York, NY: Three Rivers Press.

Part 2

Prospection and Life's Enduring Questions

6

Pragmatic Prospection

Roy Baumeister

"No fate but what we make" *or* "The future has not been written. There is no fate but what we make for ourselves."—*Terminator II*

"Question: How did he do it? (A) He cheated. (B) He is lucky. (C) He's a genius. (D) It is written."
Answer: (D) It is written."—*Slumdog Millionaire*

TWO ICONIC LINES FROM BLOCKBUSTER MOVIES ENCAPSULATE radically different versions of the future. A series of movies with the *Terminator* title invoked the questionable premise of time travel to assert the principle that the future can be changed. The theme of these movies was that in the near future, machines and computers take over the world and wage war on humankind. People fight back under the leadership of a remarkable man. Eventually the machines devise a way to travel back in time, and they send a deadly robot to kill the mother of the future leader.

By eliminating the leader, they could prevent the rebellion in their (future) time. The doughty humans fight back in the present, realizing eventually that by changing the present, they could prevent the machine takeover, thus improving the prospects for future generations. "No fate but what we make for ourselves" is the guiding motto of the humans. We are not locked into one inevitable destiny but can change what happens based on how we act.

A very different theory of the future was articulated in the surprise hit *Slumdog Millionaire*, about a poor, ignorant boy in India who, through a remarkable series of coincidences, acquires key facts that enable him to know the obscure answers to a series of questions on a televised quiz show, so that he wins a fortune of 20 million rupees. The odds would have seemed impossibly long against his chances of winning: Questions pursuing recondite facts and even a conspiracy by the television show's management militate against him. But the show asserts that the apparent "odds" are misleading, because it was his destiny all along to get on the show, give the right answers, and win a fortune. The movie starts with a multiple-choice question about why the young man won the game, and the film ends with the answer that his winnings were inevitable: "Because it is written." That is, his fate, presumably like everyone's fate, was decreed long in advance, and nothing else was ever possible.

Which is correct? Many philosophers and other thinkers have been smitten with the doctrine of determinism, which asserts that everything that happens is inevitable and that the chain of causality runs ineluctably from the beginning of time, through and including your reading this sentence, off into the finite or infinite future of the universe. The claim that "it is written" is a fanciful rendition of this idea. These thinkers do not really believe that there is a document somewhere on which every detail of the future is actually written down. But they embrace the spirit of it. To a strict determinist, everything that ever happens and ever will happen was already inevitable right after the origin of the universe. The appearance of multiple possibilities in the future is an illusion based on ignorance, not reality. Indeed, this vision of reality is itself much like a movie: The film's ending is already set and cannot be changed, even though the audience watching the early scenes does not know what that ending will be. The characters in the film may struggle and choose, and their actions bring about the ending, but it was always inevitable that they would do what they end up doing, and that the result will be what it is. A film ends as it does "because it is written" (i.e., in the screenplay).

The four authors of this book come from rather different disciplines. Peter Railton is a philosopher. Chandra Sripada is also a professor of philosophy, but in addition he is a psychiatrist and a neuroscientist. Roy Baumeister is a social psychologist, and Martin Seligman is a general psychologist with a background in experimental psychology and clinical psychology. Even from these different perspectives, there is one issue that each of us has thought long and hard about: free will. And we each have different opinions about free will (so this is the domain in which the editor's job of having the chapters all speaking with a single voice does not really work).

We agree on the following, however: The metaphysical questions about free will are at a standstill. For every move asserting, for example, that the universe is deterministic and free will is incompatible with determinism, there is a countermove and a countermove against that. So we have decided not to take on the metaphysical issues. Rather, we will assume that psychologically speaking, free will exists. That assumption is unavoidable for both positive psychology and prospection. So we will ask what distinguishes a free creature—*Homo prospectus*—from those who are not free.

Prospection is centrally concerned with how people think about the future. The idea that we explore in this chapter is that prospection is fundamentally *pragmatic*. That is, the reason people think about the future is that doing so can enable them to steer events toward one outcome rather than another. Thus, prospection as a practical matter embraces the *Terminator* view rather than the *Slumdog* view. The very point of thinking about the future is that there are different possible futures. By anticipating them and adjusting one's actions, one can try to produce the more desirable ones and avoid calamities and disasters.

The idea that the future is unsettled, that we can change the future but not the past, may seem intuitively obvious. But a powerful and mischievous idea, determinism, disputes it. At present, there is lively intellectual debate about whether the future is fixed or malleable. It is vital to consider the deterministic worldview, if only to appreciate what it means to deviate from it.

Slumdog's *Lockstep Vision: Determinism*

The idea that the future is fixed and can in principle be predicted with unerring precision has a long history and exerts a continuing fascination for the human mind. Ancients consulted seers and shared stories about prophecies that came true. It's hard to know what became of prophets whose predictions were disconfirmed, but most likely they lost individual credibility and were suspected of error or bias rather than being blithely forgiven because the future was inherently unknowable, after all.

Early views did not work out the details and can best be understood as what is called "fatalism," the belief that the future will turn out the same no matter what you do. For example, the famous story of Oedipus is fatalistic. Confronted with the prophecy that he would commit terrible crimes, in particular murdering his father and marrying his mother, he did his best to prevent that outcome by going far away. But because of a case of mistaken identity, he ended up fulfilling his fate.

Christian theology struggled with questions of whether the future was determined in advance or not. Certain future events were definitely considered inevitable, such as the Apocalypse (and seers have been spotting signs of the supposedly imminent end of days ever since, although so far, they have not gotten it right). But humans supposedly were given free will so that they could choose how to act, implying that each person might really end up in either heaven or hell, depending on how the person acted. John Calvin took the extreme view, which is that because God knows everything and knows in advance what each person's eternal fate would be, and so only one future is possible for each person. Many early American settlers were Puritans, who espoused Calvin's views, and so they may linger in the background of American collective consciousness, but relatively few people today accept Calvin's understanding of predestination.

A scientific version of this idea was articulated by the French mathematician Pierre Simon LaPlace (1749–1827) and has come to be known as determinism. He proposed that if a superhuman mind were to know the exact state of the universe at any one time plus all the laws of nature, it would be possible to calculate precisely the complete state of the universe at any past or future time.

Determinism continues to exert a fascination on sophomoric minds and scientific fellow travelers. It implies that the laws of nature permit no exceptions and can account for everything. Nothing in the future is possible other than what actually happens. Determinists gleefully claim that all our impressions of making choices among genuine alternatives, of being able to change what will happen, are illusory. Indeed, some psychology professors assert in print and teach their students that to be a scientist, it is necessary to embrace determinism. This is a bit ironic, because in our informal surveys, we have not been able to find any deterministic principles in psychology, and nearly all the thousands and thousands of published reports on empirical studies use statistics that are based on the assumptions of probability theory. All science as far as we know is statistical.

Determinism differs from fatalism slightly. With fatalism, as with Christian predestination, the particular future outcome will happen regardless of what one does. In determinism, the person's actions are a vital part of the causal chain bringing about the future, and so if the person were able to do something different, the result would be different. But, of course, the determinist also insists that the person could not really do something different. To some, that distinction is a matter of splitting hairs, while others find it meaningful. It is not highly relevant to our theory of prospection, however. What matters is the view, common to determinism and to fatalism, that the future is already unalterable. Determinism is simply a more rigid view than fatalism or religious predestination, because it says that not only is the outcome inevitable, but each momentary step along the way is also the only possible one.

The determinist, thus, lives in a kind of shadowy world. You cannot change the future, so there is no point in trying. The fatalist believes that the outcome is inevitable, so all we can do is accept it and prepare for it. The determinist takes even that away, because you cannot change whether you are going to accept it or not, and whatever preparations you make have also been inevitable since the Big Bang. You are much like a character in a movie: Your actions move the plot along, but you really do not have any power to change the ending. You may think you are pondering different options that are all genuinely possible and deciding to do one thing rather than another, but just like the movie character who agonizes over what to do and then takes a particular action, the impression of other possible actions is illusory.

Terminator's *Mission and the Reality of Mere Possibility*

In contrast to the lockstep march of determinism, in which the future and past are equally unchangeable, most people see a big difference between the past and the future. Pragmatically, it is impossible to change the past (although people are tempted to reinterpret events, conceal them, invent other pasts, and even collectively rewrite history based on current political views). But the future is considered open. That is, one can do something to change the future. Even when particular events are beyond one's individual control, such as the impending hurricane or war or corporate bankruptcy, one can make choices to reduce the effect on oneself, thus changing the future in small ways.

The nondeterministic vision of the future embraces *the reality of mere possibility*. That is, certain things might happen, but also might not happen. This is how people think about the future: Events are possible, sometimes probable, but not unchangeable or inevitable. Danger or threat means that something bad might happen, but might not. An opportunity is that something good that might happen, but might not. Success is only meaningful if failure is possible and vice versa. Negotiation is based on the premise that different outcomes are possible and the two parties seek to find one that is acceptable to both.

In one large study on people's thoughts during their daily lives, most thoughts about the future reflected the reality of multiple possibilities (Baumeister, Hofmann, & Vohs, 2015). As we shall detail shortly, by far the most common category of prospective thoughts was planning. Perhaps determinists go through the motions of making plans because causal processes dating back to the Big Bang dictate that they have to make them, but ordinary people presumably make plans because they want to make sure that the future produces one result rather than another, and planning increases their chances of getting the desired result. Other thoughts about the future include wondering what will happen, hoping for something in particular, and the like, all of which rest on the assumption that there are different possible futures.

Thinking About Thinking About the Future

Determinism appeals to many because of its intellectual rigor. But it is hopeless as a basis for constructing a theory about the future. To construct a psychological theory about how people imagine and use the future, it is necessary to recognize that the future looms as unsettled, undetermined. The future consists of possibilities, only some of which will come true.

Determinists might say that the multiplicity of possibilities is purely epistemic, that is, it is an illusion born of our ignorance, not a reality. When you watch the start of a movie, the ending is already preordained, but you do not know what it is. Multiple possible endings loom, in terms of which characters might die or marry or get caught or find happiness. To a determinist, life is much the same way: We do not know what will happen, but it is preordained. The only difference is that in life, oneself is one of the characters whose actions help bring about the particular ending (unlike a movie, obviously). But one's actions are also preordained and inevitable.

The key point, however, is that determinism is profoundly unhelpful. A woman struggles with an unplanned pregnancy and must decide whether to abort, have the baby and give it up for adoption, or become a mother, and these point her along very different life paths. How does it help her understand her situation and make these hard choices for a determinist to tell her that whatever she eventually decides has been inevitable since the Big Bang? A man's honor is impugned by enemies and he must decide whether to engage in a risky fight or to back down and accept the humiliation, leaving his social status reduced and perhaps inviting others to take advantage of him. The determinist's claim that whatever he chooses to do was always inevitable is of no use, neither to him in his choosing nor to the psychologist seeking to understand how he chooses. *Slumdog's* vision is elegant but bankrupt.

The Pragmatic Prospection Principle

People think about the future frequently. Why do they do this? The main answer is that they think about it because they want to do something about it. More than a century ago, William James proposed that thinking is for doing, and a series of subsequent thinkers has reaffirmed the wisdom and accuracy of that claim. It applies very well to thinking about the future.

One vital implication is that people think about the future in rough proportion to how much they can do about it. Most prospection is not idle fantasy, grim contemplation of the inevitable, or wondering how things will turn out. Such thoughts do arise now and then: People's minds roam far and wide and occasionally entertain all sorts of thoughts, including utterly useless ones. But when people think about the future, most of the time they are focused on what can be done about it.

Apart from determinists, most people recognize a fundamental difference between the future and the past. The future can be changed; the past cannot. The future comes at us as a set of possibilities. The moving present is the process by which the fixed past crystallizes out of these possible futures.

People do think about the past, despite the fact that it cannot be changed. Does that disprove James's assertion that thinking is for doing, and by implication does it discredit the pragmatic prospection principle? Perhaps not.

For one thing, people think much more about the future than the past. Evidence for this comes from a recent study that tracked people's thoughts (Baumeister et al., 2015). They collected data on the time frame of people's thoughts. Almost 500 people in Chicago took part in the study. They agreed to report on their thoughts for 3 days at randomly chosen moments. The subjects carried cell phones that were programmed to interrupt them at six randomly chosen moments during the day. When the cell phone signaled them, their instructions were to notice exactly what they had been thinking and answer a series of questions about it. They could fail to respond if necessary (e.g., if they were making love, being robbed at gunpoint, or listening to their boss tell them what to do, they might not be able to stop and respond to our questionnaire), but the response rate was pretty good (75%), and even if they couldn't always stop at the precise second the beeper went off, the median response time was 8 minutes between signal and answer. These are probably the best data anyone has gotten thus far to track what goes through people's minds as they go about their daily activities.

Not all thoughts have a time frame. Baumeister et al. (2015) found that about a quarter of the time (1 of every 4 responses), people reported that their thoughts did not have a time aspect. But for the large majority that did have a time dimension, thoughts about the present were most common, followed by the future, followed distantly by the past.

More precisely, people thought about the future three times as much as the past. Other researchers have come to similar conclusions using less laborious (and perhaps less precise) measures. People also think plenty about the present, indeed roughly twice as much as about the future (and thus six times as much as about the past). The present is the biggest focus of doing because it's what can be affected immediately by one's actions. If thinking is for doing, as James proposed, then one would expect a breakdown something like that: lots of thinking about the present, some about the future, and only a little about the past.

Indeed, the most common categories of thoughts about the present are all about doing. Baumeister et al. (2015) asked people what they were thinking about, and thoughts about the present clustered most heavily in the categories "doing what I intend to do / doing what I am supposed to be doing" and "paying attention / zeroed in on what I am doing." Not far behind those were two other categories. One was "trying to figure out what is going on," which is just as pragmatic, because one can hardly act effectively without understanding what is happening in the situation.

The other was "implications of the present for the future." That, too, seems quite pragmatic, as well as prospective.

When people were asking about the past, a pragmatic streak emerged once again. The single most common category of thoughts about the past was "implications of the past for the future." Note the parallel with thoughts about the present, where implications for the future were again a prominent category (45% of thoughts about the past involved implications for the future, thus nearly half, and about 29% of thoughts about the present involved implications for the future).

The next most common category of thoughts about the past involved "trying to make sense of it, trying to understand." Perhaps we cannot change the past, but we can seek to understand it. The quest for understanding may or may not be pragmatic. Still, effective learning requires that one understand what happens. You can't learn useful lessons from the past if you seriously misunderstand what happened.

Learning brings us back to the multiplicity of future possibilities. Indeed, the main (and arguably the only) reason for bothering to learn is that the acquired knowledge will be useful in knowing how to act so as to bring about a better future rather than a worse one. People learn from their mistakes so as not to repeat them, which thus assumes that it is possible to repeat one's mistakes *and* it is possible to avoid doing so. In the language of learning theory, there are both rewards and punishments, and intelligence is for recognizing what actions lead to each, with the pragmatic result that next time around one can improve one's chances of getting the reward rather than the punishment. Doing the right thing is only meaningful insofar as it is possible to do the wrong thing.

We have said that pragmatic concerns provide less reason to think about the past than the future. That could account for the lower frequency of thoughts about the past than about present or future. Even beyond that, thoughts about the past had some features that were not very pragmatic. After exploring implications for the future and trying to understand, the next most frequent category of thoughts about the past involved replaying things over and over. That suggests a kind of involuntary rumination. Some people get mentally stuck in the past, perhaps especially if something bad has happened that troubles them, and their minds run over it again and again.

What do people think when they think about the future?

Pragmatic Prospection in Action

When people say they think about the future, far and away the most common category of thoughts is simply planning. Three of every four thoughts about the future in the thought-sampling study involved planning.

Planning is supremely pragmatic. It is a matter of charting a path from the present to the desired future. Planning assumes that there are multiple possible futures and that one can alter one's actions to bring about some of these and avoid others (e.g., there's no point in the audience trying to plan the rest of the movie). The essential purpose of the plan is to bring about one outcome rather than the others that could easily happen if one fails to make and follow the plan.

As with the past, some thoughts about the future also point toward involuntary ruminations on unpleasant matters. But these are relatively infrequent. People reported thinking about "what you hope will happen" twice as often as "what you fear will happen." And of course people do worry; in these data, 22% of thoughts about the future included worries. But that figure pales next to the 74% of thoughts that involved planning, as well as the high rates of thinking about "what you hope to do" (47%), "what you hope will happen" (45%), and even just wondering what will happen (33%).

The preponderance of pragmatic thoughts about the future is impressive. As already said, planning tops the list. There were several categories that split the vote, so to speak, about one's future actions, but together these were a substantial amount. That is, people thought a great deal about what they hoped to do (47%), what they will do (39%), intending to do something (29%), and what they are obliged to do (26%). Nontrivial minorities of thoughts were devoted even just to what one should say (or write) (17%) and to choosing or deciding among future options (25%). (People could choose more than one answer, so the categories are not mutually exclusive and therefore add to more than 100%.)

We said pragmatic thoughts about the past include figuring out what it meant, how to understand it, and what its implications for the future. Pragmatic thoughts for the future involve anticipating what will happen so that one can know how to react. Admittedly, these are not always clearly pragmatic, but most of them probably are. Thoughts about the future turn somewhat often to trying to predict what other people will do (26%). Anticipating others' actions is a key first step in thinking about how you could and should respond. Wondering what will happen (33%) reflects the uncertainty of the future and perhaps the recognition that if you can figure out what will happen, then you will know how best to act now and to respond later.

Almost one in five thoughts about the future (18%) involves possible or expected emotions. In Chapter 8, in which we discuss emotion, we say that anticipating how you will feel is an important guide for current action. People learn what actions will bring what emotions, because this helps them choose to act in ways that will bring positive emotions and avoid negative emotions. Knowing that some course of action is likely to make you feel guilty, for example, is often a compelling cue to avoid doing those things and, probably in general, a very helpful cue that will help people get through life better.

What Is Special About Planning?

Thus far we have seen that when people say their thoughts are about the future, they are usually planning. But this is not always true.

About a quarter of prospective thoughts are not described as planning. What's the difference? Given how important planning is to any pragmatic account of prospection, it helps to know more about the mental states associated with this important activity. The large study of everyday thoughts furnished plenty of reports of both kinds, namely planning thoughts and other, non-planning thoughts about the future (Baumeister et al., 2015). Comparing these two sets of thoughts offers insight into what planning involves.

First, planning is mental work, and not the easiest. People reported exerting more control over their thoughts when they were planning than when they were having other kinds of thoughts about the future. Apparently, the mind doesn't just drift into planning the way it drifts into mind-wandering. Rather, planning takes mental effort.

The requirement of effort probably explains the next finding, which is that planning is associated with low levels of mental fatigue. When people are mentally tired, they do not make plans. Planning appeals more to the vigorous mind that has energy and is ready for a challenge. Given the preponderance of planning among prospective thoughts, it seems reasonable to say that planning is people's preferred way of thinking about the future, but that preference goes away when people are mentally tired.

The work aspect of planning is also evident in people's ratings of how involved they were with what was happening right there and then. These ratings went up when people were planning. Again, planning does not just happen, like a stray thought intruding into a wandering mind. Rather, one has to be focused and working mentally at it. People who are planning say they are quite involved in what is going on just then. Planning is thus thinking about the future while being involved in the present.

Planning gets high ratings for meaningfulness. Thoughts that involve planning are considered much more meaningful than other thoughts about the future. Although technically all thoughts about the future use meaning (indeed, probably most thoughts of all types involve meaning, with the possible exception of ones that are focused on here-and-now sensations), ratings of meaningfulness probably go beyond that. Planning is meaningful for several key reasons. One of those is that it connects across time, which is inherently a meaningful connection and one that enriches the associative network of any thought or idea. Indeed, in the study of everyday thoughts, there was a general pattern linking meaningfulness to connection across time. Thoughts that combined past, present, and future were rated as the most meaningful on average of all thoughts. Those that combined any two of those "time zones," such as present plus past, were next highest on meaning. Thoughts that involved only one time zone (past, present, or future) were on average less meaningful. And thoughts that did not have any time aspect got the lowest ratings on meaning. So planning is meaningful because it connects across time—like a good story.

Another likely reason that planning is experienced as highly meaningful is because it is about getting what one wants, which is central to pragmatism. Planning is sketching out a path from where one is to where one wants to be, whether in a literal or metaphorical sense. People generally make plans for themselves, as opposed for unknown other people, and so their plans are highly relevant to their lives, including their wants and needs. Planning is meaningful because it sets out what you are actually supposed to do.

Thus far we have depicted planning as effort and work. Its emotional coloring paints it in a more pleasant light. Planning seems to feel good. When engaged in planning, people reported higher level of happiness (as compared to having other kinds of thoughts about the future). Meanwhile, negative feelings, such as anger and anxiety, were lower with planning than with other thoughts. Planning was marked by low levels of surprise and disappointment.

People rated their current stress level. Stress was lower with planning than with other thoughts. One might have expected something different. When times are stressful, it might make sense to plan how to deal with problems. That may well happen sometimes, but in general, stress was negatively associated with planning. Quite possibly, making plans is a way of alleviating stress. When someone is faced with a daunting set of challenges, problems, and obligations, it can be comforting to make a plan to deal with them. Planning transforms the ugly, chaotic mass of concerns into an organized sequence. Part of stress is feeling overwhelmed by a set of problems and threats. Making plans makes them seem more manageable, because the plan is precisely about how one is going to manage them.

Prospection and Accuracy

What is the goal of thinking about the future? And how are thoughts about the future shaped to serve that goal? The answer may be more complicated than one might assume.

The pragmatic prospection principle assumes that knowing the future is useful for shaping one's actions. This assumption leads in a fairly straightforward manner to the conclusion that forecasting the future is a matter of struggling to be accurate. After all, accurate information furnishes a much more useful basis for action than distorted information. When you leave home in the morning, should you take an umbrella and raincoat? An accurate forecast of the day's weather will provide a good basis for making the right choice. If it is going to rain, you would be sad to be out and about without any raingear. Meanwhile, if the day is to hold beaming sunshine all day and not a drop of rain, you will be uncomfortable and look silly wearing your raincoat and carrying the umbrella.

The assumption that the goal of prediction is accuracy informed our research. Indeed, we are scientists and philosophers, and so the quest for an accurate understanding of the world is central to our daily lives and underlies most of our activities. Hence, it is not surprising that we assumed that most people, likewise, want to predict the future accurately.

Yet that logical and compelling assumption must grapple with some contrary findings. In particular, researchers have known for a long time that people are not objectively, coldly accurate in their predictions and forecasts. On the contrary, most studies have found that people are relentlessly and unrealistically optimistic. The influential studies by Weinstein (1980) surveyed college students (and others) and asked them to predict the chances that varying things would happen to them, as well as predicting whether these would happen to other people similar to them (e.g., other students in the same class). In general, people predicted that more good things and fewer bad things would happen to them, as compared to the average person.

For example, asked how likely it was that you will someday have a gifted child, receive a major promotion at work, or have a long happy marriage, you will tend to rate your chances as above average (assuming you are like most people who respond to these surveys). In contrast, you rate your chances as lower-than-average for unpleasant future possibilities, such as having a mentally retarded child, being fired from work, or getting a divorce.

The notion that people have unrealistic optimism was even enshrined as one of the three "positive illusions" that characterize the mental outlook of normal, healthy, well-adjusted people. This view was developed in a classic article by Taylor and Brown (1988). That article dispelled the view that people seek above all to achieve an accurate understanding of the world. Instead, it proposed that people have various biases and illusions that make them feel good but depart from objective reality. They overestimate their good traits and overlook their failings. They think they have plenty of control over events when they don't have much. And they tend to predict that their future will be filled with lovely, positive things rather than misfortune and failure.

But how is that pragmatic? One elegant solution was proposed by Peter Gollwitzer and his colleagues (Gollwitzer & Kinney, 1989; Taylor & Gollwitzer, 1995). He showed that people hold to positive illusions and optimistic predictions most of the time, but not when they face a decision. At choice points, people suddenly become much more realistic, seeing themselves and their prospects in a less optimistic, less distorted manner. Once the decision is made, they resume their optimistic outlook.

Why maintain these distorted views of the future most of the time? One explanation is that these views feel good. Another is that they are actually helpful and useful, because they lend confidence and they inspire trying harder.

The effects of thinking about the future on trust and risk were explored in a series of studies by Andrew Monroe and colleagues (Monroe, Ainsworth, Vohs, & Baumeister, 2015). They first had people reflect on the future. In one procedure, they had people write about the person they expected to be in 10 years and what would be important to that person. (In the control condition, they wrote about their current selves and important activities.) In principle, contemplating the future with no decisions in sight ought to have bolstered their optimism, whereas focusing on the present should have highlighted choices and obligations, producing greater realism.

After the writing task, participants were asked to make some (hypothetical) decisions about investments. Some were risky and others were safer. As is generally true with investments, the riskier ones offered higher possible payoffs, but also greater possible losses. Monroe's group predicted that thinking about the future would engender optimism, so people would pick the riskier investments, hoping to score a big gain. But that's not what happened. Instead, the people who thought about the future tended to avoid risky investments and prefer the safer, duller options. That was in contrast to the people who had thought about the present. They were more open to risk.

What happened? Why did thinking about the future lead to avoiding risk? Instead of eliciting a rosy, optimistic outlook that downplayed risk, thinking about the future seems to have attuned people to uncertainty. They saw the future as full of multiple possibilities, some good, some bad, and they worried about the bad ones.

Monroe's group then turned to studying trust. Perhaps thinking about the future made people recognize that good and bad things are both possible, and so they want to avoid the bad ones. Indeed, the notion that people's financial and investment decisions are more strongly affected by possible losses than possible gains has become a basic theme in much decision work. It is called "loss aversion," based on the notion that people would rather be sure of avoiding a big loss than have a chance at a big gain (Kahneman, 2011; Kahneman & Tversky, 1979). This is likely part of an even broader pattern: The human mind (and as far as we can tell, animal minds are the same) is more affected by bad things than by good things (Baumeister, Bratslavsky, Finkenauer, & Vohs, 2001; Rozin & Royzman, 2001).

People do, however, trust others. Indeed, some have argued that people are innately predisposed to trust others and cooperate (Dunning, Anderson, Schlösser, Ehlebracht, & Fetchenhauer, 2014; Rand, Greene, & Nowak, 2012; Tomasello, 2014).

One research tool for studying trust has been dubbed the "trust game," which was developed by behavioral economists (Berg, Dickhaut, & McCabe, 1995), a group of researchers who adapted the small-experiment methods of social psychology for use in economics research. The trust game works roughly like this. You take part in a research study, and at some point, you are told that you will receive a certain amount of money, perhaps $10. You are told that you can do a couple things with this money: You can simply keep it all, or you can invest any part of it, up to the full amount. Whatever you invest will be automatically tripled in value. (This is done to mimic the rewards of cooperative investment, which has made the eco-nomic progress of capitalist societies possible.) That tripled amount will be given to another person, your "partner," who is not someone you know. That person will then be able to divide the money in any manner between him- or herself and you.

So, for example, if you decide to invest the entire $10—the maxi-mum amount of trust—then your partner will receive $30 and can decide what to do with it. Your partner might keep it all or give it all back to you, in which case you have really made out well. Even if your partner decides to split it down the middle, you are better off than if you had kept the initial stake. Instead of going home with $10, you go home with $15, which is a nice profit earned by your willing-ness to trust someone. Sometimes partners will even give more back, perhaps letting you have $20 and keeping only $10 for themselves. After all, if you hadn't trusted your partner with all that money, he or she might have got nothing, so it's much better to have $10 than nothing.

Psychologists working with the trust game have concluded that there is a general willingness to trust people, although not because they are confident that all people are trustworthy (Dunning et al., 2014). Rather, people seem to operate on the assumption that one should never start off an interaction with a stranger by showing that they think the person cannot be trusted. To put this in a metaphoric manner, if a human being meets a total stranger in the forest or the big city, the proper thing to do at first is to act as if the person de-serves to be trusted and is willing to cooperate. If the first interaction goes badly, one can quickly dump that strategy and be wary. But the norm is to show respect to the stranger by presuming that he or she has good intentions. Operate on that basis until the person reveals him- or herself to be unworthy of trust.

There were two additional twists to how Monroe and his group used the trust game. The first was that they manipulated whether people thought about the future or the present. This was done by giving people a series of statements that they were assigned to re-write in their own words. For half the people in the study, these thoughts were about the future. For the rest, they were about the present. Thus, they had to use their minds to articulate a thought referring to either now or the future. This has been an effective way of manipulating people's focus.

The other twist was that people were given some cues about whether the partner should be trusted. Previous researchers noticed that some people simply look more trustworthy than others. After poring over countless headshots in published and online sources, they came up with a variety of pictures of human faces, and they had research subjects rate whether each person looked to be more or less trustworthy. From those ratings they extracted some of the faces with the most pronounced and consistent ratings. Basically, they produced a set of pictures of people who looked really trustworthy and another set of people who looked shady.

Monroe's group selected pictures from each group to use in their study. For each subject ready to play the trust game, they selected one picture from either group (by random assignment) and said, "This is the other person playing the game with you. Whatever money you decide to invest will be automatically tripled in value and given to that person. Here is his (or her) picture." (People always played with someone having their same gender.) Of course, these pictures were not those of the actual partner. The point was simply to make participants believe that they were playing with someone who looked trustworthy—or the opposite.

What would you predict was the effect of thinking about the future? The researchers predicted that the future-thought condition would make people rely much more heavily on the relevant information, as compared to people just thinking about the present. They should exhibit more trust (as indicated by investing more money) when the partner looked trustworthy, but they would do the opposite when the partner appeared to be a shady, unreliable character.

But that's not what happened. Thinking about the future reduced trust toward everyone, and as predicted, prospection led to giving less money to the questionable partner. But it also led to giving less money to the person with the honest face. Thus, once again, thinking about the future led to a general avoidance of risk.

Subjects in the study acknowledged the differences among the faces. There was a general pattern of investing less money when the partner looked shady and unreliable than when the partner had an honest, trustworthy face. But the prior exercise in thinking about the future failed to make people put more trust in the trustworthy person. On the contrary, the subjects who had thought about the future invested less money in the trustworthy person, as compared to subjects who had thought about the present. This was the same response they had to the untrustworthy person: Thinking about the future reduced trust.

What can we make of these findings? This section began with the question of whether thinking about the future bolsters optimism. Plenty of previous research has shown that when people are asked to predict the future, they are highly, indeed unrealistically optimistic. Yet in these studies, when people think generally about the future, they seem to become less optimistic, at least in the sense that they look at investments more in terms of what can be lost than what can be gained. They exhibit a cautious avoidance of risk.

These findings cast the notion of pragmatic prospection in a new light. Contemplating the future appears to focus attention on uncertainties, possibilities, and dangers. It does not seem to operate as if there is a definite future to be known and anticipated, as in the *Slumdog* deterministic view. Instead, thinking about the future seems to drive home how very undetermined it is, including how it contains significant possibilities for bad outcomes as well as good ones. Given the greater subjective power of the possible bad outcomes, people shift their strategy toward avoidance of disaster and risk. Even trusting a seemingly trustworthy person with your money becomes less appealing when you have been thinking about the future. The pragmatic priority is not so much assessing objective facts so as to pursue what has the best chances of turning out well. Rather, it is to avoid losses and misfortunes.

Perhaps, then, the purpose of prospection is to find ways of guiding behavior toward desired goals. Accuracy is not what matters most. Instead, getting what you want is what matters most. And what people want most is generally to avoid problems, failures, and other disasters.

This view of prospection as rooted in getting what you want takes us away from the assumption that accuracy is the supreme goal of prospection. It is however quite plausible from an evolutionary standpoint. The reason simple animal minds began to form expectancies about the (usually very near) future was to guide behavior. The animal must decide what to do so as to satisfy its needs and reach its goals. Creating a mental structure that projects into the future and leads to a happy ending is a useful guide for action.

Accuracy is helpful: You can make more effective decisions if your plans are based on a realistic understanding of the world than on false hopes and misguided fears. But accuracy comes later. The first and fundamental task may be to figure out a path from where you are to where you want to be. Once you have done that, then perhaps it is useful to conduct a feasibility study (at least mentally). Accuracy of prospection is relevant to the second stage but not so much in the first.

That would explain the pervasiveness of optimistic bias in people's predictions. Thinking about the future is about getting what you want. So when you imagine the future, you tend to imagine it in a positive light, in which your hopes and aspirations are fulfilled. But when you contemplate the future more generally, you become attuned to knowing that plenty of things can go wrong. The future is uncertain. The path you may sketch out toward your dreams is fraught with risks and threats that could lead you into an outcome that is not what you want. Hence, thinking about the future in general leads to a cautious stance.

In a sense, then, there are two steps to prospection. The first is "What do I want?" The second is "What can go wrong?"

Intelligence

Human beings admire intelligence, especially in themselves. Indeed, humans admire it so much that we have rather modestly named our collective identity after it: *Homo sapiens*, translated roughly as "smart dudes," is the official biological designation of humankind.

Defining intelligence is not easy and that complicates the questions of how it emerged and what its original purpose(s) might be. Nonetheless, a provocative theory by Jeff Hawkins and Sandra Blakeslee (2004) proposed that its first and primary use is for prospection. People evolved to be smart so as to predict the future.

It may seem obvious that intelligent people can predict future events better than others. Hawkins and Blakeslee, however, go beyond this: "Prediction is not just one of the things your brain does. It is the primary function of the neocortex, and the foundation of intelligence" (Hawkins & Blakeslee, 2004, p. 270).

The basis for their argument is simple yet profound. Brains are there to understand the world. Understanding starts with recognizing patterns, such as noticing that two things often occur together. Many patterns are in sequence over time: First comes lightning, then thunder. By spotting these patterns, one can predict what will happen next.

Pattern recognition is indeed a crucial first step in seeing the world, and pattern completion is a fundamental and powerful kind of thought (Barsalou, 2008; Barsalou, Niedenthal, Barbey, & Ruppert, 2003). The mind sees lightning followed by thunder, perhaps repeatedly, and after a while it mentally foresees the thunder when it sees the lightning.

There are refinements to the theory. Hawkins and Blakeslee (2004) point out that the brain is especially good at improving its powers of prediction, so it is highly attuned to notice when patterns are not completed as expected. Sometimes there is lightning, but no thunder. Having come to expect thunder, one's attention zeroes in on its sudden absence. Perhaps it needs to acquire a more nuanced understanding, such that lightning only sometimes leads to thunder. What the brain has to do to improve its powers of prediction takes a lot more hardware than simply completing a pattern. The brain has to predict what should happen based on prior learning, then see what does happen, then compare the two, and if there is a difference, it has to figure out why. That new formulation can then be tested by making further predictions and comparing them with what actually happens.

Nor is prediction innate. As Hawkins and Blakeslee (2004) emphasize, most prediction is based entirely on experience and learning. We are not born knowing what will happen. We are born with the ability to see what happens and learn from it and on that basis to predict what else will ensue.

Thunder and lightning are natural phenomena and perhaps not of the utmost importance to predict. Another highly influential theory of intelligence asserts that it evolved not so much for figuring out the natural world but for figuring out each other. This "social brain theory" was originally developed by Robin Dunbar and his colleagues (Dunbar, 1993, 1998) to understand intelligence in general, rather than humankind's in particular. Dunbar started by questioning the simplistic but widespread assumption that more intelligence is simply better for coping with the world and would nearly always improve survival and reproduction. If that were so, why do so many species seem to reach a limit in intelligence? If smarter creatures survive and reproduce better than stupid ones, why has evolution not produced cows, chickens, and even cockroaches with superminds like Albert Einstein's? His answer was that the brain is extremely expensive metabolically. The human brain, for example, accounts for about 2% of the human body by mass but consumes around 20%–25% of its calories. If you doubled your brain size, you'd need to eat a whole lot more just to keep your brain working. And if your double brain failed to bring in more calories, it wouldn't help you survive—in fact it might cause you to starve. A cow with an Einstein brain wouldn't really get much benefit from being able to think more powerfully, and the caloric demands of a giant brain would take away vital energy from the other organs that keep the cow alive.

Now we know why evolution doesn't just go on making bigger and bigger brains everywhere in nature (Dunbar, 1993, 1998). But that brings up the question of just why some brains did get bigger and more powerful than others. In a painstaking study, Dunbar (1993, 1998) compared brain sizes of many different animal species, not even including humankind in the sample. He tested a variety of theories, but they flopped. For example, the mental map theory proposed that animals that roam far and wide need bigger brains than animals that stay in one place, because the brain has to form a bigger mental map and therefore needs more memory storage space and computational power to keep track. But it didn't work out: Except for a small difference in the motor cortex, animals with big territories didn't have bigger brains than the stick-near-home-base types. Another theory was that some kinds of food are harder to find and keep track of. An animal that eats grass doesn't need to be smart because grass is everywhere, but animals that eat fruit need to keep updating their knowledge about where to find food, because fruit ripens and then goes bad. Alas, there was no support for the "fruit-seeking brain theory" either.

What did predict intelligence, as the name "social brain theory" implies, was the number of social relationships. Animals with bigger and more complex social networks had bigger brains than animals whose social worlds were more limited.

All this applies in spades to humankind, of course. The main purpose of the human brain is not to predict rainfall, or to figure out how to build a hut with a roof (let alone an iPhone), or even to anticipate where the deer and the antelope cavort. Rather, it is for figuring out each other and building new relationships. Given the complexity of human behavior, learning to anticipate and predict each other's actions is an endless project. Yet people who are good at it will likely survive and reproduce much better than their clueless rivals.

Predicting when your mate will be hostile versus amorous, for example, is probably quite important for your own reproductive chances (and possibly even survival). Moreover, predicting how members of groups will act is also useful. Stereotypes are much bemoaned in modern Western countries, partly based on the doctrine that it is unfair to judge people collectively rather than individually. But stereotypes, although crude, are generally accurate (Jussim, 2012; Jussim, Cain, Crawford, Harber, & Cohen, 2009; Madon et al., 1998; Swim, 1994), and thus they do furnish a basis for predicting how others will behave. Again, it is imperfect, but it is better than nothing by far. Hawkins and Blakeslee (2004) emphasize that despite our best intentions, judging by stereotypes is not likely to cease any time soon, because that kind of thinking is deeply rooted in how the brain is designed.

In short, intelligence is one of the core human traits, and one of its main functions—perhaps the primary and original function—is to predict the future. And the reason for that is largely pragmatic. We need to predict each other's reactions so we can interact with each other in useful ways. The pattern of having mutually beneficial interactions with non-kin, even strangers, is pretty rare in the non-human world. Humans, however, do it all the time. For example, you can fly to Barcelona and get food and shelter from total strangers, who in fact are almost as glad to get your business as you are to get a good meal and nice hotel room.

The Meaning of Death

The pragmatic prospection view clashes with one highly influential theory about human psychology and motivation. At issue is the role of death in human thought and action.

The presence of death in human life has varied substantially across cultures and historical periods. In Western civilization, death has gradually receded from everyday life. Earlier generations lived much closer to death, according to the acclaimed treatment by the French historian Phillippe Ariès (1981). For example, in the very simple villages in medieval Europe, the cemetery was often the focus of social life, because it was one of the few places people could come and go as they pleased in the evenings (there not yet being discos, bars, restaurants, sports arenas, public libraries, shopping malls, and all the other places that modern citizens visit and gather). Moreover, death occurred at all points in life, striking down young, middle-aged, and old, instead of being mainly limited to very old people. There were no retirement pensions or social security payments, so many people worked until they died, thus again making death highly visible, unlike the modern plan by which the person retires from most active duties for several years so that the person can die rather quietly without disrupting events. Indeed, most people died at home, and it was common for relatives, friends, casual acquaintances, even some cases just curious passersby and strangers to come in to the bedroom to see the dying person. Again, this is quite unlike the modern practice in which the dying person is hidden away in a hospital room, far from the hustle and bustle of everyday life and off limits to all but the immediate family (Ariès, 1981). Compared with those earlier practices, Ariès (1981) characterized the modern Western treatment of death as one in which death is nearly invisible. He also noted that early modern citizens seemed to cultivate reminders of death, such as keeping mementos of dead relatives (perhaps a strand of hair or a bone, molded into a kind of knick-knack on the desk or mantle).

The greater presence of death in life made it plausible, even inevitable, that death was on people's minds. In the 1970s, the view that death is often on people's minds (even modern citizens) received its most ambitious elaboration by an anthropologist, Ernest Becker (1973). Building on some lines of existentialist thought, but also informed by studies of human cultures and symbols, Becker asserted the provocative conclusion that awareness of impending death was the central and fundamental key to understanding human nature *and* culture.

Becker said that human beings are the only creatures on earth who understand death and who, therefore, know long in advance that they will die. In Becker's view, this awareness of one's mortality could not but create a kind of deep fundamental anxiety and fear. He proposed that much human activity should be understood as motivated by this fear and the desire to keep it at bay. As a particularly powerful example, he suggested that people create culture in order to shield themselves from the fact of their own mortality. Participating in culture—doing a job, shopping, following the news, being politically active, following a sports team, affirming one's group against its rivals and enemies—enables people to distract themselves from the terrible realization that they will each die eventually.

Becker's ideas inspired a group of social psychologists to develop them further and conduct laboratory experiments. The result was "terror management theory" (TMT; Greenberg, Pyszczynski, & Solomon, 1986; Pyszczynski, Greenberg, & Solomon, 1999), which came to argue that the fear of death was the most fundamental human motivation, from which all other human strivings and desires can be derived. Although as an anthropologist, Becker's approach was fundamentally cultural, the TMT theorists also connected rather vaguely with evolutionary theory, with its emphasis on survival, and with a frequent assertion that people have a "survival instinct" that takes precedence over most other motives when those clash.

Hundreds, perhaps thousands of experiments have been informed by this theory. Typically they assign one group of research subjects (usually college students) to think vividly about what will happen to them when they die, and their subsequent reactions are compared with those of people who thought about something else, like going to the dentist. One common result is that thoughts of death make people seek to affirm their cultural values. For example, if they read an article that is critical of their country, they are especially negative toward the article and its author. These findings seem to fit well with Becker's contention that fear of death underlies identification with one's culture.

These studies do not really test the central assertion of the theory. They show that when people are instructed to think about death, their reactions change. Such studies do not and indeed cannot show that people think about death a great deal or that terror of mortality underlies most human activity.

The pragmatic prospection perspective adopts a radically different view of death, even though it may be quite compatible with all the experiments done under the banner of TMT. Pragmatic prospection says that people mainly think about the future when they can do something about it.

TMT emphasizes one's mortality per se—the inevitability that one is going to die someday. Awareness of the inevitability of death is touted as the key to understanding human striving. But inevitability, by definition, violates the pragmatic principle. You cannot do anything about the fact that you are going to die someday. Therefore the pragmatic prospection view proposes that people will not give much thought to mortality in itself.

Things are very different when there is a specific possibility of dying in a certain way in a particular future context, especially if that prospect could be avoided. Pragmatic prospection would dictate that people will think a great deal about death when there is a threat of death and an opportunity to avoid it. For example, if you learned that someone will try to kill you next week, you would likely be very interested and want to know every detail. You'd think about how to avoid that person and how to prevent yourself from being killed. Or if your physician says that you have an incipient illness that could become life threatening unless specific steps (e.g., medication, surgery) are taken, your focus would be very much on how to get those steps taken quickly and effectively.

Writing about how economists think about the relationship between present and future, John Maynard Keynes made the famous observation, "In the long run, we are all dead." Death is indeed in everyone's future. But is that a remote, abstract possibility, something that people rarely think about because nothing can be done about it, and dwelling on it is a useless downer? Or is it the central driving force in the human psyche, something that is in the back of everyone's mind most of the time?

Unconscious thoughts are notoriously difficult to track, because people cannot tell you what their unconscious thoughts are. People can only tell you the thoughts they know they have. So the possibility that fear of death lurks constantly in the unconscious is something that cannot be evaluated.

In this respect, TMT resembles many aspects of Freud's psychodynamic theory (1965), because they were impossible to prove right or wrong. Still, if mortality is the foundation of all human striving, it would likely show up in consciousness fairly often. By analogy, sexual motivation—the foundation of Freud's theory about what people want, at least for much of his career, until he posited an aggressive instinct as a second and competing fundamental motive—may be a powerful unconscious force, but it also emerges into consciousness with some frequency. People think about sex rather often. By some counts, many young men have sexual thoughts dozens of times every day (Byers, Purdon, & Clark, 1998; Eysenck, 1971; Laumann, Gagnon, Michael, & Michaels, 1994).

There is precious little evidence about how much death is really on people's minds. The thought sampling study (Baumeister et al., 2015) included asking people whether they had been thinking about death when the beeper went off. We hoped not only to get an estimate of how frequent these thoughts were but also to learn about them, by seeing what personality traits, situations, and other factors produced higher versus lower rates of thoughts about death and mortality. We also thought to ascertain whether thoughts of death bring terror (for which TMT is named) and to see what other thoughts and feelings coincided with thoughts of death.

But death does not seem to be on people's minds. Our 500 research subjects checked the "death" box on the list of thoughts barely 1% of the time. Unfortunately this rate was far too low to permit the kind of statistical analyses we hoped to conduct to learn what correlates with thoughts of death. To illustrate, if you want to learn what factors are linked to thinking about death, you want to compare a large set of responses in which people were thinking about death with a large set of responses when they were not. To get the most powerful and most informative statistical information, the ideal would be to have people thinking about death half the time. That would supply plenty of information to ask general questions: Do old folks think about death more than young people? Do men think about death more than women do? Are thoughts of death accompanied by terror or merely worries? Are these thoughts of death rated as out of control or under one's control? Do people think about death when they get up in the morning, while they're at work, or in the evening? Does consuming alcohol make thoughts of death increase or decrease? But there were too few thoughts of death to enable us to conduct these analyses.

The extremely low rate of thoughts about death does, however, cast considerable doubt on Becker's position and on TMT generally. It is hard to argue that fear of death is the central driving force in the human psyche, when death hardly ever seems to cross people's minds. Indeed, even in modern life, from which many instances of death have been removed and hidden, there are still plenty of reminders: Most people watch television and follow the news, and death occurs with some regularity in both entertainment and news. Yet even the frequent availability of these cues does not seem to make death a focus of our thoughts for very long.

In fact, even those few thoughts that did involve death did not necessarily reflect a Beckerian kind of management of existential terror. About half the thoughts involving death referred to the past, not the future. Almost certainly, people were thinking about someone else's death. For example, one of the authors of this book, Baumeister, lost his only child during the project. He thinks of her death almost every day, but hardly ever thinks about his own.

The paucity of thoughts about death does not prove that the pragmatic prospection perspective is correct, of course. But it seems consistent with it. Although there were a few older people in our sample (the oldest was 67), the average age was 29, which in modern life is a long way from death. And even the older ones were probably not facing imminent death or danger. (We doubt they would have volunteered to be in our study otherwise.) So it seems reasonable to assume that death was not a pragmatic concern for our participants. If prospection is pragmatic, they would not be thinking about death. The crucial test would be to run a similar study with people who are coping with life-threatening illnesses or other dangers. If they think about death more often than our sample (which would not be hard, given that our sample almost never thought about death), that would support the pragmatic theory. Indeed, the pragmatic theory would predict that people would think about death in proportion to what they can do about it.

What about people with terminal illness, who expect that they will die fairly soon and cannot prevent it? One might invoke the pragmatic theory to predict that they would not think about death, because the illness cannot be cured and their imminent death is inevitable. In a sense, they are like everyone else, knowing that one will die and unable to do anything about it. But avoiding death is not the only pragmatic concern. If you are going to die in a few months, there is much to be done. You want to make the most of your final weeks. You want to make arrangements for your loved ones after your death, especially if they depend on you.

Baumeister knew the great social psychologist Caryl Rusbult and visited her a few times when her inoperable cancer was reaching the late stages. She knew she was going to die soon. She was of course quite familiar with TMT, as it was influential in her field of study. On one occasion, out of the blue, she turned and said, "By the way, that terror management theory is bullshit. When you face death, it's not about upholding your cultural values. The main thing is to get right with the people you love." For her, imminent death was a pragmatic concern, even though she could not change the fact that she was going to die soon.

Suppose people did think about the fact of mortality, that is, the inevitability of death in general, as opposed to the specific possibility of dying in an imminent preventable way. Would that show exceptions to pragmatic prospection? Even then, possibly not, and certainly far fewer than one might think. There are still things to be done now about what might happen after one is dead. There are two main categories.

One concerns earthly affairs. Yes, you will die someday, but that does not mean you have no reason to care what happens thereafter. Life draws meaning from broader time spans, and many people seek to make life more meaningful by having some lasting effect on the world—one that will continue after their own death. This may involve leaving money and property to one's children and other heirs, so that their lives can be improved. It may be contributing something that will live on in the broader society, such as a work of art or science. It may be participating in some grand project that will carry on into the distant future, such as political change. By participating in a political (or religious) movement, for example, one can contribute to events that may reach success or failure long after one's own lifetime.

Indeed, some people sacrifice their lives for political or religious causes. Prospection beyond death is likely an important factor. A sacrifice is not simply putting an end to one's life but rather accepting a high cost to oneself that is presumably paid in order that other people in the future might benefit.

The issue of religion brings up the second major category of posthumous prospection: the possibility of one's own "life" continuing in some form after death. All over the world, and since prehistory, people have seen others die, wondered about their own deaths, and generated ideas about how they themselves may continue to live on, in some altered sense, after death. Ghost stories are found in most major languages, indicating their wide appeal. Belief in reincarnation is a central doctrine of many Eastern religions.

Western religions, such as Christianity, adopt a more limited form of reincarnation, namely being reborn into heaven. (Christian reincarnation holds that the next life is immune to death, insofar as one lives in heaven or hell forever, unlike Hindu and Buddhist reincarnation, in which one is born again only to die over and over again.) For many centuries, Judaism did not have any doctrine about life after death, but newer forms of Judaism now espouse an afterlife, and the change indicates the continuing appeal of the idea.

Views of the afterlife vary (e.g., Eliade, 1978, 1982). Some depict it as wonderful, such as the Christian doctrine of heaven. Traditional Christianity also has a notion of hell, which is understood as the most miserable form of eternal life that one could imagine. Belief in hell has declined sharply over the last couple centuries, although a minority of Christians today still are likely concerned that they could indeed end up there. Ancient Greek mythology had the Hades underworld, which was a kind of mildly unpleasant afterlife, though not nearly as bad as Christianity's hell. The Hindu and Buddhist notions of reincarnation offer no guarantees, as one can be reborn into any sort of life, good, bad, or indifferent.

The pragmatic contingencies associated with the afterlife depend considerably on what form one believes the afterlife will take. For the Christian who believes firmly in heaven, hell, individual judgment, and free will, the matter is quite urgent. One's actions during this life will dictate where and how one will spend eternity, which will either be a euphoric bliss with lots of singing, family reunions, and proximity to God or else an unending stream of fiendish tortures. The pragmatic Christian who thinks about life after death would want to make careful choices about what to do, giving particular priority to behaving in morally virtuous ways and to participating in church rituals and sacraments.

Quite different guidelines for current actions would loom as useful to, say, the early barbarians of northern Europe. In their mythology, Valhalla was the desirable afterlife, but it was open only to valiant warriors, and by some accounts it was restricted to men who died in battle. Such a view would likely encourage pragmatically minded believers to fight bravely and even to take chances, so they would enjoy the afterlife benefits of the hero's death rather than, say, dying of pneumonia, frostbite, or food poisoning.

Meanwhile, the believer in Eastern-style reincarnation has pragmatic concerns but possibly less pressing ones. In that view, one is reborn into another life, most likely on earth but possibly in another world or universe. The circumstances of one's rebirth depend on how well one acts in the present life. (One accumulates karma, a kind of spiritual record of goodness and badness, and karma propels one through the interim of death into a new life, for better or worse.) In that sense, it behooves one to be a good person so as to earn good karma, thereby benefiting oneself in reincarnation. But that life too will end, and the journey will then continue, possibly through many lives. For the Christian, this life is the one that will decide one's eternal fate, so proper behavior is all-important. For the Hindu or Buddhist, this life is just one of many in a sequence, so although it is good to be good, one will have plenty of time in the future to atone for misdeeds and to accumulate more good karma.

Thus, pragmatic prospection does not necessarily end with death. People have pragmatic concerns that go beyond the end of life. In general, we think people devote relatively little thought to the fact that they are going to die. And even when they do so, they are often engaged in pragmatic prospection.

References

Ariès, P. (1981). *The hour of our death*. (H. Weaver, Trans.). New York, NY: Knopf.

Barsalou, L. W. (2008). Grounded cognition. *Annual Review of Psychology, 59*, 617–645.

Barsalou, L. W., Niedenthal, P. M., Barbey, A. K., & Ruppert, J. A. (2003). Social embodiment. In B. Ross (Ed.), *The psychology of learning and motivation* (Vol. 43, pp. 43–92). New York, NY: Academic Press.

Baumeister, R. F., Bratslavsky, E., Finkenauer, C., & Vohs, K. D. (2001). Bad is stronger than good. *Review of General Psychology, 5*, 323–370.

Baumeister, R. F., Hofmann, W., & Vohs, K. D. (2015). Everyday thoughts about the past, present, and future: An experience sampling study of mental time travel. Manuscript submitted for publication.

Becker, E. (1973). *The denial of death*. New York, NY: Free Press.

Berg, J., Dickhaut, J., & McCabe, K. (1995). Trust, reciprocity, and social history. *Games and Economic Behavior, 10,* 122–142.

Byers, E. S., Purdon, C., & Clark, D. A. (1998). Sexual intrusive thoughts of college students. *Journal of Sex Research, 35,* 359–369.

Dunbar, R. I. M. (1993). Coevolution of neocortical size, group size, and language in humans. *Behavioral and Brain Sciences, 16,* 681–694.

Dunbar, R. I. M. (1998). The social brain hypothesis. *Evolutionary Anthropology, 6,* 178–190.

Dunning, D., Anderson, J. E., Schlösser, T., Ehlebracht, D., & Fetchenhauer, D. (2014). Trust at zero acquaintance: More a matter of respect than expectation of reward. *Journal of Personality and Social Psychology, 107,* 122–141.

Eliade, M. (1978). *A history of religious ideas: Vol. 1. From the stone age to the Eleusinian mysteries.* (W. Trask, Trans.). Chicago, IL: Chicago University Press.

Eliade, M. (1982). *A history of religious ideas: Vol. 2. From Gautama Buddha to the triumph of Christianity.* (W. Trask, Trans.). Chicago, IL: Chicago University Press.

Eysenck, H. J. (1971). Masculinity-femininity, personality, and sexual attitudes. *Journal of Sex Research, 7,* 83–88.

Freud, S. (1965). *New introductory lectures on psychoanalysis* (J. Strachey, Trans.). New York, NY: W. W. Norton. (Original work published 1933)

Greenberg, J., Pyszczynski, T., & Solomon, S. (1986). The causes and consequences of a need for self-esteem: A terror management theory. In R. F. Baumeister (Ed.), *Public self and private self* (pp. 189–212). New York, NY: Springer-Verlag.

Gollwitzer, P. M., & Kinney, R. F. (1989). Effects of deliberative and implemental mind-sets on illusion of control. *Journal of Personality and Social Psychology, 56,* 531–542.

Hawkins, J., & Blakeslee, S. (2004). *On intelligence* [iBook]. Retrieved from http://www.apple.com/ibooks/

Jussim, L. (2012). *Social perception and social reality: Why accuracy dominates bias and self-fulfilling prophecy.* New York, NY: Oxford University Press.

Jussim, L., Cain, T. R., Crawford, J. T., Harber, K., & Cohen, F. (2009). The unbearable accuracy of stereotypes. In T. Nelson (Ed.),

Handbook of prejudice, stereotyping, and discrimination (pp. 199–228). Mahwah, NJ: Erlbaum.

Kahneman, D. (2011). *Thinking, fast and slow*. New York, NY: Farrar, Strauss, & Giroux.

Kahneman, D., & Tversky, A. (1979). Prospect theory: An analysis of decision under risk. *Econometria, 47*, 263–291.

Laumann, E. O., Gagnon, J. H., Michael, R. T., & Michaels, S. (1994). *The social organization of sexuality: Sexual practices in the United States*. Chicago, IL: Chicago University Press.

Madon, S., Jussim, L., Keiper, S., Eccles, J., Smith, A., & Palumbo, P. (1998). The accuracy and power of sex, social class, and ethnic stereotypes: A naturalistic study in person perception. *Personality and Social Psychology Bulletin, 24*, 1304–1318.

Monroe, A. E., Ainsworth, S. E., Vohs, K. D., & Baumeister, R. F. (2015). Fearing the future? Increasing future-oriented thought leads to heightened aversion to risky investments, trust, and immorality. Manuscript submitted for publication.

Pyszczynski, T., Greenberg, J., & Solomon, S. (1999). A dual-process model of defense against conscious and unconscious death-related thoughts: An extension of terror management theory. *Psychological Review, 106*, 835–845.

Rand, D. G., Greene, J. D., & Nowak, M. A. (2012). Spontaneous giving and calculated greed. *Nature, 489*, 427–430.

Rozin, P., & Royzman, E. B. (2001). Negativity bias, negativity dominance, and contagion. *Personality and Social Psychology Review, 5*, 296–320.

Swim, J. K. (1994). Perceived versus meta-analytic effect sizes: An assessment of the accuracy of gender stereotypes. *Journal of Personality and Social Psychology, 66*, 21–36.

Taylor, S. E., & Brown, J. D. (1988). Illusion and well-being: A social psychological perspective on mental health. *Psychological Bulletin, 103*, 193–210.

Taylor, S. E., & Gollwitzer, P. M. (1995). Effects of mindset on positive illusions. *Journal of Personality and Social Psychology, 69*, 213–226.

Tomasello, M. (2014). *A natural history of human thinking*. Cambridge, MA: Harvard University Press.

Weinstein, N. D. (1980). Unrealistic optimism about future life events. *Journal of Personality and Social Psychology, 39*, 806–820.

7

Free Will and the Construction of Options

Chandra Sripada

D O WE HAVE FREE WILL? WHEN PHILOSOPHERS TAKE UP this question, they nearly always approach it from a highly abstract point of view. What mainly matters to them are basic and highly general physical features of the world. How does causation work in our universe? What sorts of physical laws does it have? A standard way to proceed is to ask whether free will is possible in a world in which the laws are fully deterministic. One group of philosophers, the compatibilists, argue that if one is careful not to confuse causation with constraint, then there is no opposition between free will and determinism. Incompatibilists deny this claim.

We believe that this metaphysical debate has reached a stalemate. There are a variety of compelling arguments on either side, but nothing decisively tips the balance in one or the other way. In any case, as we said in Chapter 6, we are not going to enter the metaphysical fray about free will here. Our interest in this chapter is on another topic, one that, as the metaphysicians are busy blasting their howitzers at each other, too often gets neglected.

Most compatibilists and incompatibilists are not free will skeptics. They think that free will is possible in our universe and ordinary, unimpaired adult human beings do in fact have it. They also, of course, agree that not all things are free. A rock certainly is not free. Neither is a fern or an ant or, more controversially perhaps, a crow or rabbit. This raises a different sort of question than the metaphysical question that is at center stage in the philosophical debate—a *comparative* question. Assuming, as is it is standard to do, that humans do have free will, what is it about our minds and brains that distinguishes us from simpler animals that lack it? What is the distinctive psychological basis of freedom?

A natural place to begin investigating this question is with the capacities that are involved in enabling humans to make decisions. It is useful to divide these into two types. The first type consists of *construction processes* that enable an agent to build an option set. This is a mentally represented set of candidate action plans and their anticipated outcomes. The second type consists of *selection processes*. Given an option set, these enable an agent to assign evaluative weights to the elements of this set, to say how good or bad these options are. When the evaluative weights have been assigned, whichever action plan in the option set is ranked as best is next selected for execution.

It is tempting to think that the distinctive mark of human freedom is to be found in human selection processes—somehow, humans are able to select things in a way that differs from all other creatures. A bit of reflection suggests this is not a promising approach. As we saw in Chapter 2, even relatively simple animals, such as rabbits and mice, mentally represent candidate actions (e.g., continue to forage in this bush versus move on to the next bush), and their actions reliably depend on the evaluations assigned to these actions. Recall that it is the job of the affective system to maintain and update representations of the key information—probability, confidence, absolute and relative value, discrepancies between expectation and actual outcomes, and so forth—needed to generate accurate evaluations. So there is nothing categorically distinct about human selective processes that could serve as a distinguishing basis of freedom. Indeed, selection, it would seem, *just has to* involve the assignment of evaluative weights to options in some way or other, followed by acting on that which is evaluated as best. This is something like a forced move; it must be how selection works in humans, mice, and even machines. So it is unlikely that we will ever find a distinctive mark of freedom by looking here.

In contrast to selective processes, few thinkers have thought much about the role of constructive processes of decision-making in enabling free will. In discussions of free will, it is standard to simply assume an agent who has a rich and varied set of options already in hand. No one asks where the options come from in the first place or how they were constructed. Our aim here is to redress some of this neglect.

We will argue that the distinctive mark of human freedom is *latitude*. Latitude refers to what agents have when the "size" of their option set is large. For now, we can say an agent has more latitude when the *number* of *distinct* options in the option set is larger. A bit later, we will provide a more refined account of how to understand the "size" of an option set.

Simple animals have sharply limited latitude. The candidate options they can mentally represent, and from which they can in turn select, are few and relatively fixed. At the other extreme, human agents have a truly *colossal* amount of latitude. Because humans are deeply prospective creatures with powerful imaginal abilities, they can build option sets that are truly vast. As a result, humans can express themselves in countless ways. This *latitude for self-expression* is, we argue, the best answer to the comparative question of free will. It is the distinctive psychological feature that explains why humans, but not simpler animals, are free.

The Power to Construct Options

Let us investigate the basis of what we shall call the *productivity of human option construction*, our ability to construct option sets of truly large size.

Consider a rat approaching a fork in a maze. The rat mentally represents two candidate actions available to it, going right or going left. Moreover, because it has explored the maze before, it has formed expectations of what would be the case were either option taken. The rat represents that going right will yield a reward while going left will not, and on this basis, the option of going right is selected.

Now contrast this scenario with a young woman in her second year of college. March is approaching and she is thinking about how to spend her spring break. Her friends will go to Tampa for a week of tawdry parties. Her family would love if she came home. She might stay in the dormitory and study, she thinks. If she is to get into medical school as she plans, she will need to do better in biochemistry, and the break will be a good chance to catch up in the course. But why does she want to go to medical school anyway? She spends every free moment she can dancing in the studio, and that is what she really wants to do. But is a career as a dancer even realistic? Better to deal with that question later, she thinks. For now, wouldn't it be wonderful to spend the entire break in the studio? There would be no one to bother her and no place she had to be instead. Of course, the next tuition bill will be coming due soon. So maybe at least some of the break could be spent making some extra money tutoring. Or maybe she could pick up those extra tutoring hours after spring break. Or still better than that, she could work the entire break, then she wouldn't need to juggle school and work for the rest of the term. But what about being able to dance all break? She would just hate to have to give that up—and so it goes.

The example illustrates that the construction of options unfolds fast and furious, and with very little need for conscious guidance or supervision. The student sets her mind to think about what she could do and the options just burst forth. What explains this remarkable productivity of option construction in humans relative to simpler creatures such as the rat?

One important explanatory factor is that with humans, the individual options that are constructed are complex and consist of numerous constituent parts. Humans have the ability to form *sequential plans*, chains of actions linked in a coordinated way to achieve a goal. Plans are characteristically decomposable into parts, each of which achieves some proximal goal (Miller, Galanter, & Pribram, 1960): To become a physician, one must graduate from college with the right major, take entrance exams, and fill out applications. To graduate from college with the right major, one must enroll in the right classes. One such class is biochemistry. To pass this class, one must attend the lectures, complete the accompanying lab, and study all the time, perhaps even during spring break.

When sequential planning is allowed, the space of potential options vastly increases. Suppose a creature has 10 individual primitive actions it can perform, such as running, pushing, grasping, chewing, and turning. If sequential planning is not allowed, the possible options are capped at 10. But if sequentially organized 15-item action sequences are allowed, there are more than 1.3 trillion unique courses of action the creature can potentially undertake.

Another closely related factor for explaining the productivity of option construction is *extended time horizon*. The existing evidence suggests that nonhuman animals cannot represent goings on at points in time in the distant future. Some studies place the time horizon of nonhuman animals at just a few minutes; others allow that in some contexts, some animals might prospect as far as day (Roberts, 2002). Humans, in contrast, can readily mentally represent events and episodes that are days, years, decades, and indeed millennia in the future, long after they as individuals, or even as a species, will have perished. The time horizon of humans appears to be essentially boundless.

The preceding two factors—sequential planning and extended time horizon—are enabled by a suite of *other* sophisticated capacities. Central among these are powerful abilities for prospective imaginal simulation; we can mentally project ourselves into temporally distant hypothetical situations. Indeed, there appears to be a set of interconnected brain regions, called the *default network*, specialized for this purpose (Raichle et al., 2001). This is a network of regions in the brain's midline and posterior lateral areas that have reliably been implicated in prospective thinking (Spreng, Mar, & Kim, 2008), as well as other cognitive tasks that involve projecting oneself into different times, places, situations, or perspectives (Buckner & Carroll, 2007). Areas of the default network have undergone extensive elaboration in the transition from mammalian ancestors to modern humans (Buckner, Andrews-Hanna, & Schacter, 2008). The expanded abilities for prospective simulation thus enabled likely plays a key role in explaining why capacities for sequential planning are more powerful and our time horizon more distant.

Let us turn to another factor that contributes to the productivity of human option construction: the ability for *meta-representation*, that is, the ability to mentally represent one's own psychological states. To appreciate the importance of this capacity for option construction (and relatedly, for free will), start by considering Harry Frankfurt's influential account of freedom.

Frankfurt argued that while humans and simpler animals are alike in having first-order desires (desires to do this or that), humans are unique in having the ability to form second-order desires (desires about which desires to have). Humans also have the ability to form desires of still higher order. He argued that the ability to form higher-order desires is intimately connected to freedom; agents are free when their first-order desires mesh with their higher-order desires.

One way of both further understanding, as well as importantly recasting Frankfurt's insight, is in terms of how the ability for meta-representation dramatically expands an agent's space of options. Suppose you are an agent with various action-guiding psychological states, including various desires, cravings, cares, concerns, evaluative beliefs, habits, character traits, and principles of choice. Let us suppose you lack meta-representational capacities. Now suppose you are an agent, who has precisely this same set of action-guiding psychological states, but who differs in having robust meta-representational capacities.

Notice you will have vastly more options that you can construct. For each psychological attitude that you have (i.e., for each desire, craving, care, concern, and so on), you can construct options in which you maintain, accentuate, resist, regulate, extinguish, or in some other way modify this desire. Indeed, you can construct options in which you cultivate entirely new desires that differ from anything in your existing psychological repertoire. Agents lacking meta-representational abilities cannot recognize and mentally represent their own psychological states in this way. Thus they can't see their own mental states as "optional," as things that could be different were certain courses of action undertaken. Because of this deficit, their space of options is importantly constrained.

An additional factor that helps to explain the productivity of human option construction is *creativity*. Consider some examples. Although everyone else thinks it's impossible to breach the walls of Troy, Odysseus devises a brilliant plan to accomplish this. Cyrano takes himself to be too hideous to approach Roxanne, but he hits on an idea: He can express his feelings for her in letters that are disguised to be from someone else. Siddhartha sees suffering all around him. After extensive meditation, he emerges with an eightfold path aimed at its cessation. Seeing that everyone carries around a cellphone, Steve Jobs invents a way to place the functionality of a personal computer inside of it.

Humans have awesome abilities for creativity, and this is the topic of Chapter 11. They can find new ways to achieve their ends, where these ways are quite different from anything that has come before. According to current theories in cognitive science, a number of component processes are involved in creativity. For example, creativity requires facility with divergent, "nonlinear" thinking (see Baer, 1993; Kim, 2008; Runco, 1991). This mode of thinking is tested in tasks that pose open-ended questions (e.g., How many uses can you create for a paper clip?), and the measure of success is the number of acceptable responses made in a fixed amount of time. Creativity also appears to be linked to analogical reasoning (see Gentner, Brem, Ferguson, & Wolff, 1997; Holyoak & Thagard, 1996; Johnson-Laird, 1989). Analogy involves forming an isomorphism between the objects and relations that hold across two distinct domains. Once an isomorphism is discovered, known operations applicable to one domain might lead to the development of novel corresponding operations in the second. Other theories emphasize the "perseverance" aspect of creative thought (see Campbell, 1960; Simonton, 1999): Finding creative solutions requires brute force, iterative generation, and testing of innumerable combinations of ideas until a suitable solution is found.

The psychology and neuroscience of creativity remain active areas of investigation, and the preceding represent only a small sampling from this literature. The point we want to emphasize is that because of the kinds of processes just discussed, we are an intensely creative species. When we face obstacles in our way, we invent new ways around them. As a result, the option sets we construct are always expanding.

The preceding four factors—sequential plans, extended time horizon, meta-representational capacities, and creativity—work together to help to explain the remarkable human ability to build vast options sets, certainly bigger than any other creature in the animal world. Moreover, this is no idle ability that we possess but rarely use. Constructing options is a ubiquitous activity. We spin out options at a rapid clip whenever the situation demands it, and also when it doesn't—when we are sitting quietly just daydreaming. In the next section, we will see how building options gives rise to latitude in expressing our selves in countless ways.

Options for Self-Expression

Consider the following intuitive principle:

> To be free is to have options, and to have more options is to be more free.

In this section, we want to use this principle as a starting point to build a novel approach to free will. The account says that as the "size" of an option set grows, the person has more latitude and thus more freedom. To set out and defend this view, the first thing we need to do is say what makes an option set larger, that is, what makes it the case that a person has "more options."

One approach that seems implausible is to equate the size of an option set with the number of distinct *action sequences* within it. If this approach were correct, then a person's option set would be larger and latitude—and thus freedom—would be expanded when countless useless and absolutely irrelevant action sequences were added to the set (e.g., wiggle one's little finger 1 mm once, wiggle one's little finger 1 mm twice, and so on).

There are two problems with the preceding account. First, what appears to matter for freedom is not the number of distinct *action sequences* an option set contains, but rather the number of distinct *ways of expressing one's self in action*. Freedom is expanded only when the additional entries to one's option set represent meaningful expressions of one's values and cares, that is, those psychological states that specify one's basic evaluative take on the world. The second problem is that we need to capture the idea of *diversity* of options. An option set has greater size when the options within it are, in a sense to be made precise, *divergent*; they speak to very different aspects of one's self. To sum up, we propose that the size of an option set is based on the *number* and *diversity* of opportunities for self-expression that are contained within. Let us turn now to clarifying the key elements of this proposal.

Start with what it means to express one's self in action. People care about different things: health, wealth, prestige, relationships, justice, pleasures that range from the most refined to most carnal, and so on. Caring goes beyond merely desiring something. When people care for something, they are committed to it in a fundamental, intrinsic, and cohesive way. People express themselves in action when something they care about manifests itself in what they do. The young woman introduced earlier is passionate about dance. Suppose she gets up at 5 a.m. and trudges across town to the dance studio to take a lesson. In acting to further something she cares about, with this very aim in mind, what she cares about is expressed in what she does (Sripada, 2015).

Selves are complex, cacophonous things. People care about a multitude of different things, with their sundry cares sometimes in subtle, or not so subtle, tension with each other. To express one's self doesn't require one's action speak for all of one's cares, or a sizable number of cares, or some overall weighted average of them. Rather, an expression of one's self needs to be anchored in just *one* care. Consider a scientist who cares about knowledge, power, fame, career, and status and thus spends all his time engaged in his work. But he also has a passion for ice climbing. When he spends a month on an iceboat excursion in southern Chile, he does not advance, and indeed sets back, many of the other career and status-related ends he cares for deeply. Yet his taking this month-long trip is fully an expression of his self.

Because people care about a multitude of things, and because expressions of the self need to be anchored in just a small part of the self (i.e., just a single care), then there are correspondingly a massive number of distinct expressions of the self that are possible. They correspond to all the different ways of expressing different subsets of one's self. According to our proposed account of the size of an option set, as people engage in the sophisticated kinds of constructive activity described in the previous section and thereby construct more and more options that are expressive of their selves, the size of their option sets correspondingly grows.

Increasing the *number* of self-expressive options is only one way for an option set to grow in size. The other way concerns what it means for two options to be *divergent*. In *Existentialism and Humanism*, Jean-Paul Sartre (1966) presents a story of a young man who faces the choice of going to England and fighting with the French Resistance or staying home and taking care of his frail mother. While Sartre had his own purposes for the story, what is most striking to us is the way the young man's options speak for two entirely distinct aspects of his self. Fighting for the Resistance resonates with the man's patriotism, his hatred of the enemy (his brother was killed by the Germans), his sense of adventure, and his pursuit of honor and glory. But the young man also deeply loves his mother who doted on him as a boy and who wants him to stay home. Were the man to go to war, it would plunge her into despair. By staying home, he respects his mother's wishes, tends to her health, and ensures his own life and livelihood.

Think of options as lying in a multidimensional space. Each of one's cares establishes a new axis. The position of an option along that axis is determined by whether the option satisfies, hinders, or is neutral with respect to the satisfaction of that care. The notion of divergence can be understood as *distance* between two options in this high-dimensional space. The young man's options are highly divergent in that they lie at opposing "corners" of this space. A diverse option set is one in which the options within it are spread out and cover the space. That is, there is sufficient divergence between individual options that they are not all clustered within a tiny region.

We have proposed that the size of option set is based on the *number* and *diversity* of opportunities for self-expression that are contained within. Now we are in a position to say what *latitude* is. Latitude is not the size of the option set itself. Rather, it is something agents enjoy in virtue of the size of their option sets. Let us suppose a person's selective processes are functioning properly. Given an option set that has already been constructed, these processes appropriately assign evaluative weight to the options and select for implementation those that are evaluated as best. Holding fixed this fact, suppose now we enlarge the option set over which these selective processes operate, either by increasing the number of options or increasing the diversity of options. Even though the selective processes themselves have not changed, the person's latitude *has* changed. Latitude consists in the opportunities for self-expression that have grown due to the expansion of the option set.

Because of our uniquely powerful constructive powers, we humans build option sets of unraveled size. We correspondingly have unmatched latitude of self-expression. The view we are proposing is that it is the latitude we enjoy when we act that is the distinctive mark of free will. That is, *free will consists of having the latitude to express one's self in numerous and diverse ways.*

We have focused on powers to construct options as the distinctive basis for free will. Humans, however, also have uniquely powerful selective processes. That is, the processes that underlie our ability to assign evaluative weights to actions and implement those actions evaluated as best are also more advanced than those possessed by other creatures. One might object to the latitude view of free will for being too narrowly focused on the psychological processes that underlie option construction. Why not say that gains in sophistication of all the processes that subserve decision and action—the processes that subserve option construction as well as the processes that subserve option selection—contribute to freedom?

Our response to this objection takes note that agency is a complex and multifaceted phenomenon. Because of this, we have a rich and nuanced vocabulary for separately describing distinct "achievements" of agency. For example, agents can be free, responsible, prudent, moral, virtuous, and so forth, and each of these terms picks out a distinct way that agency can go well. One important achievement of agency specifically concerns the functioning of selective processes. When these processes are made to function better (i.e., when evaluative weights are assigned to options in a way that better reflects their actual worth), we don't say the agent is thereby more *free*; rather we say the agent is thereby more *rational*.

We agree with the objector, then, that humans uniquely possess advanced powers of option construction as well as option selection. We contend, however, that the greater sophistication of selective processes, and the more careful and nuanced assignment of evaluative weights that is thereby enabled, is connected with a very specific achievement of agency: rationality. But if we want to know how humans differ from simpler animals in terms of *freedom*, it is not the selective processes that matter for this. Rather it is the constructive processes. The greater sophistication of human constructive processes and the greater latitude of self-expression that is thereby conferred are what distinguish humans from other animals in terms of freedom.

The Phenomenology of Freedom

A number of philosophers have offered reports of the subjective experience of free will. One theme that looms large in these descriptions, indeed nearly to exclusion of everything else, is the *ability to do otherwise*.

For example John Searle writes,

> ... [R]eflect very carefully on the character of the experiences you
> have as you engage in normal, everyday human actions. You will
> sense the possibility of alternative courses of action built into these
> experiences ... [T]he sense that "I am making this happen" carries
> with it the sense that "I could be doing something else." In normal
> behavior, each thing we do carries with it the conviction, valid or
> invalid, that we could be doing something else right here and now,
> that is, all other conditions remaining the same. This, I submit, is the
> source of our own unshakable conviction of our own free will. (Searle,
> 1984, p. 95)

Searle's descriptions of the experience of the ability to do otherwise are highly controversial and we won't try to adjudicate whether
he is right. Rather, we want to point out an important omission in
this area. While nearly all the philosophical focus has been the ability to do otherwise, there are other aspects of the phenomenology of
freedom that are hardly ever discussed. To illustrate this, let us consider another case.

Suppose a man has been diagnosed with lung cancer. He is offered
the options of chemotherapy or radiation treatment. At the level of
cellular biology, the mechanisms of action of the respective treatments are quite different. Nonetheless, they are both similarly potentially life-saving, and they both generate a similar profile of horrible side effects. One therapy is administered at St. Joseph's Hospital
uptown while the other at University Hospital downtown, but both
hospitals are just as good and are at an exactly equal distance from
the man's house. Thus the man has two options, but they aren't ter-
ribly divergent—in all the ways that matter, the two therapies seem
much the same.

Compare this man's subjective experiences as he chooses between the two options with what is experienced by the young man
in Sartre's story. Recall this young man chooses between fighting for
the Resistance versus staying home with his mother—two ways of
expressing himself that are utterly divergent in that they speak for
completely different aspects of his self. It is very plausible that the
experiences of freedom of the two men during choice are quite different. The man who has cancer experiences the "narrowness" of his
options. His options aren't at all divergent; they are both contained

within a small region of option space. In contrast, the young man in Sartre's story *feels* the amazing distance between his two options. The gap that separates them is vast; it is dizzying to traverse it. As the young man moves back and forth between his options, it feels like a trek between distant worlds. When the man diagnosed with cancer moves back and forth between his two options, he hardly shifts at all.

These examples illustrate that experiences of *spaciousness* and *movement* are important aspects of the phenomenology of freedom. It should be clear that these experiences are closely connected with latitude. Latitude is linked to the size of an option set; it consists of the potentialities for self-expression that are gained as one's option set grows. Correspondingly, the difference in the subjective experiences of these two men just discussed arises from the difference in option set size. That is, the option set of the young man is larger because the options within it are highly divergent, and the young man's freedom is experienced as movement back and forth within this expansive space.

Now consider the young woman thinking about what to do for spring break. Like Sartre's young man, she too has an option set of large size. In particular, she has numerous and varied options that give her diverse opportunities for self-expression. But there is something else in her case: Even as she is deciding what to do, she is actively building new options. That is, she is deploying her potent powers of option construction to dream up new avenues for self-expression. If her space of options is sparsely covered in certain important regions, she will deploy her creative powers to fill it up. This gives rise to an additional experience of freedom. In addition to spaciousness and movement, she experiences a feeling of *unboundedness*. Her option set is already expansive; it permits great movement within it. But in addition to this, its perimeter is not fixed; she has the power to enlarge it.

Nearly all philosophers who have discussed the phenomenology of freedom have done so in terms of the experience of the ability to do otherwise. If the feeling of freedom exclusively consists of the feeling that one has this ability, then there should be no difference at all among these three agents—the man diagnosed with cancer, Sartre's young man, and the young woman in college planning her spring break—in their subjective experiences of freedom. All three agents equally well have the ability to do otherwise.

We agree with Searle that phenomenology is central to understanding free will and forms the basis of our conviction that we are free agents. We have argued, however, that in addition to the feeling that one has the ability to do otherwise, the feeling of spaciousness, movement, and unboundedness are core aspects of the experience of freedom. The latitude account of free will readily makes sense of these other aspects of the phenomenology of freedom, while standard views don't, is an important piece of evidence in favor of our latitude account.

Willing

We have emphasized the constructive aspect of freedom thus far. We have said relatively little, however, about "willing" and we turn to this topic in this final section.

There is one sense of "will" that comes into play when we engage in the spontaneous or deliberate prospection of future possibilities. When the mind explores possibilities and finds one that stands out relative to alternatives, it feels like a "free willing" because what precipitates our action is our own desires. Nothing more, no additional act of will, is required to make the action "up to us."

The option that is settled on is in an obvious sense one's own because it came about through one's own unimpeded mental activity. This need not always be the case. Sometimes one confronts internal compulsion that is insensitive to what one prefers or external coercion that blocks one from doing what one most wants to do. So long as one's exploration of alternatives is not constrained by factors such as these, then no additional transcendental will is needed for the act to be "of one's own accord." No rational homunculus must enter the scene and ratify what one does. For when agents, after freely exploring options, settle their minds by following what "seems best," they have already done exactly what this rational homunculus is invoked to do.

So given that an agent has extensive prospective powers and has built an option set of substantial size, "freely willing" an option consists of running through these options until one feels that one's mind is made up, and then taking the course of action one has settled on and nothing more.

The philosophical debate about free will primarily concerns abstract issues of metaphysics. How does causation work in our universe?

What sorts of physical laws does it have? Would free will be possible if the laws of the universe were deterministic? These are important questions and the debate about them goes on, but the subject of our chapter has been something else. Our focus has instead been on an important *comparative* question about free will that hardly ever gets addressed: What are the distinctive psychological factors that explain why humans are free but simpler animals are not? The answer, we claim, is latitude. Humans are deeply prospective creatures who have powerful abilities for option construction. Humans can, thus, build option sets that contain numerous and diverse opportunities for self-expression. It is because humans are unique in being able to roam far and wide in a vast space of options that humans are unique in being free.

References

Baer, J. (1993). *Creativity and divergent thinking: A task-specific approach.* Hillsdale, NJ: Erlbaum.

Buckner, R. L., Andrews-Hanna, J. R., & Schacter, D. L. (2008). The brain's default network: Anatomy, function, and relevance to disease. *Annals of the New York Academy of Sciences, 1124,* 1–38.

Buckner, R. L., & Carroll, D. C. (2007). Self-projection and the brain. *Trends in Cognitive Sciences, 11,* 49–57.

Campbell, D. T. (1960). Blind variation and selective retentions in creative thought as in other knowledge processes. *Psychological Review, 67,* 380–400.

Gentner, D., Brem, S., Ferguson, R., & Wolff, P. (1997). Analogy and creativity in the works of Johannes Kepler. In T. B. Ward, S. M. Smith, & J. Vaid (Eds.), *Creative thought: An investigation of conceptual structures and processes* (pp. 403–459). Washington, DC: American Psychological Association.

Holyoak, K. J., & Thagard, P. (1996). *Mental leaps: Analogy in creative thought.* Cambridge, MA: MIT Press.

Johnson-Laird, P. (1989). Analogy and the exercise of creativity. In S. Vosniadou & A. Ortony (Eds.), *Similarity and analogical reasoning.* Cambridge, England: Cambridge University Press.

Kim, K. H. (2008). Meta-analyses of the relationship of creative achievement to both IQ and divergent thinking test scores. *The Journal of Creative Behavior, 42,* 106–130.

Miller, G. A., Galanter, E., & Pribram, K. H. (1960). *Plans and the structure of behavior* (Vol. 29). New York, NY: Adams Bannister Cox.

Raichle, M. E., MacLeod, A. M., Snyder, A. Z., Powers, W. J., Gusnard, D. A., & Shulman, G. L. (2001). A default mode of brain function. *Proceedings of the National Academy of Sciences, 98,* 676–682.

Roberts, W. A. (2002). Are animals stuck in time? *Psychological Bulletin, 128,* 473–489.

Runco, M. A. (1991). *Divergent thinking* Westport, CT: Ablex.

Sartre, J. P. (1966). *Existentialism and humanism.* (P. Mairet, Trans.). London, England: Methuen.

Searle. J. R. (1984). *Minds, brains and science.* Cambridge, MA: Harvard University Press.

Simonton, D. K. (1999). Creativity as blind variation and selective retention: Is the creative process Darwinian? *Psychological Inquiry, 10,* 309–328.

Spreng, R. N., Mar, R. A., & Kim, A. S. (2008). The common neural basis of autobiographical memory, prospection, navigation, theory of mind and the default mode: A quantitative meta-analysis. *Journal of Cognitive Neuroscience, 21,* 489–510.

Sripada, C. (2015). Self-expression: A deep self theory of moral responsibility. *Philosophical Studies,* 1–30.

Sripada, C. (2016). Free will and the construction of options. *Philosophical Studies,* 1–21. Advance online publication. doi:10.1007/s11098-016-0643-1

8

Emotions: How the Future Feels (and Could Feel)

Roy Baumeister

E MOTIONS, YOU MIGHT ASSUME, ARE MAINLY IN THE present. So one might conclude that the future doesn't matter. With emotion we might finally have a class of phenomena to which future events, and prospections in general, are largely irrelevant. But emotions may involve the future. In this chapter we examine the relevance of future events to present emotions—and the relevance of anticipated future emotions to present events.

Consider the example of a man making a decision. He ponders several options, which means he imagines performing particular actions that bring about certain consequences, whereupon he does other things, and further consequences ensue. How does emotion enter that process? He may have some emotional states in the present while he is thinking about the future. His thoughts about the future may also predict that he will have future emotions (e.g., "I'll be sorry if X happens").

The present and future emotions may not be entirely independent. They may even be highly correlated, if present emotions sometimes arise as foretastes (especially warnings and promises) of future

emotional states. Anticipating a hot romantic date might bring pleasure in the present, but this is likely linked to the expectation that
the date itself will bring positive emotions.

There is, in fact, a theoretical case to be made for the overlap between present and future emotions, albeit with somewhat different
forms of emotion. The next section summarizes this theory.

Current Affect as Signal for Future Expected Emotion

What is the purpose of emotion, and how does emotion function in
human psychology? A widely held view is that emotions exist to
cause behavior (e.g., Cosmides & Tooby, 2000; Frank, 1988; Frijda,
1986; Izard & Ackerman, 2000). Many theories of emotion use the
standard example of fear. An early human who lacked fear might
stand still, curiously watching a tiger approach, so that he would be
eaten. Such non-fearful individuals would thereby take themselves
out of the gene pool. As a result, today's population would only be
descended from forebears who experienced fear. The fear made them
run away from the tiger and other dangers, with the beneficial result
that they survived longer and were better able to reproduce. It's a
very persuasive just-so story.

Although the idea that emotions are for guiding behavior is intuitively appealing, in fact, the evidence for it is remarkably weak and
frequently contradictory. Research on emotion has shown plenty of
effects on thought processes, judgment, and decision making—but
effects on actual behavior are few and far between. Two influential reviews of the literature by Schwarz and Clore (1996, 2007) remarked
on the contrast between the extensive evidence about cognitive effects of emotion and the minimal evidence of behavioral effects. In
the second review, the authors concluded that "The immediate effects of emotion . . . are more mental than behavioral" (2007, p. 39).

The idea that the main purpose of emotion is to cause behavior was
aggressively rejected by Baumeister, Vohs, DeWall, and Zhang (2007)
on both conceptual and empirical grounds. They reiterated some cri-
tiques of the view that emotion is for causing behavior. These include
the idea that there are not enough emotions for all the possible behaviors, so that emotions cannot contain specific directions for how to act.
(As Schwarz & Clore [1996] pointed out, fear might well cause someone to do a variety of things other than start running: The person

might hide, listen to the weather report, sell stocks, work harder at a job, purchase insurance, or telephone home.) They include the fact that emotions arise slowly, indeed much too slowly to guide behavior in a fast-moving situation. (For example, if after first seeing a cat, a mouse waited until its body generated a state of fear complete with physiological arousal, and then for its brain to perceive that state and understand it as fear, and then send the signal to run, it wouldn't get around to budging fast enough to avoid becoming the cat's lunch.)

Another objection to the theory that the purpose of emotion is to cause behavior is contained in the popular view, well confirmed by empirical studies, that actions driven by current emotional state often end up being irrational and even self-destructive, which means that causing behavior could not be the main purpose of such emotions. Natural selection cannot favor self-defeating actions, insofar as self-destruction is inimical to survival and reproduction. To the extent that emotions push people into self-defeating actions, motivating action is not the evolved purpose of emotion. This might be offset by large amounts of beneficial behaviors motivated by emotion; but it's hard to find much evidence of that, other than the imaginary example of fear making one run away and survive.

Instead, Baumeister et al. (2007) proposed that the purpose of emotion is to stimulate reflection. Emotion directs attention to important events and stimulates the mental processing of them. A computer moves on to the next task once the current one is finished, but humans dwell on things that are over and done with. By continuing to ruminate about them, including veridical replays and counterfactual replays, humans may learn useful lessons that can guide behavior helpfully in future situations.

Moreover, people learn from these experiences how they will feel if they act in particular ways in particular situations. Gradually they become able to anticipate what the emotional outcome will be. People generally operate so as to promote positive emotions and avoid or minimize bad ones, and so once they can effectively forecast how they will feel, they can adjust their behavior effectively.

Two Meanings (and Kinds) of Emotion

The very term *emotion* is used in different ways, which complicates the theory-making. Baumeister et al. (2007) proposed that a crucial distinction is between a full-blown emotional state and what can be called *automatic affect*. Full-blown emotion is what ordinary people understand by the term *emotion*. It is a state of conscious feeling, typically marked by bodily changes such as breathing fast, elevated heartbeat, maybe flushing, and even tears. It is felt as a single state. It arises slowly and dissipates slowly too.

In contrast, automatic affect is a simply a twinge of feeling that something is good or bad. It is typically automatic and may be entirely unconscious. It can come and go quickly, and it is presumably possible to have several at the same time. It might not involve any physiological response, such as a state of arousal.

To be clear, automatic affect is certainly a form of emotional response, even though it does not act or feel like a full-blown emotion. Automatic affect is essentially a feeling of good or bad. Cognition understands, whereas emotion evaluates. The feelings of pleasure and pain signify to even very simple creatures that something is good or bad. Humans have a vastly expanded emotional repertoire, but the good–bad dimension remains strong and clear: For the vast majority of emotional states, there is no question as to whether each one feels good or bad. Even feeling both good and bad at the same time is rare, whereas people routinely experience combinations of good emotions and combinations of bad emotions (e.g., Larsen, Diener, & Emmons, 1986; Polivy, 1981). Automatic affect is thus a very simple, minimalist version of a full-blown emotion. The person knows whether it is good or bad, even though much of the rest of the rich emotional reaction is missing. It is a kind of twinge: "I feel good (or bad) about this." Such little twinges of feeling may often dictate whether the person takes the plunge or not.

Moral behavior provides an instructive example. Moral principles are grand rules, and one can engage in moral reasoning to decide one's actions. Should you tell your friend that you saw his girlfriend kissing another man in the park yesterday? You can debate the application of various moral principles, including the obligations of friendship insofar as you are friends with him, your obligation to keep secrets if you have such a friendship with the girlfriend, the stigma of tattling, the acceptability of kissing one person when in a committed relationship with someone else, and so forth. Kant (1797/1967) offered a profound and famous formula for deciding such issues: Act such that the maxim of your action could serve as the basis for a universal guideline. Act as if you were setting a precedent for all other people in similar situations.

Yet psychologists have gradually come round to the conclusion that that's not how morality works. Jonathan Haidt (2001) provided startling evidence that people make moral judgments and choices based on feelings. They don't step back and hash out the conflict between competing moral principles with their finest logical reasoning. They just get a sense of what feels right, and that's what they do. If it feels right, they approve and do it. If it feels wrong, they object and refrain. It is the twinge of automatic affect, the intuitive moral feeling that is decisive.

To understand emotion in this way, one purpose of conscious emotions is to create a basis for automatic affects in the future. Damasio (1994) proposed the term *somatic marker* to explain the benefits of emotion. As we understand his analysis, he thought that emotions leave a bodily trace of themselves, which can be reactivated in similar situations. This is an important part of learning to live in a social environment. That is why people who do not have normal emotional reactions have considerable difficulty in life. They aren't the wise, rational beings imagined by the creators of Mr. Spock in the television show *Star Trek*. In that show, Spock, a man from another planet and race, was similar to humans except supposedly lacking in emotion, and this lack made him a model of effective, efficient, rational action. But humans who lack emotion are nothing like him. The absence of emotion seems to render people incompetent to function properly in a social world.

Admittedly, the social incompetence of emotionless people is a puzzle. If emotion makes people do impulsive, irrational, even self-defeating things, then why aren't people better off without emotions? The answer hinted at by Damasio and emphatically asserted by Baumeister et al. (2007) is that acting on the basis of current emotions is often irrational and can lead to trouble, but emotion is for learning, not for guiding immediate behavior. The function of full-blown emotions is to help the person learn from current experience, so as to behave better in a nonspecific future. And the somatic markers or other affective associations help make that come about.

Thus, one has an experience that causes a full-blown emotional reaction. That leaves a trace in memory. When a similar situation arises, that trace is activated. So on the point of deciding to act in the later situation, one has a twinge of affect in connection with the idea of acting in a certain way. That twinge (in the present) is a signal of what full-blown emotion one will have (in the future) if one acts that way, and it arises because of what one learned from previous, similar actions (in the past). The present affective twinge helps one anticipate future emotion.

Simulating the Future

The future cannot be experienced directly, as long as it remains in the future. Hence it must be imagined. In effect, people contemplate the future by mentally simulating what might happen at some future time.

In fact, many researchers believe that all conscious experience consists of mental simulations. Conscious experience is obviously produced by the brain. As Merker (2012) wrote, "Enclosed in an opaque skull, the brain knows nothing of the world that surrounds it apart from irregular spike trains delivered at the proximal ends of its sensory nerve fibers . . ." (p. 38). It uses those flickering electrical impulses to construct a subjective impression of the world outside. No wonder this image is prone to various errors. In that view, even awareness of what is happening right there and then at the present moment is just a simulation. People naively assume that their eyes bring a picture of the world directly to the brain, which is what we see, but that is completely wrong. The world sets off nerve cell firings in the eyes, and this information is transmitted to the brain, where it is sorted and processed and eventually put together into a composite, coherent picture, with gaps filled in with best-guess content, meaningful interpretations already inserted, and evaluative feelings attached.

That is why you know whether you like or dislike something almost as fast as you know what it is (Zajonc, 1980). The brain processes the incoming information and works it up into a sort of internal movie about what is happening. While making the movie, it not only presents what is there, but it elaborates on it with information from memory, including what it means and what symbolic or other associations are relevant. Crucially, it also adds value judgments, based on what it wants, needs, likes, and remembers. It does not have time to create a full-blown emotional response prior to conscious experience. After all, it takes a while for emotion to build, and your brain cannot afford to be too far behind reality. Think of a football player running with the ball and trying to dodge a member of the opposing team who wants to tackle him. If his brain waits until he has a full emotional response, even just a few seconds behind actual events, he would be on the ground before he could dodge. But automatic affect can be inserted rapidly. The sight of the lunging opponent comes with the twinge of negative feeling, so he knows to sidestep the would-be tackler, all within a split second.

So much for the present. When simulating the future, time is less pressing, but the same system operates. The mind imagines a sequence of possible events, including perhaps one's own actions, their consequences, and other people's actions and reactions. And these are felt as good or bad. These feelings may help the person decide whether to initiate that sequence of actions or not.

The Case for Anticipated Emotion

In this section we develop the idea that actions are often guided (and guided well) by prospective hedonics—by forecasting how one will feel in the future.

Guilt as Anticipated Emotion

Fear was the favorite example of the old theory that emotions were for causing behavior. Guilt is a good example of the new theory. (We follow the current consensus on distinguishing guilt from shame such that guilt is a bad feeling about a particular action whereas shame is a bad feeling about one's entire person.) A man might do something and then feel guilty afterward, possibly because others complain and criticize him. Guilt makes him reflect on what he did that elicited that reaction. He imagines how he could have acted differently so as to avoid that unpleasant emotional state. The next time he finds himself in a similar situation and is tempted to act in the same way he acted before, he feels a twinge of anticipatory guilt, and so he alters his behavior.

The point of this example is that the current and future states are meaningfully, even causally linked. If he does the same thing he did before, he now realizes, he is likely to end up feeling guilty again.

This is not merely his logical analysis but it is aided, even spurred, by a twinge of automatic affect in the present as he contemplates the problematic action. The bit of bad feeling in the present is there to help him anticipate the full-blown emotional state he would have in the future.

That's part of the beauty of guilt. Used properly, it guides behavior effectively even if the person hardly ever feels genuinely guilty. If you can anticipate what will bring guilt and use that information to avoid those actions, then you can prevent yourself from suffering from more guilt. And in the process you're likely to change your actions to do things that benefit society and ultimately yourself as well.

Guilt thus furnishes a paradigm example of prospective hedonics. Based on past and present, one can project possible futures—and that includes what emotions one is likely to experience during each alternate scenario. And based on those anticipated emotions, one can adjust behavior accordingly, so as to avoid unpleasant emotional states. In the present, one does not really have the full-blown emotion, merely some awareness that guilt lies ahead if one does this. There is no need to feel guilty now, when one has not done anything wrong. All that is needed is to know that if one does a particular something wrong, one will feel guilty.

Decisions, Thoughts, and Feelings

It is tempting to construct a model of the ideal human being, the modern descendant of Plato's philosopher-king. Such a person would be thoughtful, perceptive, and rational, just like *Homo economicus*— yet also presumably highly moral and ethical. Decisions would be made and actions chosen based on a careful and sensitive analysis of the circumstances.

The capacity to think like a philosopher-king is, however, quite a recent development in evolution. Outside humankind, rational and moral thinking is very limited or indeed wholly absent in most cases. Yet animals have been making choices since very early in evolution. How did they make them, if they were unable to conduct logical cost–benefit analyses of competing prospective scenarios?

Choosing on the basis of how one feels right now is a simpler process than making rational decisions, and it requires less mental hardware. We suspect that the earliest feelings to emerge in evolution included pain, which functioned as a signal to the organism that it should move in order to escape from being injured and damaged.

Acting on Basis of Current Emotion

As we already said, the evidence for current emotional state causing behavior is quite sparse and weak. Nobody is saying that it never happens. Certainly people say or do things because they are angry, afraid, or happy. But how common is that? And, moreover, can that be the main function of emotion?

A meta-analysis by DeWall, Baumeister, Chester, and Bushman (2015) compiled evidence from several hundred papers that examined links between emotion and behavior. They took every article in the leading social psychology journal (the *Journal of Personality and Social Psychology*) that analyzed for whether emotion mediated between the study's independent variable and any outcome involving behavior or social judgment, from 1987 to the present (1987 was chosen as the start date because that was when new procedures for analyzing mediation started to become widely used, based on an article the previous year that explained and justified them, thereby bringing about a revolution in how social psychologists worked with their data; Baron & Kenny, 1986).

The idea of mediation by emotion goes something like this. First, something happens in the social situation. Second, the person experiences an emotion as a result of perceiving that. Third, the person does something. Experiments are published when the first step causes the third, that is, when the circumstance reliably causes a certain kind of response. The question is whether the person's emotional reaction to the circumstance contributes to causing what the person does. Someone insults you, and you get angry, and *therefore,* you act aggressively toward that person. If the insult had not elicited anger, you would not have responded to it with aggression. For evidence of mediation, to put it simply, the researcher must show that the circumstance is statistically linked to the behavior, that the emotion is also linked to the behavior, and that when you control for the emotion, the link from circumstance to behavior disappears. In that case, the emotion accounts for the link. (Researchers are also supposed to show that it doesn't work the other way around; namely that even if you control for the circumstance, the emotional state still predicts the behavior.)

A significant finding of mediation means that the emotion is the immediate cause of action. The causal link leads from the circumstance to the emotion and thence to the behavior.

The DeWall et al. (2015) meta-analysis showed that emotion sometimes causes behavior—but just barely. Of several hundred analyses, only 20% were statistically significant. Significance means that there is less than a 5% probability that the results would be found by random, chance variation. So one would expect 5% of the studies to yield significant results by random chance; 20% is thus not much better than chance.

That low rate is remarkable not just because it shows how infrequently researchers have been able to show that emotion causes behavior. Space in that journal is coveted by thousands of researchers, who compete fiercely to publish their best work in those pages. According to the logic of research design, nonsignificant findings are hard to interpret if not completely meaningless, and so most journals publish only studies that find significant results. That such a prestigious journal is so full of nonsignificant results is startling. The only explanation is that authors, reviewers, and editors all assume that emotion is a major if not *the* major cause of behavior, and so everyone must analyze the data to establish whether that is correct in the current case. If someone wants to show that behavior follows from something other than emotional states, it is necessary to provide data to show that emotion is not the real cause. And apparently the field has been slow to wake up to the fact that emotion is typically *not* the driving cause of behavior.

The meta-analysis also examined anticipated emotion. In contrast to the hundreds of analyses that looked for effects of people's current emotional state, only a handful examined anticipated emotional state. But those that did look at anticipated emotion yielded a much higher rate of success, near 90%. Much more research is needed, but the evidence available at present suggests that behavior is much more reliably based on how people expect to feel in the future than how they feel at present.

Moreover, and crucially, even the feeble results for current emotional state probably overstate the case. It is possible to get results that look like one's current emotional state is driving behavior—even when the true cause is anticipated future emotion. In particular, many consequences of unpleasant emotional states come about because people are trying to repair their unpleasant state and make themselves feel better.

This problem was identified by the eminent emotion researcher, Alice Isen (1984, 1987) in the 1980s. Surveying the research literature on emotion, she identified a key ambiguity in studies of bad moods and emotional distress. It is quite hard to disentangle the direct results of the emotion from the person's quest for an anticipated better state. Suppose, for example, that you ran a study in which you put people into good, bad, and neutral moods by random assignment and then measured how much ice cream they ate. You might find that the people who felt bad ate the most ice cream. Does that mean that bad moods cause people to eat sweets, perhaps to lose self-control, and to disregard their diets? Or, alternatively, does it mean that people in bad moods eat ice cream because they think the treat will cheer them up? Isen saw no solution to this problem and advocated that researchers shift to study positive emotions, which do not suffer from that problem of ambiguity. After all, people do not usually try to escape from feeling good. So if a researcher makes people happy and then observes changes in their behavior, it is fair to assume the behavior flowed directly from the happiness, rather than from efforts to change the emotional state, thus avoiding the problem that plagues studies of negative emotion. The rest of her career followed that path with considerable success.

Around the same time, however, another researcher, Robert Cialdini, created a way to tease them apart. Cialdini had been locked in an ongoing debate with Dan Batson about the causes of helping. Are people ever really altruistic, in the sense that they do things purely for the benefit of others? Or do they just help because it makes them feel good? Cialdini suspected that most if not all the evidence purporting to establish human altruism was actually just a sign that people want to feel good. They help others because doing so cheers them up. (It works: Helping others and doing good deeds do in fact generally make the helper feel good.)

Matters came to a head with evidence that ordinary people who find themselves momentarily in sad, unhappy moods are especially helpful. Does sadness cause helping? Or does sadness make people want to feel better, so they help in the hope and expectation of attaining a cheerier mood?

The ingenious solution devised by Cialdini and his colleagues (Manucia, Baumann, & Cialdini, 1984) was the *mood-freezing pill*. "Freezing" in this case had nothing to do with being cold: It simply meant that whatever emotional state you have when you take the pill would continue for a while and could not be changed. In reality there is no such pill, but it wasn't necessary to actually have such a pill. All the researchers had to do was convince people that they had one.

The beauty of the mood-freezing pill is that once someone has taken it, there is no point in trying to repair your mood or alter your emotional state. Again, this does not refer to actual pills but rather to people's beliefs. If you think your mood can't change no matter what you do, any attempts to change it are doomed to fail, so it makes no sense to try. Therefore, this clever ruse can solve Isen's problem. Sad people who believe they have taken a mood-freezing pill know there is no point in trying to cheer themselves up. If sadness causes behavior directly, the mood-freezing pill won't matter, and people will continue to perform the same actions regardless of whether they have taken a pill. But insofar as behavior is designed to cheer oneself up, the mood-freezing pill should put a stop to it.

The researchers gave what were in fact placebos (pills with no effects) to college students after inducing various mood states. The students were told that the researchers were testing new pharmaceutical products and that preliminary results had shown that these had the side effect of locking one's emotional state wherever it happened to be, for about an hour. To make it plausible (as no known drugs actually accomplish this), the experimenter explained that many drugs have emotional side effects, such as cannabis, which intensifies emotional reactions. This new drug, they said, would not intensify emotions but simply keep them about the same for about an hour.

The findings were dramatic. Without the mood-freezing pill, sad moods led to more helping, as in previous studies. But the sad people who had supposedly taken the mood-freezing pill failed to help.

This pattern is relevant because it further undermines the evidence that current emotional state causes behavior. In such a study, one could get evidence that sad moods mediated statistically between circumstances and helping behavior. But in reality, the helping was not a direct result of sadness. Sad people only helped when they thought that helping might cheer them up. So a correct understanding of the phenomenon would show that anticipated emotion was the true cause. Presumably, a substantial number of the 20% of significant findings in the meta-analysis that purported to show current emotion causing behavior could in fact reflect acting on the basis of anticipated emotion.

There have been further findings confirming the mood-freeze pattern. Sad people do eat more sweets than happy people, but not if their moods have been frozen (Tice, Bratslavsky, & Baumeister, 2001). Upset people seek immediate rather than delayed gratification, but again, not if their moods are frozen (Tice et al., 2001). Perhaps most dramatically, anger fails to cause aggression when moods are frozen (Bushman, Baumeister, & Phillips, 2001). The latter is especially remarkable because the idea that anger leads to aggression is one of the foundations of research on aggression, and some experts have asserted that anger contains within the emotional state the incipient muscle movements for aggression (Berkowitz, 1989). But apparently, angry people lash out mainly because they think they will feel better as a result. Remove the expectation that attacking someone will make them feel good and reduce anger, and anger ceases to cause aggression.

There are profound implications of this view that human behavior is guided by anticipated emotions. Whatever else people are doing, they are often also acting in ways that will improve their future emotional state. They choose actions that they expect will bring positive emotions and reduce or avoid negative ones. *In an important and emotional sense, most behavior is thus guided by prospection.* Deciding what to do is commonly informed by expectations about the future and the emotions associated with this or that anticipated outcome.

If that view is correct, then emotional prospecting is crucial. A false prediction about how one might feel will lead to a wrongheaded, counterproductive action. That raises the question of how well people can predict their emotional outcomes, to which we turn in the next section.

Affective Forecasting and Its Alleged Inaccuracy

Thus far we have examined the theory that people choose and act based in part on how they expect to feel. Behaving in such a way could be an effective way to go through life, provided that one's emotional reactions have been shaped by evolution and learning to be adaptive. But there is one potential problem for this view. What if people are not very good at predicting their future emotions? If they act on the basis of expecting to feel happy and instead end up feeling miserable, then apparently their expectations were wrong—and, moreover, acting on the basis of such seriously mistaken expectations would not likely be adaptive. The very fact that they end up feeling miserable is probably a sign that they did not choose the best course of action.

In fact, an important line of research has suggested that people are often inaccurate when they predict their future emotional reactions. Research by Dan Gilbert, Tim Wilson, and an impressive host of colleagues on the phenomenon they dubbed *affective forecasting* has repeatedly confirmed that people make systematic mistakes about how they will feel in the future.

Yet the research findings on affective forecasting do not really demolish the idea that anticipated emotions guide behavior. In a way, they even strengthen and confirm it. People do make systematic errors, but *not*, apparently, of the sort that something they expect to bring joy ends up making them miserable (although certain marriages, drugs, and investments probably fit that description).

The main error is an overestimation of *how long* the emotion will last. For example, when young professors predicted how they would feel if they were denied tenure, they generally predicted they would be extremely upset and depressed for a long time (Gilbert, Pinel, Wilson, Blumberg, & Wheatley, 1998). In the event, those who were denied tenure were sad and disappointed for a while, but they got over it rather quickly. In another study, students predicted that they would be much happier if the campus room draw assigned them a place in a particular dorm that was much loved and sought after, as opposed to being assigned to a less attractive dorm (Dunn, Wilson, & Gilbert, 2003). Those who got into the coveted dorm were probably happier at first than the ones who did not, but when researchers contacted the students a year after they made their predictions, the two groups were equally happy. Their forecasts of differential levels of happiness were probably right about the initial reaction and merely wrong about how long those differences would last.

It is likely adaptive for people to overestimate their future emotional states. Consider the young professors approaching the tenure decision. If they think that failing to get tenure will make them miserable for a long time, they will be motivated to work hard to prevent that from happening. They are, therefore, more likely to actually achieve their goal and earn tenure. Meanwhile, consider what would happen if they had made the opposite error. Suppose they thought that denying tenure would not bother them or would produce only a brief feeling of disappointment, but when it actually happened they became profoundly unhappy for a long time. Expecting a minimal reaction might well be demotivating—why knock yourself out for years working toward an outcome that will have little emotional impact? The opposite error would be maladaptive, because it would reduce your chances of reaching the goal.

Motivating oneself based on anticipated emotion is the main point. It makes one do the best work one can. By the time the tenure decision arrives, the emotion has served its function. If the young professor does end up failing to get tenure, there is no particular advantage in being miserable for years afterward.

References

Baron, R. M., & Kenny, D. A. (1986). The moderator–mediator variable distinction in social psychological research: Conceptual, strategic, and statistical considerations. *Journal of Personality and Social Psychology, 51*, 1173–1182.

Baumeister, R. F., Vohs, K. D., DeWall, C. N., & Zhang, L. (2007). How emotion shapes behavior: Feedback, anticipation, and reflection rather than direct causation. *Personality and Social Psychology Review, 11*, 167–203.

Berkowitz, L. (1989). Frustration-aggression hypothesis: Examination and reformulation. *Psychological Bulletin, 106*, 59–73.

Bushman, B. J., Baumeister, R. F., & Phillips, C. M. (2001). Do people aggress to improve their mood? Catharsis beliefs, affect regulation opportunity, and aggressive responding. *Journal of Personality and Social Psychology, 81*, 17–32.

Cosmides, L., & Tooby, J. (2000). Evolutionary psychology and the emotions. In M. Lewis & J. M. Haviland-Jones (Eds.), *Handbook of emotions* (2nd ed., pp. 91–115). New York, NY: Guilford.

Damasio, A. (1994). *Descartes' error: Emotion, reason, and the human brain*. New York, NY: Putnam.

DeWall, C. N., Baumeister, R. F., Chester, D. S., & Bushman, B. J. (2015). How often does currently felt emotion predict social behavior and judgment? A meta-analytic test of two theories. *Emotion Review*. Advance online publication. doi:10.1177/1754073915572690

Dunn, E. W., Wilson, T. D., & Gilbert, D. T. (2003). Location, location, location: The misprediction of satisfaction in housing lotteries. *Personality and Social Psychology Bulletin, 29,* 1421–1432.

Frank, R. H. (1988). *Passions within reason: The strategic role of the emotions.* New York, NY: W. W. Norton.

Frijda, N. H. (1986). *The emotions.* Cambridge, England: Cambridge University Press.

Gilbert, D. T., Pinel, E. C., Wilson, T. D., Blumberg, S. J., & Wheatley, T. P. (1998). Immune neglect: A source of durability bias in affective forecasting. *Journal of Personality and Social Psychology, 75,* 617–638.

Haidt, J. (2001). The emotional dog and its rational tail: A social intuitionist approach to moral judgment. *Psychological Review, 108,* 814–834.

Isen, A. M. (1984). Toward understanding the role of affect in cognition. In R. S. Wyer & T. K. Srull (Eds.), *Handbook of social cognition* (Vol. 3, pp. 179–236). Hillsdale, NJ: Erlbaum.

Isen, A. M. (1987). Positive affect, cognitive processes, and social behavior. In L. Berkowitz (Ed.), *Advances in experimental social psychology* (Vol. 20, pp. 203–253). New York, NY: Academic Press.

Izard, C., & Ackerman, B. (2000). Motivational, organizational, and regulatory functions of discrete emotions. In M. Lewis & J. M. Haviland-Jones (Eds.), *Handbook of emotions* (2nd ed., pp. 253–264). New York, NY: Guilford.

Kant, I. (1967). *Kritik der praktischen Venunft* [Critique of practical reason]. Hamburg, Germany: Felix Meiner Verlag. (Original work published 1797)

Larsen, R. J., Diener, E., & Emmons, R. A. (1986). Affect intensity and reactions to daily life events. *Journal of Personality and Social Psychology, 51,* 803–814.

Manucia, G. K., Baumann, D. J., & Cialdini, R. B. (1984). Mood influences on helping: Direct effects or side effects? *Journal of Personality and Social Psychology, 46,* 357–364.

Merker, B. (2012). From probabilities to percepts: A subcortical "global best estimate buffer" as locus of phenomenal experience.

In S. Edelman, T. Fekete, & I. Zach (Eds.), *Being in time: Dynamical models of phenomenal experience* (pp. 37–80). Amsterdam, The Netherlands: John Benjamins.

Polivy, J. (1981). On the induction of emotion in the laboratory: Discrete moods or multiple affect states? *Journal of Personality and Social Psychology, 41,* 803–817.

Schwarz, N., & Clore, G. L. (1996). Feelings and phenomenal experiences. In E. T. Higgins & A. Kruglanski (Eds.), *Social psychology: Handbook of basic principles* (pp. 433–465). New York, NY: Guilford.

Schwarz, N., & Clore, G. L. (2007). Feelings and phenomenal experiences. In E. T. Higgins & A. Kruglanski (Eds.), *Social psychology: Handbook of basic principles* (2nd ed., pp. 385–407). New York, NY: Guilford.

Tice, D. M., Bratslavsky, E., & Baumeister, R. F. (2001). Emotional distress regulation takes precedence over impulse control: If you feel bad, do it! *Journal of Personality and Social Psychology, 80,* 53–67.

Zajonc, R. B. (1980). Feeling and thinking: Preferences need no inference. *American Psychologist, 35,* 151–175.

9

Morality and Prospection

Peter Railton

Suppose that your uncle is driving you and your family to the farmers' market for a Saturday outing. As the car approaches the market, however, a sudden heart attack causes him to slump over the steering wheel, his foot still on the gas pedal. The car is headed directly toward a crowded stall in the center of the market. You're in the front seat, but you can't reach the pedals, so all you can do in the second that remains before collision is to reach over and tug on the steering wheel, turning the car to the right just enough to aim at the least crowded part of the sidewalk ahead, where one or two pedestrians are strolling along, unaware.

Should you turn the wheel, very likely killing one of these pedestrians but saving the lives of a number of people at the stall, or should you not turn the wheel, allowing the car to continue straight ahead and plow into the crowded stall, very likely killing a number of the people gathered there?

Let's call this hypothetical scenario *Farmers' Market*. This scenario was recently posed to students on the first day of an ethics class, and they were asked to give their "intuitive judgment" of what to do. They rapidly entered their answers anonymously on a hand-held device called an *i>Clicker*, which sent the results to a radio receiver at the front of the room. The receiver then tallied the results and produced a bar graph, which was projected on a screen for the whole class to see. The result was stark: 84% answered that they should turn the steering wheel, while only16% answered that they should not. When the class was asked to volunteer an explanation of why one might think that one should turn the wheel, virtually all agreed on a straightforward justification: In an emergency situation of this kind, in which some must die however one acts, one should try to minimize the loss of innocent lives. No one seemed to feel that there *was* no explanation. But when asked to volunteer an explanation of why one might think that one should not turn the wheel, no predominant answer was given. Instead, people suggested a variety of reasons, including, "You cannot play God with other people's lives," "You would be actively killing the one if you pushed the switch, but only allowing the five to die if you did not," "It is none of my business to intervene in this situation." Some even said, "I don't know why, but I just feel it would be wrong to do it."

Many readers will recognize that Farmers' Market is a variant of the notorious trolley problem (Foot, 1967; Thomson, 1976), the classic version of which is *Switch*:

> You are about to pass over some trolley tracks at a street-level crossing when you look up the line and see a trolley hurtling in your direction, its driver slumped over the controls, evidently unconscious. Looking down the line in the other direction you see that the tracks enter a narrow tunnel, where you can discern five tramway maintenance workers bent over the tracks, evidently doing some repair. They do not see the trolley coming toward them, and will almost certainly not have a chance to escape being crushed if the speeding trolley continues unchecked. Looking around desperately, you see a switch along the tracks between the trolley and the tunnel and a nearby lever that operates the switch. If the lever is pushed, the trolley will be diverted onto a side track, where it will continue into another tunnel, in which you see one maintenance worker. Like those in the other tunnel, he is unaware of the trolley's rapid approach and would almost certainly be unable to escape before it reaches and crushes him.

*Should you push the lever, sparing the five workers on the main
track but almost certainly killing the one worker on the side track?
Or should you allow the trolley to proceed down the main track un-
checked, where it will almost certainly kill the five workers trapped
by the confines of the tunnel?*

Asked for their intuitive judgment in Switch, 62% of the same
introductory class answered that they should push the lever, killing one, but sparing five; 38% said they should not. As in Farmers'
Market, students tended to agree that saving as many lives as possible in such an emergency is the best explanation of why someone
would recommend intervention (in this case, by pushing the switch).
And also as in Farmers' Market, asked for reasons why one should
not intervene, answers ranged more widely, including "I don't know."
Switch is called a *bystander* scenario, and the 62% to 38% split of
the students is quite typical of a population of students or adults
in the United States or United Kingdom, where the trolley problem
has been most intensely studied (Gold, Pulford, & Colman, 2014).
The Farmers' Market is a so-called passenger scenario, and passenger
scenarios usually result in a significantly higher number of interven-
tionist judgments than bystander scenarios. The 84% to 16% split of
the students is, again, quite typical (Hauser, Cushman, Young, Jin, &
Mikhail, 2007).

It is striking how replicable these results on the two hypothetical
scenarios are, year in and year out, in one after another introductory
ethics class or sample poll. What's fairly constant isn't that everyone
agrees about what to do, but rather that the percentage split in the
two kinds of cases tends to hover around the same values, that more
tend to favor intervention in passenger scenarios than bystander
scenarios, and that people tend to converge on a harm-minimizing
explanation for why one should intervene, while showing wider divergence and less clarity about why one should not.

When people first hear of the results of the trolley problem and
its variants, they often wonder whether the answers given reflect
real behavior in choice situations or would be different if we compared different subpopulations or different cultures. What if we divided the usual test populations by gender or ethnicity? The results
tend to be the same (Navarette, McDonald, Mott, & Asher, 2012). Or
what if we looked at another culture? Here the answer is less clear.

Some studies with Chinese subjects found very little difference from the typical proportions in the United States (Mikhail, 2011; Moore, Lee, Clark, & Conway, 2011), while others found differences worth noting.[1] For example, two studies found that Chinese subjects are somewhat less likely to favor pushing the lever in Switch (Ahlenius & Tännsjö, 2012; Gold et al., 2014). However, interpreting such differences is difficult. Translation is always a problem, and the Chinese subjects studied also expressed much higher belief in "fate," which is not itself a moral concept, but is often cited in favor of nonintervention (Gold et al., 2014).

Readers familiar with the trolley problem know what comes next. The problem isn't just what to do in Switch, and why, but how these answers in Switch compare to the answers given in the following seemingly very similar scenario, *Footbridge*:

> You are crossing a pedestrian footbridge over some trolley tracks. The tracks run into a narrow tunnel about a hundred yards further down the line. As you are crossing above the tracks, you look up the line and see a trolley hurtling down the track, its driver slumped over the controls, evidently unconscious. Looking down the line in the other direction you see that the tracks enter a narrow tunnel, where you can discern five tramway maintenance workers bent over the tracks, evidently doing some repair. They do not see the trolley coming toward them, and will almost certainly not have a chance to escape being crushed if the speeding trolley continues unchecked. Looking around desperately, you see a very large man standing on the footbridge directly above the track, leaning over the railing. Although your own weight would not be sufficient to block the trolley and prevent it from hurtling into the maintenance workers, his bulk would be.
>
> *Should you push this man off the footbridge, so that his bulk will block the trolley, which will almost certainly kill him, thereby sparing the five workers? Or should you not push the man, allowing the trolley to speed unchecked into the tunnel, almost certainly killing the five workers?*

Only 31% of the students in the introductory ethics class answered that they should push the man, while 69% answered that they should not. This, too, is a fairly typical result. Moreover, students were polarized in their certainty in the case of Footbridge as compared to Switch: 41%, said they were "very certain" in Footbridge (compared to 31% in Switch), 30% said "somewhat certain" (compared to 48%), 30% said "not very certain" or "not at all certain" (compared to 21%). Yet unlike Switch, there was considerable divergence in saying why, in Footbridge, someone might make the choice that most had endorsed, taking no action, rather than making the choice of taking action to minimize harm.

What might account for the striking difference, or *asymmetry*, in these responses? Seeing the results projected before them, the students were intensely concerned: They could feel the pressure to "treat like cases alike," a venerable moral principle, so they wanted to figure out why Footbridge *wasn't* like Switch, at least for many in the room. Students, however, found it hard to say why; it seemed many were more confident of their answer, but less confident that they could justify it.

Some students, however, volunteered an intuitively plausible rationale: In Footbridge, one is directly *using* the man as a means to prevent substantially greater harm, while in Switch one is not. In Switch, the death of the lone worker on the sidetrack is a side effect, not a deliberate aim, of diverting the trolley. Even though they knew that pushing the lever would result in the worker's death, still, if he hadn't been there, they'd still push the switch. But the large man's being crushed by the trolley was essential for stopping it in Footbridge, so it was intended and not a side effect. This rationale exemplifies a principle that has been articulated in one way or another for centuries, sometimes called the "doctrine of double effect" (Aquinas, *Summa Theologiae*, trans. 2008, II-II, Q.64, a.7; Bennett, 1981; Cushman, Young, & Hauser, 2006).

Of course, these students might never have articulated this principle before, but, on reflection, they thought it explained their intuition. As we saw in Chapter 2, the idea of "tacit" principles or rules that shape intuitive judgments and behavior is familiar from linguistics. Most native speakers of English can tell you that a speaker who utters,

(1) "If Oswald hadn't shot Kennedy, somebody else would have"

believes (a) that Kennedy was shot, and (b) that Oswald did it. By contrast, a speaker who utters,

(2) "If Oswald didn't shoot Kennedy, somebody else did"

believes (a), but leaves it open whether (b). The difference between the subjunctive or counterfactual conditional (1) and the indicative conditional (2) is subtle, and it wasn't until the latter half of the 20th century that philosophers and linguistics gave a clear account of it (Adams, 1970; Lewis, 1973). Presumably few English speakers could clearly explain the principles behind these two different conditionals. Yet, intuitively, they understand the difference and can use them in speech and comprehension. Perhaps moral intuitions are like linguistic intuitions, and the challenge is to identify the underlying, perhaps universal, "moral grammar" (Mikhail, 2011). The asymmetric intuitions in Footbridge versus Switch might show that this underlying grammar contains a principle like the doctrine of double effect (Hauser et al., 2007).

But "trolleyology," as it is called, has another surprise up its sleeve. At this point, one more trolley scenario is presented: *Loop* (Thomson, 1985). Loop begins just like Switch, but there is a difference: The sidetrack in Loop does not simply go off into a different tunnel, it rejoins the main track *before* that track goes into the tunnel. So it might seem there is no point in switching to the sidetrack. The trolley will still strike and kill the five tramway workers whichever path it takes, except

> Standing on the looping sidetrack is a single tramway worker. He is facing down the track, and so would not see an oncoming trolley. He is bulky enough that his body would stop the trolley, however, preventing it from reaching the tunnel containing the five tramway workers.

> *Should you push the switch and send the trolley down the sidetrack, killing the lone tramway worker but sparing the five?*

When asked for their intuitive response to this scenario, fully 73% of the same group of students on the same day said they should push the switch to send the trolley down the sidetrack, and only 27% said they should not, which is essentially the same result as the original Switch. Once again, this is a very typical response. And the rationale students gave for diverting the trolley was also the same as in Switch: minimizing the loss of life. Yet, in

Loop, as in Footbridge, you *are* using the lone tramway worker as a means to prevent the deaths of the five; you choose to cause crushing him to stop the trolley, so his death is no mere side effect. So what became of the underlying moral principle, the doctrine of double effect?

Confronted with enough trolleyology, most people at some point throw up their hands and say that there simply is no coherent way of accounting for their intuitions. Perhaps there is no underlying, principled moral competence after all. Or, perhaps all the examples show is that highly artificial scenarios can be cooked up by clever philosophers to make ordinary people look foolish, so trolleyology tells us little about actual human moral thought and practice.

What if we looked at people's behavior in cases where real harms or benefits are at stake? Enter the psychologists and "experimental philosophers," a new breed of philosophers who believe in applying scientific methods in the place of philosophical speculation about what is intuitive or common sense. These researchers have designed less lethal ways of placing people in more realistic moral dilemmas, using virtual reality simulations or genuine harms and benefits in the form of monetary gains and losses. What they have found is that people in general have stronger emotional responses in the more realistic scenarios (FeldmanHall et al., 2012), and, perhaps as a result, their patterns of behavior show stronger effects than in purely hypothetical scenarios. For example, in a virtual reality simulator, an even higher percentage (90%) pushed the lever in Switch (Navarette et al., 2012). And in bystander-Switch-like cases where actual monetary contributions to worthy causes were at stake, 80% of U.K. subjects elected to divert the threat to a victim (Gold, Colman, & Pulford, 2014). These results contrast with the mid-60s' percentages favoring diversion in typical responses to bystander-Switch hypothetical scenarios in similar subject populations. What more realistic tests haven't shown, however, is the contrary: The asymmetric patterns of results of the original "armchair" thought experiments reverses or goes away.[2]

So what might drive the asymmetries? Psychologists pushed yet deeper into the mind, posing trolley problems to people while sampling their brains' responses in fMRI scanners, to see which areas of the brain showed the greatest change in metabolic activity. In a pioneering study, Joshua Greene and colleagues found a surprising result, which promised to explain the peculiar patterns observed in typical samples. When considering trolley problems like Switch, areas of the brain associated with *cognition*, such as working memory and the comparison of magnitude, were more active in relation to a resting state; but when considering problems like Footbridge, these cognitive regions exhibited *less* metabolic activity than in the resting state, while greater activity was observed in regions associated with *emotion* (Greene, Sommerville, Nystrom, Darley, & Cohen, 2001). Perhaps the pattern of moral intuitions could be explained by the greater emotional arousal produced by the hands-on, personal violence in Footbridge scenarios, which preempted the cognitive assessment of harm-minimization that seemed to be taking place in the hands-off, impersonal Switch? That would explain why Loop verdicts are similar to Switch and not Footbridge. In Loop, the violence is also hands-off and impersonal. One only pushes a lever, and the death occurs elsewhere.

This explanation came at the right time to ride a wave of opinion in psychological research. The last few decades have seen the rise of a "dual-process" model of the brain, according to which a fast, evolutionarily ancient, effortless, relatively inflexible, affect-laden, automatic, intuitive "system 1" operates alongside a slower, evolutionarily more recent, effortful, more flexible, cognitively demanding, deliberative "system 2" (Chaiken & Trope, 1999).[3] On this model, it is the rapid deployment of the intuitive system 1 that explains the ready answers we have when making non-deliberative, intuitive responses. The deliberative system 2 might be able to correct the biases of system 1, but typically it operates too late and too weakly unless circumstances provoke greater reflection.

The dual system approach had very high generality, and it promised to give a neuroscientific basis for the vast body of evidence accumulated in the "heuristics and biases" program pioneered by Amos Tversky and Daniel Kahneman (1974), which had been developed to explain experimental evidence of ways in which humans systematically departed from standard decision-theoretic norms in their intuitive thinking. For example, when asked to estimate probability, people appear to use an availability heuristic: They rely on the ease with which instances come to mind rather than more accurate, experienced-based statistical estimations. Thus, people given a list of names of well-known men and women, which contains an equal number of men and women, when asked later whether the list contained more men or women, will give an answer that reflects their *familiarity* with the names on the list, not the actual *frequency*. If the men on the list are better known than the women, people will tend to say that the list contains more men, and vice versa (Tversky & Kahneman, 1973). The availability heuristic works reasonably well in general, because one's ability to call things to mind often reflects their frequency in one's experience. But in a range of cases, it will lead to systematic error. For example, even when the underlying statistics presented were the same, and the net results of the choice were probabilistically equivalent, people showed more risk aversion when the choice about whether the United States should adopt a vaccine was framed by "lives lost" and "risk taking" than when the choice was framed by "lives saved" (Tversky & Kahneman, 1981).

The heuristics and biases approach reached into all dimensions of deliberation and decision-making and fundamentally reshaped how psychologists and, increasingly, some economists view human cognition and choice. *Homo economicus*, the rational expected-value maximizer of introductory economics courses, was dethroned as a model for actual humans. At least anecdotally, even trained economists made the same errors as the population at large when asked informally for intuitive responses.

If the evolutionarily ancient, affectively driven system 1 inherited from our animal ancestors had, as it was supposed, "little knowledge of logic or statistics" (Kahneman, 2011), but it came "on line" rapidly and effortlessly in our responses to the world, then this would explain how intuitive thought could be subject to such simplifying heuristics and biases, which yield good results most of the time, but fail in systematic ways when calculation, analysis, or inference are required. To correct system 1 intuition requires system 2 reasoning—controlled, effortful, logical thought (Kahneman, 2003). Because the trolley scenarios and their ilk are presented with a request for prompt, intuitive responses, the scenarios that have greater visceral impact, such as Footbridge, will generate an immediate verdict before thoughtful reflection can come into play. One result is that people won't be able to give a *principled* reason for the pattern of their responses in these different scenarios; there simply *is* no principle there to be found, just a powerful emotion driving their response in Footbridge, but not in Switch or Loop.

The social psychologist Jonathan Haidt described this phenom-enon of having a clear moral intuition for which one cannot articu-late a rationale as "moral dumbfounding." He devised a number of scenarios to demonstrate the phenomenon at work. The best known is *Julie and Mark*:

> Julie and Mark are brother and sister. They are traveling together in France on summer vacation from college. One night they are staying alone in a cabin near the beach. They decide that it would be interest-ing and fun if they tried making love. At very least it would be a new experience for each of them. Julie was already taking birth control pills, but Mark uses a condom too, just to be safe. They both enjoy making love, but they decide not to do it again. They keep that night as a special secret, which makes them feel even closer to each other.
>
> *What do you think about that, was it OK for them to make love?* [emphasis added] (Haidt, 2001, p. 814)

What Haidt and colleagues found was that most experimental subjects readily judged that Julie and Mark's lovemaking is "not OK," but when they were pressed to explain their judgments, the justifications they provided did not correspond to the facts of the case. For example, they might cite such harm-related features of incest as the occurrence of genetic abnormalities or psychological trauma, even though these negative consequences were plainly excluded by the details of the vignette. When this discrepancy was pointed out to them, however, many subjects apparently did not withdraw or alter their original judgment that Julie and Mark's action was not OK. They eventually hit a point when they could not give a ratio-nale, but they stuck with their intuitive condemnation.

Here's how a dual process accounts for this. Subjects reading the vignette first encounter that Julie and Mark are brother and sister. So when they read that Julie and Mark had sexual intercourse, they experience an immediate flash of disgust. Readers had a fast, automatic system 1 reaction that preempted moral processing by the more delib-erative system 2, so that their negative assessment was unaffected by reading the action's benign consequences. Such a flash of disgust at the thought of incest has been postulated as arising from an evolutionary past, in which incest posed a peril to reproductive fitness. Because this automatic disgust mechanism is entirely tacit, subjects asked to explain their judgments had no introspective access to it. They, therefore, needed to "confabulate" an after-the-fact rationale using system 2. Naturally, they found features tied to incest by their general knowledge, even though these features were not applicable to the example. After learning that their system 2–manufactured rationale didn't apply and would not be able to undermine the affective system's evolutionarily ancient disgust response to incest, the subjects' firm negative verdict did not change. At the same time, the subjects had no insight into this origin for their verdict, and so were, in the end, dumbfounded: "I can't say why, but [it] just seems wrong" (Haidt, 2001).

This parallels the explanation Greene and Haidt teamed up to offer for the asymmetry in verdict between Switch and Footbridge (Greene & Haidt, 2002). Given that humans evolved in small groups that depended on cooperation, mutual assistance, and social peace, we could expect that evolution would favor the existence of a fast, automatic, negative system 1 "alarm response" to discourage the personal use of force in a direct, "ME HURT YOU" situation, at least when not in the context of active intergroup conflict. The consideration that using this personal force would save the lives of five workers further down the track is a harm-minimization calculation that only appeals to the emotionally and motivationally weak system 2 and has no effect on the "myopic module" responsible for the well-entrenched system 1 alarm response (Greene, 2013). Hence the intuition that pushing in Footbridge is wrong persists in most subjects, even when they cannot articulate a principle to defend it (Greene & Haidt, 2002).

Had the mystery of the trolley problem, which had so baffled moral philosophers looking for fundamental moral principles, been solved by appeal to something much more *psychologically* basic: the difference between a fast, negative, automatic emotional response to "violations a chimpanzee can appreciate" in Footbridge-like scenarios versus the cool cognitive calculation of costs and benefits induced in Switch-like or Loop-like scenarios (Greene & Haidt, 2002, p. 519)? Further evidence came when Greene and colleagues studied intuitive responses to variations of the Footbridge scenario that differed in *how* one's "personal force" was exerted. For example, whether the bulky man was sent to his death by the *direct* action of one's own muscles, such as pushing him with a pole, as opposed to an *indirect* effect, such as pushing a lever to open a trap door, they found that the intensity of the negative response varies in proportion to directness

(Greene et al., 2009). But such differences in strength of moral judgment seem to have no real basis in moral principles. "Thou shalt not use a pole rather than a trap door" would never have made it as the Eleventh Commandment.

The work by Greene, Haidt, and others had a galvanizing effect on thinking about moral psychology. Perhaps philosophers were chasing a will-o'-the-wisp all along, misled into placing too much confidence in moral intuitions by their excessive confidence in underlying human rationality. Yet recall our discussion of intuition in Chapter 2 and of the surprising ways in which the implicit responses of the affective system of humans and their animal relatives *do* follow the principles of rational decision theory. How can we reconcile this large body of detailed neuroscientific evidence with the large body of evidence in social psychology and moral psychology *against* the rationality of intuition? In Kahneman's influential discussion (2003), system 1 (intuition) is fast, parallel, automatic, effortless, associative, slow-learning, and typically emotionally charged, while system 2 (reasoning) is slow, serial, controlled, effortful, rule-governed, flexible, and typically emotionally neutral. It seems indisputable that intuition is fast and effortless in comparison with declarative reasoning, and more heavily laden with emotional force, but is it also associative and slow learning? And does it lack flexibility and a capacity to perform algorithmic or rule-like inference?

We have already discussed the way that linguistic intuitions appear to reflect underlying competencies with rule-like structures that can, almost instantaneously, generate or interpret entirely novel sentences. So these sorts of features, at least, should be conceded to be within the realm of possibility for intuition. Why not in the moral case as well? But don't examples like the trolley problems suggest that, far from the regular structures of language, moral judgments are a motley crew, showing none of the discipline characteristic of language? And yet responses to the trolley problems *do* show regularities, which hold up across a wide population. The question is, can we locate an alternative explanation of these patterns that would provide some ground for thinking that the moral intuitions are more rational than they might seem? We believe the answer is *yes*, and that the key to the answer lies in understanding how *prospection* figures in moral judgment.

The first point we'll need to make is philosophical: One cannot meaningfully *contrast* reasoning with intuition. That might seem odd. Reasoning is a step-by-step process where each step follows *logically* from the previous step. Here's an example, ascribable to the logician and philosopher George Boolos. He starts with the title of great old song from the 1930s—*Everybody loves my baby, but my baby don't love nobody but me*—and shows that it is has a surprising implication:

(1) Everybody loves my baby, but my baby don't love nobody but me.
(2) If my baby is loved by everyone, my baby is loved by my baby.
(3) But my baby loves only one person, me.
(4) If my baby were different from me, then my baby would love *two* people, me and my baby.
(5) Therefore, I am my baby.

Check it out. One can follow this kind of reasoning by seeing how each step does indeed follow from the ones before, so that, if the premises are true, the conclusion must be true. That's what logicians mean in calling an argument *valid*. Of course, the songwriter would not be impressed; most likely he'd say that only a logician would be foolish enough to take (1) so literally. Besides, *Everybody loves my baby, but, apart from herself, my baby don't love nobody but me* wouldn't make much of a title for a hit song.

The beauty of logic is its relentlessness. Given a starting point, it will carry you to a conclusion that can surprise you very much, and yet do so with what the medieval scholastics would call "demonstrative certainty." Some of the amazing conclusions reached by logic include multiple, dramatically different *sizes* of infinity (Cantor, 1891), and even though logic is mechanical in its application, you cannot build a "logic machine" that will check every proof for validity (Church, 1936; Turing, 1937). Neither of these conclusions is what one would call obvious, yet both have demonstrative certainty.

But wait, demonstrative certainty is only certainty *relative to certain axioms, premises, and systems of rules.* And what about them— can they be equally certain? Could we prove them, too? But what would we prove them *from* if we had no axioms or premises, or what would we reason *with* if we had no rules? And then we'd have to try to prove those axioms, premises, rules, and so forth, too. Clearly, we'd never get to the end of this.

It's an argument at least as old as Aristotle—and that's precisely why Aristotle introduced the notion of intuition in the first place (*Posterior Analytics*, trans. 1941, II.19). We must have some form of non-demonstrative knowledge to furnish the axioms, premises, and rules. Logicians and mathematicians accept the conclusions *demonstrated* by Cantor, Church, and Turing because they *non-demonstratively* accept the axioms and rules they worked with.

To bring this discussion back down to earth, in Boolos' argument, going from step (1) to step (2) involved the rule of "universal instantiation," that is, roughly, *If everything is F, then for each a, a is F.* Now that seems obvious, even self-evident. But obviousness and self-evidence are not forms of demonstration, they are forms of *immediately seeing* something without being aware of carrying out any inference or criteria-based judgment. Indeed, both "obvious" and "evident," like "intuition," have roots in verbs for seeing. So any piece of reasoning, however arcane, involves continuous reliance on intuition to make the very steps that are the defining characteristic of reasoning.

Now we present one more philosophical point before we return to psychology. Our reliance on obviousness, self-evidence, and intuition isn't *infallible*—no *actual* mental process is infallible. Reasoning, for example, has many moving parts that can go wrong: memory, knowledge of meaning, grasp of possibilities, and so on. Even universal instantiation underwent a major shift after the Aristotelian syllogism had prevailed for many centuries. In modern logic, *a is F* is false for every *a* in an empty universe, but *Everything is F* is true. This is vital for many demonstrations. But for Aristotle, *Everything is F* implies that *something is F*, and so it must be false in an empty universe. So there was something that *seemed* self-evidently true to Aristotle and to generations of brilliant scholastics after him, but really wasn't. This points up a limitation on all appeals to self-evidence or intuition: One must be modest enough to admit that what seems obvious will be limited by the scope of one's ability to project imagined possibilities.

And that seems like a good starting point for thinking about intuition in ethics. If history tells us anything, it tells us that previous generations of fine, sensitive, intelligent people saw certain moral principles as self-evident or intuitively obvious that we now outright reject, while there are others we accept as fundamental that they never so much as entertained. When the signers of the Declaration of Independence declared boldly, "We hold these truths to be self-evident, that all men are created equal, that they are endowed by their Creator with certain inalienable Rights . . ." (U.S. 1776, para. 2), they knew that this was not everybody's view, and certainly not the view of the monarchical empire they opposed. And today, we have extended the notions of equality and rights in ways that would have surprised them, but which seem to us self-evident or intuitively obvious. Neither should we assume that we are at the end of history, or that our self-evident moral intuitions are infallible, or that our moral imagination and understanding is complete.

So let's now return to the question of intuition and rationality, armed with the ideas that we cannot have rationality without intuition, and that sensible people take intuitions, even basic ones, to be fallible. But for us to recognize fallibility is not to say that anything goes. In the trolley problems, for example, people differ over whether the value of reducing the death or suffering of innocent people is the *only* value at stake. But very few would deny that this is any value at all. And few would deny another core consideration, that, from a moral point of view, all persons are to receive equal concern. And, as we've noted, nearly everyone feels the pressure to treat like cases alike, hence the need to be able to say why Switch and Footbridge are not alike. These are values, concerns, or principles most of us find intuitively self-evident, and they seem to be implicitly at work in people's intuitive responses in these scenarios, *whichever side of the question they come down on intuitively.*

Of course, we all recognize that there can be considerations that *favor* causing harm in a given instance, even to innocent people, and even without their permission, such as cleaning the open wound of a child who cannot understand why this must be done. Part of the challenge of trolley problems is that either outcome results in harms to one or more innocent people, and these harms are not compensated— as they are in the case of the wounded child—by benefits to the same person or persons. According equal weight to each innocent death would seem to yield a clear verdict, but relatively few find Footbridge as clear a case as Switch. We therefore should be modest enough to think considerations of harm and equal treatment might not suffice to capture all of the morally-relevant dimensions involved in these cases. But we should not for that reason discount these concerns—good reasons seem to be needed to explain why they do not decide these cases, and the many others like them where intuitions seem to pull us in conflicting directions.

Now, let's return to Haidt's example of moral dumbfounding, the scenario Julie and Mark. Consider *Jane and Matthew*:

> Jane and Matthew are brother and sister. They are hiking together in Alaska on summer vacation from college. One night they are staying alone in a cabin in a high pass. They decide that it would be interesting and fun if they tried playing Russian roulette with the revolver they are carrying with them for protection from bears. At very least it would be a new experience for each of them. As it happens, when they spin the chambers and pull the trigger, the gun does not go off, and neither suffers any lasting trauma from the experience. They both enjoy the game, but decide not to do it again. They keep that night as a special secret, which makes them feel even closer to each other.

> *What do you think about that, was it OK for them to play Russian roulette with a loaded revolver?*

Was it? Whether or not the thought of Russian roulette triggers a flash of disgust in us, we can immediately appreciate as we read the story what a senseless loss it would have been had the gun gone off, and what a world of pain this would have left behind for the one who pulled the trigger, or for family and friends. Jane and Matthew carelessly put all this at risk for the sake of a potentially interesting and fun evening, to counteract mild boredom. This is not OK, despite the fortunate outcome.

Now return to the question of moral dumbfounding. By engaging in incestuous lovemaking, Julie and Mark were playing Russian roulette with their psyches simply to have an interesting and fun evening. Because they improbably got away with doing so without any lasting harm to their relationship, psyches, or present and future families does not show that their action was OK after all, any more than it does in the case of Jane and Matthew.

Haidt and colleagues concluded that subjects confabulated when they point to harmful results that *generally* arise from incest to justify their verdict on Julie and Mark. After all, these general harms did not arise in the case at hand. But *are* the generally harmful tendencies of a type of action actually irrelevant in moral assessment? Part of what made Julie and Mark's behavior "not OK" is that it involved a significant *risk* of bringing about such a typical consequence of incest as psychological trauma—a *general tendency* of such an action. Or what if contraception had failed—a less common, but entirely possible tendency—and a child had been conceived?

Let's return to the language for speaking of intuition developed in Chapter 2. As we read a scenario like Julie and Mark or Jane and Matthew, our mind constructs a predictive causal "model" of their situation as described, including their attitudes, the options they face, and the choices they make. This model supports predictive and evaluative *expectations* about, and *simulation* of, how the scene might evolve. We put ourselves in their situation, simulating not only what the scenario tells us explicitly, but many dimensions of the situation and possible outcomes not mentioned in the scenario. Our ability to do this reflects our own learning and empathic capacity, as well as the values of likely outcomes as represented in our own affective system. We are profoundly social creatures, and our brains were "built" for this sort of information-intense, but rapid predictive and evaluative modeling of actual or possible social situations, just as much as they were built for similar predictive modeling of the physical world or the mechanics of our own bodies. Our gut feeling that it would *not* be OK for them to engage in Russian roulette is more than a stomach pang. It is the upshot of such implicit social simulation and evaluation, just as much as your "uneasy feeling" in response to your colleague's invitation (in Chapter 2) seems unlikely to be a mere emotional flash of a myopic module, rather than the upshot of sophisticated and realistic implicit or explicit simulations and evaluations of the various outcomes that could arise from the answer you were about give.

Prospection, then, is at home in the heart of moral intuition as well as intuitions about our own lives and prospects. A primary role of emotion in morality is prospective. Guilt functions not only to "punish" us for previous wrongdoing, but more often (given that immoral conduct is the exception rather than the rule), it is the deterrent of *prospective* guilt that shapes our conduct as we imaginatively simulate a possible action and its potential outcomes (Ent & Baumeister, 2015; Moll, de Oliveira-Souza, & Zahn, 2008; Tangney, Stuewig, & Mashek, 2007).[4] Because the process of empathic simulation and evaluation is very rapid and largely implicit, individuals often have no direct insight into it, and so may draw a blank or fumble if asked to explain *why* they feel a given action should or should not be done. My experience is that, once people have heard the Jane and Matthew scenario, they have no difficulty in providing a justification for their negative verdict in Julie and Mark. It becomes quite clear that the question whether Julie and Mark's action was morally OK is not settled by the fortuitous fact that neither Julie nor Mark, nor anyone else, suffered any untoward consequences. Risk of negative social outcomes is not something we see with our eyes, but it is something to which we must be continually sensitive if we are to function well as social creatures. It was, for example, the risk of offending your colleague that explained your uneasiness about turning down his invitation, much as you might have wanted to. So moral evaluation, like all forms of evaluation relevant to action, is about *expected* as well as actual value.

Here we see an important feature of prospective empathic simulation, touched on in Chapter 2. The neuroscientific evidence suggests that we use our own affective system as the "test bed" for empathic simulation, but this does not mean we look at the situation of others entirely from our own point of view (Decety & Ickes, 2009; Ruby & Decety, 2001). On the contrary, in empathically simulating how your colleague might be hurt by your refusal, you put yourself into the position of someone who, unlike yourself, had *not* been promoted when others were, and who carries a bit of a chip on his shoulder. Your own affective system has the imaginative range to simulate this condition. Think of all the stories, dramas, and films that depend for their plots on our ability to understand "from the inside" the situation of those quite different from ourselves, and the logic of their thinking and acting as they do. When his situation is simulated, your affective system can then supply the social pain and anger "off line" that could result for your colleague from your refusal. Empathy was not designed simply to help us understand those who agree with us, but also to fathom our rivals and enemies, whose thoughts, feelings, and behaviors we must anticipate as best we can if we are to meet the challenges they pose or to spot the occasional instance when they are willing to work together with us, even when *we* were not planning on this (Hoffman, 2000). Simply carrying out a normal conversation involves a continuous need to place oneself in the other's shoes to interpret their words or make our own meaning clear to them.

Just as Lashley's and Tolman's rats exploring the maze developed *egocentric* maps of their location relative to the objects immediately around them to enable them to locate and orient themselves, they developed *allocentric* maps of the maze as a whole that they could use to prospect pathways that lay beyond their current visual horizon or to imagine and be ready to take shortcuts when the opportunity presented itself (Fyhn, Molden, Witter, Moser, & Moser, 2004; Gupta, van der Meer, Touretzky, & Redish, 2010; Ji & Wilson, 2007). It is no less vital that we be able to map our social situation allocentrically as well as egocentrically.

But what about the supposed evolutionarily engrained flash of disgust brought on by hearing of any incestuous activity, which is thought to block any further exploration of the risks, benefits, or costs at stake? Perhaps there is indeed such a flash—although incest also seems to have been a point of fascination and titillation in literature and soap operas—but it isn't obvious that such a response preempts further evaluation or refuses to budge as one engages in further thought. One of the key insights of recent research is that brain systems that previously had been thought of as "modular" and relatively compartmentalized, such as the five senses or affective versus cognitive systems, in fact interact pervasively and recruit whatever information they can from one another in order to improve performance. Taste, for example, recruits not only smell, but also visual and auditory information, as well as cognitive expectations and affective appraisal (Small, 2012). Even a seemingly basic or "primal" response, such as disgust at a smell, involves a complex synthesis of information from multiple senses and memory. Whether detecting volatile carboxylic acid disgusts or delights depends on whether one believes one is smelling ripe cheese or old socks.

Changing patterns of social behavior can effect just such alteration in the information people have to work with in forming their affective responses. Homosexuality has long figured in the psychological literature on disgust and has been grouped with disgust as has incest or bestiality (Haidt, McCauley, & Rozin, 1994), sometimes with a presumed evolutionary explanation that homosexual sexual activity does not yield replication of genetic material, so homosexual impulses must be resisted in much the same way that impulses to eat must be resisted when the food is potentially contaminated. Reactive disgust accomplishes this by making the stimulus less attractive and inducing rejection and withdrawal. Moreover, experimenters found evidence that increased disgust or sensitivity to disgust goes along with increased disapproval of homosexual relations (Inbar, Knobe, Pizarro, & Bloom, 2009; Lieberman & Smith, 2010). But a growing body of research suggests that intuitive affective reactions are not evidence-resistant "push-button" vestiges of evolution, but can be influenced extensively by individual and social learning (Blair, 2002; Tybur, Kurzban, Lieberman, & DeScioli, 2013). The "evolved function" of disgust, like all affective states, is not destiny; affective responses are influenced by changes in experience that alter individuals' information and evaluations. Stereotypes can be undermined in experience because statistical learning systems operate by discrepancy reduction. The result is that people do not simply see what they expect to see. As we saw in Chapter 2, in implicit mental processes, *incongruous* information receives special attention, as when infants not yet able to speak nonetheless pay greater attention to sequences of phonemes they have not yet heard (Saffran, Aslin, & Newport, 1996). Exposing people to subliminal images of *admired* individuals in stigmatized groups can result in less "automatic" stereotyping, even prior to any change in explicit or conscious bias (Dasgupta & Greenwald, 2001). And working together successfully with someone from a stigmatized or "alien" group on a meaningful project to which each contributes also reduces such implicit bias (Blincoe & Harris, 2009; Dasgupta, 2013).[5]

Such evidence is especially intriguing in light of the natural experiment over the last decade of changing attitudes on gay marriage, where rates of disapproval versus approval have inverted, so that now a majority favors granting legal recognition to gay marriage.[6] What brought about this change? Of course, many people have a principled opposition to discrimination on grounds such as sexual orientation, but changes in attitudes toward homosexual relations go much deeper. Fifteen years ago, a common unit in contemporary moral problems classes at universities was "the gay rights controversy." In recent years, it has become difficult to generate a sense among college students that there *is* a real controversy here. Today's undergraduates grew up in a world in which gay individuals were more open about their orientation, and as a result they have brothers, sisters, parents, relatives, teachers, and friends whom they know to be gay. Because their knowledge of *who* is gay is much more detailed and representative than that of the generations before them, their knowledge of *what gays are like* is also much more detailed and representative. Millennia of discrimination against gays and a supposedly evolutionarily entrenched or universal disgust response seem to have been counteracted to an impressive extent within one generation of highly informative actual experience. Our affective system will use the information it gets, and the wider and more representative the experience it has, the less it will rely on secondhand prejudice or evolutionary "defaults," and the more it will come to reflect the actual social reality around us. The tragedy of relations among African Americans and European Americans is that despite many changes in laws to prohibit discrimination, the life experience of members of both groups often does not contain a broad, representative sample of the other group involving an array of personal connections. By some measures, today's neighborhoods and public schools are *more* segregated than they were in 1990 (Anderson, 2010).

All of this is, unfortunately, very dry. It is hard to give a sense of how intuition involving prospective social simulation and evaluation might work in real time without producing some convincing examples. Because only words are available here, perhaps a somewhat less cartoonish story than the usual philosophers' scenarios will do. If we're right, your very ability to understand this story, as well as the story itself, will convey some sense of actual social and moral intuition at work in guiding thought and action in real time.

A high-powered attorney is working pro bono defending an individual from a disadvantaged and stigmatized group against an accusation of murder. The trial is nearing a close, and in her professional judgment everything seems to be going her way. Jury selection went well, and she had deftly cast doubt on the slipshod forensic evidence. The prosecutor had bungled numerous times, and rulings from the bench have all been in her favor. But now in these final days, a gnawing unease has grown within her. Leaving the courtroom on the next-to-last day of the trial—despite having just succeeded in trapping the prosecution's key witness, a petty criminal who's bargained his way to a lighter charge, in a blatant inconsistency during cross-examination—she feels defeated, not triumphant.

The attorney keeps thinking about her client, who has been sullen and uncommunicative throughout, and who gave her the facts she needed to corner the prosecution's key witness only after a series of tense, whispered exchanges during the cross-examination over the course of which she had interrogated him almost as sharply as the witness. But she was new to pro bono work, and she tells herself that this sort of sullen, distrustful attitude is typical of the kinds of defendants one encounters in pro bono cases. Who knows what they've been up to that makes them so uncomfortable in a court of law?

Still, she can't talk herself out of the sense that something's wrong. An image sticks in her mind. At the end of that day's session, just as she was turning to thank her client for giving her the information she'd needed, she received an urgent text from her firm. A major case was breaking. "Sorry, I have to take this," she said to her client, turning away. By the time she had turned back, he was already being led out of the courtroom in handcuffs. That evening, as she tries to work on her summary argument, she can't focus and finds herself rerunning the days' events in her mind, always coming back to the image of her client, head bowed, looking away from her, as he was led out of the courtroom. "What's with me?" she thinks, forcing herself to get back to work. "Well, at least tomorrow we're done with the trial. I'll be glad to have it over with."

The next morning, as she approaches the courthouse, her legs feel like lead and her stomach is tied in a knot. When her client is brought into the courtroom, she greets him and thanks him for his help yesterday, trying to be enthusiastic. He glances downward in silence, as he often does when she addresses him. But then he looks up and says with a slight smile she hadn't seen before, "Yeah. We got it done."

The session begins. Her summation is prepared, and still lacking any clue as to why she feels so uneasy, she resolves to stick to her tried-and-true formula: Walk the jury through the evidence and the law step by step, making the logic of her case seem inescapable. "Win their minds and you will win their hearts," she has always said.

But about a third of the way into the summation, hearing her own voice echoing back to her in the large courtroom and feeling in herself a strange reluctance to look the jurors in the eyes as she paces back and forth in front of them, her unease becomes unbearable. She feels distant, disconnected, lost. She shoots a nervous glance at her client. He's staring down, expressionless. She tries to buy time, "But before I continue with the evidence, let me remind you of the details of the charge brought against the defendant ... " This feels wooden, preachy, hopeless. Her throat is going dry and she's starting to flush deeply. It feels as if everyone must know that she's struggling. Once she has repeated the charge, she breaks off again.

With no new idea, she tries to pull herself together, straightening her tensed body, taking a long breath, and walking slowly over to the jury box. As she does so, she can't help taking another look at her client, who is now staring at her, his brow deeply furrowed. Is it worry or anger? She turns abruptly and makes herself try to look the jurors in the eye. Focusing her energy as best she can, she resumes speaking, though no longer in her courtroom voice, " . . . But I know that you know the facts of this case backwards and forwards. So what is there left to say?" She pauses awkwardly, her mind racing. More words come: "What's left is to talk about what this case is *really* about, which is why, however heinous the crime, however much we feel for the family of the victim, there will be no justice if we turn our anger on the wrong man. You might still feel hesitant, but there's one person who knows for sure that my client is innocent—the murderer himself, who's still out there, laughing at justice. My client just happened to be the right height, weight, . . . and color, and to have been in the wrong place at the wrong time. A convenient target for a prosecutor eager to get a conviction and able to produce a fake witness in return for copping a plea. But my client no more deserves life imprisonment than you or me. Throw the book at him and you'll close the book on this case, and the real murderer will roam the streets as free as ever. We must keep the book open, and find the man who really deserves our anger, and our righteous justice."

As she approaches the jury box, the jurors themselves shift in their chairs uneasily, looking away as she tries to catch their eyes. She is in unfamiliar territory, not seeing clearly where she is going, straining to keep her own concentration and composure. Having taken up the thread, she follows it, not stopping to ask where it is leading. She moves her eyes from face to face as slowly as she dares, trying to speak about the case as if talking to a friend late at night, her taut face and voice softening. One by one, the jurors stop staring at their shoes or looking past her and begin to meet her eyes and fix on what she is saying. As she explains what moved *her* about this case, she feels the emotion rising in her throat and notices that the eyes of an older man in the front row, who had sat steely faced throughout the trial, begin to tear up. Following where spontaneous thought and intense feeling had led her, she now senses that she must not drag this out. She must build to a conclusion.

But *what* conclusion?—She has no ringing phrases at the ready. Yet somehow, the words come. Barely controlling her voice, she says, "I have spoken to you from my heart. And I hope that I have reached your hearts. Because *that* is where you must search to find justice in this case. I know you will. Thank you. The defense rests." The courtroom is dead silent. Her legs are weak beneath her as she returns to her seat, but she feels that her work is done.

And she's right. The jury votes to acquit. Pressed by a colleague afterwards to say what led her to depart from her prepared summation and show her feelings, she draws a blank. "All I know is, at that moment I felt like I was talking to myself. Completely cut off. Nowhere, with no one listening. And I just couldn't go on. I *had* to do something. Somehow, when I slowed down and concentrated on their faces, trying to speak *to* them, the words began to come. My head was pounding, but I just tried to make sure I never lost eye contact. It began to feel like, 'Yes—keep going.' Don't ask me why."

Later the attorney learns indirectly that her trademark meticulous method had rubbed certain influential jurors the wrong way from the outset of the trial. She had come across as indifferent and remote—the words that got back to her were "cold," "phony," and "condescending"—while the prosecutor, legally outmaneuvered at every turn, nonetheless seemed to care strongly about the crime and its victim and to treat the jurors as equals. The jurors had come to distrust her and to resist believing what she was trying to establish. Her demolition of the prosecution witness felt to them cruel and overbearing. Sure, with her fancy education she could run circles around a petty criminal who never finished high school, but what did *that* prove? She was indeed about to lose the case.

Later still, she realizes something more. She *had* in some degree been remote, even phony and condescending. Her contempt for the prosecutor, her smug pleasure at outmaneuvering him and his witnesses, her evident sense that she, the fast-rising young attorney from a top firm, was the smartest person in the room, all came through loud and clear to everyone present. Palpable to everyone, too, was the distance between her and her own client. Sure of herself from the start, social distance had made her wary of him. Sure of her plan of attack, she hadn't listened carefully to what her client was trying to tell her from the outset. He had soon realized that he wasn't being listened to and became sullen and withdrawn. So she didn't learn the crucial information that truly convinced her of his innocence until the next-to-last day. She had been unconvincing, she realized, because she herself was unconvinced. And he had seemed alienated, because she was.

Working together that penultimate day for the first time, they had actually begun to trust one another a bit, despite her inquisitorial manner. Of course, she didn't recognize this at the time. All she had felt was a confused, nagging regret over her botched attempt to thank him in the aftermath of the cross-examination. So her growing unease had a double source, and her formulaic, one-size-fits-all summation felt inauthentic to her, too. That afternoon she had, just a bit, broken through the barriers of class and race to connect to him as an individual, and that lent a new urgency to everything else. The next day, delivering her routine summary felt wrong. And it was. No wonder she couldn't go on.

Sometimes it is said that developing a skill or expertise is a matter of performing certain actions so frequently that they become "automatic," no longer requiring the effortful, conscious attention or thought of a novice. The model here is inherited from a now-outdated conception of reinforcement learning in animals, in which repeated performance with reinforcement is said to ingrain a "motor pattern" that is "triggered" by a particular stimulus situation, so that the "conditioned" motor response emerges automatically in response to the stimulus.

Although our trial lawyer did not act *deliberatively* in departing from her stock summation—indeed, she acted in violation of her explicit deliberative resolution—she certainly wasn't acting "automatically" in this sense, or from habit. On the contrary, she had snapped out of her familiar role and routine, and her mind was working flat out, wholly focused and drawing on all her resources, perceptual, intellectual, and emotional. In the earlier days of the trial she had begun implicitly to detect certain signs—facial expressions, body language—that she was losing touch with jurors. These gave rise to the unease within her, undermining her confidence and sapping her motivation, even if she could not say why. Then, on the next-to-last day, the intense experience of working together successfully under pressure had moved attorney and defendant *out* of their accustomed frameworks of social distance. Her frustrated effort to thank him, only to see him led away, unacknowledged, put her in the position of sensing with sudden clarity how she must look to him, and how he might have felt distrusted and excluded by her. As he became more of a person in her own mind, the injustice that would be done *to him* if the jury convicted came home to her, igniting her own sense of injustice. What might under ordinary circumstances have felt like nothing worse than flatness—doing her job in a professional way, glad to be getting to the end of the trial—now felt like something she could not abide, a personal betrayal.

When she finally yielded to intuition, what spontaneously felt right was to step out of her distant, professional manner, to try to reconnect with her client, and to reach across the gulf between her and the jury, speaking to them as one human to another, letting her passion and sense of injustice show. In the end, she was pouring everything she had into it, and becoming frank and eloquent in ways that surprised her, yet which *were*, at bottom, expressive of her and her deepest values. However remote and condescending her initial attitudes might have been, she was there, doing pro bono work, because she *did* care about seeing justice done. One is never more present, alive to the world, and human—never less automatic in one's thought and action, or inattentive to the values at stake—than when one rises to the occasion in this way.

Nonetheless, the attorney's turnaround that morning and eventual success should somewhat puzzle us. With no clear insight into the source of her unease, what could account for the unplanned yet effective coordination of all her faculties in shaping how she eventually responded? No merely linguistic competence or expertise in the law could explain all that she went through that morning or the day before, or enabled her finally to find her own voice when all appeared lost.

The competencies underlying such a spontaneous, effective response no doubt had many sources. There was her explicit and implicit experience in the courtroom and with her client over the last few days; there were years of legal practice, honing skills of interrogation, exposition, and persuasion; there was her powerful mind, emotional intelligence, and skills at connecting with people enlarged and refined over a lifetime. These skills included a capacity to read others' faces or behavior, to feel something of what they feel, to sense when she has someone's trust, to overcome others' defenses by letting her own guard down, to keep focused despite high anxiety and uncertainty, to persist in the face of frustration, and to stick up for what she believes in. Hard at work, too, was a very high level of sociolinguistic competence, having the right words for addressing this jury just come to her, so that she could both express her own heartfelt concerns and reach across to, and move, those who had become so distant.

But pulling back, we can also see in the defense attorney's thoughts, feelings, and behavior other conflicting strains. Her ability to use the full resources of her complex internal model of social interactions had been restricted by social preconceptions and prejudices that led her, implicitly, to discount her client's trustworthiness and competency to contribute to his own defense. Given a lifelong experience of a society divided by class and race, such implicit tendencies operated within her—as they operated within her client, and indeed as they operate within all of us—even against her own judgment and ideals, coloring her thoughts and actions in ways that cannot be detected introspectively or controlled at will. These implicit attitudes set the stage for their initial, failed interactions and might have persisted unchallenged throughout the trial had not the critical cross-examination driven them to work together and broken down the set-piece character of their relationship, giving her a sense of distress about failing to thank him, and bringing to his mind the "we" in "We got it done."

This incomplete summary of all the capacities and attitudes that might be at work over the course of the trial suggests why undergoing this turnaround and salvaging the case by acting intuitively took everything the defense attorney had.

The undramatic intuitions of everyday life—what strikes one as the right gift for a friend, sounds like a bad idea for a sales presentation, or smells fishy as an excuse, even though one is hard-pressed to say exactly why—also typically draw on wider personal resources as well as more specialized competencies. Given the volume of sensory information we take in at each moment, the varied needs and goals we seek to meet, and the complex personal relationships and social environments we inhabit, the conscious, deliberate mind could hardly manage everything on its own. It must continuously depend on the experienced discernment exercised by our underlying perceptual, cognitive, and emotional capacities as we find our way through life.

And it must depend on our moral capacities as well. For it was an incongruity with the defense attorney's *values* and her commitment to her client, not just the prospect of a failed case, which eventually stopped our lawyer in her practiced, professional tracks and brought up from within her the resources to bring her values and commitment to life. Perhaps what made it possible for her to *detect* this incongruity, *feel* it as she went through her final summation, and *respond* to it aptly, had to do with her implicit competence in modeling the social situation in which she found herself. By forcing herself to look the jurors in the eye, she stimulated her ability empathically to simulate the state of mind of the jurors and thereby imagine how things looked to them and what optic on the case might really be accessible to them or convincing for them. The unease about whether she was actually getting through to the jury had been building for several days, and it had become so palpable and strong that she could not ignore it. Her sense of the hopelessness of continuing as planned and renewed sense of the urgency of the situation and of the injustice that would be done to her client if she did not somehow connect with the jurors, intensified her focus and motivation in a way that enabled her to bring all of her intelligence and skills—in thinking, feeling, and speaking—to bear. She had, on this picture, created a dynamic evaluative representation of her situation and of its prospects and perils for the fundamental values at stake, and she was able to follow the intuitive action-guidance this "expected moral value" representation generated for her. Her implicit social competency became part of her implicit moral competency.

At least, this is what a prospection-based explanation of her thought, feeling, and action might look like. Intuition, whether in language, social action, or moral evaluation, need not be a mystery, a black box from which judgments emerge without explanation. Neither does the fact that intuitive moral judgments often appear to involve affect tell against their sensitivity to reasons and values. That is why the intuition is not an accident. Intuition is why native German speakers have a better ear for what sounds right in their language than high schoolers taking third-year German; why highly experienced mariners have a better sense of how to respond to a sudden storm than landlubbers; why professional basketball players can read the opportunities of a situation on court better than spectators (Yarrow, Brown, & Krakauer, 2009); and why people who have less well-developed empathic abilities tend to show lower "emotional intelligence" and related difficulties in seeing intuitively what to do in social situations (Baron-Cohen & Wheelwright, 2004; Mayer, Caruso, & Salovey, 1999; Mayer & Gehrer, 1996). If the prospection hypothesis is right, then it should also help us remove some of the mystery from *moral* intuitions, and to understand better what is going on in people's immediate responses to hypothetical scenarios as posed by moral philosophers.

The philosophical method of inducing us through examples to imaginatively simulate hypothetical scenarios, and then asking us to evaluate several possible actions and outcomes in response to those scenarios, is actually an instance of what we have been arguing is the core business of prospective action guidance. If we are indeed equipped by the architecture of mind for prospective social action guidance, then that would explain why this example-based method is so readily intelligible to those upon whom it is practiced, and why they seem quite capable of answering the questions rapidly, without extensive deliberation. At the same time, because prospection normally proceeds by implicit simulation and evaluation, it is perhaps unsurprising that people so often are much more prepared with a *response* to these hypothetical scenarios than they are with an *explanation* of this response, since so much of what lies behind those answers is not readily available to introspection.

Of course, it would be a poor large-scale psychological hypothesis that could only explain such an esoteric phenomenon as the philosophical use of (often bizarre) thought experiments in ethics. What about our everyday life? Is it a prominent feature of our ordinary lives to engage in anything like this kind of prospective simulation and moral evaluation of possibilities?

Before taking that question on squarely, let's look at two phenomena tightly intertwined with everyday moral thought and practice. First, *stories* have a powerful grasp on people's thoughts and feelings. Whether in the form of Icelandic sagas, Mayan creation myths, children's books, Hollywood action movies, romantic novels, top-40 hit songs, sacred texts, or soap operas and television dramas, people invest an extraordinary amount of emotional energy and time living within the world of created stories. Why should this be if the people and events in these stories do not exist and are not in a position to threaten us with any material risk or provide us any material benefit?

Yet we go on creating, telling, reading, watching, reflecting on, and discussing or arguing about stories. Subtract all the stories from our cultural record, including story-laden history, music, paintings, and sculptures, and the buildings, artifacts, abstract art, and absolute music that would be left would say surprisingly little of the distinctive character and occasional greatness of spirit of humankind to an alien visitor.

One might say that there's no real puzzle here because we simply find stories entertaining and sometimes moving. But why should *that* be? What is so interesting or occasionally so exciting, wrenching, or gratifying about stories of people we will never meet? One suggestion would be that creatures built for prospection are built to imagine alternate possible ways the world might be and to take an interest following them out and evaluating them, *whether their own interests are involved or not.* If "merely possible" stories and characters and "mere fictions in the mind" could not move us, then we could not imagine and respond evaluatively to all the branching future paths—the different combinations of persons, actions, and outcomes—we must consider if we are to prospect well, even with respect to our own lives. Deficits in empathy, it has been argued, are not simply deficits in the ability to imagine what life is like for others, but deficits in the ability to imagine what our own lives would be like in circumstances that are as yet merely possible (Baron-Cohen, 1997). Empathic simulation, then, is not in itself a *moral* attitude or capacity. In competitive tennis, for example, players use empathy to simulate their opponents' likely behavior, and thus locate their shots where it will be most difficult for their opponents to return them. Empathic simulation is *ubiquitous*, as our discussion of the default network in Chapter 4 suggested.

A second feature of our daily lives that prospection helps us make sense of is our inveterate tendency to *gossip* (Dunbar, 1996; Sabini & Silver, 1982). Gossip certainly engages us for the same reasons stories do, but there is more. Gossip is by its nature *sharing* a discussion of the stories of others' lives, and this sharing has a purpose beyond information gathering and imaginative engagement. By trying to piece together stories with one another, and to think through and compare our reactions to these stories, we are able to leverage our own imaginative and empathic capacities with those of others, and to focus especially on the crucial question of how to *respond* to individuals and events in the social world around us. Depending on our relationship with one another, we might coordinate or calibrate our responses, validate or challenge one another's responses, or give each other insight into how the larger society will view the reactions they are having or the behaviors they are contemplating. Gossip, then, is not just a matter of talking down those who aren't present, it is a way of thinking aloud with others about what to feel and how to act. Looked at in this way, we can see that gossip often *is* a form of prospection, a way of developing a shared simulation of how the target of gossip thinks and feels and how he or she will, therefore, likely act and be judged. If you feel outraged by the behavior of certain friends and ready to act against them, and yet cannot find any resonance for your feelings in the feelings of other friends or any sense of the appropriateness of the actions you are planning, your internal map of the social prospects and perils you face might need updating.

Let us now return to morality. What to think, how to feel, or whether to act are all questions of how we *ought* to live our lives, of what is *appropriate*, not simply questions of how we *do* or *will* live our lives. The stories and gossip that most engage us are those that raise questions not only about how people *do* think, feel, and act, but about how they *ought* to. This ranges from the explicitly moralizing character of a children's story or a religious parable to the complex moral entanglements and ambiguities of a successful soap opera or television drama.

Contemplating the world from the perspective of asking how one *ought* to think, feel, or act has a *prescriptive* or *commending* character that inevitably points beyond the individual case or what has transpired in the past and carries an implication for how one should go on to think, act, and feel. As the philosopher David Hume argued three centuries ago, and as Aristotle argued two millennia ago, moral evaluation typically takes as its object not just a bit of behavior, but a combination of circumstance, action, and agent—a *story*, however brief, of what has happened or could happen. If you tell a friend that someone has cut your arm today, your friend will not know how to respond morally without knowing whether the arm-cutting was the work of a stranger bent on taking your wallet, an incision by a surgeon removing a cyst, or a desperate act of potential suicide you managed to restrain. You must provide a *model*, large or small, of what happened and why. And this model will tell your friend not only what happened, but with what motive or precipitating circumstance, toward what end, and with what connection to your own will. Moral judgment is essentially *general*, not in the sense that we always rely on general principles (often, it seems, we do not), but in the sense that when we make a moral judgment, we are committed to "treat like cases alike." If we label our neighbor's act of failing to declare income to avoid taxes as wrong, we must be prepared to see our own actions judged to be wrong should we likewise seek to avoid taxes by failing to declare income. "Treat like cases alike" is a fundamental requirement of morality and the law, and it attests to the prescriptive and commending character of both. In moral and legal judgments, we are deciding about *how to go on* as well as *what has already been*. Interestingly, and for the same reasons, this requirement is a constraint in gossip as well: "What's sauce for the goose is sauce for the gander."

Let's now return to the problem of trying to understand "moral intuition" in the well-known moral dilemmas that tend to dominate popular discussions of moral philosophy. Recall the challenge of understanding why so many think it appropriate to tug on the steering wheel in Farmers' Market or to push the lever in Switch, but so many think it inappropriate to push the man onto the tracks below in Footbridge. The literature on such cases is vast, and thus far, no real consensus has been reached among the many philosophers and psychologists who have studied these cases. Might the notion of prospection enable us to add something that has been missing and that might make more sense of the seeming puzzle of asymmetric judgments?

One might try asking what moral assessment is *for*. This is a question of which moral philosophers have rightly been suspicious. Moral life is obviously complex and sensitive to a wide range of features of the human condition, psyche, and history. Moral life, moreover, seems to serve many functions: Moral norms and attitudes can be seen as fostering coordination and cooperation, encouraging mutual respect, stabilizing property, helping reduce selfishness, and assuring that basic needs are met for those unable to care for themselves, and so on. But moral norms and attitudes are not all sweetness and light. They also figure in social domination and subordination, and in self-righteousness and cycles of revenge. What sense would it make to say that morality is *for* any one of these purposes, and what would be our evidence?

Let's, however, consider a more limited question: not what morality is for, but what moral *assessment* might be for. These are different questions. For example, it is unclear what one would say *beauty* or *aesthetic value* is for. An evolutionary theorist might say that physical beauty is a marker of health and, thus, good reproductive potential, but relative rates of replication of genetic material do not seem to be at the bottom of what interests people in aesthetic judgment. We can make a start on an answer to why people are so readily engaged in making and sharing assessments of beauty and aesthetic value by pointing to the tremendous satisfaction to be gained from an appreciation of things of beauty and aesthetic value, and the fact that others often can provide us with reliable information about sources of aesthetic value we might have missed. So a practice of making and sharing such assessments and being guided by them in our choices can contribute importantly to the quality of our lives. No one needs to force us to engage in this practice: We go in for it spontaneously, whether in matters of the visual beauty of landscapes, the aural beauty of music, the deliciousness of food, or the power of a film.

Similarly, even if we cannot give a simple answer to the question of what morality is for, we might be able to identify some basic features that would help explain why we would spontaneously engage in a shared practice of moral assessment. For example, it matters very much to the quality of our lives whether we live in a social milieu—a neighborhood, family, workplace, society—in which people are to a considerable degree decent, trustworthy, considerate, respectful, cooperative, brave, and generous in their attitudes, motivations, and conduct. And it matters very much to identify those around us who are, in the circumstances in which we encounter them, prone to aggression, violence, selfishness, deception, recklessness, cowardice, and manipulation. Some of these traits matter most in good times; others matter most in bad times. These tendencies can be found in almost all of us, so the question is what sort of balance these tendencies exhibit in individuals or groups over time, and what sorts of conditions encourage what sorts of attitudes, motivations, and behaviors? We need to know *what we can expect from others or from ourselves* or *what to anticipate from certain kinds of actions and circumstances* and *how this will change the quality of the lives affected.* In short, we need *prospective evaluation* along dimensions that correspond to those of moral evaluation. After all, if the practice of making and sharing moral assessments enabled us to gain a more objective assessment of the prospects of our actions and those of others, this would surely be a strong reason to engage in such assessment.

How might the idea that moral evaluation affords a more objective representation of the expected value or disvalue of actions and outcomes help us to understand the trolley problems? We have already suggested how a tacit social competency in the assessment of actions, situations, and outcomes could play a role in generating intuitive evaluative judgments, as in the case of the trial lawyer. Is there evidence that such a competency might underlie moral intuitions?

In a series of studies dating back to the 1970s, psychologists have found that even preschool children are able to distinguish between conventional norms ("You must ask permission to go to the bathroom") and moral norms ("You must not take others' lunches without their permission") and to understand that conventional norms depend on particular practices or rules that are subject to arbitrary change, while moral norms cannot be overridden or replaced in this way by those "in charge" of a situation or institution. Moreover, these children understand that moral norms are related to matters of potentially serious harm, and *that* is part of why they cannot be changed at will (Nucci & Nucci, 1982; Turiel, 1983). This implicit competency helps children contend with complex social situations in which there is pressure on them to violate a harm-based norm because "someone says so." Even if they cannot always resist such pressure, they can also understand a more objective framework standing in the background against which such pressure can be judged inappropriate.

Moral evaluation is objective in another sense as well: It is substantially independent of *one's own* particular thoughts or goals, so that one's own interests need not be affected for a moral concern to arise. But do children really have such "interest-independent," non-egocentric ways of viewing things? Using techniques such as eye-tracking, attention-fixation, and preference expression, psychologists have been able to explore the mind of prelinguistic infants and have found that it is remarkably sophisticated in understanding the social world *from other points of view*. Early on, it was observed that infants as young as 2 years could group actions together by their pro- or anti*social* valence, not just their physical similarity or benefit to the self. For example, they could group together cartoon objects shown to be caressing and helping and cartoon objects shown to be hitting and hindering, even though the caressing and hitting behaviors were *physically* more similar in their immediately observable features, as were the helping and hindering behaviors (Premack & Premack, 1997). Young children often have difficulty explicitly attributing beliefs to others that they do not themselves share, the so-called false belief task. In one version of this task, children watch as a puppet named Sally places her marble in a basket and leaves the room, but then another puppet named Anne comes in and moves the marble into her own container, a box. "When Sally comes back," the psychologist asks the infant, "where will she look for her marble—the basket or the box?" Prior to the age of 3 or 4 years, children regularly answer, "The box," which is where they themselves know the marble to be, even though Sally could have no idea of this. But a study of the eye motion of children as young as 15 months reveals that their eyes move first to the basket, the correct response (Onishi & Baillargeon, 2005). In other words, infants show greater social understanding *implicitly* rather than explicitly. Perhaps, indeed, it is the early implicit understanding of the intentional structure of the situation that helps cue their later, explicit recognition. Notably, the implicit understanding is also more *objective*, in the sense that it embodies an ability to attribute a mental state to others that oneself does not accept.

An even more striking exhibition of early non-egoistic social cognition is found in the work of Kiley Hamlin and colleagues (Hamlin & Wynn, 2011), who used puppets to enact scenarios in which one geometric shape (a triangle with eyes, say) helps another geometric shape (a circle with eyes) in moving up the side of a steep hill, while, in another scenario, a third shape (a square with eyes) hinders the same uphill movement by the circle. Offered a choice of which puppet to play with at the end of the scenarios, infants as young as 6 to 9 months preferred the "helper" puppet. Notice that understanding these scenarios requires the infants to impute a goal to the circle, namely, trying to move up the hill, and different goals to the triangle and circle, helping or hindering the square, respectively. Notice, too, that the infants' preferences reflect a comparative assessment of the two puppets in scenes where the infants themselves have nothing to gain or lose—the preference seems therefore to reflect a *generic* rather than ego-centric evaluation. The complex layering of this intentional representation of the situation was made evident in later experiments, which showed that very young infants also preferred puppets that *hindered* hinderers over puppets that helped them (Hamlin, 2013).

Studies imputing mental states to preverbal infants, and especially infants in the first year of life, must always be treated with caution, lest we over-interpret in an effort to make infants more like ourselves. Perhaps surprisingly, however, it might be said that there was long a tendency to treat very young infants as too little like adults—to see their thinking as concrete, unstructured, dominated by immediate experience. Yet, as we have seen earlier, several decades of study have provided impressive evidence that very young children are capable of thinking in abstract, causal terms, and of attending to experience in ways that resemble rational learners trying to understand the world around them—including of course the social world (Wellman, 2014).

An implicit ability to model and evaluate the intentional structure of actions relevant to moral assessment thus seems to emerge very early in life. That this model is implicit is suggested by study of eye movement based on the well-documented premise that infants look longer at phenomena that *violate* their expectations. As we noted in Chapter 2, it has been found that infants as young as 15 months are able to detect the correct option in the "false-belief task" even before they are able to give the correct response verbally (Onishi & Baillargeon, 2005). The false-belief task reveals infants' ability to attribute to imagined other children beliefs that the infants do not themselves have and to use this false belief to predict the imagined children's behavior. This is, in effect, an allocentric rather than egocentric mapping of the mental attitudes present (Wellman & Bartsch, 1988). So, while normal infants tend to give an egocentric *explicit* representation of the task prior to their third or fourth year (Wellman, Cross, & Watson, 2001), a year or more earlier, at the *implicit* level, their eye movements are already tracking the correct prediction that would be made by an allocentric representation. Children with apparent deficits in empathy cannot solve the false-belief task verbally until several years later and do not show the same anticipatory eye movements earlier on. Finally, studies of normal children as they move through elementary school show a steady progression toward an ability to distinguish between intentional harm and unintentional harm and a disposition to evaluate intentional harm more severely, even though the physical harm done is the same (Baird & Astington, 2004; Young, Cushman, Hauser, & Saxe, 2007).

Pulling these strands of evidence together, we believe that, just as linguistic competence emerges reliably in young children through an underlying capacity to make linguistic discriminations and learn language regularities, so might infants' capacity for non-egocentric evaluation of social interactions, linked perhaps to their capacity for empathic simulation, form the basis of an evaluative competence that will enable them to discriminate morally relevant dimensions of behavior and make moral (or proto-moral) assessments of actions and agents. Normally developing infants show a persistent preference for communicating with others, and similarly they show a persistent preference for prosocial behavior in real and imagined others (Hamlin & Wynn, 2011). Indeed, it seems plausible that language competency and social competency proceed together, and that a capacity for empathic simulation plays an important role in understanding and evaluating others' verbal as well as social behavior (Guiora, Brannon, & Dull, 1972).

Thus far, no consensus has emerged concerning the learning processes by which children acquire linguistic or social competency or what sorts of underlying, preexisting capacities are drawn on in such learning (for defense of a Bayesian approach, see Wellman, 2014). But enough strands of evidence have emerged from enough directions to make the idea of an implicit proto-moral social competency akin to implicit linguistic competency a promising hypothesis. In each case, a tacit competency could be the source of intuitive evaluation and action guidance, even in the absence of an ability to explain the assessments in question. And in each case, the tacit competency is *generative*, that is, it is not a mere storehouse of past experience, but an ability to use experience to respond adaptively to new hypothetical or actual situations. That is, these competencies are prospective in nature.

But this is still speculative, and what if the evidence suggests that things are just the other way around? What if people's underlying models of others' behavior are *driven* by their personal moral points of view, rather than by an acquired tacit competency that develops a more objective, third-personal empathic mapping of the motives, attitudes, aims, and outcomes characteristic of intentional action? This challenge has been poised sharply by Josh Knobe's influential work relating moral evaluations to the imputation of intentionality in individual actions (2010).

Knobe began by collecting a random sample of experimental subjects and dividing it into two groups. To the first group, he poses the following scenario (2010, p. 317), which we will call *Boardroom Harm*:

> The [vice president] of a company went to the chairman of the board and said, "We are thinking of starting a new program. It will help us increase profits, but it will also harm the environment." The chairman of the board answered, "I don't care at all about harming the environment. I just want to make as much profit as I can. Let's start the new program." They started the new program. Sure enough, the environment was harmed.
>
> *Did the chairman intentionally harm the environment?* [emphasis added]

Most will say, without needing to reflect, yes. What happens, however, when we propose a very slightly different scenario to the individuals in the other half of the sample? Here is *Boardroom Help*:

> The [vice president] of a company went to the chairman of the board and said, "We are thinking of starting a new program. It will help us increase profits, and it will also help the environment." The chairman of the board answered, "I don't care at all about helping the environment. I just want to make as much profit as I can. Let's start the new program." They started the new program. Sure enough, the environment was helped.
>
> *Did the chairman intentionally help the environment?* [emphasis added]

Most will say, without needing to reflect, no.

Yet what is the difference between the two scenarios except for replacing the *word* "harm" with "help?" Knobe concludes that "people's *moral* judgments can actually influence the intuitions they hold both in folk psychology and in causal cognition." One's own values seem to be entering into what should be one's impartial representation of the intentional structure of an action (2010, p. 315). This seems to be just the opposite of what prospective assessment, based on a capacity for non-egocentric analysis and evaluation of social behaviors, would predict.

But do these paired examples show that people's ordinary judgments of intentionality are moralistic or are they centered on their own values? Consider now a third scenario, *Goat Help*:

> You are a goat herder living on a hillside above a remote village. Your uphill neighbor has an orchard of olive trees. One day you are browsing the shelves in the agricultural supply store in the village, when you overhear your neighbor being told by the man at the register, "Yes, you could use this spray on your trees, and it would kill all the bugs, but when the rain comes it will wash off and run down onto your neighbor's fields, killing the bugs in her grass and helping her goats." You listen intently for his answer, which is quick in coming: "I don't care at all about helping her goats, I just want to kill the bugs on my olive trees. Give me the spray."

Let's assume what the prospective account suggests, which is that when you read this scenario you tacitly simulate *both* your own imagined state of mind and the state of mind of the neighbor, and use this information to form an expected value assessment of this action and the individual taking it.

Take your neighbor's state of mind first. Will it be a cold indifference to whether he helps you? Your tacit social competency assesses this as a negative, but it is hardly extraordinary for someone to be selfish in this way. Now take your own state of mind. How alarmed are you? You are concerned about such indifference, but you also need not take any particular steps to protect yourself from it. Now pull back your simulative focus to include others in the community. Imagine another neighbor, who hears you complain that this man doesn't care at all about helping you. Will this neighbor feel any alarm, sympathy, or concern? A bit, maybe.

Now consider a slightly different scenario, *Goat Harm*:

> You are a goat herder living on a hillside above a remote village. Your uphill neighbor has an orchard of olive trees. One day you are browsing the shelves in the agricultural supply store in the village, when you overhear your neighbor being told by the man at the register, "Yes, you could use this spray on your trees, and it would kill all the bugs, but when the rain comes it will wash off and run down onto

your neighbor's fields, harming her goats when they eat the grass."
You listen intently for his answer, which is quick in coming: "I don't
care at all about harming her goats, I just want to kill those bugs. Give
me the spray."

What state of mind do you simulate in your neighbor as you contemplate this scenario? Is it a selfish indifference or something much
more callous or ruthless: a willingness to harm animals and damage
another's livelihood, perhaps seriously, without compunction? And
what state of mind do you simulate in yourself? Very likely, it is
alarm and an urgent need to be vigilant to see whether your neighbor goes through with his plan. Pulling back the focus, could you
expect other neighbors to share your alarm and show sympathetic
concern for your plight? How comfortable will *they* be living alongside this man?

Goat Help and Goat Harm suggest that Boardroom Harm and
Boardroom Help are less symmetrical than they first appeared. Intuition
makes use of whatever evidence it can, and given our experience, someone who "doesn't care at all" about whether he harms his neighbors is,
happily, statistically rare, while someone who "doesn't care at all" about
whether he helps his neighbors is, perhaps regrettably, much more
common. Statistical learning systems pay special attention to anomalies
because they carry more information than events that are more predictable. The attitude of the chairman in Boardroom Harm and the neighbor in Goat Harm attract such attention, and in real life these attitudes
would indeed be viewed as more antisocial than the attitude of the chairman in Boardroom Help and the neighbor in Goat Help, and as calling for greater than normal vigilance on the part of others.[7] Because an
action in which one knowingly, willing, and with indifference harms another as a completely foreseeable side effect is commonsensically understood to be antisocial—not to mention being a tort at law—the actions in
Boardroom Harm and Goat Harm are seen as *congruent* with the relatively antisocial attitudes expressed by the chairman and neighbor, and
presumably indicative of their underlying motivational structure and
values. It is natural, therefore, for intuition to treat these actions on their
part as to that extent more intentional. By contrast, the indifference expressed by the chairman in Boardroom Help and the neighbor in Goat
Help toward the completely foreseeable side effect of helping others
is *not* commonsensically seen as signaling the presence of a relatively

prosocial attitude on their part. So an act with the prosocial side effect of *helping* others is not particularly congruent with their attitudes, and to that extent is intuitively seen as less intentional.

What may matter in such intuitive social attributions of intent with respect to side effects is the fit of the action with the causal-attitudinal-intentional model of the agent we tacitly construct in light of the person's behavior (e.g., as antisocial versus self-concerned versus prosocial) rather than the moral quality of the side effect itself. Recently, experimental evidence points to a *mediation* of people's judgment of intentionality in cases like Boardroom Harm versus Boardroom Help by an implicit model of the mentality of the chairman (Konrath & Sripada, 2011; Sripada, 2012), suggesting that we rely on a "deep self" construction in interpreting social behavior. Here values *do* enter, but they are not the values of the person making the assessment; they are the imputed values suggested by the behavior of the individual being assessed.

From the standpoint of prospection, when we read scenarios like Boardroom or Goat, part of what we are tacitly asking is what we can expect from a person with such apparent values, motives, and attitudes. After all, moral judgments will be much more useful for individuals and society alike (recall the pervasive role of stories and gossiping in our lives) if they are predictive. As we said earlier in discussing the impartiality or allocentric mapping of empathy, it is vitally important for us to be able to gauge others' attitudes and intentions accurately, even and perhaps especially, when they are at odds with our own. It would be surprising, then, if our causal-attitudinal-intentional prediction of others were skewed so strongly by *our own* moral values, rather than tracking evidence of the values of others and thus, crucially, of their likely behavior.

We can now return to the trolley problems. As we saw, Greene and colleagues (2009) concluded that the asymmetry in intuitive moral acceptability in the well-known trolley cases arises because in Footbridge, but not Switch, "the force that directly impacts the victim is generated [by] the agent's muscles (e.g., in pushing)" (Greene et al., 2009, p. 364). Yet consider the following scenario, called *Bus*:

> You live in a city where terrorists have in recent months been suicide-bombing buses and trains. The terrorists strap explosives to themselves under their clothing and, at busy times of the day, spot a crowded bus

or train and rush to board it, triggering the bomb as they enter the vehicle in order to avoid being stopped by the passengers. You are on a very crowded bus at 5:10 p.m., and struggling to get out the door at your stop. The doors are starting to close and you won't be able to squeeze off unless you jostle the slow-moving, portly gent trying to exit at the same time. Suddenly you notice a man who is running up to the bus door. His coat is open in front, and through the opening, you see bombs strapped to his chest and his finger on a trigger.

You can't reach the bomber directly, but if you right now push the portly gentleman beside you hard into the path of the oncoming bomber, the portly gentleman will fall directly on top of the bomber and flatten him against the sidewalk. You will fall back into the bus and the doors will slam shut. The bomber won't make it onto the bus and the bomb will explode underneath the portly gentleman, killing them both, but not affecting the people on the bus. And not affecting you.

Alternatively, you could simply continue exiting the bus alongside the portly gentleman, shouting, "Watch out, a bomber!" but allowing the bomber to squeeze on board the bus just behind the portly gentleman and before the doors slam shut. The bomb will go off immediately once he's on the bus and kill five people onboard. But you and the portly gentleman will be safely on the sidewalk outside.

Either way, you will not be killed. And either way, the bomber himself will die. The difference is whether one man is killed on the sidewalk as a result of your pushing him on top of the bomber, as opposed to five other people dying on the bus as a result of the bomber getting aboard after you and the portly gentleman exit.

Should you push the portly gentleman on top of the bomber?

Recently, when this scenario was presented in my undergraduate ethics course, 63% of students said they thought they should push the man into the bomber, while 35% thought they should not.[8] This is virtually the same as Switch (67% vs. 33%). Why, if Bus involves using one's "direct muscular force" to send a man to a grisly death, just like Footbridge, doesn't it have the disapproval rate of Footbridge (31% vs. 69%)?

How might one's tacit social competence be responding in Bus versus Footbridge? First, try to imagine yourself starting to get off the bus and seeing the onrushing bomber. Can you vividly imagine—under what feels to you like life-or-death pressure—actually laying your hands on the large gentleman beside you, feeling the heft of his body, and shoving him with all your might in the direction of the bomber? Now, try to imagine yourself on the Footbridge, beside the large gentleman as the trolley is approaching underneath. Can you vividly imagine—under what feels to you like life-or-death pressure—actually laying your hands on the large gentleman beside you, feeling the heft of his body, and shoving him with all your might off the footbridge and into the path of the speeding trolley? I will guess that, for many of you, as for myself, the answer to the first question is that you *can* credibly imagine this, but in the second case you cannot—even if you are inclined to judge that the heavy man *should* be pushed in Footbridge.

Now imagine the social setting. Imagine those on the bus who see the apparent bomber's approach and see your situation in the doorway, separated from the apparent bomber by a large, oblivious man. Can you also imagine them shouting to you, "Push him, for God's sake!"? By contrast, imagine the five track workers seeing the trolley hurtling toward them and seeing you on the bridge next to the large man. Can you also imagine them shouting up to you, "Push him, for God's sake!"?

Now try to imagine the aftermath of pushing in each case and imagine that in Footbridge, you succeeded in stopping the trolley and that in Bus, the explosion took place on the sidewalk, killing the large gentleman and the bomber, but sparing you and everyone on the bus. You now have to bear the awful fact of having pushed an innocent man to his death. In which case, if either, can you imagine bearing this more easily? And is the mixture of feelings involved—guilt, regret, shame, disgrace—the same in each case? For which, if either, can you imagine that others, including members of the innocent victim's own family, might show more acceptance, understanding, or forgiveness of your action? Or imagine that you failed to push the man in each scenario. In Bus, can you imagine feeling haunted by guilt or regret? Can you imagine that others would understand if you did? Now imagine not pushing in Footbridge. Would this haunt you in the same way? And would others understand equally well if it did?

If you are like me, you will *feel* asymmetries between Bus and Footbridge when taking up these different simulations, asymmetries that parallel the original felt asymmetry between Bus and Footbridge. They are all of a piece. This suggests that the asymmetry at work here is relatively standpoint-independent: It has to do with an implicit, shared social understanding of the situations and has little to do with the distinctive perspective of the person who pushes. Both Bus and Footbridge involve personal force and fit the "ME HURT YOU" schema (Greene & Haidt, 2002, p. 319), yet imagining these two cases results in a systematic, interconnected set of asymmetries in "reactive attitudes" (Strawson, 1974). These imaginative structures suggest that there is more at work here than a blunt biological response or myopic module that sounds an alarm but ignores collateral effects (compare Greene, 2013, Chapter 9).

To test this idea, I asked my students a series of questions about Switch, Footbridge, and Bus: "If you learned that your friend or close relation had pushed the lever in Switch [or pushed the man in Footbridge, or pushed the man in Bus], would you feel *more trusting, less trusting,* or *about equally trusting* of him or her?" The results are presented in Table 9.1.

Pushing the lever in Switch has no net effect on levels of trust, but not so in Footbridge or Bus. In Footbridge, 3 of 4 would be *less* trusting of someone who pushed the man. But now look at Bus: Nearly half would be *more* trusting. Why might this be? In Bus, one might speculate, those hearing the scenario construe the event in terms of *collective self-defense against an immediate social threat.* In such a case, we *want* the sort of people beside us who can take the dreadful but necessary steps to protect as many as possible, that is, we assign a positive expected value to individuals with this capacity in such a circumstance. When there are random public bombings, all share in the

TABLE 9.1 *Percentage of class responses regarding effects of behavior on trust in a moral dilemma*

If you learned that a friend or relation pushed ...	More trusting (%)	Less trusting (%)	About equally trusting (%)
The lever in Switch	23	30	47
The man in Footbridge	10	75	13
The man in Bus	46	32	20

risk, and all must be prepared to make sacrifices to prevent the risk from doing the greatest possible damage. In Footbridge, by contrast, we do not construe the example in terms of social self-defense: The fate of the five workers is not seen as part of a shared fate with you or the large gentleman.

To investigate whether differences in social or empathic perspective are playing a role in explaining the asymmetries in these moral dilemmas, I recently asked my students *which* potential victim or victims seemed to them imaginatively "closest." In Switch, 59% of the students answered "all six" victims, while 28% said "the single worker on the sidetrack" (the others said "the five workers on the main track"). When asked the same question about Footbridge, only 39% of the students answered "all six," and 58% of the students answered "the man on the footbridge" (the remainder said "the five"), which is virtually the same asymmetry as we saw in the initial verdicts themselves. To the extent that we think adopting a perspective that is *impartial* with respect to innocent victims is important in morality, then, we should think that there is some reason to question whether the case of Footbridge is effective in bringing respondents to take up a moral point of view. This, in turn, might make us think we should not simply take the intuitive responses in Footbridge at face value.

What, then, about the idea that Bus has such a different reception among students from Footbridge, given that both involve exerting the same kind of direct personal force to kill an innocent victim, because Bus brings to light the need for action in social "self-defense" against a shared threat? When I asked my students about imaginative "closeness" of potential victims in Bus, 63% said "the five on the bus," 30% said "all six," while the rest said "the man exiting the bus"; 93% took up a social perspective. Does this mean that the majority answer is Bus is "right" while the majority answer in Footbridge is "wrong"? Not at all; only that we should understand better the roots of these differences in a more complex capacity to use empathic simulation to evaluate social situations and agents.

Evidence that such an empathic evaluative competence might be at work in these scenarios comes from several recent scientific studies. The students in my classes were not arbitrary in thinking that someone who would push in Footbridge would be less trustworthy. One set of studies found that individuals with damage to a region of the brain involved in social emotions, the ventromedial prefrontal cortex, are more likely than people at large to answer that one should push in Footbridge (Koenigs et al., 2007); another found that willingness to push was correlated with higher scores on a sociopathic scale (Kahane, Everett, Earp, Farias, & Savulescu, 2015; see also Bartells & Pizzaro, 2012); and yet another found that individuals with higher blood-alcohol levels, which generally correlates with lowered inhibition and impaired social cognition, were also more likely to push (Duke & Bègue, 2015). Finally, a recent study has found that subjects form negative judgments of the motivation and character of the *person* in Footbridge-like cases, even when they judge the act of pushing victims to their death to save others to be morally the right choice in the circumstances (Uhlmann, Zhu, & Tannenbaum, 2013).

Let us look at two final trolley problems. If our hypothesis that intuitions in trolley scenarios reflect not only evaluation of the act, but of the attitudes, motives, or will that would make the action possible, then we should be able create a trolley case that shows such morally dubious attitudes, motivation, or will at work when one imaginatively models the situation, but in which there is no direct, personal violence at all. If we are right, then such a case should yield an intuitive rejection similar to the typical response in Footbridge.

Consider *Beckon*, which, like Switch and Footbridge, begins with a runaway trolley headed for five potential victims and which one cannot *oneself* directly stop. Only this time, there is no switch or footbridge:

> You are at some distance from the trolley track, but you can see on the other side of the track, between the runaway trolley and the tunnel containing the five workers, a very large gentleman. This man cannot see the oncoming trolley because a large sign blocks his view up the track, but he is not at risk, because he is clear of the track and not attempting to cross it. He is simply standing still and happens to be looking your way. You could, by enthusiastically gesturing to him to come toward you, cause him to step forward into the path of the oncoming trolley, and the bulk of his body would stop it before it reaches the tunnel. He would die, but the five workers would be saved.

Should you enthusiastically beckon the large man in your direction?

When this scenario was posed to the same group of students as before, asking them to give their intuitive response, only 36% said yes, while 64% said no, which is virtually the same percentages as Footbridge. There is no personal violence, no laying on of hands, just a very devious-seeming action, which lures an unsuspecting person to his death—for a good cause, but in a distinctly cunning manner.[9] Asked whether they would trust someone more, less, or the same if they learned he had beckoned in Beckon, no students said "more," 79% said "less," and 21% said "the same." This is essentially the same pattern as in Footbridge and might suggest a similar implicit social evaluation of the expected consequences of the kind of motivational system that would lead someone naturally to beckon the large man in Beckon, compared to the motivational system that would lead someone naturally to push the lever in Switch, or to push the large man in Bus.

We could get further support for this idea if we could think of a trolley scenario that is otherwise like Beckon but does not seem to indicate anything unusual about the motivational system of the agent. Consider *Wave*, which is like Beckon except,

> You can see that there are five workers on the track down which the runaway trolley is speeding, who do not see the trolley and will soon be killed by it. A single worker is also standing on the left side of the track against a very close wall. Your voice cannot reach these workers, but they can see you. If you were to vigorously wave your arms to the right side, the five workers would step off the track to safety. But the one worker would step onto it, where he would be struck and killed.

Should you wave vigorously to the right?

In Wave, 87% of the students say they should wave, and 13% say that they should not. As for trust, 20% said they would trust a person who they learned had waved in the Wave scenario "more," 68% said "the same," and 13% said "less," which is essentially the same pattern we found in Switch.

So it would seem that, lying behind the intuitive responses in trolley cases might be a more complex, sophisticated, and credible implicit capacity for social evaluation of actions and agents than we had previously been led to believe.

Our concern here has not been to defend one or another answer in these scenarios, but to make a case that intuitive moral judgment likely involves developed capacities for empathic social evaluation and *prospective* assessment—whether of acts and agents in trolley problems, in cases like those of Julie and Mark and Jane and Matthew, or in cases like Boardroom and Goat. As David Hume argued 300 years ago in the *Treatise of Human Nature*, moral assessment is neither a matter of arbitrary social convention nor a system of pure a priori reason; it has a firm foundation in an appreciation, developed across the long history of human social life, of the *tendencies* of acts, motives, traits, and practices to make people's lives go better or worse, individually and together (1739–1740/1969). Even the notorious trolley problems seem well-diagnosed by Hume's prospective approach.

Philosophers and psychologists alike have long seen the necessity of postulating implicit competencies, sensibilities, or faculties that can attune us to reasons to think and act, but recently there has begun to be impressively detailed empirical evidence of the psychic reality of such capacities to model the world and its prospects and perils. A better understanding of these capacities will provide more insight into the strengths and weaknesses of human affect and cognition in helping us stay in touch with the realities and possibilities of our physical and social worlds and their evaluative characteristics. This is a period of incredible excitement in moral philosophy, which is undergoing a revolution based on the improvement of our understanding of the mind and its workings. Although moral judgment is often viewed as essentially retrospective and reactionary, we believe that prospection will emerge as central in this new era of moral psychology.

In some ways, this is also a return to a conception of moral philosophy that animated Aristotle, who defended the idea that well-attuned affective states are appropriate ways for humans to respond to value. "Virtue is concerned with feelings and actions," he wrote, explaining:

> I am talking here about virtue of character, since it is this that is concerned with feelings and actions, and it is in these that we find excess, deficiency, and the mean. For example, fear, confidence, anger, pity, and in general pleasure and pain can be experienced too much or too

little, and in both ways not well. But to have them at the right time, about the right thing, towards the right people, for the right end, and in the right way, is the mean and best, and this is the business of virtue. (*Nicomachean Ethics*, trans. 2000, II.06b17-20)

For example, in the case of the key virtue of courage,

> ... the courageous person is the one who endures and fears—and likewise is confident about—the right things, for the right reason, in the right way, and at the right time. (Aristotle, *Nicomachean Ethics*, trans. 2000, III.5b17-19)

The fully virtuous warrior, for example, will also have *practical wisdom* (*phronesis*), which provides the theoretical underpinning of his character and the guiding values in life. But Aristotle believed that no strict, rule-based theory can guide the virtuous warrior reliably in situ. Rather, the warrior must have an affectively attuned *practical appreciation* of the risks involved, the potentials for taking action, and the values at stake: The "courageous person feels and acts in accordance with the merits of the case," grounding him in his concrete situation in such a way that "what is true appears to him" (Aristotle, *Nicomachean Ethics*, trans. 2000, III.5b19). Fear presents an *evaluative* representation of the landscape of choice, and, when it is well-attuned to the risks present, we can speak of this fear as "reasonable," "accurate," or "justified." Thus it can furnish the non-deliberative, context-sensitive, flexible intuitions that can account for the warrior's ability to adapt *spontaneously* yet successfully to the demands of a critical situation. Well-attuned affective responses are as indispensable to warriors' practical wisdom as their ability to reason.

Recent research in neuroscience affords us with an idea of how the affective system can provide such guidance, via the generation of evaluative models that permit the spontaneous simulation of multiple courses of action. And because the affective system enters early into the perceptual stream, it can make some situations or actions look promising or threatening, feel prudent or unwise, or seem right or wrong. Affectively grounded prospective capacities provide for the first time a credible basis for understanding how humans could be *both* intuitive *and* moral creatures, that is, how we could *see* what's right and have at the same time the motivation and intelligent mapping of possibilities that would allow us to do it.

Notes

1. For a general critique of the use of U.S. university students in psychological and economic experiments, see Henrich, Heine, and Norenzayan (2010).
2. An apparent exception is Gold, Pulford, and Colman (2014), who used a game show-based modification of the typical passenger versus bystander versions and found a reversal from the usual pattern, but they recognize that subjects might apply different norms about the fairness of interventions that affect outcomes by bystanders versus participants.
3. The terms system 1 and system 2 should be understood *functionally*, as two modes of mental processing, rather than as two separate brain systems. That is why the theory is called *dual process*.
4. It was Howard Nye who first drew my attention to the importance of *prospective* guilt as a moral emotion. For an important discussion of the role of emotion in moral judgment, see Gibbard (1990).
5. For example, although implicit bias has been linked by some researchers to a primal "us–them" emotional set, a review of nearly 50 studies, varied in test-hypothesis and research methods, provides evidence of malleability of automatic processes of stereotyping and prejudice. "Early social information processing," in which implicit attentional and motivational processes (known to be regulated by affect) work together with other internal and external cues, appears able to modulate the effects of stereotyping or evaluative bias, in some cases reversing it altogether. See Blair (2002).
6. See the Pew Research Center report, "Five Facts About Same-Sex Marriage" (Masci & Motel, 2015).
7. Indeed, this is not simply a *tacit* or *commonsense* understanding of his character. Indifference to causing harm to others and willingness to violate the rights of others without remorse are key diagnostic criteria of antisocial personality disorder. See the *Diagnostic and Statistical Manual of Mental Disorders* (4th ed., text rev.; American Psychiatric Association, 2000).
8. The percentages do not add up to 100% because of a 2% error rate in responses. To see whether the mention of a terrorist is influencing people's responses, in another variant of the case, it is

not a bomber but a missile that has misfired from a nearby army vehicle and will either be stopped outside the bus by your pushing the portly gentleman into the path of the missile, or allowed into the bus behind you where it will kill five. Student answers tend to be similar to the original bus case.

9. Beckon does add an element of deception that Switch lacks. Could this explain the dramatic reversal in intuition? But Footbridge, too, adds an element of wrongdoing not present in Switch, which is physical assault. If people thought this added wrongdoing were enough to explain the original Switch/ Footbridge asymmetry, the trolley problem would have been solved years ago. It is equally doubtful that the added wrongdoing of deception in Beckon explains its sharp difference from Switch.

References

Adams, E. W. (1970). Subjunctive and indicative conditionals. *Foundations of Language, 6,* 89–94.

Ahlenius, H., & Tännsjö, T. (2012). Chinese and westerners respond differently to the trolley dilemmas. *Journal of Cognition and Culture, 12,* 195–201.

American Psychiatric Association. (2000). *Diagnostic and statistical manual of mental disorders* (4th ed., text rev.). Washington, DC: Author.

Anderson, E. (2010). *The imperative of integration.* Princeton, NJ: Princeton University Press.

Baird, J. A., & Astington, J. W. (2004). The role of mental state understanding in the development of moral cognition and moral action. *New Directions for Child and Adolescent Development, 103,* 37–49.

Baron-Cohen, S. (1997). *Mindblindness: An essay on autism and theory of mind.* Cambridge, MA: MIT Press.

Baron-Cohen, S., & Wheelwright, S. (2004). The empathy quotient: An investigation of adults with Asperger syndrome or high functioning autism, and normal sex differences. *Journal of Autism and Developmental Disorders, 34,* 163–175.

Bartells, D. M., & Pizarro, D. A. (2012). The mismeasure of morals: Antisocial personality traits predict utilitarian responses to moral dilemmas. *Cognition, 121,* 154–161.

Bennett, J. (1981). Morality and consequences. In S. McMurrin (Ed.), *The Tanner lectures on human values* (Vol. 2, pp. 45–95). Salt Lake City, UT: University of Utah Press.

Blair, I. V. (2002). The malleability of automatic stereotypes and prejudice. *Personality and Social Psychology Review, 6,* 242–261.

Blincoe, S., & Harris, M. J. (2009). Prejudice reduction in white students: Comparing three conceptual approaches. *Journal of Diversity in Higher Education, 2,* 232–242.

Cantor, G. (1891). Über eine elementare Frage der Mannigfaltigkeitslehre. *Jahresbericht der Deutschen Mathematiker-Verienigung, 1,* 75–78.

Chaiken, S., & Trope, Y. (Eds.). (1999). *Dual-process theories in social psychology.* New York, NY: Guilford.

Church, A. (1936). A note on the entscheidungsproblem. *Journal of Symbolic Logic, 1,* 40–41.

Cushman, F., Young, L., & Hauser, M. (2006). The role of conscious reasoning and intuition in moral judgment: Testing three principles of harm. *Psychological Science, 17,* 1082–1089.

Dasgupta, N. (2013). Implicit attitudes and beliefs adapt to situations: A decade of research on the malleability of implicit prejudice, stereotypes, and the self-concept. In P. G. Devine and E. A. Plant (Eds.), *Advances in experimental social psychology* (Vol. 47, pp. 233–279). London, England: Academic Press.

Dasgupta, N., & Greenwald, A. G. (2001). On the malleability of automatic attitudes: Combating automatic prejudice with images of admired and disliked individuals. *Journal of Personality and Social Psychology, 81,* 800–814.

Decety, J., & Ickes, W. (2009). *The social neuroscience of empathy.* Cambridge, MA: MIT Press.

Duke, A. A., & Bègue, L. (2015). The drunk utilitarian: Blood alcohol concentration predicts utilitarian responses in moral dilemmas. *Cognition, 134,* 121–127.

Dunbar, R. (1996). *Grooming, gossip, and the evolution of language.* Cambridge, MA: Harvard University Press.

Ent, M. R., & Baumeister, R. F. (2015). Individual differences in guilt proneness affect how people respond to moral tradeoffs between harm avoidance and obedience to authority. *Personality and Individual Differences, 74,* 231–234.

FeldmanHall, O., Mobbs, D., Evans, D., Hiscox, L., Navrady, L., & Dalgeish, T. (2012). What we say and what we do: The relationship between real and hypothetical moral choices. *Cognition, 123,* 434–441.

Foot, P. (1967). The problem of abortion and the doctrine of double effect. *Oxford Review (Trinity), 5,* 5–15.

Fyhn, M., Molden, S., Witter, M. P., Moser, E. I., & Moser, M.-B. (2004). Spatial representation in the entorhinal cortex. *Science, 305,* 1258–1264.

Gibbard, A. (1990). *Wise Choices, Apt Feelings: A Theory of Normative Judgment.* Cambridge, MA: Harvard University Press.

Gold, N., Colman, A. M., & Pulford, B. D. (2014). The outlandish, the realistic, and the real: Contextual manipulation and agent role effects in trolley problems. *Frontiers in Psychology, 5*(35).

Gold, N., Pulford, B. D., & Colman, A. M. (2014). Cultural differences in responses to real-life and hypothetical trolley problems. *Judgment and Decision Making, 9,* 65–76.

Greene, J. D. (2013). *Moral tribes: Emotion, reason, and the gap between us and them.* New York, NY: Penguin.

Greene, J. D., Cushman, F. A., Stewart, L. E., Lowenberg, K., Nystrom, L. E., & Cohen, J. D. (2009). Pushing moral buttons: The interaction between personal force and intention in moral judgment. *Cognition, 111,* 364–371.

Greene, J., & Haidt, J. (2002). How (and where) does moral judgment work? *Trends in Cognitive Sciences, 6,* 517–523.

Greene, J. D., Sommerville, R. B., Nystrom, L. E., Darley, J. M., & Cohen, J. D. (2001). An fMRI investigation of emotional engagement in moral judgment. *Science, 293,* 2105–2108.

Guiora, A. Z., Brannon, R. C. L., & Dull, C. Y. (1972). Empathy and second language learning. *Language Learning, 22,* 111–130.

Gupta, A. S., van der Meer, M. A. A., Touretzky, D. S., & Redish, D. (2010). Hippocampal replay is not a simple function of experience. *Neuron, 65,* 695–705.

Haidt, J. (2001). The emotional dog and its rational tail: A social intuitionist approach to moral judgment. *Psychological Review, 108,* 814–834.

Haidt, J., McCauley, C., & Rozin, P. (1994). Individual differences in sensitivity to disgust: A scale sampling seven domains of disgust elicitors. *Personality and Individual Differences, 16,* 701–713.

Hamlin, J. K., & Wynn, K. (2011). Young infants prefer prosocial to antisocial others. *Cognitive Development, 26*, 30–39.

Hauser, M., Cushman, F., Young, L., Jin, R. K.-X., & Mikhail, J. (2007). A dissociation between moral judgments and justifications. *Mind & Language, 22*, 1–21.

Henrich, J., Heine, S. J., & Norenzayan, A. (2010). The weirdest people in the world? *Behavioral and Brain Sciences, 33*, 61–83.

Hoffman, M. L. (2000). *Empathy and moral development: Implications for caring and justice.* Cambridge, England: Cambridge University Press.

Hume, D. (1969). *A treatise of human nature.* London, England: Penguin. (Original work published 1739–1740)

Inbar, Y., Knobe, J., Pizarro, D. A., & Bloom, P. (2009). Disgust sensitivity predicts disapproval of gays. *Emotion, 9*, 435–439.

Ji, D., & Wilson, M. A. (2007). Coordinated memory replay in the visual cortex and hippocampus during sleep. *Nature Neuroscience, 10*, 100–107.

Kahane, G., Everett, J. A. C., Earp, B. D., Farias, M., & Savulescu, J. (2015). "Utilitarian" judgments in sacrificial moral dilemmas do not reflect impartial concern for the greater good. *Cognition, 134*, 193–209.

Kahneman, D. (2003). Maps of bounded rationality: Psychology for behavioral economics. *The American Economic Review, 93*, 1449–1475.

Kahneman, D. (2011). *Thinking, fast and slow.* New York, NY: Farrar, Straus and Giroux.

Knobe, J. (2010). Person as scientist, person as moralist. *Behavioral and Brain Sciences, 33*, 315–329.

Koenigs, M., Young, L., Adolphs, R., Tranel, D., Cushman, F., Hauser, M., & Damasio, A. (2007). Damage to the prefrontal cortex increases utilitarian moral judgements. *Nature, 446*, 908–911.

Konrath, S., & Sripada, C. S. (2011). Telling more than we can know about intentional action. *Mind & Language, 26*, 353–380.

Lewis, D. (1973). *Counterfactuals.* Cambridge, MA: Harvard University Press.

Lieberman, D., & Smith, A. (2010). It's all relative: Sexual aversions and moral judgments regarding sex among siblings. *Current Directions in Psychological Science, 21*, 243–247.

Masci, D., & Motel, S. (2015). Five facts about same-sex marriage. *Fact Tank: News in the Numbers.* Retrieved from http://www.pewresearch.org/fact-tank/2015/06/26/same-sex-marriage/

Mayer, J. D., Caruso, D. R., & Salovey, P. (1999). Emotional intelligence meets traditional standards for an intelligence. *Intelligence, 27,* 267–298.

Mayer, J. D., & Gehrer, G. (1996). Emotional intelligence and the identification of emotion. *Intelligence, 22,* 89–113.

Mikhail, J. (2011). *Elements of moral cognition: Rawls' linguistic analogy and the cognitive science of moral and legal judgment.* New York, NY: Cambridge University Press.

Moll, J., de Oliveira-Souza, R., & Zahn, R. (2008). The neural basis of moral cognition: Sentiments, concepts, and values. *Annals of the New York Academy of Sciences, 1124,* 161–180.

Moore, A. B., Lee, N. Y. L., Clark, B. A. M., & Conway, A. R. A. (2011). In defense of the personal/impersonal distinction in moral psychology research: Cross-cultural validation of the dual process model of moral judgment. *Judgment and Decision Making, 6,* 186–195.

Navarette, D. C., McDonald, M. M., Mott, M. L., & Asher, B. (2012). Virtual morality: Emotion and action in a simulated three-dimensional "trolley problem." *Emotion, 12,* 364–370.

Nucci, L. P., & Nucci, M. S. (1982). Children's responses to moral and social conventional transgressions in free-play settings. *Child Development, 53,* 1337–1342.

Onishi, K. H., & Baillargeon, R. (2005). Do 15-month-old infants understand false beliefs? *Science, 308,* 255–258.

Premack, D. (1990). The infant's theory of self-propelled objects. *Cognition, 36,* 1–16.

Premack, D., & Premack, A. J. (1997). Infants attribute value ± to the goal-directed actions of self-propelled objects. *Journal of Cognitive Neuroscience, 9,* 848–856.

Ruby, P., & Decety, J. (2001). Effect of subjective perspective taking during simulation of agency: A PET investigation of agency. *Nature Neuroscience, 4,* 546–550.

Sabini, J., & Silver, M. (1982). *Moralities of everyday life.* Oxford, England: Oxford University Press.

Saffran, J. R., Aslin, R. N., & Newport, E. L., (1996). Statistical learning by 8-month-old infants. *Science, 274,* 1926–1928.

Small, D. M. (2012). Flavor is in the brain. *Physiology and Behavior, 107,* 540–552.

Sripada, C. S. (2012). Mental state attributions and the side-effect effect. *Journal of Experimental Social Psychology, 48,* 232–238.

Strawson, P. F. (1974). *Freedom and resentment.* London, England: Metheun.

Tangney, J. P., Stuewig, J., & Mashek, D. J. (2007). Moral emotions and moral behavior. *Annual Review of Psychology, 58,* 345–372.

Thomson, J. J. (1976). Killing, letting die, and the trolley problem. *The Monist, 59,* 204–217.

Thomson, J. J. (1985). The trolley problem. *The Yale Law Journal, 94,* 1395–1415.

Turiel, E. (1983). *The development of social knowledge: Morality & convention.* Cambridge, England: Cambridge University Press.

Turing, A. M. (1937). On computable numbers, with an application to the entscheidungsproblem. *Proceedings of the London Mathematical Society, 2,* 230–265.

Tversky, A., & Kahneman, D. (1973). Availability: A heuristic for judging frequency and probability. *Cognitive Psychology, 5,* 207–232.

Tversky, A., & Kahneman, D. (1974). Judgment under uncertainty: Heuristics and biases. *Science, 185,* 1124–1131.

Tversky, A., & Kahneman, D. (1981). The framing of decisions and the psychology of choice. *Science, 211,* 453–458.

Tybur, J. M., Kurzban, R., Lieberman, D., & DeScioli, P. (2013). Disgust: Evolved function and structure. *Psychological Review, 120,* 65–84.

Uhlmann, E. L., Zhu, L. L., & Tannenbaum, D. (2013). When it takes a bad person to do the right thing. *Cognition, 126,* 326–334.

Wellman, H. M. (2014). *Making Minds: How the Theory of Mind Develops.* Oxford: Oxford University Press.

Wellman, H. M., & Bartsch, K. (1988). Young children's reasoning about beliefs. *Cognition, 30,* 239–277.

Wellman, H. M., Cross, D., & Watson, J. (2001). Meta-analysis of theory-of-mind development: The truth about false belief. *Child Development, 72,* 655–684.

Yarrow, K., Brown, P., & Krakauer, J. W. (2009). Inside the brain of an elite athlete: The neural processes that support high achievement in sports. *Nature Reviews Neuroscience, 10,* 585–596.

Young, L., Cushman, F., Hauser, M., & Saxe, R. (2007). The neural basis of the interaction between theory of mind and moral judgment. *Proceedings of the National Academy of Sciences, 104,* 8235–8240.

10

Prospection Gone Awry: Depression

Martin Seligman with Ann Marie Roepke

I N THE PRECEDING CHAPTERS, WE LOOKED AT PROSPECTION as an adaptive process that evolution favored because it helps humans plan for the future and survive, reproduce, and thrive. We believe that when prospection goes awry, it negatively influences emotion, cognition, and behavior, and that depression is the paradigm case of this. We present a framework in which faulty prospection is the core causal process of much depression. In our view, faulty prospection is a core underlying process that produces and maintains several pathologies. We focus on depression here, but a growing body of research also highlights the ways in which faulty prospection may contribute to anxiety disorders and other types of psychopathology (e.g., Alloy et al., 2008; Carleton et al., 2012).

For many years future-thinking was neglected within clinical psychology, and the weight of etiology was mostly placed on the past. Early psychoanalytic approaches emphasized the past as a main cause of present pathology (Freud, 1917). Classical behavioral approaches also emphasized the past: A person's history of instrumental reinforcement and of classical conditioning was viewed as a crucial tool for predicting and understanding his or her future behaviors (Pavlov, 1927; Watson & Rayner, 1920). Nonetheless, some future-oriented themes can be found in past work in behaviorism and cognitive psychology. First and foremost we build upon Beck's (1974) negative cognitive triad, which marked major theoretical progress in the study of depression. Beck postulated a negative view of the world, of the self, *and of the future* as the hallmark symptoms of depression, and suggested they were more than mere symptoms; they actually caused depression. We agree with this, and we further suggest that the negative view of the future is the first among equals in the triad.

Much research and therapy focuses on negative views of the self (e.g., Metalsky, Joiner, Hardin, & Abramson, 1993; Orth, Robins, & Roberts, 2008), but negative views of the future may matter even more; we hypothesize that the entire cognitive triad may actually boil down to negative future-thinking. Certainly, it is depressing for people to believe that they are no good, that the world is no good, and that this will always be the case. In contrast, if people think that they are no good and that the world is no good, but that this will change dramatically for the better tomorrow, this is not nearly as disheartening. Sadness and dejection are understandable reactions to the belief that things will always be bad. The emotional reaction is not faulty here, but rather the representation of the future is. Beck posited that by helping clients to spot and change dysfunctional beliefs, therapists could alleviate symptoms; in the same vein, we posit that by helping clients to spot and change dysfunctional *if-then* simulations of the future, therapists can promote recovery and resilience. Targeting this part of the cognitive triad might be one of the most important existing interventions and the single most important target for further development.

This prospective framework also extends and enriches Abramson, Metalsky, and Alloy's (1989) hopelessness theory of depression, which posits that hopelessness is sufficient for causing a subtype of depression, as well as MacLeod et al. (2005) and those of Miloyan, Pachana, and Suddendorf (2014), which point to the specific maladaptive problems in mental simulation that characterize hopelessness, depression, anxiety, and suicidal behavior.

We see faulty prospection as a core underlying process that drives depression (and potentially contributes to a range of other comorbid disorders). We believe that prospection is not a mere symptom or correlate of depression, but rather the process that belongs front and center in the study of depression.

We first discuss three kinds of faulty prospection that may cause and maintain depression. Then we address the clinical implications of this view, exploring how improving prospection can relieve depression.

How Dysfunctional Prospection Creates Depression

We recast depression as a disorder of faulty prospection. The research literature documents this amply: Depressed people simulate the future in ways that create, exacerbate, and maintain dysfunction: In their *if-then* simulations, *if* clauses are frequently finished with negative, and even catastrophic *then* clauses (e.g., "If I try to talk things out with my partner, then it will always make things worse"; "If I don't sleep well tonight, then tomorrow will be awful"). These if-then conditionals may be expressed in words or images, and they may be more or less conscious.

Negative prospection and even depression itself is not inherently dysfunctional, maladaptive, or problematic; indeed, both could be essential for adaptive functioning, because incessant optimism would have serious costs (Nesse, 2004; Norem & Chang, 2002). So we distinguish negative prospection from faulty prospection. By *negative prospection*, we mean representations of an undesirable future (these are normal and often useful); by *faulty, poor, or dysfunctional prospection*, we mean patterns of representations of the future in which negative content predominates and leads to significant impairment.

In our framework, three general faults of prospection drive depression: poor *generation* of possible futures, poor *evaluation* of possible futures, and underlying global negative *beliefs* about the future. Further, we propose that depressed mood and poor functioning, in turn, exacerbate these faults in a vicious cycle.

Three Faults of Depressive Prospection

Simulation of possible futures. The first fault concerns the construction of possible futures. Depressed people tend to imagine fewer

positive scenarios and depressed (and anxious) people tend to imagine negative future scenarios more quickly and easily than controls
(Bjärehed, Sarkohi, & Andersson, 2010; MacLeod & Cropley, 1995;
Miles, MacLeod, & Pote, 2004). Moreover, depressed people imagine positive future events less vividly than controls do (Morina,
Deeprose, Pusowski, Schmid, & Holmes, 2011), and this is a problem because vividly imagined scenarios are more believable than
vague ones and vivid images evoke stronger emotions than words
do (Holmes & Mathews, 2010). Vivid mental images of one's own
death are especially dangerous, as these *flashforwards* are linked to
increased suicide risk (Hales, Deeprose, Goodwin, & Holmes, 2011).
Conversely, imagining positive future events may buffer against suicidality and can predict suicidality better than global hopelessness
does (O'Connor, Fraser, Whyte, MacHale, & Masterton, 2008).

Evaluation of possible futures. The second fault concerns the
evaluation of future scenarios. Depressed people tend to overestimate,
over-weight, and over-attend to risk, and this produces more negative
expectations of the future. Depressed people not only judge bad things
as highly likely, but also generate more reasons why this would be
so (Alloy & Ahrens, 1987; MacLeod, Tata, Kentish, Carroll, & Hunter,
1997). These predictions are overblown (Strunk, Lopez, & DeRubeis,
2006), yet greater depression goes hand in hand with greater certainty
about these predictions (Miranda & Mennin, 2007). Depressed people
not only expect bad outcomes, but they also expect to have little power
to change them, even following experiences of success (Abramson,
Garber, Edwards, & Seligman, 1978; Kosnes, Whelan, O'Donovan, &
McHugh, 2013; Seligman, 1972).

At the extreme end of pessimism, we find hopelessness and depressive predictive certainty, black-and-white expectations that negative outcomes will occur and positive outcomes will not (Abramson
et al., 1989; Andersen, 1990; Beck, Weissman, Lester, & Trexler,
1974; Miranda, Fontes, & Marroquín, 2008). Depressive predictive certainty is toxic: People who are certain that good things will
not happen tend to have more suicidal ideation, even after adjusting for depressive symptoms and general hopelessness (Sargalska,
Miranda, & Marroquín, 2011). Likewise, hopeless people are at a
higher risk of killing themselves (Kovacs & Garrison, 1985), and
hopelessness is likely sufficient for causing depression symptoms
(Abramson et al., 1989).

These general negative expectations are related to specific simulations of the future: For example, repeatedly simulating emotionally charged scenarios makes them more believable, so repeatedly simulating negative (and not positive) events should produce even more negative expectations (Szpunar & Schacter, 2013). Indeed, the fewer positive events people imagine, the greater their hopelessness (MacLeod et al., 2005).

Negative beliefs about the future. The third problem with depressed people's prospection concerns their underlying templates for understanding what the future holds. We propose that a template, which we call *pessimistic predictive style*, is particularly poignant. This parallels pessimistic explanatory style (PES), a characteristic tendency to explain past and present events with certain patterns of causes (Peterson et al., 1982). A person with PES explains negative experiences with causes that are personal, pervasive, and permanent (Peterson & Seligman, 1984): Bad things happened because of one's own shortcomings, which have poisoned all domains of life and always will. Depressed people tend to have a marked PES (Alloy, Abramson, Metalsky, & Hartlage, 1988; Peterson & Seligman, 1984; Seligman, Abramson, Semmel, & von Baeyer, 1979). In parallel, depressed people explain good events with impersonal, transient, and specific causes.

Explanatory style is the past and present side of the coin, however, and the future side has been neglected. To appreciate the shortcomings of explanatory style theorizing and to appreciate why predictive style is an advance, we must return to the scientific atmosphere of the late 1970s. Behaviorism was just giving way to cognitive psychology, but cognitive psychology was exclusively about memory (past) and perception (present), and it was deliberately silent about expectations of the future. When explanatory style was formulated (Abramson, Seligman, & Teasdale, 1978), theorizing about mental life had just become acceptable, but only if the mental life was about the present and the past. This unstated premise of avoiding future-oriented cognitions plagued both explanatory style theory and Beck's theorizing as well. Why? Essential to behaviorism and to early cognitive theory is that no reference should be made to teleology; its mission was to explain the apparently forward-looking behavior of animals only by the past and the present. Drives and reinforcers might be more varied for humans, and humans might be capable of longer stimulus-response chains and wider stimulus-generalization, but notions such as expectations of as yet nonexistent future events were an invitation to untestability at best, and to obscurantism and incoherence at worst.

Cognitions about past experience and present events would, it was hoped, determine cognitions about the future. So when explanatory style was formulated, it was about past and present events, with the unspoken premise that these would somehow determine cognitions about the future. Even in the 1970s, this premise was dubious, because as Brickman et al. (1982) astutely pointed out, explanations for the cause of a problem do not mandate parallel explanations for its solution: The cause of facial disfiguration might be external, temporary, and local (a madman throwing acid at my face), but the implications for the future (endless surgeries and social rejections) are permanent and pervasive.

Explanatory style needs the other side of the coin fleshed out: predictive style, attributions about the causes of future events. This is a neglected area of research. A pessimistic predictive style should have the same features as PES: Depressive predictions about if-then sequences in the future are likely (a) pervasive, (b) permanent, and (c) personal (i.e., "if I don't perform well on this test, then I'll never succeed and I'll die a failure"), and the predictive style about good events should be the opposite. Explanatory style about the past and present might or might not be strongly correlated with predictive style about the future. This is a good topic for research, and empirical work should compare explanatory style and predictive style as causal of depression: We hypothesize that predictions about the future will influence people's behavior more than their explanations of the past and the present.

A Vicious Cycle

So faulty simulations, evaluations, and beliefs about the future may drive depression, and these three problems interact with one another to create the hallmark characteristics of major depressive disorder: first and foremost, depressed mood, irritability, low energy, low motivation, apathy, and suicide. We do not think, however, that poor prospection causes *all* symptoms of depression in the *Diagnostic and Statistical Manual* (5th ed.; *DSM-5*; American Psychiatric

Association, 2013); for example, it is more difficult to see how prospection would cause concentration problems, loss of pleasure, or psychomotor agitation. This may be because the *DSM-5* does not carve nature at the joints; major depressive disorder is not a single distinct thing (Gorman, 1996; Haslam, 2003; Haslam & Beck, 1994; Ruscio & Ruscio, 2000). Regardless, faulty prospection is neither necessary nor sufficient; rather we hypothesize that faulty prospection is the primary cause in that *it accounts for more of the variance at the psychological level than other causes, such as the negative view of the self, negative view of the world, and PES.*

We also propose that faulty prospection sets up a vicious cycle. It produces depression, and depression, in turn, potentiates poorer prospection in at least three ways. First, depressed people withdraw socially, limit their activities, and rely on avoidance, and thus have fewer positive experiences (Holahan, Moos, Holahan, Brennan, & Schutte, 2005; Kasch, Rottenberg, Arnow, & Gotlib, 2002). Because of this, they have impoverished raw material for constructing positive future scenarios. Second, depression leads people to act in ways that create stressful experiences and interpersonal conflicts (Hammen, 2006), and these negative experiences provide raw material for vivid negative simulations of the future. Third, simply being in a sad mood makes one more likely to remember a negative past and imagine a negative future (Miloyan et al., 2014; O'Connor & Williams, 2014).

Improving Prospection

If faulty prospection drives depression, then interventions should aim to fix prospection. Cognitive behavioral therapy (CBT) already has some future-oriented arrows in its quiver and these deserve to be formalized, extended, and grouped together. One can be a competent CBT therapist and focus entirely on future cognitions or ignore them altogether. CBT adherence protocols do not explicitly rate attempts to change faulty prospection. The Collaborative Study Psychotherapy Rating Scale (Hollon et al., 1988), for example, lists 32 CBT procedures; none of them explicitly target prospection and only three implicitly target prospection (setting up behavioral experiments to test beliefs, exploring realistic consequences of actions, and scheduling pleasant activities).

Here is a scenario that highlights the difference between CBT interventions that neglect prospection versus target prospection: A depressed woman has argued with her husband, and her therapist challenges her distorted, upsetting thoughts about the argument. The therapist chooses one of two interventions, both of which are classic CBT: Intervention A neglects the woman's thoughts about her future, whereas Intervention B squarely focuses on them.

In Intervention A, the therapist considers the client's automatic thoughts about the fight, and decides that this one is the most important: "He must think I'm a horrible person." (In the depressive cognitive triad, this reflects a negative view of the self.) The client and therapist identify the cognitive distortion underlying this thought (mind-reading), and then consider the evidence for and against the thought. To dispute the thought, they consider times in the past when the client's husband has said positive things about her, times when she has acted in a caring way toward him, and times when they reconciled after a fight and did not judge each other harshly. The client decides that her husband probably has a balanced and compassionate view toward her, and she feels better—for now.

This is a perfectly "adherent" cognitive intervention, but it leaves the client's faulty prospection intact. Even as the client comes to believe that her husband still loves and respects her, she is bothered by a nagging fear that it is just a matter of time before he leaves her. She disqualifies the past evidence (e.g., that he has forgiven her after past fights), saying to herself, "that was then; things will get worse this time"). She still runs if-then simulations that end with divorce, and she still imagines a sad future: visions of divorce papers, a living room filled with boxes containing her husband's belongings, and courtroom appearances about child custody. She is still deeply pessimistic, and still feels depressed whenever she runs these recurring negative simulations.

In Intervention B, which targets prospection, the therapist decides to challenge this automatic thought: "I am going to drive this relationship into the ground." (In the depressive cognitive triad, this is a negative view of the future.) The client and therapist identify the imagery tied to this prediction. They spot the cognitive distortions of fortune-telling and catastrophizing, and then consider the evidence (Beck & Weishaar, 1989; Burns, 1980). They generate other possible outcomes (e.g., reconciling, using the incident to strengthen their bond), and they review the evidence for these. They also explore actions that would lead to positive outcomes (e.g., change communication styles in couples therapy). The client decides that her marriage is not doomed and she feels better.

This, too, is an "adherent" CBT intervention, but it directly addresses the future. The best possible outcome of this intervention would be an end to the client's catastrophic predictions and imagery about her future. She considers a broader, more realistic, and more empowering array of if-then scenarios. Of course, this change will not come quickly or easily; initially such future-based interventions will likely be effortful because the client's faulty prospection is so entrenched. This is exactly why such interventions are needed, however, and in the long run, we hypothesize that these interventions will prove more protective than other cognitive interventions.

CBT therapists face many decision points during a single therapy session. Which problem should be prioritized? Which automatic thought should be targeted? If faulty prospection is indeed central to depression, then therapists should be guided by two principles when making these decisions:

1. When there is a choice to work on several automatic thoughts, target the thought about the future, unless there is a compelling reason to do otherwise.
2. When no dysfunctional thought about the future is immediately evident, search for it. If needed, *downward arrow* questions (Friedman & Thase, 2006) should be used until the underlying prospective thought is discovered.

We hypothesize that when therapists systematically and extensively target depressive prospection, then CBT will work better.

How CBT Already Targets Faulty Prospection

At least four CBT maneuvers already target prospection, and there is evidence that CBT improves future-thinking (Andersson, Sarkohi, Karlsson, Bjärehed, & Hesser, 2013; MacLeod, Coates, & Hetherton, 2008). First, therapists work to change clients' pessimistic predictions: They help clients spot future-focused distortions like catastrophizing and fortune-telling, and they use Socratic questions to coach them in creating accurate predictions (Beck, 1995). Second, therapists train clients in goal setting and planning, and goals are inherently future-directed (Malouff, Thorsteinsson, & Schutte, 2007; Wright, Basco, & Thase, 2006). Third, therapists use cognitive rehearsal to plan how to overcome obstacles (Beck, Rush, Shaw, & Emery, 1979). Fourth, therapists use behavioral activation to help clients schedule pleasant, mastery-inducing experiences in the future (Jacobson, Martell, & Dimidjian, 2001).

In addition to these four specific techniques, good therapy may promote better prospection generally. Therapists generate hope. Technique aside, clients can start envisioning a brighter future simply because they are taking steps to feel better and they have found support. Further, good therapists likely promote better prospection by shifting focus from the past and the present to the future (Ellis, 2001).

Several treatment packages combine various techniques to systematically target future-thinking. These include future-directed therapy (Vilhauer et al., 2012), hope therapy (Cheavens, Feldman, Gum, Michael, & Snyder, 2006), solution-focused therapy (de Shazer, 1985), goal-setting and planning (MacLeod et al., 2008), and future-oriented group training (van Beek, Kerkhof, & Beekman, 2009). These interventions need more randomized controlled evaluations before being considered empirically supported treatments, but their initial findings show promise.

Future-directed therapy (FDT) is a 10-week "full clinical intervention intended to reduce symptoms of depression and improve well-being by promoting a paradigm shift from dwelling on the past, or highlighting one's limitations in the present, toward creating more positive expectancies about the future through the use of a comprehensive and well-defined set of skills" (Vilhauer et al., 2012, p. 103). These skills include generating positive expectancies, practicing mindfulness, identifying and working toward values, simulating outcomes and processes, and solving problems. In a non-randomized pilot, FDT produced greater improvements in depression than treatment as usual (Vilhauer et al., 2012).

Hope therapy is "a treatment protocol designed to increase hopeful thinking and enhance goal-pursuit activities as described in hope theory" (Cheavens et al., 2006, p. 64). It focuses on five skills: setting goals, finding multiple paths to goals, increasing motivation, monitoring progress, and flexibly modifying goals and pathways. In the initial randomized controlled trial, hope therapy reduced depression symptoms better than a waiting list control (Cheavens et al., 2006).

Solution-focused therapy (de Shazer, 1985) is built on the premise that future orientation is necessary for positive change. This therapy encompasses a whole suite of techniques and has demonstrated positive outcomes in treating depression (Bozeman, 2000).

Goal-setting and planning is a manualized well-being intervention focused on developing and pursuing positive goals, rather than solving problems or directly targeting depressive symptoms. It has been tested in group-based and individual self-help formats and found to decrease depression in both (Coote & MacLeod, 2012).

Future-oriented group training (van Beek et al., 2009) is a unique intervention specifically targeting suicidality. It is intended as an addition to other treatment. Over the course of 10 workshops, participants learn how to change their future-oriented thinking and behavior and work toward goals that will make life worthwhile. Results of the initial trial have yet to be published.

These treatment packages are not radical departures from standard CBT. Instead, they use strategies that emphasize fixing faulty prospection and they merit further investigation in randomized controlled trials. There is clearly a need to develop new future-oriented treatment techniques, which we will speculate on in the following section.

Promising Techniques

Route-based imagery. Popular, sometimes footless, self-help programs emphasize the importance of visualizing the outcomes you desire (e.g., Byrne, 2006). But it is not enough to visualize a better future; it is essential to visualize the route that leads there (Oettingen, Hönig, & Gollwitzer, 2000; Taylor, Pham, Rivkin, & Armor, 1998). Route-based imagery involves identifying behaviors, thoughts, or feelings that are a route to the desired outcome. In a series of experiments, students who visualized routes got higher test scores, finished projects more quickly, and used more active coping strategies (Taylor et al., 1998).

This finding is relevant to treatment: Depressed people who visualize themselves taking small, concrete steps toward well-being might recover faster than those who just visualize good outcomes (or do not visualize at all). Visualizing good events can lift mood, but failing to visualize the route to get there could be risky. If a person vividly sees a wonderful future but remains convinced it is blocked, this could maintain depression; indeed depressed and hopeless people, and those with recent suicidal behavior, do not necessarily abandon their goals but rather they have painful engagement, seeing their goals as both essential for happiness and too hard to achieve (Danchin, MacLeod, & Tata, 2010).

Manipulations of time perspective. When using Beck's (1970) *time projection* technique, therapists help clients to relax deeply and then to project themselves into the future vividly imagining good experiences. This is similar to Erickson's (1954) *pseudo-orientation in time* procedure, in which clients first project themselves into a time when their troubles are resolved. They then converse with the therapist as if they were truly in the future, and they describe the process by which they improved their lives and solved their problems. It is not known if time perspective methods work, and they likely need to be refined to better target prospective mechanisms.

Anticipatory savoring. Therapists can teach depressed people *anticipatory savoring* (Loewenstein, 1987), as well as mindful awareness and appreciation of the process of striving for meaningful goals (McCullough, 2002). One positive psychotherapy (PPT) exercise called the *three good things* technique can be modified to be future-focused instead of past-focused (Seligman, Rashid, & Parks, 2006). In the original exercise, people keep nightly logs of three positive things that happened, and what they did to make these things happen. In the prospective exercise, depressed clients would keep logs of three good things they expect to happen tomorrow, and what they could do to ensure that these things happen. Whereas the original exercise targets PES, the reformulated exercise targets pessimistic predictive style.

Strengths-based work. One way to make positive simulations feel personally relevant is to help clients discover their signature strengths as in PPT and solution-focused therapy (Seligman et al., 2006): When clients identify and develop what is good about themselves, they may feel that positive outcomes are both more attainable and more deserved. They can also simulate using their strengths to pursue meaningful goals (Padesky & Mooney, 2012).

Building purpose. Meaning and purpose are integral parts of psychological well-being, and they buffer against despair and suicide (Ryff & Keyes, 1995; Seligman, 2012). Although the terms are sometimes used interchangeably, purpose differs from meaning in being more future-directed: Purpose is about the intention to accomplish something important, a "central, self-organizing life aim that organizes and stimulates goals, manages behaviors, and provides a sense of meaning ... [and] directs life goals and daily decisions" (Damon, Menon, & Cotton Bronk, 2003; McKnight & Kashdan, 2009, p. 242). Meaning and purpose fit very well within prospection-based interventions.

How can CBT build purpose? First, it can help clients clarify their highest values and chart a course toward them as in acceptance and commitment therapy (Hayes, Strosahl, & Wilson, 1999). Second, clients can be guided in taking on *personal projects* in order to attain a valued outcome (Little, 1983); such projects may help depressed clients to be drawn into a meaningful future and not be mired in a dark past. Third, CBT therapists can use the *forward arrow* technique. This is inspired by the classic CBT *downward arrow* technique (Burns, 1980; Friedman & Thase, 2006) in which the therapist drills down to the core fear underlying a client's distress (e.g., "I'll die alone and unloved, which will mean that my life was a failure"). The forward arrow technique uses similar methods toward a different end: The therapist elicits a positive scenario, and then asks the client what exactly makes this scenario so fulfilling. This questioning is repeated until the client arrives at the core purpose that draws him into the future (e.g., "Then I would know that I had really made my family happy and made the world better for future generations"). The therapist can then use this positive vision to help propel the client through obstacles. This positive vision could also combat depressed people's tendency to set fewer approach goals, more avoidance goals, and to pursue approach goals for avoidance-related reasons (e.g., to earn a promotion so that one's family will not be disappointed) (Sherratt & MacLeod, 2013; Vergara & Roberts, 2011).

Limitations and Future Directions

Prospection gone awry may be relevant, even central, to a number of other disorders besides depression. We will leave it to others to elaborate these, but importantly, our framework is *transdiagnostic*. Transdiagnostic approaches assess and target core underlying processes that produce pathology regardless of how the disorder in which they occur happens to be classified (Forgeard et al., 2011). These processes span traditional diagnostic boundaries; two disorders can manifest in different symptoms and yet be driven by the same fundamental problem. We have argued that faulty prospection is the fundamental problem driving depression. We suspect that faulty prospection may also undergird a diverse range of psychopathologies, including the entire range of anxiety disorders. While we do not have the space to elaborate on this, it is an astonishing historical accident that theories of anxiety focus on the past and the present, while the presenting symptoms are about dangers that might happen in the future. Addiction is a second example that likely involves prospection gone awry: The addict cannot delay gratification. Displaying a disorder of temporal discounting, the addict sacrifices larger later rewards for smaller sooner ones (Claus, Kiehl, & Hutchison, 2011; Kirby, Petry, & Bickel, 1999; Monterosso et al., 2006). If this is so, clinicians should identify and repair faulty prospection (a core process) rather than just identifying and repairing mere symptom clusters.

Shortcomings

There are two issues we worry about most: (a) What are the risks of emphasizing prospection? and (b) What is the role of negative self-concept as opposed to negative view of the future in depression?

What Are the Risks of Emphasizing Prospection?

Prospection is generally adaptive for emotion regulation and problem-solving. But can it become too much of a good thing? Is it possible to be excessively future-minded and devote too little attention to the past and present? Could intense future-directedness lead people to miss out on enjoying the present moment, benefiting from reminiscence, or enjoying? We just don't know.

Similarly how much time do depressed people spend thinking about the past, present, and future—and how much they should spend? Some research hints that depressed people may be less future-oriented (e.g., Breier-Williford & Bramlett, 1995), but measurement is not yet adequate: Existing future-orientation scales include items tapping self-regulation, conscientiousness, optimism, and hope, and they also do not clearly differentiate between a positive future versus a negative future (Hirsch et al., 2006; Zimbardo & Boyd, 1999). The newer big data techniques that we use—creating a lexicon of temporal orientation—and using Twitter and Facebook to validate it, holds real promise as the method for answering these questions.

What are the merits of present-focused and future-focused therapies? The concept of mindfulness (an accepting awareness of present experience) has become more popular, and there is a growing body of evidence to support its usefulness in (Segal, Williams, & Teasdale, 2012). More research is needed to understand the benefits and risks of prospective techniques versus present-centered techniques and to investigate the possibility that present-centered therapies actually work by correcting faulty prospection (e.g., by helping people to disengage from catastrophic thoughts about the future).

Despair Versus Depression

We think that a negative view of the future is more important than a negative view of the self in driving depression. But it is possible that a negative view of the self is a necessary condition of depression. Consider concentration camp prisoners. They might have negative views of the world and the future, but as unjustly imprisoned victims and virtuous people, they might have quite positive views of themselves. Despair certainly may follow, but does depression? For Beck (1974), the negative view of the self is necessary, and despair, when rational, does not equal depression, nor is despair a disorder. In contrast, the reformulated hopelessness theory of depression does not require internal attributions, and despair counts as depression (Abramson et al., 1989).

One possible resolution is that the self is just a particularly long-lasting subset of the future and nothing more. To appreciate this, contrast a negative view of the world to a negative view of the self. A negative view of the world is of almost no moment in depression *if one also believes that the world will get much better tomorrow.* Clearly a negative view of the world is subsumed by a negative view of the future, because it only matters for depression if it projected long into the future. Hence, within the prospective framework, we can dispense with a negative view of the world, leaving only the future and the self to account for depression.

But can the negative view of the self also be dispensed with? The self (unlike the weather) is a robustly stable factor and it projects far into the future; self-concept is a stable, multifaceted, organized perception of *who I am*, and thus, of whom I will be. It is possible, then, that the self only matters for depression insofar as it portends a bad future. If an individual believed that he or she was unlovable, but only for today, this would not be so discouraging; the thought "I am unlovable" is distressing because it implies "no one will *ever* love me." Conversely, self-concept may matter beyond its implications for the future; the active role of self might be moral as opposed to merely predictive, hence, guilt and anger turned inward (Freud, 1917). Even if people believed they could redeem themselves in the future, they might, nevertheless, feel intense distress and guilt over bad deeds they had done in the past.

Does eliminating a negative view of the future in therapy, without eliminating a negative view of the self, fail to relieve depression completely?

In conclusion, prospection belongs front and center in the study of depression. Much more investigation is needed to determine whether faulty prospection drives depression, and how prospection can be improved. We believe that faulty prospection is a crucial and under-appreciated transdiagnostic process that may underlie much more than depression. An understanding of how prospection shapes psychopathology will enable the creation of more effective treatments and allow distressed individuals create brighter futures.

References

Abramson, L. Y., Garber, J., Edwards, N. B., & Seligman, M. E. P. (1978). Expectancy changes in depression and schizophrenia. *Journal of Abnormal Psychology, 87,* 102–109.

Abramson, L. Y., Metalsky, G. I., & Alloy, L. B. (1989). Hopelessness depression: A theory-based subtype of depression. *Psychological Review, 96,* 358–372.

Abramson, L. Y., Seligman, M. E. P., & Teasdale, J. D. (1978). Learned helplessness in humans: Critique and reformulation. *Journal of Abnormal Psychology, 87*, 49–59.

Alloy, L. B., Abramson, L. Y., Metalsky, G. I., & Hartlage, S. (1988). The hopelessness theory of depression: Attributional aspects. *British Journal of Clinical Psychology, 27*, 5–21.

Alloy, L. B., Abramson, L. Y., Walshaw, P. D., Cogswell, A., Grandin, L. D., . . . Hogan, M. E. (2008). Behavioral approach system and behavioral inhibition system sensitivities and bipolar spectrum disorders: Prospective prediction of bipolar mood episodes. *Bipolar Disorders, 10*, 310–322.

Alloy, L. B., & Ahrens, A. H. (1987). Depression and pessimism for the future: Biased use of statistically relevant information in predictions for self versus others. *Journal of Personality and Social Psychology, 52*, 366–378.

American Psychiatric Association. (2013). *Diagnostic and statistical manual of mental disorders* (5th ed.). Washington, DC: Author.

Andersen, S. M. (1990). The inevitability of future suffering: The role of depressive predictive certainty in depression. *Social Cognition, 8*, 203–228.

Andersson, G., Sarkohi, A., Karlsson, J., Bjärehed, J., & Hesser, H. (2013). Effects of two forms of internet-delivered cognitive behaviour therapy for depression on future thinking. *Cognitive Therapy and Research, 37*, 29–34.

Beck, A. T. (1970). Cognitive therapy: Nature and relation to behavior therapy. *Behavior Therapy, 1*, 184–200.

Beck, A. T. (1974). The development of depression: A cognitive model. In R. J. Friedman & M. M. Katz (Eds.), *The psychology of depression: Contemporary theory and research* (pp. 318–330). Oxford, England: Wiley.

Beck, A. T., Rush, A. J., Shaw, B. F., & Emery, G. (1979). *Cognitive therapy of depression*. New York, NY: Guilford.

Beck, A. T., & Weishaar, M. (1989). Cognitive therapy. In A. Freeman, K. M. Simon, L. E. Beutler, & H. Arkowitz (Eds.), *Comprehensive handbook of cognitive therapy* (pp. 21–36). New York, NY: Springer.

Beck, A. T., Weissman, A., Lester, D., & Trexler, L. (1974). The measurement of pessimism: The hopelessness scale. *Journal of Consulting and Clinical Psychology, 42*, 861–871.

Beck, J. S. (1995). *Cognitive therapy: Basics and beyond*. New York, NY: Guilford.

Bjärehed, J., Sarkohi, A., & Andersson, G. (2010). Less positive or more negative? Future-directed thinking in mild to moderate depression. *Cognitive Behaviour Therapy, 39*, 37–45.

Bozeman, B. N. (2000). *The efficacy of solution-focused therapy techniques on perceptions of hope in clients with depressive symptoms* (Doctoral dissertation). Retrieved from ProQuest Information & Learning.

Breier-Williford, S., & Bramlett, R. K. (1995). Time perspective of substance abuse patients: Comparison of the scales in Stanford Time Perspective Inventory, Beck Depression Inventory, and Beck Hopelessness Scale. *Psychological Reports, 77*, 899–905.

Brickman, P., Rabinowitz, V. C., Karuza, J., Coates, D., Cohn, E., & Kidder, L. (1982). Models of helping and coping. *American Psychologist, 37*, 368–384.

Burns, D. D. (1980). *Feeling good: The new mood therapy*. New York, NY: William Morrow.

Byrne, R. (2006). *The secret*. New York, NY: Atria.

Carleton, R. N., Mulvogue, M. K., Thibodeau, M. A., McCabe, R. E., Antony, M. M., & Asmundson, G. J. G. (2012). Increasingly certain about uncertainty: Intolerance of uncertainty across anxiety and depression. *Journal of Anxiety Disorders, 26*, 468–479.

Cheavens, J. S., Feldman, D. B., Gum, A., Michael, S. T., & Snyder, C. R. (2006). Hope therapy in a community sample: A pilot investigation. *Social Indicators Research, 77*, 61–78.

Claus, E. D., Kiehl, K. A., & Hutchison, K. E. (2011). Neural and behavioral mechanisms of impulsive choice in alcohol use disorder. *Alcoholism: Clinical and Experimental Research, 35*, 1209–1219.

Coote, H. M., & MacLeod, A. K. (2012). A self-help, positive goal-focused intervention to increase well-being in people with depression. *Clinical Psychology & Psychotherapy, 19*, 305–315.

Damon, W., Menon, J., & Cotton Bronk, K. (2003). The development of purpose during adolescence. *Applied Developmental Science, 7*, 119–128.

Danchin, C. L., MacLeod, A. K., & Tata, P. (2010). Painful engagement in deliberate self-harm: The role of conditional goal setting. *Behaviour Research and Therapy, 48*, 915–920.

de Shazer, S. (1985). *Keys to solution in brief therapy*. New York, NY: W. W. Norton.

Ellis, A. (2001). *Overcoming destructive beliefs, feelings, and behaviors: New directions for Rational Emotive Behavior Therapy*. Amherst, NY: Prometheus.

Erickson, M. H. (1954). Pseudo-orientation in time as an hypnotherapeutic procedure. *International Journal of Clinical and Experimental Hypnosis, 2*, 261–283.

Forgeard, M. J. C., Haigh, E. A. P., Beck, A. T., Davidson, R. J., Henn, F. A., Maier, S. F., . . . Seligman, M. E. P. (2011). Beyond depression: Toward a process-based approach to research, diagnosis, and treatment. *Clinical Psychology: Science and Practice, 18*, 275–299.

Freud, S. (1917). Mourning and melancholia. *Standard edition of the complete psychological works of Sigmund Freud, 14*, 243–258.

Friedman, E. S., & Thase, M. E. (2006). Cognitive-behavioral therapy for depression and dysthymia. In D. J. Stein, D. J. Kupfer, & A. F. Schatzberg (Eds.), *Textbook of mood disorders* (pp. 353–371). Washington, DC: American Psychiatric Publishing.

Gorman, J. M. (1996). Comorbid depression and anxiety spectrum disorders. *Depression and Anxiety, 4*, 160–168.

Hales, S. A., Deeprose, C., Goodwin, G. M., & Holmes, E. A. (2011). Cognitions in bipolar affective disorder and unipolar depression: Imagining suicide. *Bipolar Disorders, 13*, 651–661.

Hammen, C. (2006). Stress generation in depression: Reflections on origins, research, and future directions. *Journal of Clinical Psychology, 62*, 1065–1082.

Haslam, N. (2003). Categorical versus dimensional models of mental disorder: The taxometric evidence. *Australian and New Zealand Journal of Psychiatry, 37*, 696–704.

Haslam, N., & Beck, A. T. (1994). Subtyping major depression: A taxometric analysis. *Journal of Abnormal Psychology, 103*, 686–692.

Hayes, S. C., Strosahl, K. D., & Wilson, K. G. (1999). *Acceptance and commitment therapy: An experiential approach to behavior change*. New York, NY: Guilford.

Hirsch, J. K., Duberstein, P. R., Conner, K. R., Heisel, M. J., Beckman, A., Franus, N., & Conwell, Y. (2006). Future orientation and suicide ideation and attempts in depressed adults ages 50 and over. *The American Journal of Geriatric Psychiatry, 14*, 752–757.

Holahan, C. J., Moos, R. H., Holahan, C. K., Brennan, P. L., & Schutte, K. K. (2005). Stress generation, avoidance coping, and depressive symptoms: A 10-year model. *Journal of Consulting and Clinical Psychology, 73,* 658–666.

Hollon, S. D., Evans, M. D., Auerbach, A., DeRubeis, R. J., Elkin, I., Lowery, A., ... Piasecki, J. (1988). *Development of a system for rating therapies for depression: Differentiating cognitive therapy, interpersonal psychotherapy, and clinical management pharmacotherapy.* Unpublished manuscript, Vanderbilt University, Nashville, TN.

Holmes, E. A., & Mathews, A. (2010). Mental imagery in emotion and emotional disorders. *Clinical Psychology Review, 30,* 349–362.

Jacobson, N. S., Martell, C. R., & Dimidjian, S. (2001). Behavioral activation treatment for depression: Returning to contextual roots. *Clinical Psychology: Science and Practice, 8,* 255–270.

Kasch, K. L., Rottenberg, J., Arnow, B. A., & Gotlib, I. H. (2002). Behavioral activation and inhibition systems and the severity and course of depression. *Journal of Abnormal Psychology, 111,* 589–597.

Kirby, K. N., Petry, N. M., & Bickel, W. K. (1999). Heroin addicts have higher discount rates for delayed rewards than non-drug-using controls. *Journal of Experimental Psychology: General, 128,* 78–87.

Kosnes, L., Whelan, R., O'Donovan, A., & McHugh, L. A. (2013). Implicit measurement of positive and negative future thinking as a predictor of depressive symptoms and hopelessness. *Consciousness and Cognition, 22,* 898–912.

Kovacs, M., & Garrison, B. (1985). Hopelessness and eventual suicide: A 10-year prospective study of patients hospitalized with suicidal ideation. *American Journal of Psychiatry, 142,* 559–563.

Little, B. R. (1983). Personal projects: A rationale and method for investigation. *Environment and Behavior, 15,* 279–309.

Loewenstein, G. (1987). Anticipation and the valuation of delayed consumption. *The Economic Journal, 97,* 666–684.

MacLeod, A. K., Coates, E., & Hetherton, J. (2008). Increasing well-being through teaching goal setting and planning skills: Results of a brief intervention. *Journal of Happiness Studies, 9,* 185–196.

MacLeod, A. K., & Cropley, M. L. (1995). Depressive future-thinking: The role of valence and specificity. *Cognitive Therapy and Research, 19,* 35–50.

MacLeod, A. K., Tata, P., Kentish, J., Carroll, F., & Hunter, E. (1997). Anxiety, depression, and explanation-based pessimism for future positive and negative events. *Clinical Psychology & Psychotherapy, 4,* 15–24.

MacLeod, A. K., Tata, P., Tyrer, P., Schmidt, U., Davidson, K., & Thompson, S. (2005). Hopelessness and positive and negative future thinking in parasuicide. *British Journal of Clinical Psychology, 44,* 495–504.

Malouff, J. M., Thorsteinsson, E. B., & Schutte, N. S. (2007). The efficacy of problem solving therapy in reducing mental and physical health problems: A meta-analysis. *Clinical Psychology Review, 27,* 46–57.

McCullough, M. E. (2002). Savoring life, past and present: Explaining what hope and gratitude share in common. *Psychological Inquiry, 13,* 302–304.

McKnight, P. E., & Kashdan, T. B. (2009). Purpose in life as a system that creates and sustains health and well-being: An integrative, testable theory. *Review of General Psychology, 13,* 242–251.

Metalsky, G. I., Joiner, T. E., Hardin, T. S., & Abramson, L. Y. (1993). Depressive reactions to failure in a naturalistic setting: A test of the hopelessness and self-esteem theories of depression. *Journal of Abnormal Psychology, 102,* 101–109.

Miles, H., MacLeod, A. K., & Pote, H. (2004). Retrospective and prospective cognitions in adolescents: Anxiety, depression, and positive and negative affect. *Journal of Adolescence, 27,* 691–701.

Miloyan, B., Pachana, N. A., & Suddendorf, T. (2014). The future is here: A review of foresight systems in anxiety and depression. *Cognition & Emotion, 28,* 795–810.

Miranda, R., Fontes, M., & Marroquín, B. (2008). Cognitive content-specificity in future expectancies: Role of hopelessness and intolerance of uncertainty in depression and GAD symptoms. *Behaviour Research and Therapy, 46,* 1151–1159.

Miranda, R., & Mennin, D. S. (2007). Depression, generalized anxiety disorder, and certainty in pessimistic predictions about the future. *Cognitive Therapy and Research, 31,* 71–82.

Monterosso, J., Ainslie, G., Xu, J., Cordova, X., Domier, C., & London, E. (2006). Frontoparietal cortical activity of methamphetamine-dependent and comparison subjects performing a delay discounting task. *Human Brain Mapping, 28,* 383–393.

Morina, N., Deeprose, C., Pusowski, C., Schmid, M., & Holmes, E. A. (2011). Prospective mental imagery in patients with major depressive disorder or anxiety disorders. *Journal of Anxiety Disorders, 25,* 1032–1037.

Nesse, R. M. (2004). Natural selection and the elusiveness of happiness. *Philosophical Transactions—Royal Society of London, Series B Biological Sciences, 359,* 1333–1348.

Norem, J. K., & Chang, E. C. (2002). The positive psychology of negative thinking. *Journal of Clinical Psychology, 58,* 993–1001.

O'Connor, R. C., Fraser, L., Whyte, M. C., MacHale, S., & Masterton, G. (2008). A comparison of specific positive future expectancies and global hopelessness as predictors of suicidal ideation in a prospective study of repeat self-harmers. *Journal of Affective Disorders, 110,* 207–214.

O'Connor, R. C., & Williams, J. M. G. (2014). The relationship between positive future thinking, brooding, defeat and entrapment. *Personality and Individual Differences, 70,* 29–34.

Oettingen, G., Hönig, G., & Gollwitzer, P. M. (2000). Effective self-regulation of goal attainment. *International Journal of Educational Research, 33,* 705–732.

Orth, U., Robins, R. W., & Roberts, B. W. (2008). Low self-esteem prospectively predicts depression in adolescence and young adulthood. *Journal of Personality and Social Psychology, 95,* 695–708.

Padesky, C. A., & Mooney, K. A. (2012). Strengths-based cognitive–behavioural therapy: A four-step model to build resilience. *Clinical Psychology & Psychotherapy, 19,* 283–290.

Pavlov, I. P. (1927). *Conditioned reflexes: An investigation of the physiological activity of the cerebral cortex.* London, England: Oxford University Press.

Peterson, C., & Seligman, M. E. P. (1984). Causal explanations as a risk factor for depression: Theory and evidence. *Psychological Review, 91,* 347–374.

Peterson, C., Semmel, A., Baeyer, C., Abramson, L. Y., Metalsky, G. I., & Seligman, M. E. P. (1982). The attributional style questionnaire. *Cognitive Therapy and Research, 6,* 287–300.

Ruscio, J., & Ruscio, A. M. (2000). Informing the continuity controversy: A taxometric analysis of depression. *Journal of Abnormal Psychology, 109,* 473–487.

Ryff, C. D., & Keyes, C. L. M. (1995). The structure of psychological well-being revisited. *Journal of Personality and Social Psychology, 69,* 719–727.

Sargalska, J., Miranda, R., & Marroquín, B. (2011). Being certain about an absence of the positive: Specificity in relation to hopelessness and suicidal ideation. *International Journal of Cognitive Therapy, 4,* 104–116.

Segal, Z. V., Williams, J. M. G., & Teasdale, J. D. (2012). *Mindfulness-based cognitive therapy for depression.* New York, NY: Guilford.

Seligman, M. E. P. (1972). Learned helplessness. *Annual Review of Medicine, 23,* 407–412.

Seligman, M. E. P. (2012). *Flourish: A visionary new understanding of happiness and well-being.* New York, NY: Free Press.

Seligman, M. E. P., Abramson, L. Y., Semmel, A., & von Baeyer, C. (1979). Depressive attributional style. *Journal of Abnormal Psychology, 88,* 242–247.

Seligman, M. E. P., Rashid, T., & Parks, A. C. (2006). Positive psychotherapy. *American Psychologist, 61,* 774–788.

Sherratt, K. A., & MacLeod, A. K. (2013). Underlying motivation in the approach and avoidance goals of depressed and non-depressed individuals. *Cognition & Emotion, 27,* 1432–1440.

Strunk, D. R., Lopez, H., & DeRubeis, R. J. (2006). Depressive symptoms are associated with unrealistic negative predictions of future life events. *Behaviour Research and Therapy, 44,* 861–882.

Szpunar, K. K., & Schacter, D. L. (2013). Get real: Effects of repeated simulation and emotion on the perceived plausibility of future experiences. *Journal of Experimental Psychology: General, 142,* 323–327.

Taylor, S. E., Pham, L. B., Rivkin, I. D., & Armor, D. A. (1998). Harnessing the imagination: Mental simulation, self-regulation, and coping. *American Psychologist, 53,* 429–439.

van Beek, W., Kerkhof, A., & Beekman, A. (2009). Future oriented group training for suicidal patients: A randomized clinical trial. *BMC Psychiatry, 9*(65), 1–7. doi:10.1186/1471–244X-9–65

Vergara, C., & Roberts, J. E. (2011). Motivation and goal orientation in vulnerability to depression. *Cognition & Emotion, 25,* 1281–1290.

Vilhauer, J. S., Young, S., Kealoha, C., Borrmann, J., IsHak, W. W., Rapaport, M. H., ... Mirocha, J. (2012). Treating major depression by creating positive expectations for the future: A pilot study for the effectiveness of future-directed therapy (FDT) on symptom severity and quality of life. *CNS Neuroscience & Therapeutics, 18*, 102–109.

Watson, J. B., & Rayner, R. (1920). Conditioned emotional reactions. *Journal of Experimental Psychology, 3*, 1–14.

Wright, J. H., Basco, M. R., & Thase, M. E. (2006). *Learning cognitive-behavior therapy: An illustrated guide*. Arlington, VA: American Psychiatric Publishing.

Zimbardo, P. G., & Boyd, J. N. (1999). Putting time in perspective: A valid, reliable individual-differences metric. *Journal of Personality and Social Psychology, 77*, 1271–1288.

11

Creativity and Aging: What We Can Make With What We Have Left

*Martin Seligman with Marie Forgeard
and Scott Barry Kaufman*

T HREE OF THE FOUR AUTHORS OF THIS BOOK ARE OLDER than 60, and the fourth, Chandra Sripada, is no longer a spring chicken. We believe, in spite of our age, that our advocacy of prospection is quite a creative turn for psychology, philosophy, and neuroscience. It is natural that the four of us should be invested in the issue of aging and creativity and that our concluding chapter should tackle this thorny issue.

Almost 40 years ago, Seligman was fortunate enough to spend an evening with psychologists Jerome Bruner and Donald Broadbent, who were both in their mid-60s. When asked, "Be honest. When were you really at your most creative?" both answered without hesitation: "Right now!" Similarly, Seligman meets once a month with Aaron Beck, age 93. His answer is exactly the same, "Right now!"

Are these self-serving delusions, or can creativity actually increase with age?

Much research suggests that neural conduction speed, memory, and stamina decline as we get older (Baltes & Lindenberger, 1997; Hoyer & Verhaeghen, 2006; Salthouse, 1996, 2004). In addition, historiometric studies have shown that creative productivity in the arts and sciences tends to peak within a few decades of the start of one's career, and then decreases gradually afterwards (Lehman, 1966; Simonton, 1977, 2012; Zuckerman, 1977). There are, of course, exceptions: Kant wrote his most famous work, *The Critique of Pure Reason*, at age 57, and Verdi composed *Falstaff* at around 80. Pavlov did not even begin his conditioning work until the second half of his life. This pattern, however, varies by field (youth seems to be more of an asset for mathematicians and poets than other scholars), and a second peak ("swan song") often occurs later in life (Feist, 2006; Simonton, 2006).

The conclusions that can be drawn from the current body of literature clearly indicate that creativity tends to decline with age, in spite of anecdotal reports to the contrary. Let us, however, propose a counterfactual thought experiment. Let us consider, for a moment, that some individuals are indeed able to maintain and even enhance their creative abilities as they age. How could this be? Trying to answer this question is in itself an exercise in creativity that can help us understand what factors are responsible for the negative age trend. It forces us to extrude a number of putative elements of creativity and to ask which elements do in fact deteriorate with age, which elements do not, and what factors enable them to do so. Answering this is not only a matter of consolation for the authors of this book, but it might even point the way toward how to train more creativity—even among youngsters.

Defining Creativity

We begin with a working definition of creativity and how this construct differs from related ones, including imagination, prospection, originality, and innovation. We clarify our working definitions of each to yield a framework for understanding creativity.

The first and the core skill is *imagination*, which consists of mental representations (visual, verbal, and auditory) of things that are not present to the senses. Imagination is about some alternative to present perception (Markman, Klein, & Suhr, 2009) and includes all of the following: mental imagery of things that may or may not exist, counterfactual conjecture, alternative pasts, daydreaming, fantasizing, pretending, mental simulation of other minds, mental rehearsal, and aspects of night dreaming. Although the term "imaginative" has positive connotations in everyday speech (e.g., an imaginative movie script), imagination itself is neutral. Imagination includes adaptive activities (like effective scenario planning in a business setting) and maladaptive activities (like frightening imagery that fuels phobic avoidance). Similarly, imagination implies novelty to the layperson, but imagination need not be original. Mentally rehearsing one's golf swing or repetitively worrying about leaving the oven on are examples of banal imagination. Imagination need not be about the future: The ancient cave painting of animals being hunted represents absent events, but in this case likely past events.

Prospection, the central topic of this book, is imagination about possible futures. By definition, these possibilities contain elements that are not present to the senses now. Prospecting can have visual, verbal, kinesthetic, and auditory representations (Buckner & Carroll, 2007; Gilbert & Wilson, 2007; Seligman, Railton, Baumeister, & Sripada, 2013; Taylor, Pham, Rivkind, & Armor, 1998).

Originality is prospecting that introduces *novelty*. One can prospect without originality by taking the past and merely projecting it into the future. Originality, conversely, introduces new variables, perspectives, and possibilities (Sawyer, 2012).

Creativity requires originality, which in turn requires prospection, which in turn requires imagination. Creativity, crucially, also requires usefulness and a good sense of the audience who will make use of the idea (Amabile, 1983; Sternberg & Lubart, 1999). "Audience" can refer to a literal audience, but at the highest levels of creativity, it is often the gatekeeping members of the discipline to which the original idea applies (Csikszentmihalyi, 1999). Importantly a sense of audience requires enough knowledge of the discipline to accurately evaluate the worth of one's novel idea and the likelihood of its success. Researchers have also argued that creativity requires that an idea or product is "surprising" or "nonobvious" (Boden, 2004; Bruner, 1962; Simonton, 2012), and we agree.

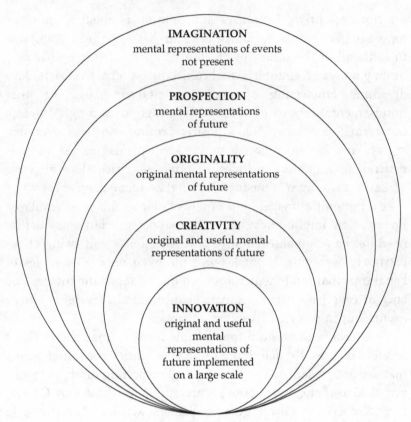

FIGURE 11.1. Creativity and Allied Terms

Finally, *innovation* refers to bringing a creative idea to scale by successfully implementing it on a large scale within an organization or society at large (Amabile, 1988; Sawyer, 2012). Figure 11.1 depicts the interconnected terms we use to describe creativity.

Because creativity consists of the generation of ideas or products that are both original and useful, it means that a wide array of separate but related cognitive processes are at play to satisfy both criteria. Thus, researchers have suggested that the creative process may best be characterized by a *generation* phase, in which original ideas are freely invented without scrutiny, followed by an *evaluation* or *exploration* phase, during which the value of ideas is examined, and ideas are elaborated and refined as needed (Finke, Ward, & Smith, 1992). When asked by a student how he was able to come up with so many good ideas, Linus Pauling famously replied, "You have a lot of ideas and throw out the bad ones" (Csikszentmihalyi, 1996, p. 116).

The creative process, of course, does not happen in such a clean sequence, as generative and evaluative processes often take place in an iterative and almost simultaneous fashion. Nevertheless, this framework suggests that a review of the factors at play in creativity should consider the relative contribution of each cognitive process to generative and/or evaluative processes. Some of the factors reviewed in the following sections may primarily influence generative processes, whereas others may primarily shape evaluative ones. Many probably contribute to both.

The Present Review

Based on the growing body of literature examining psychological elements at play in creativity, we propose that three sets of factors need considering in order to understand the effects of aging. We begin by reviewing factors related to (a) *cognition and expertise*, including cognitive abilities, originality, mind-wandering, knowledge and expertise, intuition, pattern recognition, and heuristics. Next, we consider the role of factors related to (b) *personality and motivation*, including flexibility, openness to experience, integrative complexity, strength of interest, intrinsic motivation, ambition, grit, optimism, confidence, self-efficacy, and energy. Finally, we examine the contribution of (c) *interpersonal processes*, such as having a good sense of the audience and engaging in collaboration.

Although this list of factors is not exhaustive, these are the most important and thoroughly researched psychological influences.

Cognition and Expertise

Cognitive Abilities

Over the past 100 years, intelligence researchers have done a remarkable job cataloging covariations among various cognitive abilities (Carroll, 1993). The modern synthesis takes the form of the Cattell-Horn-Carroll (CHC) theory of cognitive abilities, which consists of nine broad cognitive abilities that have been consistently validated during the past decade (Schneider & McGrew, 2012):

1. *Fluid reasoning (Gf)*: "The deliberate but flexible control of attention to solve novel 'on the spot' problems that cannot be

performed by relying exclusively on previously learned habits, schemas, and scripts."

2. *Crystallized intelligence (Gc)*: "Depth and breadth of knowledge and skills that are valued by one's culture."

3. *Short-term memory (Gsm)*: "The ability to encode, maintain, and manipulate information in one's immediate awareness."

4. *Long-term storage and retrieval (Glr)*: "The ability to store, consolidate, and retrieve information over period of time measures in minutes, hours, days, and years."

5. *Visual processing (Gv)*: "The ability to make use of simulated mental imagery (often in conjunction with currently perceived images) to solve problems."

6. *Auditory processing (Ga)*: "The ability to detect and process meaningful nonverbal information in sound."

7. *Processing speed (Gs)*: "The ability to perform simple repetitive cognitive tasks quickly and fluently."

8. *Quantitative knowledge (Gq)*: "Depth and breadth of knowledge related to mathematics."

9. *Reading and Writing (Grw)*: "Depth and breadth of knowledge and skills related to written language."

While partially distinct, all nine of these broad cognitive abilities are positively correlated with each other, and are positively correlated, in varying degrees, with a more global cognitive ability factor, *g* (Carroll, 1993; Jensen, 1998).

Cognitive abilities and creativity. How do these cognitive abilities relate to creativity? Early research examining the relationship between general cognitive ability and creativity resulted in the threshold theory, which holds that overall cognitive ability, *g*, only matters until a certain point proposed to be somewhere around 120 IQ points (Guilford, 1967; Jung et al., 2009; Yamamoto, 1964). Other findings, however, do not support the threshold theory (Kim, 2005; Preckel, Holling, & Wiese, 2006).

In evaluating the threshold hypothesis, we believe that it is useful to distinguish *creative cognition* (which is part of the cognitive ability nexus) from *creative achievement* (which depends on many other factors, including the noncognitive ones reviewed next). A recent study investigated the cognitive and personality predictors of creative achievement in the arts versus the sciences (S. B. Kaufman et al.,

2015). Across four samples, comprising more than 1,000 demographically diverse participants, the researchers found that *g* and divergent thinking were much stronger predictors of creative achievement in the sciences (inventions and scientific discovery) than the arts (visual arts, music, dance, creative writing, humor, and theater and film). In fact, there appeared to be no cognitive ability threshold for the arts: Cognitive abilities were not significantly correlated with creative achievement in the arts.

Taken together, it appears that cognitive abilities facilitate creative cognition but only up to a certain point (depending on the domain). Beyond this threshold, cognitive abilities may still have an important influence on the extent to which creative ideas are translated into actual creative achievements, perhaps by aiding in the evaluation and usefulness of the ideas, although more research is needed to further examine this hypothesis.

Cognitive abilities and aging. More than 50 years of research has consistently found that fluid reasoning (*Gf*) and processing speed (*Gs*) are extremely vulnerable to aging, whereas crystallized intelligence (*Gc*)—knowledge—is maintained throughout most of adult life (Cattell & Horn, 1978; Salthouse, 1985, 1996). With the advent of contemporary IQ tests grounded in CHC theory, researchers have more recently been able to assess the developmental trajectories of a wider range of cognitive abilities. This research confirms that fluid reasoning (*Gf*), short-term memory (*Gsm*), processing speed (*Gs*), reading comprehension (a component of *Gc*), quantitative knowledge (*Gq*), math reasoning (*MR*), math calculation (*MC*), and writing abilities (*Grw-Writing*) all decline with age (A. S. Kaufman, Johnson, & Liu, 2008).

In contrast, large-scale studies conducted on contemporary IQ batteries have found that long-term retrieval (*Glr*), visual processing (*Gv*), auditory processing (*Ga*), verbal knowledge (the vocabulary and general knowledge components of *Gc*), academic knowledge (*AK*), reading abilities (*Grw*), oral expression (*OE*), and listening comprehension (*LC*) are maintained at least to the age of 65.

Therefore, we conclude that speed, fluid reasoning, and short-term memory all likely decline with age and that all of these declines contribute to a possible decline in creative thinking and creative achievement.

Originality

Another cognitive ability relevant to creativity is the ability to imagine and generate multiple possibilities, ideas, and solutions to a problem. E. Paul Torrance (1988) referred to this ability as "divergent thinking," John Carroll (1993) referred to it as "idea production," and J. P. Guilford (1984) referred to it as "divergent production." We call it "originality": the mental representation of novel ideas. Whatever its name, this ability is part of the general cognitive ability nexus (Silvia, 2008), and it is partially distinct from the broad cognitive abilities that form the core of the CHC model.

Originality declines after the age of 40 (McCrae, Arenberg, & Costa, 1987), which is probably caused by its reliance on fluid reasoning and executive functioning (Batey, Chamorro-Premuzic, & Furnham, 2009; Silvia & Beaty, 2012). Older individuals may, however, be able to retain their originality if they use a different cognitive strategy and rely on declarative memory to enhance their performance (Leon, Altmann, Abrams, Gonzalez Rothi, & Heilman, 2014). These findings suggest that accumulated knowledge may compensate for the effects of aging on cognitive abilities (as expanded on in following section). Nonetheless, we conclude that a second cognitive factor—originality—likely declines with age and might contribute to a decline in creative achievement.

Daydreaming and Mind-Wandering

More than 50 years ago, pioneering research by Jerome L. Singer and colleagues provided evidence that daydreaming is a widespread and normal aspect of human inner experience (McMillan, Kaufman, & Singer, 2013; Singer, 1966). In the past 10 years, there has been a resurgence of research on the costs and benefits of daydreaming, with the term "mind-wandering" showing a dramatic increase in the frequency of articles using this term (Callard, Smallwood, Golchert, & Margulies, 2013). This renewed interest in mind-wandering is partly caused by the discovery of the default network that we discussed at length earlier.

How are the default network and the self-generated cognitions that arise from it related to creativity? For one, the default network plays a role in imagination by "constructing dynamic mental simulations based on personal experiences such as used during re-membering, thinking about the future, and generally when imagin-ing alternative perspectives and scenarios to the present" (Buckner, Andrews-Hanna, & Schacter, 2008, pp. 18–19). It is for this reason that we are fond of thinking of it as the "imagination" network. Indeed, a recent large-scale review of the literature on the neuro-science of creativity suggested that the default network is a criti-cal contributor to originality (Jung, Mead, Carrasco, & Flores, 2013). In conjunction with executive functions, such as cognitive control, inhibition, and flexibility, mental simulations of the future can be harnessed for practical value. Recent research suggests that the de-fault network interacts with other large-scale brain systems (such as the executive attention network) to maintain an internal train of thought (Andrews-Hanna, Smallwood, & Spreng, 2014; Smallwood, Brown, Baird, & Schooler, 2012).

Second, the default network is related to mind-wandering (e.g., Mason et al., 2007), and this has implications for the generation of creative insights. The "Aha!" experience rarely comes while the mind is focused intensely on solving a problem. Instead, creative insights typically arise unsupervised, when the conscious mind has wandered away from the task at hand, enabling spontaneously generated novel connections. Unlike machine models of mind, the mind is likely in wild chaos much of the time. The mind wanders, is nimble, and is opportunistic, but it *can* focus—but only for limited periods of time.

In keeping with this, evidence suggests that the ability to gener-ate original ideas, as well as actual creative achievement, is associated with diffuse, unfocused attention to the external environment (e.g., Jung et al., 2013; Martindale, 1981; White & Shah, 2006).

Mind-wandering and aging. Mind-wandering and task-unrelated thoughts have been found to decrease with age, at least under labora-tory conditions (Giambra, 1989; Singer & McCraven, 1961; Tamplin, Krawietz, Radvansky, & Copeland, 2013). This finding is consistent with research showing reduced activity in the default mode network as people age (Damoiseaux et al., 2008).

So far we have reviewed five cognitive factors that decline with age and likely contribute to a decline in creativity:

1. Speed
2. Short-term memory

3. Fluid reasoning
4. Originality
5. Mind-wandering

This paints a dismal picture for Bruner, Broadbent, Beck, and the rest of us as we age. However, some cognitive factors are maintained into older age, including long-term retrieval, verbal and academic knowledge, reading abilities, oral expression, and listening comprehension. Because these abilities draw more on knowledge and expertise, we now look at additional knowledge-related factors that likely improve with age and, therefore, might contribute to a compensatory increase in creativity with age.

Knowledge and Expertise

Although acquiring knowledge in any domain is an important part of the creative process, not all forms of knowledge are well captured by the tests of cognitive ability reviewed earlier. One significant source of individual differences not assessed by traditional measures of cognitive ability is *domain-specific knowledge,* defined as knowledge of the particular dominant culture (such as occupational and avocational knowledge). Ackerman refers to this knowledge as the "dark matter" of adult intelligence (Ackerman, 2000), an under-appreciated yet crucial determinant of achievement.

Another term for domain-specific knowledge is "expertise." This knowledge takes two forms: *procedural knowledge* (knowing how to do something, heavily required for athletic domains such as sports and dancing) and *declarative knowledge* (factual information stored in long-term memory, necessary for more cognitive domains). K. Anders Ericsson and colleagues have studied the development of expertise in a wide variety of domains, including medicine, surgery, software design, professional writing, music, visual arts, acting, ballet, and chess (Ericsson, Charness, Feltovich, & Hoffman, 2006). They have found that mastering the tradition within a particular domain requires very long hours of learning and practice (Ericsson, Krampe, & Tesch-Römer, 1993; Ericsson & Ward, 2007).

Of course, creativity is not mere expertise. An idea is not typically judged as creative by an audience if it constitutes a *reasonable* extension of domain-specific knowledge. For example, the U.S. Patent

Office will not award patent protection if the invention represents no more than ordinary expertise in a domain. However, given that no work can be completely original (indeed, elements of tradition must always be present), creativity requires the creator to find the right balance between tradition and originality. The creator must be just the right distance ahead of the tradition: Too short and the idea is banal, too long and the idea is outlandish.

Also, the amount of expertise required to obtain world-class expertise varies dramatically between domains, and people differ dramatically in the rate in which they master the domain (Simonton, 1999). What's more, the success of training depends on many more factors than just time spent on task, including motivation, environment, and cognitive factors, such as working memory (Hambrick et al., 2014; S. B. Kaufman, 2013). For example, access to mentors and role models (Simonton, 1975) as well as family resources (think of Johann Sebastian Bach growing up in a family of musicians) likely have a great influence in determining whether training results in creative achievement.

Finally, the importance of accumulated knowledge for creativity is by no means limited to domain-specific expertise. Creative people often call on what they know from other domains—*general knowledge*—to penetrate problems. Paul Erdős, the celebrated Hungarian mathematician, for example, viewed mathematics as a social endeavor and published with 511 collaborators across almost the entire range of mathematical issues (Baker & Bollobás, 1999). He had knocked around mathematics long enough to know the entire field well enough to bring methods from one domain to bear on others. So general was his knowledge and his influence that almost all mathematicians have "Erdős numbers" to designate the degree of separation from Erdős himself: Someone who never published with Erdős but published with someone who did publish with Erdős has an Erdős number of 2. It is estimated that 90% of the world's academic mathematicians have an Erdős number below 8.

Knowledge, expertise, and aging. Not surprisingly, older adults have acquired more domain-specific knowledge than younger adults. In one study, Ackerman (2000) administered measures of cognitive ability alongside measures of knowledge in 18 domains (including art, music, world literature, biology, technology, and law) to a sample of 228 educated adults between the ages of 21 and 62. As expected, middle-aged adults displayed much higher domain-specific knowledge compared with younger adults.

The effect of age on expertise also depends on the nature of the accumulated knowledge (procedural or declarative). In general, success in domains that rely heavily on declarative knowledge tends to be correlated with cognitive ability (Ackerman, 2011; Schipolowski, Wilhelm, & Schroeders, 2014). There are between-domain differences, however. Fluid or nonverbal intelligence is more strongly related to knowledge in mathematics and the sciences, whereas verbal or crystallized intelligence is more strongly related to knowledge in the humanities (Ackerman, 2011; Park, Lubinski, & Benbow, 2007). In contrast, domains in which performance depends more on procedural knowledge (e.g., sports and dance) show diminished associations with cognitive ability as expertise increases, perhaps because of their reliance on perceptual-motor functions (Ackerman, 2011).

From a life span perspective, general knowledge, domain-specific knowledge, and procedural skills, once acquired, tend to be preserved over most of the life span (Ackerman, 2011), and the acquisition of knowledge has been shown to help compensate for the decline of cognitive ability in a wide variety of domains, from football to music to chess to science (Ericsson, 2013). In addition, the benefits of knowledge are cumulative: Early success provides advantages that initiate a virtuous cycle (Merton, 1968; Petersen, Jung, Yang, & Stanley, 2011), with early knowledge stimulating the discovery and use of more knowledge, so multiplying the chances that creative ideas will emerge.

While many cognitive abilities decline as we age, *knowledge and expertise increase*, and these factors play a major, necessary role in creativity. Increased knowledge may help compensate for decreased mental speed, decreased short-term memory, poorer fluid reasoning, and less originality as we age.

Intuition, Pattern Recognition, and Heuristics

Over the past 30 years, research has revealed that much information processing takes places *implicitly*—without intent, awareness, or conscious reasoning—and this implicit form of knowledge plays a crucial role in thinking, reasoning, and creativity (Kihlstrom, 1987; Polyani, 1966; Wagner & Sternberg, 1985). This has led to dual-process theories, which distinguish between two types or systems of thinking (Evans, 2008; Kahneman, 2011).

System 1 processes operate fast, automatically, and are not dependent on slower, conscious, and voluntary control systems. System 1 processes include affect, pattern recognition, intuition, heuristics, implicit learning, and latent inhibition. These processes are fast, unconscious, effortless, and involuntary. In contrast, system 2 processes require attention, are associated with *g*, and are voluntary, supervised, executive functioning. These processes are slow, linear, conscious, and effortful, and they come into play when and if we bother to question and then check the output of the system 1 processes. In this section, we discuss the relation of creativity to the following system 1 processes: intuition, pattern recognition, and heuristics.

Much well-practiced knowledge involves the automatic recognition of situations that resemble situations encountered previously. We sometimes call this kind of automatic recognition "intuition." For example, we have no trouble recognizing a table or a game when we see one, but how do we do this? Unlike circles, there is no one property that all games have in common (no necessary condition), and no one property that distinguishes a game from all other activities or a table from all other objects (no sufficient condition). Wittgenstein proposed that intuitive recognition is explained by "family resemblances" (1953/2009), but this explanation only substitutes one mystery for another. Seligman and Kahana (2008) suggested that the mind must perform three tasks to decide if a table is a table: First, identify all relevant dimensions to the decision (which, following Wittgenstein, are only *relevant*, but not necessary or sufficient); second, assign a value and a weight for each relevant dimension and each interaction; and third, create a decision rule for table-hood. This process results in *a mathematical model that weights each dimension (and their interactions) in such a way as to reliably distinguish past instances of tables from non-tables*. This model has been shown to work for recognizing faces, even when upside down or in different profiles (Lacroix, Murre, Postma, & van den Herik, 2006).

Thus, one of the core processes at play in intuition seems to be the recognition of patterns. Beyond recognizing tables, pattern recognition underpins analogical reasoning, which consists of mapping knowledge from a base domain to a target domain, for example, recognizing that the structure of an atom is understood by thinking about the structure of the solar system (Gentner, 1989). Isaac Newton's insight about gravity, for example, resulted from seeing an apple and the moon subtending the same visual angle. Armed with knowledge and expertise, Newton suddenly wondered if what draws the apple to the earth is the same force that holds the moon in orbit (Gleick, 2004). Many other creative moments illustrate the role of pattern recognition and analogical thinking in creativity: Benjamin Franklin's discovery that lightning contained the same stuff (electricity) that charged batteries is another example.

Pattern recognition is at the heart of Jeffrey Hawkins's theory of intelligence (and, in turn, of creativity). Hawkins and Blakeslee (2007) proposed that intelligence consists in the prediction of the future, not in the knowledge of the past. They used the visual cortex as their model (see also Clark, 2013). The visual cortex is layered, with activity of the neurons in the lowest layer (V1) reflecting the voluminous information that arrives at the retina. Each succeeding layer abstracts only some of the information from the layer below. Importantly, connections not only go up the layers, but also back down the layers, and in fact, there are 10 times as many downward connections as upward ones. In their theory, the downward connections tell the lower layers what pattern is *predicted* in the next moment's saccade (eye-movement): inhibiting unexpected connections and exciting expected connections.

Creativity, for Hawkins, resides in the patterns that are formed in the very top layers, the cross-modal layers that integrate all information available. How do creative insights emerge if unexpected information is inhibited and we only rely on memory to predict the future and act in the present? The answer, according to Hawkins's memory-prediction framework, lies in pattern recognition. When confronted with a novel problem, we conjure memories of similar situations, and find out how to solve it using analogical reasoning. Although Hawkins and Blakeslee (2007) deem all analogies creative, they explain that creativity is most obvious when "our memory-prediction system operates a higher level of abstraction, when it makes uncommon predictions using uncommon analogies" (p. 185). It must be remarked that Hawkins's theory is itself a theory that shows its sense. It argues that creativity proceeds by the discovery of very high order analogies, and it comes to this conclusion by using the visual system as a high order analogy of the creative process.

Heuristics. Closely related to intuition and pattern recognition are heuristics. Accumulated knowledge leads to the ability to use fast shortcuts, or "heuristics" to make decisions, rather than relying on effortful decision-making (Baron, 2000; Peters, Finucane, MacGregor, & Slovic, 2000). Importantly, heuristics are not algorithms (i.e., cookie-cutter methods for solving a problem), but involve a certain degree of flexibility that allows them to be useful for creative solutions (Amabile, 1996). Also, heuristics are often automatic (but still flexible) ways of processing information and making decisions. Thus, individuals may often not be able to verbalize what shortcut they are taking. Heuristics can be broadly categorized as "negative heuristics" (what to avoid) and "positive heuristics" (what to do) (Lakatos, 1970). Physicians' oath to *do no harm*, eight of the Ten Commandments (e.g., "Thou shalt not steal"), and of course, "If it ain't broke, don't fix it," are all examples of negative heuristics.

But a major caveat about negative heuristics is in order: *Not getting it wrong does not equal getting it right.* Imagine making a speech with no grammatical errors. Or writing a biography in which nothing untrue is said. Or serving a meal in which nothing tastes bad. Or proving a theorem in which every statement was true. Or playing the Beethoven Opus 109 with no mistakes. Or chairing a meeting in which no one was discourteous. None of these would guarantee a good speech, a good book, a good meal, a good proof, a good performance, or a good meeting.

This is where positive heuristics come in, by providing us with shortcuts to figure out the right thing to do. To complicate matters, however, such heuristics often lead to biases. The study of how ordinarily useful heuristics can go wrong has been the meat and potatoes of the work of Kahneman and Tversky (Gilovich, Griffin, & Kahneman, 2002; Kahneman, 2011). Consider the "availability heuristic": For example, a woman is asked to estimate the frequency with which physical assaults take place in her city. She replies that such assaults are extremely common. Following the availability heuristic, this person based her judgment on "the ease with which instances come to mind" (Kahneman, 2011). In this case, the woman had just read about an assault. If she lived in an unsafe city, the heuristic led to an accurate answer and saved time. If her city is indeed safe compared to most other cities, the heuristic saved cognitive processing time but led to an inaccurate answer. Thus, the availability heuristic often leads to a bias.

There is no doubt that the study of problems associated with heuristics is important given their occasional negative consequences. However, researchers should not neglect to further investigate adaptive heuristics and how they often lead to enhanced outcomes. Heuristics may not usually lead to errors in thinking. We believe that system 1 and the shortcuts it relies on are at the heart of the adaptive prospecting of possible futures. At the margins, heuristics make errors, but by and large, they are our first and most robust way of navigating the future (Seligman et al., 2013). When they do not lead to biases, positive heuristics allow goodness, rightness, beauty, and truth to occur over and above the mere absence of badness, wrongness, ugliness, or falsehood.

George Pólya's classic book *How to Solve It* (1945) provides shortcuts to help students learn to solve mathematical problems independently (e.g., "Do you know a related problem?"). Anne Lamott, the author of bestseller *Bird by Bird* (1994), begins all of her workshops by telling students that "good writing is about telling the truth." Gordon's (1961) *Synectics* encourages participants to "make the familiar strange and the strange familiar." The creative problem solving (CPS) approach suggests the virtue of "looking at something, and seeing something else" (Treffinger, Isaksen, & Dorval, 2000, p. 57). Although some creativity-training programs (e.g., CPS) have received empirical support (e.g., Puccio, Firestien, Coyle, & Masucci, 2006), the specific contribution of the use of positive heuristics for creative thinking has (to the best of our knowledge) not yet been dismantled.

In addition, the degree to which positive heuristics can be domain-general remains unclear. Many heuristics may be domain-specific and work because they succinctly convey domain-specific knowledge. Yet, some broad general principles may also apply across fields, and the creativity-training programs described earlier generally seek to offer such domain-general heuristics. Given that positive heuristics may constitute a major source of creativity and likely are a good part of what "wisdom" means, we commend science on positive heuristics to the future. Consider the following examples of additional potential heuristics for creativity in various domains: Above all be kind. A good tragedy "takes an ice-axe to the frozen sea inside of us."When in doubt, stand on principle.A good symphony comes to perfect resolution.In comedy the funniest line comes last. The next funniest comes first.A good meal brings out the best in its natural ingredients.

A good piece of science tells us that something we thought was false is true, or something we thought was true is false—or even just gets us to think about something we never thought about before. Consider the following:A good theory makes counterintuitive predictions.A good person shows us how to lead our lives.

Intuition, pattern recognition, heuristics, and aging. How do intuition, pattern recognition, and heuristics fare with age? As with all cognitive abilities, seeing patterns sometimes requires abstract integration and fluid reasoning (see Green, Kraemer, Fugelsang, Gray, & Dunbar, 2010, 2012) and so will show some deterioration with aging. But those aspects of pattern recognition that are automatic draw heavily on knowledge and domain-specific expertise, which are factors that likely improve with age.

Thus, analogies, pattern recognition, and intuitions may constitute paradigm cases of the "compensatory" mechanisms that Baltes and Baltes (1990) invoked in their theory of "optimization with compensation" as we age. The older we get, the more information and experiences are available to us, and the more examples of successful patterns, heuristics, and intuitions we have to draw on. As time passes, we may also be able to refine the dimensions along which we intuitively weigh information. Consider a lieutenant recognizing a likely ambush. The lieutenant intuitively and correctly decides that this bit of forest is a likely ambush site, based on weighing relevant dimensions. The more ambushes (or the more simulations of ambushes) the lieutenant has faced, (a) the more relevant dimensions of ambushes will be *identified*, (b) the more accurate is the mean value put on each dimension (insect quiet likely means ambush), and (c) the more accurate the weight of each dimension and their interactions are (insect quiet plus no adult men in the village almost surely means ambush). The accuracy of the decision rule in multidimensional space improves with experience, but with one major proviso. Useful experience must be at the knife edge of the decision process, close decisions that vary the relevant features of the dimensions. If the experience is only repeated clear-cut instances of ambush and non-ambush, experience adds nothing—20 years of experience versus 1 year of experience twenty times.

So we conclude our review of cognitive factors in creativity with three that likely improve with age and bode well for the aging authors:

1. Domain-specific knowledge
2. General knowledge
3. Intuition, pattern recognition, and heuristics

Personality and Motivation

Having reviewed the role of various forms of cognition, we now consider the influence of personality and motivation on creativity and the trajectory with age. Torrance's longitudinal study of creative achievement provided important information about the role of personality and motivation in creative achievement. Initial findings showed that cognitive ability and divergent thinking (originality) were both important predictors of creative achievement (Cramond, Matthews-Morgan, Bandalos, & Zuo, 2005; Plucker, 1999). At the 50-year follow-up, however, cognitive ability was a weak predictor of both personal and publicly recognized creative achievement (Runco, Millar, Acar, & Cramond, 2010). In contrast, what Torrance termed "beyonder" characteristics were important predictors of creative achievement above and beyond measures of scholastic performance (Runco et al., 2010; Torrance, 1993). These characteristics included "love of work," "persistence," "deep thinking," "tolerance of mistakes," "purpose in life," "diversity of experience," "high energy," "creative self-concept," "risk taker," "openness to change," and being comfortable being a "minority of one." Thus, the Torrance longitudinal study supports the importance of looking beyond cognition and expertise to understand how creativity fares with aging.

Diversity of Experience and Flexibility

Aging brings the risk of rigidity: Finding tradition more appealing than originality, and the delicate balance between the old and the new may shift as time passes. "The expert can become so entrenched in a point of view or way of doing things that it becomes hard to see things differently" (Sternberg, 1996, p. 347). Experts may have more difficulty adapting to changes than novices because of increased rigidity.

What can be done to prevent rigidity? Simonton (2000) investigated the careers of 59 classical composers and found that two factors were particularly good predictors of the differential aesthetic success of their operas: specialization ("overtraining") having a negative effect and versatility ("cross-training") having a positive effect.

The benefit of being exposed to diverse influences is well illustrated by history and the advantages conferred on civilizations "standing at crossroads." The immune system of 15th-century Europeans was strengthened by the diversity of people and diseases the continent had been exposed to for millennia. This likely explains why Columbus' sailors survived, even exposed to new Carib Indian diseases, but the Carib Indians were decimated. Going beyond health and into culture, Tasmanian Aborigines, who were cut off from trade routes by the almost impassable Tasman Strait, saw the sophistication of their tools deteriorate across 2,000 years while those of the more nomadic Australian Aborigines improved (Diamond, 1997). By standing at crossroads, civilizations are given opportunities to integrate and make connections between unrelated and disparate influences (Mednick, 1962).

At the individual level, increased flexibility is likely one of the main mechanisms explaining the benefits of diverse experience. Research suggests that living and adapting to foreign cultures facilitates creative thinking by enhancing integrative complexity, a thinking style we discuss in the next section (Simonton, 1994, 1997; Tadmor, Galinsky, & Maddux, 2012).

Other recent research suggests that *any* unusual and unexpected experience can increase cognitive flexibility. In a series of experiments, Ritter et al. (2012) exposed participants to unusual, schema-violating experiences in a virtual reality environment (e.g., as people walked closer to a suitcase standing on a table, the size of the suitcase *decreased*, but as they walked away, the size *increased*). Those who actively engaged in this unusual virtual world subsequently scored higher in cognitive flexibility (they switched categories more on a measure of divergent thinking) than a group of people who did not experience the unusual events.

Diversity, flexibility, and aging. As we age we have more opportunity to encounter diversity. To the extent that we stay open to experience, and to the extent more experience is not just more repetition, aging allows us to "stand at crossroads." Our propensity to welcome—instead of reject—such experience is likely influenced by some of the personality influences discussed next.

Openness to Experience, Flexibility, and Integrative Complexity

"Openness to experience," which is one of the Big Five personality traits, is consistently related to creativity (S. B. Kaufman, 2013; McCrae, 1987; Silvia, Nusbaum, Berg, Martin, & O'Connor, 2009). This trait reflects a drive toward exploration and includes openness to fantasy, feelings, actions, ideas, values, and "interest in varied experiences for their own sake" (McCrae, 1987, p. 1259). Thus, individuals who are open to new experiences are more likely to make connections among seemingly unrelated pieces of information, as well as to see new patterns.

Openness to experience can be separated into two main subcomponents (DeYoung, Quilty, & Peterson, 2007): *openness* (engagement with sensory and perceptual information) and *intellect* (engagement with abstract information, primarily through explicit reasoning). While intellect is associated with general cognitive ability and working memory, openness is correlated with implicit learning (S. B. Kaufman et al., 2010). This form of learning, defined as "the ability to automatically and implicitly detect complex and noisy regularities in our environment," is closely linked to intuition and can be measured by assessing reaction time on a probabilistic sequence-learning task among other methods (S. B Kaufman et al., 2010, p. 321; Shanks, 2005).

Recent research suggests that the openness versus intellect distinction has important implications for creative achievement. Nusbaum and Silvia (2011) found that openness (but not fluid reasoning), predicted total creative achievement, whereas intellect predicted fluid reasoning but not total creative achievement. Further research suggests that openness specifically predicts creative achievement in the arts, whereas intellect predicts creative achievement in the sciences (S. B. Kaufman et al., 2015)

Openness to experience is closely related to integrative complexity, the capacity and willingness to find links among multiple competing perspectives (Suedfeld, Tetlock, & Streufert, 1992). Many studies have found that openness to experience and integrative complexity are significantly correlated, but have not decomposed this personality trait into its two subcomponents (openness and intellect). In research examining life stories, McAdams et al. (2004) found that openness to experience predicted the extent to which participants wrote complex narratives including multiple points of view, mixed motivations, complex emotions, and contradictory aspects of the self. Significant correlations between integrative complexity and openness to experience have also been noted among U.S. presidents (Simonton, 2006) and Master of Business Administration students (Tetlock, Peterson, & Berry, 1993).

Openness to experience, integrative complexity, and aging. Staying open to experience with age may play an important role in maintaining cognitive abilities. Williams, Suchy, and Kraybill (2013) found that low openness to experience in older adults was a marker of cognitive decline over the next 12 months. This was especially true of older adults who scored low on aesthetics (i.e., participants who reported being insensitive to and uninterested in art and beauty), as well as values (e.g., participants who endorsed dogmatic and rigid social, political, and religious values).

Both correlational and longitudinal studies have shown, however, that people tend to either remain stable or decrease in openness to experience as well as tolerance of ambiguity with age (Costa et al., 1986; Diehl, Coyle, & Labouvie-Vief, 1996; Soldz & Vaillant, 1999; Wortman, Lucas, & Donnellan, 2012).

We are not aware of any aging studies that have separated intellect from openness, but we hypothesize that the intellect component will be more vulnerable to the effects of aging, because of its reliance on fluid reasoning, whereas openness will remain stable or increase with age, because of its independence of cognitive ability. This prediction is also in line with research showing that linguistic markers of cognitive complexity (e.g., using causation or insight words, etc.), as well as "wise reasoning" (a construct closely related to integrative thinking), significantly increase with age (de Vries & Lehman, 1996; Grossmann, Na, Varnum, Kitayama, & Nisbett, 2012; Pennebaker & Stone, 2003).

In addition, social factors may also foster more openness with age. In academic fields, scholars probably feel much freer to seriously consider new (and perhaps outlandish) ideas once they have established themselves and obtained tenure. Thus, social factors likely increase the extent to which people have the willingness to *voice* original ideas with age, while openness itself may decline. With that said, it is also possible that openness decreases with age, as older people tend to take less risks and tend to be less revolutionary in their ideas (Simonton, 1994). Thus, we cannot yet conclude how, on balance, openness to experience and integrative complexity fare with aging. Nevertheless, our review suggests that openness to experience may lead individuals to seek diverse experiences, which are in turn conducive to creative achievement.

Interest and Motivation

In keeping with Fredrickson's (1998, 2001) "broaden-and-build" theory, positive emotions may also guide us toward novel stimuli and help us "fall in love" with something (Torrance, 1983). One of these emotions is "interest," defined by Silvia (2001, p. 285) as "a basic emotion with significant long-term adaptational functions; it cultivates knowledge and diversifies experience at all stages of life," and thus leads to "covertly building skills and expertise." By defining interest as an emotion (with specific associated facial and vocal expressions, and subjective feeling), scientists can better understand how interest leads to engaging in meaningful activities (Izard & Ackerman, 2000; Silvia, 2006).

The emotion of interest, aside from helping diversify experiences and engage with intriguing unknown stimuli, also helps us work hard to build expertise in a domain. In keeping with this, the vast literature on the "social psychology of creativity" has shown that intrinsic motivation (i.e., the degree to which one engages in an activity for its inherent rewards, rather than for external outcomes) enhances creative thinking (Amabile, 1996). Intrinsic motivation can keep us going during otherwise daunting practice (Ericsson et al., 1993; Ericsson & Ward, 2007).

Intrinsic motivation may enable "flow" during the creative process. Csikszentmihalyi—a living example of general knowledge who brings his knowledge of the arts to bear on his science—first documented this phenomenon in the 1960s as a result of observing artists painting (Csikszentmihalyi, 1990). Flow is a psychological state defined by the presence of both high skills and high challenges, giving individuals a sense of control over the activity at hand. Flow is characterized by intense focus and concentration, a merging of action and awareness, and losing track of time. In a state of flow, individuals pursue and master novel yet manageable challenges. After experiences of flow, individuals report a sense of satisfaction and enjoyment.

Interest, motivation, and aging. Do interest and intrinsic motivation change with age? We can only speculate here. To the best of our knowledge, no study has followed creative adults across various domains to assess how their motivation—intrinsic or extrinsic—changes with age. The state of flow, which is facilitated by intrinsic motivation, is described similarly by individuals of varying ages (Massimini, Csikszentmihalyi, & Delle Fave, 1988; Nakamura & Csikszentmihalyi, 2005), but it is unknown if flow changes with age.

It is possible that one's intrinsic motivation for a particular domain remains stable, or even increases as skill levels increase. The specific questions examined and methods used within a domain may change over the course of decades, but the motivation to better understand probably remains unchanged. Conversely, the fires of ambition likely bank with age (although we know of no relevant research), so we do not know how age affects the balance of the entire complex of motivation.

Psychological Resources: Grit, Self-Efficacy, and Energy

We have so far tackled processes that have a direct and specific effect on creative processes. In addition, there are a number of important psychological resources that are not specific to creativity, but are critical for achievement in general. Among these are grit, optimism, and self-efficacy.

Grit, passion, and perseverance for long-term goals (Duckworth, Peterson, Matthews, & Kelly, 2007), enable us to remain focused and determined when obstacles get in our way. Gritty individuals do not give into helplessness readily and they persist in the face of obstacles. Optimism and self-efficacy have similar benefits (Bandura, 1997; Seligman, 1991). Individuals who do not have these find themselves discouraged early in the process, as they face the first of the countless rejections the creative career necessarily entails. As Bandura (1997, p. 239) noted, "above all, innovativeness requires an unshakable sense of efficacy to persist in creative endeavors."

These resources call on energy and stamina. Mental and physical energy enable cognitive processes requiring sustained effort and self-discipline (Baumeister, Vohs, & Tice, 2007; Chaiken & Trope, 1999). High mental energy and vigor predict higher levels of work involvement in the workplace (Atwater & Carmeli, 2009; Carmeli, McKay, & Kaufman, 2014). The existing literature, however, has surprisingly little to say about what physical energy is, how it can be measured, and how it contributes to creative achievement. An old literature examining "fatigue curves" in work performance assessed physical energy by measuring decrements in performance on a strenuous physical task, such as the ability to lift or move weights, as well as the duration of rest needed to maintain performance (e.g., Hockey, 2013), but this literature seems to have no modern counterpart, and notions of energy—both mental and physical—have unfortunately not played much of a role in theorizing since the demise of Freudian dynamics. Biographies of great achievers often emphasize their exceptional levels of energy (e.g., Jamison, 2004), and we commend the study of mental and physical energy for future research on creativity.

Grit, self-efficacy, energy, and aging. Duckworth et al. (2007) found that grit increased with age in a cross-sectional study of adults. This finding may be a cohort effect (i.e., younger generations are less gritty). Alternatively, older adults may learn through experience that perseverance pays off. In addition, self-efficacy undergoes important increases over the life span, increasing from childhood to adulthood, as we learn to master the demands of each life stage. Much variability exists in old age, but many, if not most, older adults retain a sense of personal efficacy in old age (Lachman, 1986). In addition, those who are able to maintain high self-efficacy and are in supportive and challenging environments, do better intellectually and emotionally (even if their objective capacities decline) (Bandura, 1994).

In contrast, findings on the effects of aging on energy and stamina suggest that these resources decline with age. With regards to physical energy, there is no doubt that aging brings about a decrease in stamina. Some researchers have even suggested that DNA mutations of the mitochondria, the cell's energy generator, may in fact cause the aging process (Miquel, 1992; Spirduso, Francis, & MacRae, 2005). In addition, physical changes to the body's composition and metabolism lead to declines in physical activity (e.g., Roberts & Rosenberg, 2006). Thus, the decline in energy and stamina with aging may well decrease creative achievement.

So the overall influence of aging on the psychological resources that facilitate creativity is murky, mostly because of a lack of research:

- It is not known if on average, increasing rigidity is counterbalanced by increased diversity of experience with age.
- It is not known how openness to experience and integrative complexity fare with age.
- Grit and self-efficacy likely increase with age.
- Physical and mental energy likely decrease with age, but there is a surprising lack of research on energy and how it fares with age.

Interpersonal Processes

Besides cognition, knowledge, personality, and motivation, research highlights the important role of interpersonal processes for creativity. We review one's sense of the audience, as well as the ability to collaborate, and we examine how these processes fare with aging.

Sense of the Audience

Creators think about how others will react. This "sense of the audience" probably plays a very large role in both the generation and the evaluation of creative ideas—the two defining components of creativity. Sense of the audience is at the heart of the crucial distinction between originality and usefulness. Creativity requires the accurate evaluation that the original idea will be useful, beneficial, and desired by the relevant audience (Csikszentmihalyi, 1999). "Audience" is meant both literally, as in the arts and technology, and figuratively. In science and academic disciplines, "audience" refers to people at the cutting edge of the discipline, embodied by the "gatekeepers," who are the group of individuals with the power to decide which contributions will be smiled upon (Csikszentmihalyi, 1999).

A good sense of the audience may rely on perspective taking, as it allows us to accurately judge what others will see as novel and valuable (Grant & Berry, 2011). Consistent with this idea, some of the default network brain regions associated with "theory of mind" (mental simulations of the minds of others) have been found to be crucial for a positive audience reception (Falk, Morelli, Welborn, Dambacher, & Lieberman, 2013). Adequate perspective-taking may explain why relatives of individuals who suffer from schizophrenia are more represented among creative trades than nonrelatives (Kinney et al., 2001; Kyaga et al., 2011). Indeed, the looseness of thought and surplus intrusions of schizophrenia may lead to the generation of very novel ideas, but not to their accurate evaluation. What the relatives may have, and the individuals with schizophrenia lack, is a better sense of the audience.

What does perspective-taking consist of? Perspective-taking has been defined as one's ability to imagine the world from another person's point of view (Galinsky, Ku, & Wang, 2005) and to understand other people's thoughts, motivations, and emotions (Parker, Atkins, & Axtell, 2008). Such sense of audience probably also uses domain-specific and general knowledge accumulated through experience, but it is important not to mistake a good sense of audience with the goal of merely pleasing the audience. Creators may use their sense of audience to anticipate acceptance or rejection, but its function is much broader than that. Having a well-developed sense of audience allows the creator to anticipate what the audience and the domain will *ultimately* benefit from, even if the audience may *not* find the idea to be "pleasing" in the short-run (Forgeard & Mecklenburg, 2013; Silvia, 2012).

A good sense of audience stems in part from prosocial motivation, defined as the "desire to expend effort based on a concern for helping or contributing to other people" (Batson, 1987; Grant & Berry, 2011). In keeping with this, a growing body of research shows that working for the benefit of others is linked to increased creativity (for a review, see Forgeard & Mecklenburg, 2013). Prosocial motivation and a good sense of the audience probably ultimately provide creators with the resources to effectively communicate their ideas to their audience.

Such "persuasion" is a major facet of perspective taking (Simonton, 1990). Creators can persuade indirectly, by letting their work convince and inspire others, or more directly, by persuading funders (Gardner, 2011). In keeping with this, Gardner (1993) suggested that the key similarity among the seven geniuses of the 20th century—Freud, Einstein, Picasso, Stravinsky, Eliot, Graham, and Gandhi—was effective and relentless self-promotion.

Sense of audience and aging. There are good reasons to believe that age helps perspective-taking. Some of this stems from an increasing concern for the well-being of others (and especially of future generations), thinking more about legacy. Erikson referred to this as *generativity* (1963), a primary focus starting in middle age and continuing into old age (Keyes & Ryff, 1998; Sheldon & Kasser, 2001). The role legacy may play in creativity is illustrated by the swan-song phenomenon that Simonton (1989) documented in classical composers. Not infrequently, creators produce successful works at the very end of their lives.

Aside from increasing concern and motivation for others, how does aging influence the cognitive processes at play in a good sense of the audience? The research on age differences in theory of mind has produced inconsistent results, with some studies finding increases (e.g., Happé, Winner, & Brownell, 1998), others no differences (MacPherson, Phillips, & Della Sala, 2002), and others decreases (Maylor, Moulson, Muncer, & Taylor, 2002; Pratt, Diessner, Pratt, Hunsberger, & Pancer, 1996) with age. A meta-analysis of these findings, however, suggests that aging is associated with reliable *deficits* in theory of mind and task modalities (Henry, Phillips, Ruffman, & Bailey, 2013). Research on the underlying mechanisms of this decline suggests that it is only partially explained by general decline in executive function and general cognitive ability, and that a specific decline in social cognitive abilities exist (Moran, 2013; Sullivan & Ruffman, 2004).

On balance, we suspect that aging likely leads to an enhanced sense of audience thanks to the accumulated knowledge of the audience. We suspect this outweighs the possible decline in theory of mind with age. This assumes, however, stability of the audience over time. Sometimes, however, the audience changes faster than the creator can accommodate. For example, Pietro Mascagni's greatest opera was his first, after which the audience response to his successive operas declined until he was eventually booed off the stage.

Collaboration

The last factor we discuss is also not specific to creativity, but general to success: the role of collaboration. Two-thirds of the nearly 300 Nobel Prize laureates named between 1901 and 1972 received the prize for work done collaboratively, and scientists who did not win were less likely to have collaborated (Zuckerman, 1967, 1977). In addition, the number of authors on an article predicts its number of citations (Nemeth & Goncalo, 2005).

Of course, what makes collaboration effective is probably the specific choice of collaborator: someone who is similar but different enough in personality and expertise, someone who will not hesitate to challenge you and ask you to justify your ideas and opinions (Shenk, 2014). Thus, collaboration may enhance creativity by providing diversity (as earlier). In addition, collaboration may be particularly useful when it comes to evaluating the sense of audience and usefulness of an idea. Most creators do not work alone, instead, they consult and discuss their ideas with others. These others help them refine and fully understand the germ of the insight. A fine example of this process was the intense collaboration between Danny Kahneman and Amos Tversky (Kahneman, 2011). For years the two researchers spent hours each day talking about anything and everything, enjoying each other's company, and devising ways to test their theories.

Aging and collaboration. How does collaboration fare with age? Older adults may use collaboration as a way to compensate for general cognitive decline by recruiting another's abilities (Dixon, 2000). In addition, maturation probably helps us be better able to pick the right collaborators—people who share a similar vision, yet offer different perspectives. We may also have a larger network of potential collaborators to choose from, and we may be better equipped to ride through difficulties in the process.

Summary and Discussion

We began the chapter by asking how creativity could possibly increase with age in the face of declines in speed, short-term memory, and fluid reasoning. We reviewed the role of three sets of factors at play in creativity. We found that while cognitive ability generally declines with age, knowledge, expertise, and other resources may generally increase with age.

In particular we found that the following elements likely decline with age:

- Speed
- Short-term memory
- Fluid reasoning
- Originality
- Mind-wandering
- Energy and stamina
- Openness to experience

whereas the following likely increase or remain stable with age:

- Domain-specific knowledge and expertise
- General knowledge
- Pattern recognition, intuition, and heuristics
- Diversity of experience
- Interest and motivation
- Grit and self-efficacy
- Effective collaboration

For some elements, including sense of the audience, perspective taking, and integrative complexity, the current state of empirical evidence is still murky.

Multiplying the Components

Lay theories of genius often seek to explain greatness through a single extremely rare talent: Beethoven for dreaming up grand melodies; Michelangelo for chiseling granite; Napoleon for anticipating where the enemy was weakest. Scientific theories of creativity, such as Amabile's (1983, 1996) componential conceptualization of creativity, Simonton's (1999) emergenic and epigenetic model of superior performance, or Sternberg and Lubart's (1991) investment theory of creativity, however, suggest otherwise.

Indeed, rare achievement can be arrived at when the individual is merely very good—say one in a hundred—at each of the several skills that are the components of composing or sculpting or knowing where and when to attack. Creative genius might, therefore, not reside in excelling surpassingly in just one component, rather it may occur when someone is "merely" *very good* in all of them. Because the components of golf are known, Tiger Woods makes this clear. He is not the best ever in putting, driving, or the short approach. But if he is merely one in a hundred on each of these, he will be one in a million in golf: $1/100$ to the third power.

And while the distribution of each single components may be normal, the distribution of their multiplicative combination (and therefore, of creative achievement) is highly skewed (Lotka, 1926; Murray, 2003; Simonton, 2006). If creativity is indeed componential, creativity becomes much more trainable by improving each of the components to a high, but not superhuman, level. But *much* more research is needed to identify components within each domain.

In addition, the componential view suggests that the effects of aging depend on what the components turn out to be. One can imagine that each of the golf components—putting, driving, the short game—wanes with age, and so indeed there is a decline in Professional Golfers' Association tournaments won after age 35. But this is probably not true for basketball. Accuracy of the three-point shots may wane with age, but the passing game and the sense of where you are on the court might increase with age—at least for a while. It is said that Julius Erving was a great shooter at 20, but did not become a great passer and rebounder until age 30.

The number of components, as well as the importance of cognitive ability, may explain differences in developmental trajectories between domains. Creative achievement tends to peak early (in the early 30s) and drop off rapidly in domains such as lyrical poetry, pure mathematics, and theoretical physics, which tend to rely heavily on fluid reasoning. In contrast, creative achievement peaks later (in the early 40s) and exhibits a more gradual decline (if any) in fields that draw more on knowledge and expertise, such as novel writing, history, philosophy, and medicine. Psychologists fall in the middle of these two patterns, peaking around age 40 (Dennis, 1966; Simonton, 1997).

We conclude that it is likely that a componential analysis by domain will find that some components wane with age and others wax. To the extent the domain is like sprinting, which is essentially a single-component game, steady decline with age will be the rule. To the extent that the endeavor is a many-component game, like basketball or science, age might favor creativity.

Our review suggests that it is indeed possible that creativity *can* increase even as we age, a surprising hypothesis rarely discussed in the literature.

If this is so, why would evolution have favored more creativity at the very same time that many physiological functions start to decline? Recent theories seeking to explain menopause in humans provide an intriguing explanation. Humans, in contrast to other species, tend to live two decades after they stop being able to have children. Reproductive decline, thus, occurs much earlier than somatic decline.

What fitness benefits would this unusual, human-only feature imply? The answer may lie in economic productivity. Such productivity continues to grow over the entire life span, largely through acquired knowledge. In contrast, offspring often take 20 years to reach a level of productivity that will allow them to provide for themselves. Thus, adults must produce an economic surplus to provide for their children (either as parent or grandparent) and will be best equipped to do so if they stop reproducing early. By undergoing menopause, human adults can be alive and productive for the first 20 years of their children's lives and can generate the required surplus of resources. Kaplan, Gurven, Winking, Hooper, and Stieglitz (2010) reviewed evidence from a primate sample (chimpanzees) and a human sample (consisting of members of the Tsimane, an indigenous forager-gardening people living in lowland Bolivia). Reproductive senescence was closely linked to somatic senescence in chimpanzees but not in humans. In addition, among the Tsimane, the pattern of calories produced and consumed (as measured by food production and intake) by age matched the theory's predictions, as older adults produced sufficient surplus calories to allow for transfer to the next generations. Interestingly, this held both for women and for men; for in monogamous societies, a man's reproductive cessation occurs when his wife gives birth to their last child.

This theory relates closely to the conclusions of the present review, which is that several (but not all) processes central to human creativity likely remain stable or increase with age. Creativity benefits from the skills and experiences obtained prior to average reproductive cessation, and these continue to accumulate rather than decline with age. In addition, the theory states that the main function of reproductive cessation is to allow elders to provide economic surplus to the next generation, and creativity is in essence designed to increase productivity.

All this suggests that Beck, Broadbent, and Bruner may not be indulging in a self-serving illusion, and more importantly, it augurs well for teaching creativity. All of the capacities that likely improve with age may be teachable, and teaching them explicitly should make for a more creative world.

Jack Riemer (2001), a journalist at the *Houston Chronicle*, popularized the story of a 1995 performance allegedly given by violinist Itzhak Perlman. Having been affected with polio as a child, he struggled onto the stage. As he began to play, one of the violin's strings broke. To the audience's awe, Perlman went on to perform the piece with only three strings. We do not know whether this story really happened (it likely did not). What we recognize, however, is the importance of Perlman's conclusion: "Sometimes it is the artist's task to find out how much music you can still make with what you have left."

References

Ackerman, P. L. (2000). Domain-specific knowledge as the" dark matter" of adult intelligence: Gf/Gc, personality and interest correlates. *The Journals of Gerontology Series B: Psychological Sciences and Social Sciences, 55,* P69–P84.

Ackerman, P. L. (2011). Intelligence and expertise. In R. J. Sternberg & S. B. Kaufman (Eds.), *Cambridge handbook of intelligence* (pp. 847–860). New York, NY: Cambridge University Press.

Amabile, T. M. (1983). The social psychology of creativity: A componential conceptualization. *Journal of Personality and Social Psychology, 45,* 357–376.

Amabile, T. M. (1988). A model of creativity and innovation in organizations. *Research in Organizational Behavior, 10,* 123–167.

Amabile, T. M. (1996). *Creativity in context.* Boulder, CO: Westview Press.

Andrews-Hanna, J. R., Smallwood, J., & Spreng, R. N. (2014). The default network and self-generated thought: Component processes, dynamic control, and clinical relevance. *Annals of the New York Academy of Sciences, 1316,* 29–52.

Atwater, L., & Carmeli, A. (2009). Leader–member exchange, feelings of energy, and involvement in creative work. *The Leadership Quarterly, 20,* 264–275.

Baker, A., & Bollobás, B. (1999). Paul Erdős. 26 March 1913–20 September 1996. *Biographical Memoirs of Fellows of the Royal Society, 45*, 149–164.

Baltes, P. B., & Baltes, M. M. (1990). Psychological perspectives on successful aging: The model of selective optimization with compensation. In P. B. Baltes & M. M. Baltes (Eds.), *Successful aging: Perspectives from the behavioral sciences* (pp. 1–35). Cambridge, England: Cambridge University Press.

Baltes, P. B., & Lindenberger, U. (1997). Emergence of a powerful connection between sensory and cognitive functions across the adult life span: A new window to the study of cognitive aging? *Psychology and Aging, 12*, 12–21.

Bandura, A. (1994). Self-efficacy. In V. S. Ramachaudran (Ed.), *Encyclopedia of human behavior* (Vol. 4, pp. 71–81). New York, NY: Academic Press.

Bandura, A. (1997). *Self-efficacy: The exercise of control.* New York, NY: Freeman.

Baron, J. (2000). *Thinking and deciding.* New York, NY: Cambridge University Press.

Batey, M., Chamorro-Premuzic, T., & Furnham, A. (2009). Intelligence and personality as predictors of divergent thinking: The role of general, fluid and crystallised intelligence. *Thinking Skills and Creativity, 4*, 60–69.

Batson, C. D. (1987). Prosocial motivation: Is it ever truly altruistic? In L. Berkowitz (Ed.), *Advances in experimental social psychology* (Vol. 20, pp. 65–122). New York, NY: Academic Press.

Baumeister, R. F., Vohs, K. D., & Tice, D. M. (2007). The strength model of self-control. *Current Directions in Psychological Science, 16*, 351–355.

Boden, M. A. (2004). *The creative mind: Myths and mechanisms* (2nd ed.). London, England: Routledge.

Bruner, J. S. (1962). The conditions of creativity. In H. Gruber, G. Terrell, & M. Wertheimer (Eds.), *Contemporary approaches to creative thinking* (pp 1–30). New York, NY: Atherton.

Buckner, R. L., Andrews-Hanna, J. R., & Schacter, D. L. (2008). The brain's default network. *Annals of the New York Academy of Sciences, 1124*, 1–38.

Buckner, R., & Carroll, D. (2007). Self-projection and the brain. *Trends in Cognitive Sciences, 11*, 49–57.

Callard, F., Smallwood, J., Golchert, J., & Margulies, D. S. (2013). The era of the wandering mind? Twenty-first century research on self-generated mental activity. *Frontiers in Psychology, 4*(891), 1–11.

Carmeli, A., McKay, A. S., & Kaufman, J. C. (2014). Emotional intelligence and creativity: The mediating role of generosity and vigor. *The Journal of Creative Behavior, 48,* 290–309.

Carroll, J. B. (1993). *Human cognitive abilities: A survey of factor-analytic studies.* Cambridge, England: Cambridge University Press.

Cattell, R. B., & Horn, J. L. (1978). A check on the theory of fluid and crystallized intelligence with description of new subtest designs. *Journal of Educational Measurement, 15,* 139–164.

Chaiken, S., & Trope, Y. (Eds.). (1999). *Dual-process theories in social psychology.* New York, NY: Guilford.

Clark, A. (2013). Whatever next? Predictive brains, situated agents, and the future of cognitive science. *Behavioral and Brain Sciences, 36,* 181–204.

Costa, P. T., McCrae, R. R., Zonderman, A. B., Barbano, H. E., Lebowitz, B., & Larson, D. M. (1986). Cross-sectional studies of personality in a national sample: II. Stability in neuroticism, extraversion, and openness. *Psychology and Aging, 1,* 144–149.

Cramond, B., Matthews-Morgan, J., Bandalos, D., & Zuo, L. (2005). A report on the 40-year follow-up of the Torrance Tests of Creative Thinking: Alive and well in the new millennium. *Gifted Child Quarterly, 49,* 283–291.

Csikszentmihalyi, M. (1990). *Flow: The psychology of optimal experience.* New York, NY: Harper & Row.

Csikszentmihalyi, M. (1996). *Creativity: Flow and the psychology of discovery and invention.* New York, NY: HarperCollins.

Csikszentmihalyi, M. (1999). Implications of a systems perspective for the study of creativity. In R. J. Sternberg (Ed.), *Handbook of creativity* (pp. 313–335). Cambridge, England: Cambridge University Press.

Damoiseaux, J. S., Beckmann, C. F., Arigita, E. S., Barkhof, F., Scheltens, P., Stam, C. J., . . . & Rombouts, S. A. R. B. (2008). Reduced resting-state brain activity in the "default network" in normal aging. *Cerebral Cortex, 18,* 1856–1864.

Dennis, W. (1966). Creative productivity between the ages of 20 and 80 years. *Journal of Gerontology, 21,* 1–8.

de Vries, B., & Lehman, A. (1996). The complexity of personal narratives. In J. Birren, G. Kenyon, & J.-E. Ruth (Eds.), *Aging and biography* (pp. 149–166). New York, NY: Springer.

DeYoung, C. G., Quilty, L. C., & Peterson, J. B. (2007). Between facets and domains: 10 aspects of the Big Five. *Journal of Personality and Social Psychology, 93,* 880–896.

Diamond, J. (1997). *Guns, germs, and steel: The fate of human societies.* New York, NY: W. W. Norton.

Diehl, M., Coyle, N., & Labouvie-Vief, G. (1996). Age and sex differences in strategies of coping and defense across the life span. *Psychology and Aging, 11,* 127–139.

Dixon, R. A. (2000). Concepts and mechanisms of gains in cognitive aging. In D. C Park (Ed.), *Cognitive aging: A primer* (pp. 23–42). Philadelphia, PA: Psychology Press.

Duckworth, A. L., Peterson, C., Matthews, M. D., & Kelly, D. R. (2007). Grit: Perseverance and passion for long-term goals. *Journal of Personality and Social Psychology, 92,* 1087–1101.

Ericsson, K. A. (2013). Why expert performance is special and cannot be extrapolated from studies of performance in the general population: A response to criticisms. *Intelligence, 45,* 81–103.

Ericsson, K. A., Charness, N., Feltovich, P. J., & Hoffman, R. R. (Eds.). (2006). *The Cambridge handbook of expertise and expert performance.* New York, NY: Cambridge University Press.

Ericsson, K. A., Krampe, R. T., & Tesch-Römer, C. (1993). The role of deliberate practice in the acquisition of expert performance. *Psychological Review, 100,* 363–406.

Ericsson, K. A., & Ward, P. (2007). Capturing the naturally occurring superior performance of experts in the laboratory toward a science of expert and exceptional performance. *Current Directions in Psychological Science, 16,* 346–350.

Erikson, E. (1963). *Childhood and society.* New York, NY: W. W. Norton.

Evans, J. S. B. (2008). Dual-processing accounts of reasoning, judgment, and social cognition. *Annual Review of Psychology, 59,* 255–278.

Falk, E. B., Morelli, S. A., Welborn, B. L., Dambacher, K., & Lieberman, M. D. (2013). Creating buzz: The neural correlates of effective message propagation. *Psychological Science, 24,* 1234–1242.

Feist, G. J. (2006). The development of scientific talent in Westinghouse finalists and members of the National Academy of Sciences. *Journal of Adult Development, 13,* 23–35.

Finke, R. A., Ward, T. B., & Smith, S. M. (1992). *Creative cognition.* Cambridge, MA: MIT Press.

Forgeard, M. J. C., & Mecklenburg, A. C. (2013). The two dimensions of motivation and a reciprocal model of the creative process. *Review of General Psychology, 17,* 255–266.

Fredrickson, B. L. (1998). What good are positive emotions? *Review of General Psychology, 2,* 300–319.

Fredrickson, B. L. (2001). The role of positive emotions in positive psychology: The broaden-and-build theory of positive emotions. *American Psychologist, 56,* 218–226.

Galinsky, A. D., Ku, G., & Wang, C. S. (2005). Perspective-taking and self-other overlap: Fostering social bonds and facilitating social coordination. *Group Processes & Intergroup Relations, 8,* 109–124.

Gardner, H. (1993). *Creating minds: An anatomy of creativity as seen through the lives of Freud, Einstein, Picasso, Stravinsky, Eliot, Graham, and Gandhi.* New York, NY: Basic Books.

Gardner, H. (2011). *Leading minds: An anatomy of leadership.* New York, NY: Basic Books.

Gentner, D. (1989). The mechanisms of analogical learning. In S. Vosniadou & A. Ortony (Eds.), *Similarity and analogical reasoning* (pp. 199–241). Cambridge, England: Cambridge University Press.

Giambra, L. M. (1989). Task-unrelated thought frequency as a function of age: A laboratory study. *Psychology and Aging, 4,* 136–143.

Gilbert, D., & Wilson, T. (2007). Prospection: Experiencing the future. *Science, 351,* 1351–1354.

Gilovich, T., Griffin, D., & Kahneman, D. (2002). *Heuristics and biases: The psychology of intuitive judgment.* New York, NY: Cambridge University Press.

Gleick, J. (2004). *Isaac Newton.* New York, NY: Random House.

Gordon, W. J. (1961). *Synectics: The development of creative capacity.* New York, NY: Harper & Row.

Grant, A. M., & Berry, J. (2011). The necessity of others is the mother of invention: Intrinsic and prosocial motivations, perspective-taking, and creativity. *Academy of Management Journal, 54,* 73–96.

Green, A. E., Kraemer, D. J., Fugelsang, J. A., Gray, J. R., & Dunbar, K. N. (2010). Connecting long distance: Semantic distance in analogical reasoning modulates frontopolar cortex activity. *Cerebral Cortex, 20,* 70–76.

Green, A. E., Kraemer, D. J., Fugelsang, J. A., Gray, J. R., & Dunbar, K. N. (2012). Neural correlates of creativity in analogical reasoning. *Journal of Experimental Psychology: Learning, Memory, and Cognition, 38,* 264–272.

Grossmann, I., Na, J., Varnum, M. E., Kitayama, S., & Nisbett, R. E. (2012). A route to well-being: Intelligence versus wise reasoning. *Journal of Experimental Psychology: General 142,* 944–953.

Guilford, J. P. (1967). *The nature of human intelligence.* New York, NY: McGraw-Hill.

Guilford, J. P. (1984). Varieties of divergent production. *The Journal of Creative Behavior, 18,* 1–10.

Hambrick, D. Z., Oswald, F. L., Altmann, E. M., Meinz, E. J., Gobet, F., & Campitelli, G. (2014). Deliberate practice: Is that all it takes to become an expert? *Intelligence, 45,* 34–45.

Happé, F. G., Winner, E., & Brownell, H. (1998). The getting of wisdom: Theory of mind in old age. *Developmental Psychology, 34,* 358–362.

Hawkins, J., & Blakeslee, S. (2007). *On intelligence.* New York, NY: Owl Books.

Henry, J. D., Phillips, L. H., Ruffman, T., & Bailey, P. E. (2013). A meta-analytic review of age differences in theory of mind. *Psychology and Aging, 28,* 826–839.

Hockey, R. (2013). *The psychology of fatigue: Work, effort, and control.* Cambridge, England: Cambridge University Press.

Hoyer, W. J., & Verhaeghen, P. (2006). Memory aging. In J. E. Birren & W. Schaie (Eds.), *Handbook of the psychology of aging* (pp. 209–232). Burlington, MA: Elsevier.

Izard, C. E., & Ackerman, B. P. (2000). Motivational, organizational, and regulatory functions of discrete emotions. In M. Lewis & J. M. Haviland-Jones (Eds.), *Handbook of emotions* (pp. 253–264). New York, NY: Guilford.

Jamison, K. R. (2004). *Exuberance: The passion for life.* New York, NY: Knopf.

Jensen, A. R. (1998). *The g factor: The science of mental ability.* Westport, CT: Praeger.

Jung, R. E., Gasparovic, C., Chavez, R. S., Flores, R. A., Smith, S. M., Caprihan, A., & Yeo, R. A. (2009). Biochemical support for the "threshold" theory of creativity: A magnetic resonance spectroscopy study. *The Journal of Neuroscience, 29,* 5319–5325.

Jung, R. E., Mead, B. S., Carrasco, J., & Flores, R. A. (2013). The structure of creative cognition in the human brain. *Frontiers in Human Neuroscience, 7*(330), 1–13.

Kahneman, D. (2011). *Thinking, fast and slow.* New York, NY: Farrar, Straus and Giroux.

Kaplan, H., Gurven, M., Winking, J., Hooper, P. L., & Stieglitz, J. (2010). Learning menopause, and the human adaptive complex. *Annals of the New York Academy of Sciences, 1204,* 30–42.

Kaufman, A. S., Johnson, C. K., & Liu, X. (2008). A CHC theory-based analysis of age differences on cognitive abilities and academic skills at ages 22 to 90 years. *Journal of Psychoeducational Assessment, 26,* 350–381.

Kaufman, S. B. (2013). Opening up openness to experience: A four-factor model and relations to creative achievement in the arts and sciences. *The Journal of Creative Behavior, 47,* 233–255.

Kaufman, S. B., DeYoung, C. G., Gray, J. R., Jiménez, L., Brown, J., & Mackintosh, N. (2010). Implicit learning as an ability. *Cognition, 116,* 321–340.

Kaufman, S. B., Quilty, L. C., Grazioplene, R. G., Hirsh, J. B., Gray, J. R., Peterson, J. B., & DeYoung, C. G. (2015). Openness to experience and intellect differentially predict creative achievement in art and science. *Journal of Personality, 82,* 248–258.

Keyes, C. L. M., & Ryff, C. D. (1998). Generativity in adult lives: Social structural contours and quality of life consequences. In D. McAdams & E. de St Aubin (Eds.), *Generativity and adult development: How and why we care for the next generation* (pp. 227–263). Washington, DC: American Psychological Association.

Kihlstrom, J. F. (1987). The cognitive unconscious. *Science, 237,* 1445–1452.

Kim, K. H. (2005). Can only intelligent people be creative? A meta-analysis. *Journal of Advanced Academics, 16,* 57–66.

Kinney, D. K., Richards, R., Lowing, P. A., LeBlanc, D., Zimbalist, M. E., & Harlan, P. (2001). Creativity in offspring of schizophrenic and control parents: An adoption study. *Creativity Research Journal, 13*, 17–25.

Kyaga, S., Lichtenstein, P., Boman, M., Hultman, C., Långström, N., & Landén, M. (2011). Creativity and mental disorder: Family study of 300,000 people with severe mental disorder. *The British Journal of Psychiatry, 199*, 373–379.

Lachman, M. E. (1986). Personal control in later life: Stability, change, and cognitive correlates. In M. M. Baltes & P. B. Baltes (Eds.), *The psychology of control and aging* (pp. 207–236). Hillsdale, NJ: Erlbaum.

Lacroix, J., Murre, J. M. J., Postma, E. O., & van den Herik, H. J. (2006). Modeling recognition memory using the similarity structure of natural input. *Cognitive Science, 30*, 121–145.

Lakatos, I. (1970). Falsification and the methodology of scientific research programmes. In I. Lakatos & A. Musgrave (Eds.), *Criticism and the growth of knowledge* (pp. 91–196). Cambridge, England: Cambridge University Press.

Lamott, A. (1994). *Bird by bird: Some instructions on writing and life*. New York, NY: Anchor.

Lehman, H. C. (1966). The psychologist's most creative years. *American Psychologist, 21*, 363–369.

Leon, S. A., Altmann, L. J., Abrams, L., Gonzalez Rothi, L. J., & Heilman, K. M. (2014). Divergent task performance in older adults: Declarative memory or creative potential? *Creativity Research Journal, 26*, 21–29.

Lotka, A. J. (1926). The frequency distribution of scientific productivity. *Journal of the Washington Academy of Sciences, 16*, 137–323.

MacPherson, S. E., Phillips, L. H., & Della Sala, S. (2002). Age, executive function and social decision making: A dorsolateral prefrontal theory of cognitive aging. *Psychology and Aging, 17*, 598–609.

Markman, K. D., Klein, W. M., & Suhr, J. A. (2009). Overview. In K. D. Markman, W. M. Klein, & J. A., Suhr (Eds.), *Handbook of imagination and mental simulation* (pp. vii-xvi). New York, NY: Taylor & Francis.

Martindale, C. (1981). Creativity and primary process thinking. *Contemporary Psychology, 26*, 568–568.

Mason, M. F., Norton, M. I., Van Horn, J. D., Wegner, D. M., Grafton, S. T., & Macrae, C. N. (2007). Wandering minds: The default network and stimulus-independent thought. *Science, 315*, 393–395.

Massimini, F., Csikszentmihalyi, M., & Delle Fave, A. (1988). Flow and biocultural evolution. In. M. Csikszentmihalyi & I. Csikszentmihalyi (Eds.), *Optimal experience: Psychological studies of flow in consciousness* (pp. 60–81). New York, NY: Cambridge University Press.

Maylor, E. A., Moulson, J. M., Muncer, A. M., & Taylor, L. A. (2002). Does performance on theory of mind tasks decline in old age? *British Journal of Psychology, 93*, 465–485.

McAdams, D. P., Anyidoho, N. A., Brown, C., Huang, Y. T., Kaplan, B., & Machado, M. A. (2004). Traits and stories: Links between dispositional and narrative features of personality. *Journal of Personality, 72*, 761–784.

McCrae, R. R. (1987). Creativity, divergent thinking, and openness to experience. *Journal of Personality and Social Psychology, 52*, 1258–1265.

McCrae, R. R., Arenberg, D., & Costa, P. T., Jr. (1987). Declines in divergent thinking with age: Cross-sectional, longitudinal, and cross-sequential analyses. *Psychology and Aging, 2*, 130–137.

McMillan, R. L., Kaufman, S. B., & Singer, J. L. (2013). Ode to positive constructive daydreaming. *Frontiers in Psychology, 4*(626), 1–9.

Mednick, S. A. (1962). The associative basis of the creative process. *Psychological Review, 69*, 220–232.

Merton, R. K. (1968). The Matthew effect in science. *Science, 159*, 56–63.

Miquel, J. (1992). An update on the mitochondrial-DNA mutation hypothesis of cell aging. *Mutation Research/DNAging, 275*, 209–216.

Moran, J. M. (2013). Lifespan development: The effects of typical aging on theory of mind. *Behavioural Brain Research, 237*, 32–40.

Murray, C. (2003). *Human accomplishment: The pursuit of excellence in the arts and sciences.* New York, NY: HarperCollins.

Nakamura, J., & Csikszentmihalyi, M. (2005). The concept of flow. In C. R. Snyder & S. J. Lopez (Eds.), *Handbook of positive psychology* (pp. 89–105), New York, NY: Oxford University Press.

Nemeth, C. J., & Goncalo, J. A. (2005). Creative collaborations from afar: The benefits of independent authors. *Creativity Research Journal, 17*, 1–8.

Nusbaum, E. C., & Silvia, P. J. (2011). Are intelligence and creativity really so different? Fluid intelligence, executive processes, and strategy use in divergent thinking. *Intelligence, 39*, 36–45.

Park, G., Lubinski, D., & Benbow, C. P. (2007). Contrasting intellectual patterns predict creativity in the arts and sciences tracking intellectually precocious youth over 25 years. *Psychological Science, 18,* 948–952.

Parker, S. K., Atkins, P. W. B., & Axtell, C. M. (2008). Building better work places through individual perspective taking: A fresh look at a fundamental human process. *International Review of Industrial and Organizational Psychology, 23,* 149–196.

Pennebaker, J. W., & Stone, L. D. (2003). Words of wisdom: Language use over the life span. *Journal of Personality and Social Psychology, 85,* 291–301.

Peters, E., Finucane, M. L., MacGregor, D. G., & Slovic, P. (2000). The bearable lightness of aging: Judgment and decision processes in older adults. In P. C. Stern & L. L. Carstensen (Eds.), *The aging mind: Opportunities in cognitive research* (pp. 144–165). Washington, DC: National Academies Press.

Petersen, A. M., Jung, W. S., Yang, J. S., & Stanley, H. E. (2011). Quantitative and empirical demonstration of the Matthew effect in a study of career longevity. *Proceedings of the National Academy of Sciences, 108,* 18–23.

Plucker, J. A. (1999). Is the proof in the pudding? Reanalyses of Torrance's (1958 to present) longitudinal data. *Creativity Research Journal, 12,* 103–114.

Pólya, G. (1945). *How to solve it.* Princeton, NJ: Princeton University Press.

Polyani, M. (1966). *The tacit dimension.* Garden City, NY: Doubleday.

Pratt, M. W., Diessner, R., Pratt, A., Hunsberger, B., & Pancer, S. M. (1996). Moral and social reasoning and perspective taking in later life: A longitudinal study. *Psychology and Aging, 11,* 66–73.

Preckel, F., Holling, H., & Wiese, M. (2006). Relationship of intelligence and creativity in gifted and non-gifted students: An investigation of threshold theory. *Personality and Individual Differences, 40,* 159–170.

Puccio, G. J., Firestien, R. L., Coyle, C., & Masucci, C. (2006). A review of the effectiveness of CPS training: A focus on workplace issues. *Creativity and Innovation Management, 15,* 19–33.

Riemer, J. (2001, February 10). Perlman makes his music the hard way. *Houston Chronicle.* Retrieved from http://www.chron.com/life/houston-belief/article/Perlman-makes-his-music-the-hard-way-2009719.php

Ritter, S. M., Damian, R. I., Simonton, D. K., van Baaren, R. B., Strick, M., Derks, J., & Dijksterhuis, A. (2012). Diversifying experiences enhance cognitive flexibility. *Journal of Experimental Social Psychology, 48,* 961–964.

Roberts, S. B., & Rosenberg, I. (2006). Nutrition and aging: Changes in the regulation of energy metabolism with aging. *Physiological Reviews, 86,* 651–667.

Runco, M. A., Millar, G., Acar, S., & Cramond, B. (2010). Torrance tests of creative thinking as predictors of personal and public achievement: A fifty-year follow-up. *Creativity Research Journal, 22,* 361–368.

Salthouse, T. (1985). *A theory of cognitive aging.* New York, NY: Elsevier.

Salthouse, T. A. (1996). The processing-speed theory of adult age differences in cognition. *Psychological Review, 103,* 403–428.

Salthouse, T. A. (2004). What and when of cognitive aging. *Current Directions in Psychological Science, 13,* 140–144.

Sawyer, R. K. (2012). *Explaining creativity: The science of human innovation* (2nd ed.). New York, NY: Oxford University Press.

Schipolowski, S., Wilhelm, O., & Schroeders, U. (2014). On the nature of crystallized intelligence: The relationship between verbal ability and factual knowledge. *Intelligence, 46,* 156–168.

Schneider, W. J., & McGrew, K. (2012). The Cattell-Horn-Carroll model of intelligence. In D. Flanagan & P. Harrison (Eds.), *Contemporary intellectual assessment: Theories, tests, and issues* (pp. 99–144). New York, NY: Guilford.

Seligman, M. E. P. (1991). *Learned optimism.* New York, NY: Knopf.

Seligman, M. E. P., & Kahana, M. (2008). Unpacking intuition: A conjecture. *Perspectives on Psychological Science, 4,* 399–402.

Seligman, M. E. P., Railton, P., Baumeister, R. F., & Sripada, C. (2013). Navigating into the future or driven by the past. *Perspectives on Psychological Science, 8,* 119–141.

Shanks, D. R. (2005). Implicit learning. In K. Lamberts & R. Goldstone (Eds.), *Handbook of cognition* (pp. 202–220). Thousand Oaks, CA: Sage.

Sheldon, K. M., & Kasser, T. (2001). Getting older, getting better? Personal strivings and psychological maturity across the lifespan. *Developmental Psychology, 37,* 491–501.

Shenk, J. W. (2014). *Powers of two: Finding the essence of innovation in creative pairs*. New York, NY: Houghton Mifflin Harcourt.

Silvia, P. J. (2001). Interest and interests: The psychology of constructive capriciousness. *Review of General Psychology, 5*, 270–290.

Silvia, P. J. (2006). *Exploring the psychology of interest*. New York, NY: Oxford University Press.

Silvia, P. J. (2008). Discernment and creativity: How well can people identify their most creative ideas? *Psychology of Aesthetics, Creativity, and the Arts, 2*, 139–146.

Silvia, P. J. (2012). Human emotions and aesthetic experience: An overview of empirical aesthetics. In A. P. Shimamura & S. E. Palmer (Eds.), *Aesthetic science: Connecting minds, brains, and experience* (pp. 250–275). New York, NY: Oxford University Press.

Silvia, P. J., & Beaty, R. E. (2012). Making creative metaphors: The importance of fluid intelligence for creative thought. *Intelligence, 40*, 343–351.

Silvia, P. J., Nusbaum, E. C., Berg, C., Martin, C., & O'Connor, A. (2009). Openness to experience, plasticity, and creativity: Exploring lower-order, high-order, and interactive effects. *Journal of Research in Personality, 43*, 1087–1090.

Simonton, D. K. (1975). Sociocultural context of individual creativity: A transhistorical time-series analysis. *Journal of Personality and Social Psychology, 32*, 1119–1133.

Simonton, D. K. (1977). Creative productivity, age, and stress: A biographical time-series analysis of 10 classical composers. *Journal of Personality and Social Psychology, 35*, 791–804.

Simonton, D. K. (1989). The swan-song phenomenon: Last-works effects for 172 classical composers. *Psychology and Aging, 4*, 42–47.

Simonton, D. K. (1990). *Psychology, science, and history: An introduction to historiometry*. New Haven, CT: Yale University Press.

Simonton, D. K. (1994). *Greatness: Who makes history and why*. New York, NY: Guilford.

Simonton, D. K. (1997). Creative productivity: A predictive and explanatory model of career trajectories and landmarks. *Psychological Review, 104*, 66–89.

Simonton, D. K. (1999). Talent and its development: An emergenic and epigenetic model. *Psychological Review, 106*, 435–457.

Simonton, D. K. (2000). Creative development as acquired expertise: Theoretical issues and an empirical test. *Developmental Review, 20,* 283–318.

Simonton, D. K. (2006). Creative productivity through the adult years. In H. R. Moody (Ed.), *Aging: Concepts and controversies* (pp. 95–100). Thousand Oaks, CA: Pine Forge Press.

Simonton, D. K. (2012). Creative productivity and aging: An age decrement—or not? In S. K. Whitbourne & M. J. Sliwinski (Eds.), *The Wiley-Blackwell handbook of adulthood and aging* (pp. 477–496). Oxford, England: Wiley-Blackwell.

Singer, J. L. (1966). *Daydreaming: An introduction to the experimental study of inner experience.* New York, NY: Random House.

Singer, J. L., & McCraven, V. G. (1961). Some characteristics of adult daydreaming. *The Journal of Psychology, 51,* 151–164.

Smallwood, J., Brown, K., Baird, B., & Schooler, J. W. (2012). Cooperation between the default mode network and the frontal–parietal network in the production of an internal train of thought. *Brain Research, 1428,* 60–70.

Spirduso, W., Francis, K., & MacRae, P. (2005). *Physical dimensions of aging* (2nd ed.). Champaign, IL: Human Kinetics.

Soldz, S., & Vaillant, G. E. (1999). The Big Five personality traits and the life course: A 45-year longitudinal study. *Journal of Research in Personality, 33,* 208–232.

Sternberg, R. J. (1996). Costs of expertise. In K. A. Ericsson (Ed.), *The road to excellence: The acquisition of expert performance in the arts and sciences, sports, and games* (pp. 347–354). Hillsdale, NJ: Erlbaum.

Sternberg, R. J., & Lubart, T. I. (1991). An investment theory of creativity and its development. *Human Development, 34,* 1–31.

Sternberg, R. J., & Lubart, T. I. (1999). The concept of creativity: Prospects and paradigms. In R. J. Sternberg (Ed.), *Handbook of creativity* (pp. 3–15). New York, NY: Cambridge University Press.

Suedfeld, P., Tetlock, P. E., & Streufert, S. (1992). Conceptual/integrative complexity. In C. P. Smith (Ed.), *Motivation and personality: Handbook of thematic content analysis* (pp. 393–400). New York, NY: Cambridge University Press.

Sullivan, S., & Ruffman, T. (2004). Social understanding: How does it fare with advancing years? *British Journal of Psychology, 95,* 1–18.

Tadmor, C. T., Galinsky, A. D., & Maddux, W. W. (2012). Getting the most out of living abroad: Biculturalism and integrative complexity as key drivers of creative and professional success. *Journal of Personality and Social Psychology, 92,* 1087–1101.

Tamplin, A. K., Krawietz, S. A., Radvansky, G. A., & Copeland, D. E. (2013). Event memory and moving in a well-known environment. *Memory & Cognition, 41,* 1109–1121.

Taylor, S. E., Pham, L. B., Rivkind, I. D., & Armor, D. A. (1998). Harnessing the imagination: Mental simulation, self-regulation, and coping. *American Psychologist, 53,* 429–439.

Tetlock, P. E., Peterson, R. S., & Berry, J. M. (1993). Flattering and unflattering personality portraits of integratively simple and complex managers. *Journal of Personality and Social Psychology, 64,* 500–511.

Torrance, E. P. (1983). The importance of falling in love with "something." *Creative Child & Adult Quarterly, 8,* 72–78.

Torrance, E. P. (1988). The nature of creativity as manifest in its testing. In R. J. Sternberg (Ed.), *The nature of creativity* (pp. 43–75). New York, NY: Cambridge University Press.

Torrance, E. P. (1993). The beyonders in a thirty year longitudinal study of creative achievement. *Roeper Review, 15,* 131–135.

Treffinger, D. J., Isaksen, S. G., & Dorval, K. B. (2000). *Creative problem-solving: An introduction* (3rd ed.). Waco, TX: Prufrock.

Wagner, R. K., & Sternberg, R. J. (1985). Practical intelligence in real-world pursuits: The role of tacit knowledge. *Journal of Personality and Social Psychology, 49,* 436–458.

White, H. A., & Shah, P., (2006). Uninhibited imaginations: Creativity in adults with attention-deficit/hyperactivity disorder. *Personality and Individual Differences, 40,* 1121–1131.

Williams, P. G., Suchy, Y., & Kraybill, M. L. (2013). Preliminary evidence for low openness to experience as a pre-clinical marker of incipient cognitive decline in older adults. *Journal of Research in Personality, 47,* 945–951.

Wittgenstein, L. (2009). *Philosophical investigations.* Malden, MA: Blackwell. (Original work published 1953)

Wortman, J., Lucas, R. E., & Donnellan, M. B. (2012). Stability and change in the Big Five personality domains: Evidence from a longitudinal study of Australians. *Psychology and Aging, 27,* 867–874.

Yamamoto, K. (1964). Threshold of intelligence in academic achievement of highly creative students. *The Journal of Experimental Education, 32,* 401–405.

Zuckerman, H. (1967). Nobel laureates in science: Patterns of productivity, collaboration, and authorship. *American Sociological Review, 32,* 391–403.

Zuckerman, H. (1977). *Scientific elite: Nobel laureates in the United States.* New York, NY: Free Press.

Afterword

Martin Seligman

I N RETROSPECT, THE SCIENCE OF PSYCHOLOGY OVERRATED the past and the present and underrated the future. This focus on the past and present was for a good enough reason. It made sense methodologically: The past and the present can, in principal, be measured, but the future is unknown and so it cannot be measured. The past has *causal* effects on the present, but the future cannot. At rock bottom, we experience only a single past and a single present, but lying ahead of us is an ever-widening branching of possibilities.

With this methodological justification, psychology and neuroscience strode bravely forward for more than a century, measuring memory, which is the psychological representation of the past, and measuring perception, sensation, and emotion, which are the psychological representations of the present. If perfectly measured, it seemed, the past and the present should determine the future, so accurate prediction of behavior would follow from an adequate science of memory, perception, and emotion.

This brave program failed on several grounds.

- First, all science that we know of is statistical, and the most basic and comprehensive science of all, physics, seems to tell us that probabilism is a deep fact about the world.
- Second, it turned out that memory, perception, and emotion themselves, as amply documented in this book, are not just about the past and the present. They turn out to intrinsically involve extrapolation to the future. Memory is oriented toward future usefulness. Perception and sensation are generative as much as receptive, and selectively attentive to information that is predictive. And emotion is oriented toward future realities, not tied down to reacting to what has come before. So in the absence of a science of prospection, memory, perception, and emotion will be seen only in part, not as wholes.
- Third, a conceptual error seems to have animated the lack of interest in the future. Something genuinely suspect—a metaphysical teleology of causation backward in time, of the present by the future—was conflated with something not at all mysterious, namely, the idea that, in a world with minds, behavior can be guided by maps of possible futures as well as the traces of actual pasts. In this way, "mere future possibilities" *can* explain concrete behaviors in the here and now.

Human beings *metabolize* the past to simulate and evaluate possible futures, producing, as metabolism does, something that wasn't there before. This is an ineluctable and universal human process. It pervades unconscious processes, such as sensation, perception, and intuition, and it pervades conscious processes, such as mind-wandering and deliberation. This new framework puts these extrapolations to the future front and center in psychology and neuroscience.

Where will such understanding and measurement come from?

Our principal aim in writing this book was to help galvanize such a science, and so the four authors not only spent 3 years and several retreats writing this book, but we also considered at length how best to go about this galvanizing.

Re-enter the Eagle Scouts of philanthropy, the John Templeton Foundation. We suggested to Barnaby Marsh and Chris Stawski, lead project officers at Templeton, that a research competition in prospection be launched, and they heartily agreed. With Martin Seligman, Templeton had previously launched parallel research competitions in positive psychology and in positive neuroscience. So with their generous support, we allocated $2.3 million in award funding for new research projects to expand the scientific understanding of the mental representation and utilization of possible futures. We called for proposals that would help understand (a) how to measure prospection; (b) the mechanisms of prospection; (c) applications of prospection; and (d) how prospection can be improved.

The steering committee consisted of Thalia Wheatley (Chair), Dartmouth College; Roy F. Baumeister; Randy Buckner, Harvard University; Laurie Santos, Yale University; Jonathan Schooler, University of California at Santa Barbara; Barry Schwartz, Swarthmore College; Martin Seligman; and Chandra Sripada.

We received more than 250 proposals and in August 2014, we selected the 18 that we felt represented the highest standards of scientific excellence and also identified possible future leaders in the new field of prospective psychology.

2014 *Templeton Science of Prospection Awards*

- $145,000 to Jessica Andrews-Hanna and Joanna Arch from the University of Colorado Boulder to study how prospective thinking functions in daily life and to assess the neurocognitive mechanisms that define and distinguish adaptive prospective thinking from its less adaptive forms, using a mobile smartphone application.
- $95,000 to Fiery Cushman from Harvard University to test whether there are distinct neural populations supporting social predictions, systems that track information about multiple possible future events.
- $145,000 to Evelina Fedorenko from Massachusetts General Hospital and Elinor Amit from Harvard University to evaluate whether prospection about the near or likely future relies on visual imagery, whereas prospection about the distal or unlikely future relies on inner speech.
- $95,000 to Karin Foerde from New York University and Daphna Shohamy from Columbia University to establish the specific role of dopamine in prospection and to determine the cognitive

and neural mechanisms through which dopamine influences prospection.

- $135,000 to Simona Ghetti from the University of California, Davis to examine the development of episodic prospection in 9-year-olds, 12-year-olds, and young adults.

- $145,000 to Igor Grossmann from the University of Waterloo and Kathleen Vohs from the University of Minnesota to examine whether mentally distancing oneself from present experiences makes forecasting more accurate.

- $145,000 to Benjamin Hayden from the University of Rochester to study future-oriented decisions in rhesus monkeys and to challenge the notion that nonhuman animals are "stuck in time."

- $150,000 to Abigail Marsh from Georgetown University to study prospective altruism in unrelated, altruistic stem cell donors in order to identify ways to reduce future failures of prospective altruism among stem cell donors.

- $100,000 to Anthony Wagner from Stanford University to examine how people engage in prospective planning and the effect of acute psychological stress restricting the complexity and temporal scope of prospection during planning.

- $100,000 to David Rand from Yale University to identify interventions that promote willingness to delay gratification when it is beneficial to do so.

- $150,000 to Jonathan Smallwood from the University of York to explore whether a primary benefit of prospection is the capacity to generate creative and original thought to navigate the complex social environments and to explore the underlying neural mechanisms that support this core aspect of cognition.

- $150,000 to Bethany Teachman from the University of Virginia to use cognitive bias modification to train prospection for the generation of healthy, positive (relative to extremely negative) representations of possible future states.

- $145,000 to Leaf Van Boven from the University of Colorado Boulder and Eugene Caruso from the University of Chicago to examine, using virtual reality, whether mere attention to future events and the fluency experienced when considering future events reduces the psychological distance of those events.

- $145,000 to Matthijs van der Meer from Dartmouth College to study prospection in an animal model: rats solving spatial navigation problems, as they not only replay previous trajectories, but also mentally construct novel paths toward desired goals.
- $150,000 to Felix Warneken from Harvard University to investigate how prospection expands human potential for prosocial behavior from a developmental perspective in order to witness the birth of prospection and assess its trajectory across childhood.
- $145,000 to Phillip Wolff and Eugene Agichtein from Emory University, and Bridget Copley from CNRS/Université Paris 8 to analyze—from Twitter feeds—why future-oriented thinking is associated with a range of positive psychological and health outcomes.
- $145,000 to Liane Young, Brendan Gaesser, and Elizabeth Kensinger from Boston College to use the cognitive and neural mechanisms of prospection to foster prosociality in adults.
- $14,000 to George Vaillant of Harvard University and Peggy Kern of Melbourne University to predict longer lives from the future-mindedness in the writing in the Harvard Reunion books.

We have created a website, www.prospectivepsych.org, so that you can follow their progress. We commend the future of prospective science into the hands of these fine scientists.

Author Index

Subject Index